The Law and Economics of Child Support Payments

To Joan

The Law and Economics of Child Support Payments

Edited by

William S. Comanor

University of California, Santa Barbara, USA

Edward Elgar

Cheltenham, UK • Northampton, MA, USA

Published by
Edward Elgar Publishing Limited
Glensanda House
Montpellier Parade
Cheltenham
Glos GL50 1UA
UK

Edward Elgar Publishing, Inc.
136 West Street
Suite 202
Northampton
Massachusetts 01060
USA

A catalogue record for this book
is available from the British Library

ISBN 1 84376 121 1

Printed and bound in Great Britain by MPG Books Ltd, Bodmin, Cornwall

Contents

Figures

Tables

Boxes

Contributors

Heather Antecol is Assistant Professor of Economics at Claremont McKenna College. Her research interests include the effects of family structure on children and gender differences in labor market outcomes.

Kelly Bedard is Assistant Professor of Economics at the University of California, Santa Barbara. She has written widely on the effects of family structure on youth outcomes.

Donald J. Bieniewicz is a policy consultant for the Children Rights Council in Washington DC and the author of their model child support guidelines. He is also a member of the Economic Analysis Staff, Office of Policy Analysis, US Department of the Interior.

Sanford L. Braver is Professor of Psychology at Arizona State University. He is the author of *Divorce Dads: Shattering the Myths*, published in 1998.

William S. Comanor is Professor of Economics at the University of California, Santa Barbara, and Professor of Health Services at UCLA. He served as Chief Economist at the US Federal Trade Commission between 1978 and 1980, and was the recipient of the Distinguished Fellow Award of the Industrial Organization Society in April 2003.

Ira Mark Ellman is the Willard Pedrick Distinguished Research Scholar and Professor of Law at Arizona State University College of Law. He was the Chief Reporter of the American Law Institute's ten-year study of Family Law, and is the senior author of the leading family law text, now going into its fourth edition.

Ronald K. Henry is a partner in the law firm of Kaye, Scholer, Frierman, Hays & Handler in Washington, DC. He has testified on numerous occasions before Congressional Committees on family matters, and also appeared on radio and television broadcasts.

Cynthia A. McNeely is an attorney and Executive Director of the With Arms Wide Open Foundation of Tallahassee, Florida, which is designed to promote healthy relationships between parents and children.

Robert A. McNeely is a shareholder in the law firm of McFarlain & Cassedy in Tallahassee, Florida. He is a founding member of the Florida Commission on Responsible Fatherhood.

Geoffrey P. Miller is the William T. and Stuyvesant P. Comfort Professor of Law at New York University Law School. His research has emphasized the relation between law and culture.

Llad Phillips is Professor of Economics at the University of California, Santa Barbara. He is a labour economist who has studied the impact of family structures.

R. Mark Rogers is a private economic consultant in metropolitan Atlanta, Georgia. He was a commissioner on the Georgia Commission on Child Support in 1998.

David Stockburger has taught quantitative analysis and software development for many years at Southwest Missouri State University.

Robert J. Willis is Professor of Economics and Senior Research Scientist in the Survey Research Center at the University of Michigan. He has written widely on the economics of the family.

Preface

William S. Comanor

This book originated with the complaints that have appeared in both the popular press and the academic literature as to the conduct of divorced and separated fathers. In the absence of marriage ties, these reports have suggested that many fathers have little interest or concern for their children. Many are even unwilling to make any financial provision for them. They are labelled 'Deadbeat Dads', and regarded as the worst type of villain. While they may not have physically harmed their children, you would never know that from the vitriolic tone of the published reports.

The evidence of this behaviour was well documented. Government statistics showed that most single mothers received no child support whatsoever from the fathers of their children. This absence was particularly common among never-married mothers, who are an increasingly high proportion of the total. Even among formerly married mothers, fewer than half received any support at all. Absent, non-paying fathers were an important social problem.

While one could not refute the statistical evidence, the conventional explanation seemed incomplete. If married fathers were concerned for their children, what explains the dramatic shift in their attitudes when marriage ties are broken? One answer, of course, is that most fathers did not really care about their children when married, and that this lack of concern simply becomes more apparent in the absence of marriage. But that explanation was not consistent with much of what I saw. Could there be another, more subtle explanation?

The attack on Deadbeat Dads was pursued with increasing vigour. In California, there was widespread agreement that the local district attorneys had not done enough to promote child support payment because so many of these obligations remained unpaid. The solution was to remove enforcement responsibility from these local officials and replace them with a centralized authority within the state government. A new Department of Child Support was created to serve that function. Henceforth, the full offices of the California state government would be used to ensure that these payments were made. If Deadbeat Dads were the problem, increasing government action would be the solution.

At about this time, I happened across a provocative paper by Yoram Weiss and Robert Willis in the *Journal of Labor Economics.*[1] Among the findings presented there was that of every $5 of child support paid to the custodial parent, only about one dollar was actually used to support the child.[2] That conclusion startled me, for it suggested a $4 'tax' on every dollar of support actually provided. That ratio is an effective tax rate of 400 per cent. Perhaps that was the reason that so much child support went unpaid. If this finding was even approximately correct, there is clearly a substantial incentive against making these payments. Could that be the source of the 'Deadbeat Dad' phenomenon?

These issues cried out for the methods of law and economics. The function of this increasingly important hybrid discipline was to apply economic tools to legal issues. A particular methodological approach suggested itself. Using this method, the investigator assumes that preference functions remain unchanged as between alternate circumstances, and investigates if there are external factors that may have led to any observed differences in behaviour. Rather than making the easy assumption that preferences have changed, and that people are different when placed in new situations, this methodology presumes that the actors are unchanged and asks what else may have led to the different responses. Applied to the case at hand, this approach would assume, correctly or not, that most fathers' concerns for their children are the same inside and outside of marriage, and then examines how incentives may have changed when they are asked to make child support payments.

These motivating factors are critically important for devising appropriate policies. If the conventional wisdom is correct, and the interests and preferences of fathers in marriage and outside are simply different, then there may be little recourse but to impose increasingly stringent sanctions on behaviour we seek to discourage. On the other hand, if the problem is not due to a shift in interests or preferences but rather to rearranged incentives, then the appropriate policies may be quite different. The solution may instead be to shift incentives and find a way to make child support payments more incentive-compatible. The methodology of law and economics is drawn to this second approach.

Following my encounter with the Weiss and Willis article, I published a column in the *Los Angeles Times* that raised some of these issues.[3] There were discussions with lawyers and economists on these issues, but little more. Then in March of 2001, I received notice of a UCSB campus project on Critical Issues in America. An endowment existed to support a conference to explore issues that had become critical for our society. Clearly, the ongoing problem of child support payments fell in that category. I submitted a proposal for a conference on this topic, which was approved. I am deeply indebted to Provost Aaron Ettenberg and Carole Self of the College of Letters and Science at UCSB for their support. I also received support from Chancellor Henry Yang, which I appreciate very much. We would not be at this stage in our work without this help.

The conference on this topic was held on the UCSB campus on 20 September, 2002. There were four papers presented by economists, four by attorneys, and one by a psychologist. They all dealt with different facets of the child support system. For the most part, those who attended were the authors of the papers, although there were also a small number of invited guests. I am particularly indebted to Professor H.E. Frech of the Department of Economics at UCSB, Dean Scott Altman of the Law School at the University of Southern California and Penny Mathison of the Santa Barbara Bar for their assistance. Apart from the opening chapter of this volume, the others were all presented at the conference. Each was subject to considerable discussion and debate, and was later revised. My introductory chapter was not presented there, but rather relies on the results and findings of the original papers and discussions.

There is an increasing need for further consideration of the child support system. My goal for this volume is that it provides an impetus for this effort. The current system cries out for needed change.

NOTES

1. Yoram Weiss and Robert J. Willis (1993) 'Transfers among divorced couples: evidence and interpretation', *Journal of Labor Economics*, **11**(4).
2. Ibid., p. 665.
3. *Los Angeles Times*, 22 February, 1999.

1. Child support payments: a review of current policies*

William S. Comanor

INTRODUCTION

There are two systems of belief regarding child support payments. The first system, which dominates academic discussions, considers these payments an important component of social insurance policy. Single-mother headed households represent a large share of all low-income households, and many believe it is the responsibility of the absent fathers to contribute to their support. Indeed, some writers assert that 'one of the major causes of poverty in single parent families is the inadequate amount of child support' (Del Boca and Ribero, 1998, p. 471).

Even where single-mother households have higher incomes, many believe that support payments are still needed to raise living standards. When the father is absent, income levels are invariably lower since there is now only a single wage earner. Page and Stevens find that in the first year following divorce, pre-tax family income falls on average by about 42 per cent, and post-tax income by about 32 per cent[1] (p. 17). To be sure, the absent father's consumption spending is also removed from the household budget so these differences do not necessarily mean lower living standards. Despite that fact, a commonly stated objective is to assure the same household income with one parent as would exist with two.

An important dimension of this belief system is that the costs of the children and those of the mother cannot really be distinguished. Incomes refer to the household, and the living standards of a mother and her children are inseparable. As a result, all consumption expenditures are effectively for household collective goods. In this setting, the only constraint is the ability and willingness of the non-resident father to make his payments.

In contrast to the first approach, there is a second system of belief in which child support payments have a more limited objective. Their purpose is not to provide a general income supplement for single-parent households. Instead, support payments are designed only to help pay the costs of the children. Its proponents acknowledge that both parents are responsible for

1

their children, and agree that absent fathers should contribute to their support. However, in this belief system, the costs of the children must be distinguished from those of the parent. Once determined, child costs should then be apportioned between the parents according to their relative incomes and the amount of time that each spends with the children.

While both systems of belief recognize the need for child support payments, they have very different implications for the level of payments. Proscribed payments are much higher under the first belief system than the second.

To expand the volume of child support payments, federal and state governments have intervened since 1975 with increasing vigour on the side of potential recipients. While previously these payments were considered private obligations, to be enforced through conventional legal processes, they are now viewed quite differently and the subject of major policy interventions. Yet, these efforts have not generally been successful. Despite widespread acceptance of the need for these payments, most support payments are not paid, which is a pattern that has not changed very much for the past 25 years.

Many believe this pattern arises simply from 'deadbeat dads', men who refuse to make their required payments. A recent statement from the *Journal of Human Resources* testifies to that viewpoint:

> If the NCP (non-custodial parent) is altruistic, he will receive utility from expenditures on the children, and even in the absence of any laws about child support, he will voluntarily transfer income to the custodial parent (CP) to increase child expenditures. Some NCPs, however, may wish to contribute little or nothing in support of their children, perhaps due to weak emotional attachment, antagonism toward the ex-spouse, inability to pay, or even the perception of alternative income available to the CP and child. It is in these cases that the role of the State is most important.[2]

The explanations given there for non-payment are conventional. Most discussions of these issues say little more.

These descriptions, however, are unsettling. Why should an attentive father within a family shift to being so inattentive when the household dissolves? How can we explain so striking a shift in his actions, that where he was once happy to support his child, he is now unwilling to do so?

Particularly striking is the widespread prevalence of civil disobedience. Except for the anti-liquor laws during the Prohibition era and the anti-drug laws more recently, there has not been such a general unwillingness to follow the law. Child support is a required obligation, and yet most non-custodial parents do not make their required payments. Why?

The purpose of this volume is to offer some tentative answers to these questions. We shall find that these answers relate directly to the two systems of belief regarding these payments.

GOVERNMENT POLICIES AND RESULTS

The federal government first intervened significantly in child support policy with the passage of Title IV-D of the Social Security Act in 1974. This action created the US Office of Child Support Enforcement and also provided matching funds to assist state collection efforts.

With the substantial increase in divorce rates and the expanding number of single-parent families that occurred in the 1970s, the cost of the AFDC (Aid to Families with Dependent Children) programme had exploded. There was a need to find new revenues for the AFDC programme without limiting services. Child support payments seemed a promising source. For these cases, payments would be intercepted by government agencies. Instead of the taxpayers, the absent parent would assume financial responsibilities for his family. To a great extent, the leading motivation behind the new child support policies was not to provide additional support for single-parent households as much as to reimburse government agencies for welfare payments already provided.

To be sure, the original bill permitted state agencies to assist with non-AFDC cases, where government intercepts of child support payments were not applicable. However, that provision was authorized for only a single year, in contrast to the permanent authorization for AFDC cases. It was extended through a series of yearly additions, and became permanent only in 1980.

The original focus of the new policies – reimbursing government for prior outlays – has continued to influence their direction and enforcement. Even when the AFDC programme was replaced in 1996 by TANF (Temporary Assistance for Needy Families), this emphasis continued. Primary efforts continue to be directed at households on welfare.

From this beginning, Congress has repeatedly expanded the authority of state enforcement agencies. In further legislation, it mandated various state actions on pain of losing federal support.[3] Among the actions now required of these agencies are those to restrict, suspend or deny driving and/or professional licenses for those delinquent in their child support obligations. In addition, many states now require employers to report the names and addresses of newly hired employees. This information is then used specifically to find absent fathers and levy assessments. There are also programmes to intercept income tax refunds from delinquent parents. And finally, in 1998, Congress created two new categories of federal felonies for the wilful failure to pay child support. Child support obligations are now treated far more harshly than any other form of debt.

As policy actions expanded, the immediate withdrawal of support obligations from an obligor's paycheque – wage withholding – became a favoured tool. Although originally employed only in cases where there were delinquent obligations, it soon was used pre-emptively even where there was no delinquency. Congress authorized 'immediate' wage withholding in the Family Support Act of 1988, which became effective in November 1990 for all new or modified support orders. There was the presumption that many support orders would not be obeyed, and the solution was to treat them as taxes and withdraw them directly from the parent's paycheque.

Originally, the federal government required that the first $50 of support payments each month be paid to families rather than retained by government as reimbursement for prior assistance. The purpose was to provide at least a token impact of child support payments on the child's family, for otherwise there would be no relationship at all between what a non-custodial father paid and what a custodial mother received. However, in 1996 that requirement was removed, and states were no longer obliged to 'pass through' the first $50 of payments each month. Accordingly, a large number of states stopped doing so.

Finally, the federal government, first in 1984 and more forcefully in 1988, required states to adopt child support guidelines that would provide the basis of court-ordered obligations. The states were required to create guidelines that judges would be expected to follow. Although advisory in 1984, by 1988 judges were permitted to depart from these guidelines only when they provided a written finding as to why they were doing so. As expected, most judges followed the established guidelines.

An important feature of the new guidelines was not so much their uniformity as the size of the awards. Support levels imposed on non-custodial parents were now much higher than previously. By one estimate, the adoption of the various state guidelines increased child support obligations by more than double from what they were before: from $10 billion to approximately $27 billion for the year 1979 (Garfinkel, 2001, p. 443).

As Congress continued to legislate in this area, the states have generally followed the federal provisions. Figure 1.1 reviews trends in child support policies that have been adopted by the various states through 1997. As can be seen, except for providing directories of new hires, nearly all states have closely followed the federal requirements.

Along with this substantial expansion in the collection efforts of state agencies, there has been a major increase in government expenditures used for these purposes. As reported in Figure 1.2, federal and state governments spent nearly $3.4 billion on the child support enforcement programme in 1997 as compared with $389 million in 1976, expressed in 1997 dollars. By 2001, they had grown to $4.8 billion. When reported as total expenditures per single mother, these outlays increased from $71 in 1976 to $458 in 1997, and were even higher by 2001. The child support collection effort had become a major government enterprise.

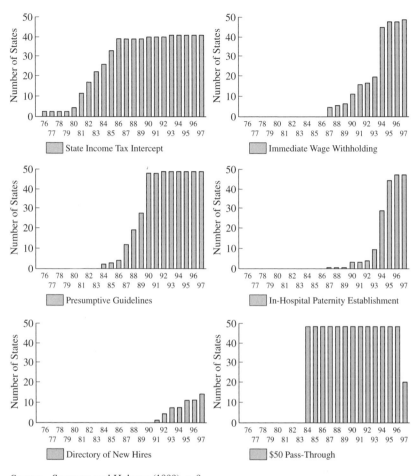

Source: Sorensen and Halpern (1999), p. 9.

Figure 1.1   Trends in child support policies

As with all such efforts, the critical question is, what are the results? What has been the effect of this major expansion in government powers and expenditures? The most telling response to this question is provided by statistics on the proportions of single mothers receiving child support payments. Government data from 1976 through 2001 are provided in Figure 1.3. As can be seen, the average percentage is only slightly higher in 2001 than it was 25 years earlier. It increased from 31 per cent in 1976 to 35 per cent in 2001. On an overall basis, the new policies have had a relatively small effect. Only about one-third of all single mothers receive their support payments.

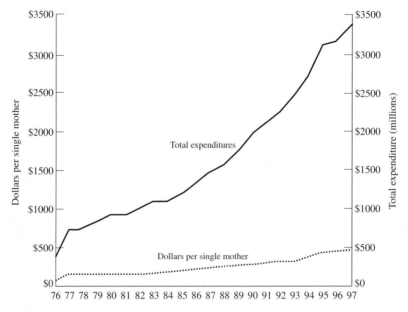

Note: Values expressed in 1997 dollars.

Source: March Current Population Surveys, as reported in Sorensen and Malpern (1999), p. 24.

Figure 1.2   Federal and state child support expenditures

To be sure, these overall results disguise larger effects in sub-groups of the population. For single mothers in the AFDC or TANF programmes, there has been increase in the proportions receiving child support payments. For those previously married, the percentage nearly doubled, from 15 per cent in 1976 to 28 per cent in 2001; while for single mothers who were never married, this percentage increased from 3 per cent to 19 per cent. For those cohorts, however, support payments made by the absent fathers are not generally received by custodial mothers. Except for the $50 'pass through' mentioned above, these payments are intercepted by the collecting agencies. For women in these cohorts, government support payments are received whether or not the non-custodial parent makes his mandated payments. And whether the funds received are considered welfare or child support is of little consequence.

The primary beneficiaries of the new policies, apart from the taxpayers, appear to be never-married women not on welfare. While child support collection rates are still quite low, they did increase from 8 per cent in 1976 to nearly 25 per cent by 2001.

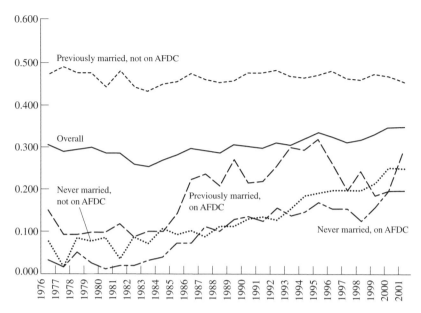

Source: US Bureau of Labor Statistics, Current Population Surveys, March.

*Figure 1.3   Percentage of unmarried mothers receiving child support by
                 marital and AFDC status*

For the largest cohort of single mothers, however, those previously
married and not receiving AFDC or TANF benefits, the new policies have
had little effect. The percentage receiving child support payments declined
from 47 per cent to 46 per cent over this 25-year period.

Another approach to this issue is through the results presented in Figure
1.4, although these data end in 1997. For previously married women, the
proportions receiving child support increased from 36 per cent in 1976 to
42 per cent in 1997, but this increase mainly applied to women receiving
government assistance. As for never-married women, the proportions
receiving child support remained far lower, although they did increase from
5 per cent to 18 per cent during the same period. Despite the major increase
in the number of single mothers who had never been married, and who are
most likely to be the source of government policies, this expansion was not
sufficient to provide an overall increase in child support receipt rates.

The striking feature of these findings is that the new policies have been
most successfully applied to single mothers who receive government assistance. Yet, in those cases, a very small share of total child support payments
is actually forwarded to these households. In fiscal year 2001, out of total

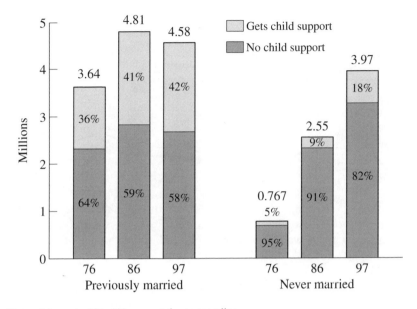

Note: May not add to 100 per cent due to rounding.

Source: March Current Population Surveys, as reported in Sorensen and Halpern (1999), p. 4.

Figure 1.4   Number of single mothers by marital status and receipt of child support

AFDC/TANF collections of $2.6 billion, only $355 million, or just under 4 per cent, was actually paid to these families. The rest was used to reimburse federal and state governments for previous assistance.[4]

THE COST-EFFECTIVENESS OF THE CHILD SUPPORT COLLECTION SYSTEM

With the advent of immediate wage withholding, the number of dollars passing through the government collection system exploded. In the six years between 1994 and 2001, total collections nearly doubled from $9.9 billion to $19 billion. Most of this increase did not apply to 'welfare' cases. AFDC/TANF collections remained stable at $2.5 billion in 1994 and $2.6 billion in 2001.[5]

From a longer time perspective, the growth in collections encompassed by the enforcement system is striking. Expressed in 1996 dollars, aggregate collections jumped from $2.6 billion in 1978 to $13.8 billion in 1998, or by an increase of more than five times during this 20-year period.[6] Despite this considerable increase, however, the proportion of single mothers receiving support changed very little over this period, and also average collections in constant dollars have not changed very much.[7] What is apparent is that the enhanced collection system has brought increasing numbers of dollars within its structure without changing very much the total volume of payments actually received by single mothers.

On the other side of the ledger, total administrative expenditures in 2001 were $4.8 billion, including both state and federal outlays, up from $2.6 billion six years before in 1994. The Office of Child Support Enforcement compares the $19.0 billion figure for total collections with these total administrative cost amounts, and reports a 'cost-effectiveness ratio' of 3.9.

Ronald Henry emphasizes the problem with this conclusion in Chapter 5. The reported cost-effectiveness ratio requires the assumption that none of these payments would have been collected in the absence of these policies, so that one can attribute every dollar to their presence. However, as we saw above, apart from their effect on low-income households, largely AFDC/TANF single mothers, the primary impact of this programme has been to bring an increasing volume of payments within its confines rather than expand the number of recipients.

Henry argues that most of the child support dollars collected under the new system would have been paid anyway. If the primary purpose of the programme is instead to recoup prior government outlays, then there are total expenditures of $4.8 billion used to obtain reimbursed expenses of $2.2 billion, which hardly describes a cost-effective programme.

Earlier studies of the cost-effectiveness of these policies have reached similar conclusions. Beller and Graham (1993), examined interstate differences in the resources devoted to child support enforcement. They concluded:

> In summary, variations in state government efforts in this child support enforcement program have no impact on the magnitude of child support payments among women overall. Variations in government spending have no impact on child support receipt rates, either, but more efficient IV-D agencies do appear to raise receipt rates by a small amount. (p. 183)

Another study, by Garfinkel and Robins in Garfinkel et al. (1994), employed a regression model to study child support outcomes. These authors report:

> For every dollar spent for a female-headed family, approximately 52 cents more in child support is collected, implying that the expenditures are not cost-effective. (p. 142)

They urge caution, however, in interpreting these results as the underlying policy variables are held constant.

Although there are specific areas where the recent acceleration in collection efforts has led to increased receipts, the broader picture is that these payments have been quite resistant to policy actions. Particularly for the previously married non-welfare segment of the population, there has been little increase in child support collections. And also, there is no indication that net receipts have increased as rapidly as government expenditures designed to expand those receipts.

SETTING CHILD SUPPORT OBLIGATIONS

What is apparent from these results is that the support obligations imposed on many non-custodial parents exceed their willingness to pay. A likely reason is the conflict between the alternative belief systems described above. While the proponents of recent policies may have the first objective in mind, the second is more acceptable to absent parents. Indeed, delinquent payers often explain their actions by asserting that these payments are used largely for the custodial parent rather than the children. In return, those who advance the first system maintain that these payments are needed for the children, and the unwillingness to make them by absent parents represents irresponsible behaviour.

Another explanation for the high degree of non-payment may be the process through which these obligations are set. In many cases, they are made without the knowledge or input of the absent parent. As Ronald Henry points out, personal service of child support orders is not generally required, but rather it is sufficient to provide service 'at the last known address'. As a result, he continues, 'tens of thousands of men . . . accrue years of unmodifiable arrearages before they even learn that they have been named as fathers' (p. 147).

Henry cites evidence for Los Angeles County that 53 per cent of the cases do not provide personal service and 70 per cent of non-custodial parents are not present in court when child support obligations are set. Although the experience of Los Angeles County may offer an extreme example, still a reliance on one-sided procedures, particularly in the case of parents who are not married, could be the source of non-payment in a large number of cases.

Even if both parents do participate in the process, the basic structure of awards might not be much different. The Family Support Act of 1988 required states to establish guidelines that judges would apply, and for the most part, those guidelines are followed. A concomitant objective of the new guidelines was to increase substantially support obligations over what they were before. These higher payments, following the first system of belief, were needed to improve living standards for custodial parents, and we consider now whether that objective was achieved.[8]

Chapter 4 by Sanford Braver and David Stockburger deals directly with the implications of the current guidelines for living standards of both the custodial and non-custodial parents. Although these authors reject this purpose for child support payments, they examine the extent to which the support standards embodied in the guidelines have the effect of equalizing living standards between the parents.

These authors account specifically for the relative tax effects and child care expenses of non-custodial parents. They determine support obligations under various scenarios dealing with the relative incomes of the two parents, the number of children, and their absolute incomes. From their computations, they conclude 'that the majority of custodial parents [now] have higher standards of living than their matched non-custodial parents' (p. 122). This result, however, differs substantially among states depending on the specific details of the guidelines employed. They find, for example, that it applies to Massachusetts but not to Missouri.

Chapter 3 by Rogers and Bieniewicz also examines this issue, although it employs a different methodology. The authors use the poverty thresholds for 2001, as published by the US Bureau of the Census, to determine relative living costs in differently sized households. By these values, a household with one parent and one child requires a 32 per cent higher income to reach the same living standard as a single-adult household, and a family with two children and one parent requires a 55 per cent higher income.

Rogers and Bieniewicz apply the presumptive support awards indicated in state guidelines, but also account for the differential tax effects of the payments and assume that the absent father has direct children's expenditures associated with a 25/75 parenting time division. On this basis, they report: 'the custodial parent typically ends up with a substantially higher standard of living than the non-custodial parent – even when the non-custodial parent starts with higher gross earnings' (p. 61). Their conclusions are thereby similar to those of Braver and Stockburger.

In addition, Rogers and Bieniewicz review the various state guidelines and point out that nearly all states employ one of two alternative methods. Thirty-three states use guidelines based on income shares, which rest on the incomes of both parents, while an additional 13 states set awards by a fixed percentage of the non-custodial parent's income. Although both sets of guidelines are designed in principle to measure the costs of raising children, these authors point out that neither deals with actual expenditure patterns but rather use an indirect means to estimate the cost of children.

Given the arbitrary nature of the methods used to determine support awards, it is hardly surprising that different states provide quite different amounts. These authors compare child support awards in four different states, each using different methods, and report differences of approximately 30 per cent between the highest and lowest amounts. Furthermore, they note that all methods in current use provide much higher payments than the more direct approach of determining the actual cost shares of children's expenses. Rogers and Bieniewicz describe this latter method and provide relative award levels in Tables 3.14 and 3.15.

In determining support obligations, there is an important distinction between the costs of the children and the appropriate size of the award. This distinction is important, according to the second belief system. To be sure, differences between costs and awards would not exist in cases where a custodial parent has no outside income and a non-custodial parent sees his children very little and so has no direct child costs.

However, by this second belief system, child support awards should be lower when family circumstances are different.[9] If we assume, for example, that the custodial parent has an income that is half that of the non-custodial parent, so that the latter earns two-thirds of total family income, and that the non-custodial parent cares for his children directly for one-quarter of the time, then the appropriate obligation is only 42 per cent of the total child costs.[10] These two factors are therefore critical for setting appropriate child support obligations.

The distinction between costs and expenditures lies at the heart of Chapter 6 by Robert and Cynthia McNeely. As a matter of economics, costs describe the minimum level of expenditures needed to achieve a particular set of results. Translated to the child support arena, the economic costs of children would provide only for basic necessities. In contrast, expenditures describe actual outlays, which may be far higher. The McNeelys point out that federal legislation requires that support payments should go beyond basic needs, and specifically declares that 'to the extent either parent enjoys a higher than subsistence-level standard of living, the child is entitled to share in the benefit of that improved standard' (p. 171). They observe that a federally imposed entitlement has thus been created, which applies only to absent parents.

The McNeelys argue that creating this entitlement is unjust. Under common law, parents are required merely to provide a minimum level of support. The federally imposed entitlement thereby applies only to a subset of children; those with unmarried parents. It would not apply, for example, to circumstances where the two parents together provided only minimal support for their children.

These three chapters focus on the mandated guidelines through which child support obligations are currently set. While each looks at this process from a different vantage point, together they describe one with unexpected consequences. In particular, Rogers and Bieniewicz maintain that child support awards are generally much higher than needed to pay for actual expenditures on the children, particularly when relative income levels and parenting time are taken into account. The ostensible purpose of those payments is instead to improve living standards in the custodial parent's household; and when paid, that is precisely what occurs.

The critical provision, of course, is that child support payments have this effect only when they are paid. And as we noted above, those obligations are not paid in a large number of cases. A major reason for that result may be the recognition that these payments provide an income supplement and exceed the amounts actually used for the children.

THE COST OF CHILDREN

At this point, we return to the question of how the costs of children are determined. These costs, of course, are the ostensible reason for child support payments.

For some items, determining children's consumption is readily done. For example, one can distinguish between clothing expenditures for the child and for the parent, and there is survey data available that make this distinction. Such goods are private rather than collective goods. In other cases, however, this distinction is not easily made. The classic example of a household collective good is housing. For such items, the two systems of belief diverge sharply in their judgment of what are appropriate levels of support.

Within the first system of belief, housing is the quintessential household good that should be provided through child support payments. Both parent and child benefit from their residence, and support payments should legitimately cover all housing costs. In contrast, those who support the second belief system observe that a custodial parent would have housing costs even without children, so the children's housing outlays should be limited to the additional expenditures used for the larger housing unit needed because of them. For example, if a mother would provide herself with a one-bedroom apartment, then her child's housing costs are measured by the additional outlays associated with a two-bedroom apartment. The relevant economic concept is marginal rather than average cost.[11] In principle, marginal outlays can be measured by the additional expenditures in particular consumption categories made by a household with children as compared to an identical household without them.

Although all members of a household, children as well as adults, jointly consume all collectively provided items, such as housing or transportation, that fact does not mean that their marginal valuations are the same. Indeed, we expect that adults value certain attributes of a collective good more strongly than children, and *vice versa*. An example might be proximity of the household's dwelling to shopping or fine restaurants as compared to playgrounds and schools. The benefits derived from these factors, and the proportions of total costs attributable to different household members, turn on the underlying utility functions of each member, which of course are unobservable.

A recent review of the economic literature on child costs considers the problem of household collective goods (Van Praag and Warnaar, 1997). Merely allocating these costs equally to all members would not be correct since different members invariably spend different amounts. In particular, there is evidence that much less is spent on children than on adults.

Lazear and Michael (1998) examine consumption spending within the household from data collected by the Bureau of Labor Statistics in the 1972–73 Consumer Expenditure Survey. They assume that joint costs are allocated within the household in the same ratio as private goods. On this basis, they find that the average family spends only 38 per cent as much on a child as on an adult (p. 87). Stated differently, these authors write that 'an adult commands about 2.5 times the resources enjoyed by a child in a typical family' (p. 87).

A striking feature of the child support figures embodied in the guidelines currently in use is that they do not rest on any allocation of household expenditures among its members, and thus avoid the problem of allocating joint costs. Instead, they employ an indirect approach. This alternate method attempts to measure the income equivalence of a child, and then defines that value as the costs of children. It measures child costs by the answer to the following question: how much must a one-child couple be compensated in order to be equally well off economically as without the child?[12] Because that method serves as the foundation for the current guidelines, we consider it in some detail.

To make this question operational, we employ the economic concept of an indirect utility function, which is defined by the following expression:

$$V(p, y_1, z_1) = V(p, y_2, z_2) \tag{1}$$

In this equation, V represents the utility or well-being of the adult decision-makers within the household. The variable p indicates the prices faced by the household, which are assumed constant under all circumstances. In situation I, described on the left-hand side of this expression, the household has income of y_1 and a demographic composition of z_1. Let z_1 represent a household of two adults and no children.

Now consider an alternate household with the same utility function, which is indicated as situation II on the right-hand side of this expression. Because of the equality sign, it has the same level of utility or well-being as the first household. One can consider the two situations as describing the same family before and after having a child, since the demographic composition in the second situation is indicated by z_2, a household consisting of two adults and one child. The demographic difference between the two households is therefore the presence of a child in the second case. If the two households have the same incomes, indicated by y_1 and y_2 respectively, their utility levels may still not be the same since their compositions are different. Now let y_2 be varied until the utility levels on the two sides of the equation become equal. Despite their different compositions, the two households must have the same levels of utility or well-being for this equation to hold. Consider the likely values that y_2 might take in order to bring the two sides into balance, as compared with the original income level of y_1.

Suppose the adult decision-makers in the second household sought to have the child, and it brings them greater utility despite any additional costs or burdens that accompany the child. In that case, the variable z like the variable y provides them with positive utility. Then a higher value of z would require a lower value of y on the right-hand side to make the two sides of the equation equal. y_2 is now lower than y_1 as the adult decision-makers implicitly accept a lower income level as compensation for having the child. This lower income level is needed to retain equality between the two sides of the equation. Clearly, in these circumstances, the difference in income levels between the two situations cannot measure the costs of a child because they would here be negative.

For this approach to be used to measure the costs of children requires the additional assumption that children provide no utility at all for the adults, and that the adults in their roles as parents receive no utility from the consumption levels of their children. Both costs and benefits of children are ignored. While this may be a dubious assumption, it is required by this approach.

Under those restrictive conditions, consider again how this equation can be used. Again, let z_2 describe the second demographic situation where there is a child along with the two adults. However, there is now no additional utility that results from the child. Still, there are costs of children, which are represented here by c_2. We then have a new expression:

$$V(p, y_1, z_1) > V(p, (y_2 - c_2), z_2) \tag{2}$$

$$\text{where } \frac{\partial V}{\partial z_1} = \frac{\partial V}{\partial z_2} = 0$$

The partial derivatives below this equation merely represent the assumption that the demographic status of the household has no effect on the utility levels of the two households. The net income level in situation II, $(y_2 - c_2)$ is now lower than y_2 alone. If the original income levels were the same, the second household now has lower income and thereby a lower level of utility. The only point of difference between the two situations is that the income available for adult consumption in the second case is reduced by c_2. Only by increasing income by this amount to compensate for the child's costs can utility be returned to its earlier level, and equality be achieved. This additional income supplement, necessarily equal to c_2, describes the Income Compensation method used to determine the costs of children.

This approach relies critically on various assumptions. In particular, it requires that children provide no value to their parents. In a review of the economic literature dealing with this method, the authors acknowledge that these estimates 'have only meaning if you accept the hypothesis that utility is not conditioned by the number of children in the household. If you do not assume that, it is hard to make any meaning out of the [values obtained]' (Van Praag and Warnaar, 1997, p. 259).

An earlier paper by Pollak and Wales (1979) makes that point even more strongly. They write:

> The usual practice is to base welfare comparisons on equivalence scales esti-
> mated from observed differences in the consumption patterns of households
> with different numbers of children. This is illegitimate. The expenditure level
> required to make a three-child family as well off as it would be with two children
> and $12000 depends on how the family feels about children. Observed differ-
> ences in the consumption patterns of two- and three-child families cannot even
> tell us whether the third child is regarded as a blessing or a curse. (p. 216)

Pollak and Wales emphasize that children influence utility levels, and also that parents' well-being is affected by the consumption levels of their children. For this reason, an approach which requires that both effects be absent cannot provide accurate figures on the costs of children.

To be sure, as Van Praag and Warnaar point out, this critique assumes that children are available to the adults in each household, which may not be the case. Not all adults have the option of changing the demographic status of their household. In some cases, the prospect of childlessness poses few implications for utility, while in others these effects can be substantial. However, it still makes little sense simply to assume these effects are absent and then derive estimates that require such unrealistic assumptions.

Further problems exist. Even making the assumptions required to use equation (2), one needs to find some means to equate the two sets of util-ities. How can one know whether a particular dollar compensation amount would bring the two utility levels into balance? Two methods have been used. The first deals with the share of food in the household budget, and the second deals with the share of adult goods, typically adult clothing, tobacco and alcoholic beverages. The reasoning here is that when a household with a child spends the same amount on these commodities as it would spend, or did spend, when childless, then the two households have the same levels of utility. Since utility levels are not measurable, the shares of food or of adult goods are used as proxies. The investigator merely assumes that utilities are the same when these expenditure shares are the same.

As Van Praag and Warnaar observe, although these methods look plausible, they are based on rather dubious assumptions (p. 249). They point out that consumption patterns for both food and adult goods invariably shift as the demographic composition of the household changes. As we all know, parents behave differently, and gain utility in very different ways, from childless couples. The attempt to equate utility levels with consumption shares is therefore illegitimate.

One study explored this issue by examining outlays on adult clothing in relation to the number of children in the household. The author reports that 'the existence of children reduces the marginal propensity to consume adult clothing by one-quarter' (Gronau, 1991, p. 217). That finding runs directly counter to the required assumption that income shares for adults can be used to represent utility levels.

While it is understandable that analysts have sought indirect means to measure the costs of children in order to avoid the problem of dealing with household collective goods, there is wide recognition among economists that this effort has failed. Particularly as applied to the determination of child support guidelines, we should examine expenditure patterns by families with and without children. Instead of indirect methods, the guidelines should employ consumer survey data directly to determine the costs of raising children.

THE PROPENSITY TO SPEND INCOME ON CHILDREN

In the previous sections, we reviewed the standards used to set current child support levels. At this point, we consider a different dimension of this issue, which is the propensity of custodial parents to spend these payments, however determined, on their children. The critical feature of child support payments is that they provide an income supplement to the custodial parent, who has no requirement to spend the funds received on any particular purpose. The question examined here is the extent to which child support payments are likely to be spent on the children.

Even where the purpose of these payments is limited to supporting the children rather than contributing to a broader income maintenance programme, there are two rationales for these payments. They can be labelled alternatively the 'economic' and the 'equitable'. The first of these concerns the allocation of resources to the children, and reflects the extent to which support payments lead to increased spending on children. In contrast, the 'equitable' rationale deals with the distribution of support burden between the parents, which may have little effect on total spending for the children. If support payments are used to reimburse a custodial parent for outlays already made, and do not lead to any increased spending, they may satisfy the equitable justification even if they have no economic effect.

To explore these issues, we review some aspects of the model of economic behaviour offered by Robert Willis in his chapter. His analysis has important implications for the question of how child support payments are actually used, and thereby on the incentives faced by non-custodial parents when making these payments.

An underlying premise of his analysis is that the preferences of the two parents in regard to their children are the same in the original situation where they lived together with their children and a new situation where they live apart. Recall the earlier quotation from Argys et al. that the leading reason for non-payment is that non-custodial parents develop antipathy towards their ex-spouses and reduced concern for their children. Whether or not these factors lead to non-payment, they do not propel the results that follow. In this analysis, the absent father's preferences are the same whether he lives with or apart from his children.

A second premise of this discussion is that the preference functions of both parents in regard to preferred spending levels on their children are the same. Although this assumption is made for expository convenience, the essential conclusion of the analysis would be the same without it. In the example below, we assume that both parents willingly spend one-third of their income on their children.[13] Recall that Lazear and Michael reported actual expenditures on children that were somewhat lower.

Consider the example described in Table 1.1, which follows the Willis analysis. As noted before, it assumes that both parents, together and separately, provide one-third of their income for their children's consumption, leaving the remaining two-thirds for themselves. On this basis, as described in Case A of the table, the children's annual consumption outlays are $20000 out of total after-tax income of $60000 in the household. That allocation includes the value that the parents place on the additional children's welfare from household collective goods as well as from private goods. In addition, a *pro forma* division of each parent's income is also indicated, which again includes outlays on both collective and private goods. In this

Table 1.1   Incentives for child support payments: an example

	Custodial parent	Non-custodial parent	Both parents
CASE A: Intact family			
Income	$20000	$40000	$60000
Adult's consumption (2/3)	$13333	$26667	$40000
Child's consumption (1/3)	$6667	$13333	$20000
CASE B: Divided family; child support of $13333			
Income	$33333	$26667	$60000
Adult's consumption (2/3)	$22222	$26667	$48889
Child's consumption (1/3)	$11111	–	$11111

example, we assume that the non-custodial parent has twice the after-tax income of the custodial parent.[14]

Now consider the case of a divided family, and assume that the level of child support is set equal to the same amount that was spent originally by the non-custodial parent from his individual income.[15] As indicated in Table 1.1, these payments would equal $13333. When that amount is added to the custodial parent's income, the resulting figure is $33333, which exceeds the non-custodial parent's net income. While it would be possible for the custodial parent to spend the same $20000 on the children as both parents spent originally, that would reduce her consumption to $13333, which is the amount available from her income alone. Note that this consumption level is much lower than it was when the family was together. Spending the original $20000 on the children would leave her with much reduced consumption.

More likely, and consistent with our assumed preference function, the custodial parent continues to allocate two-thirds of her augmented income to herself and one-third to her children. Willis suggests that the custodial parent may sometimes set a minimum level below which she would not permit her child's consumption to fall. While that may be so, we assume here that this constraint is satisfied when she allocates one-third of her income to the children, including their share of all collective goods.[16]

Note the implications of the values given in Case B, where child support payments that equal past spending levels are levied and paid. The consumption levels of both parents are increased as compared to the assumed $20000 consumption level that each had with an intact family. This increase in consumption, however, may be illusory since it ignores any additional costs from supporting two households where previously there was only one.

Such costs could absorb any increase in consumption that is suggested by this example.

On the other hand, we see that the children's consumption levels are substantially lower than they were before: $11 111 as compared with $20 000. While adult consumption levels increase, children's consumption levels decline despite the payment of adequate child support. They decline here by 44 per cent.

Note also that the children's consumption level of $11 111 is less than total child support payments of $13 333. By simply following her own preferences and allocating one-third of her augmented income to her children, not only does she not spend all of the child support payments on the children, but also she now spends nothing from her own income on them. While formerly she spent $6667 from her income of $20 000 for this purpose, she now allocates nothing at all, and even absorbs for her own use a share of the child support payments received.

Now assume alternatively that the non-custodial parent refuses to make any support payments, and is not forced to do so by the government. The child's consumption falls to $6667, which not only is below the original consumption amount of $20 000 but also lower than the consumption level of $11 111 that would be reached if child support payments were paid. From the children's vantage point, that is the worst outcome of all. That prospect lies behind the argument that 'government intervention to . . . specify support obligations and collect payments are ways to raise spending by non-custodial parents closer to efficient levels' (Lerman and Sorensen, 2001, p. 13).

While the children benefit from the presence of these payments, for example, an increase in their consumption from $6667 to $11 111 levels, there are negative incentive effects for the payer. In order to increase his children's consumption by $4444 [$11 111 – $6667], the absent father must pay $13 333, which is three times larger [$4444 × 3 = $13 333]. Thus, it costs him $3 in child support to increase his children's consumption by $1. The reason, of course, is that the custodial parent, following her own preferences, reduces her support of the children by 67 cents for every dollar received in support payments from the non-custodial parent. In effect, she pushes most of the support burden onto him. This ratio of three to one follows from the expenditure patterns implicit in the assumed preference functions of the two parents. These figures may in fact understate actual incentive effects.[17]

From the non-custodial parent's viewpoint, increasing his children's consumption by one dollar within marriage costs him only a 67-cent decline in his own consumption spending.[18] However, it is associated with a $3 decline in his own consumption when accomplished through child support payments in our example and a $5 decline in the data reported by Willis. We would expect a typical non-custodial parent to react differently in the new circumstances, even if his concern for his children is unchanged.

Willis suggests that although absent fathers may be willing to make support payments when their children's consumption levels are low despite these disincentive effects, they are likely to be increasingly less willing to do so as the custodial parent's income increases and her outlays on the children from her own income increase. At some point, he finds the trade-off not worth the result, and refuses to make further payments. According to his own preference function, which again is the same as it was in the intact family, the absent father now finds it optimal to pay nothing. The economic incentives lead directly to that result.

There is a further important implication to be drawn from this example. Assume as we did before that each parent's consumption within the intact family was one-half of total adult consumption, or $20 000. For the custodial parent, her own consumption would decline with separation to $13 333 without child support payments, but increase to $22 222 with support payments. Child support payments thus lead to an increase in her consumption standards as compared to what they were before, although admittedly one must now deduct any additional costs of supporting a separate household. Apart from this factor, consumption levels are higher out of marriage than they are within marriage as a direct result of child support payments.

Willis concludes that an overly generous system of child support payments 'would create an incentive for divorce by the custodial mother which, in turn, would cause an actual reduction in the welfare of the child' (p. 42). To the extent that child support payments serve to destabilize marriages that are already tenuous, they provide an incentive for divorce, which in turn leads to much lower welfare levels for the children. In an effort to be more generous to the children, such provisions may actually make them worse off.

In Chapter 6, the McNeelys discuss the principles embodied in the 1984 legislation that the state guidelines were directed to follow. These principles include the requirement that 'a guideline should not create extraneous negative effects on major life decisions of either parent'. As this example makes clear, high child support schedules increase the incentives for divorce by the intended recipient, and thereby violate that principle.

CHILD SUPPORT AND VISITATION

Despite the considerable disincentives that are present, child support payments are often paid. As reported in Figure 1.4, the proportion of single mothers receiving support in the largest cohort, those previously married and not on welfare, has been fairly stable for the past 25 years at between 45 and 50 per cent. This stability suggests that the new policies were not responsible for these payments.

While one explanation for support payments by non-custodial parents is of course a desire to support their children despite the adverse incentives that are present, another is the objective to secure ready access to them. Visitation time is invariably controlled by the custodial parent, whatever the legal requirements. Courts rarely overrule a custodial parent's position that for one reason or another, her child's interests are better served by disrupting visitation schedules. The willing participation of the custodial parent is typically required for visitation to proceed.

In a voluntary setting, visitation schedules and child support payments are closely tied. Thus, a recent study simply presumes that 'the amount of time the children spend with each parent is the outcome of an exchange between mother and father after divorce, where the mother controls the time of the child and the father acquires this time with his income' (Del Boca and Ribero, 1999, p. 3). These authors model that type of exchange and offer supporting empirical evidence. They suggest that non-resident fathers voluntarily pay child support in order specifically to secure visitation rights.[19]

Another study reaches the same conclusions. The authors write:

> Divorce contracts can be self-enforcing because money and custody are linked inextricably in a strategic bargaining game. The NCP (non-custodial parent) controls the actual payments of child support. The CP (custodial parent), on the other hand, determines the ease with which the NCP spends time with the children. Thus each parent has some influence over the other's well-being, and in fact can retaliate if the other parent is not complying with his or her part of the bargain. (Peters et al., 1993, p. 721)

For these reasons, many divorce settlements are self-enforcing, although of course that is not always the case.

Although most single-mother headed households rest on sole custody arrangements, a smaller number have joint custody arrangements, which provide both enhanced visitation and some greater authority to the non-resident parent for decisions regarding the children. Both factors should lead to more regular support payments, which in fact is reported in a recent study (Del Boca and Ribero, 1998). The authors find that 'joint custody increases the regularity of voluntary transfers by 19 percent and the regularity of mandated child support by 8 percent' (p. 477). In this context as well, visitation arrangements have an important influence on child support.

Despite the clear relationship between these factors, current government policies treat them very differently. While there has been a great expansion in policy actions and government expenditures towards the enforcement of child support payments, there have been few government actions taken to enforce visitation rights. For the most part, current policies towards the latter are not much different than they were in 1974 when Title IV-D of the Social Security Act was passed. Although custodial parents can receive considerable help to obtain support payments, non-custodial parents must pay the full legal costs themselves to secure access and visitation rights.[20]

This disparity is also evidenced by reports that 'the federal Office of Child Support Enforcement has made annual awards of $10 million in 1997 and 1998 to states to provide services that promote access between non-custodial parents and their children'.[21] By way of contrast, the federal share of child support collection expenses in 1998 was approximately $2.4 billion. The grants reported above thereby account for less than one-half of one per cent of total federal expenditures on child support matters.

There is general acknowledgement that the problem of visitation disruption by custodial parents is widespread. In a survey of custodial mothers, Wallerstein and Kelly found that nearly half of the custodial parents interviewed acknowledged interfering with visitation arrangements at least occasionally (Wallerstein and Kelly, 1980, p. 125). These authors reported that 30 per cent of their respondents actively tried to sabotage meetings between their children and the non-custodial parent. Another study presented results from a survey of grown children whose parents had divorced. The author writes that '42 percent of the respondents said that their mother tried to prevent them from seeing their father after the divorce' (Walker, 1986, p. 83). Others have offered different estimates, but in no case is there any suggestion that this problem is unimportant (Pearson and Thoennes, 1998, pp. 221–2).

Payments of child support and visitation activities are complementary (Veum, 1992). There is evidence that fathers who see their children more frequently make these payments, while fathers who rarely see them are much less likely to do so. Data from a 1987–88 national survey indicate that among fathers who do not see their children at all, only 16.2 per cent pay any child support, while among fathers who see their children more frequently than several times a year, 64.2 per cent make these payments (Seltzer, 1991, p. 86).

While the correlation between these two factors is acknowledged, what remains unclear is the direction of causality. Does increased visitation promote increased payment of child support, or does the nonpayment of child support lead to withholding visitation? Does the absence of visitation signal a lack of interest by the non-custodial parent in the child, which is associated also with an unwillingness to pay child support? Alternatively, are there common factors such as hostility between the parents that lead both factors to be low, or mutual respect that leads them both to be high? The available studies do not provide answers to these questions. While arguments can be made in all directions, there are no accepted conclusions.

Whatever the actual relationship between these two factors, current legal rules treat them as separate and independent obligations. In particular, they do not allow for any *quid pro quo* arrangement between parents in regard to child support and visitation. Thus, a father who is denied visitation is not permitted to withhold child support payments. And similarly, a mother who has not received these payments is not authorized to withhold access to the children. There is a question of whether the current separation is good policy, or whether the payment of child support and visitation frequency would not both be enhanced by linking them more closely together.

Ellman's chapter provides an extensive review of current legal standards on the relationship between child support and visitation. He starts by quoting a Wyoming Supreme Court decision as offering the typical rationale for the current approach: 'The welfare of the child is a primary concern and the duty of a non-custodial parent to support his or her child cannot depend on that parent's opportunity to exercise visitation rights.'[22] This explanation, however, rests on the assumption that child support payments are used largely for the support of the children.

That rationale has questionable foundations. As reported above, the amounts specified under the current guidelines generally exceed those required for the children's direct expenses, and are primarily used to improve the living standards of the custodial parent. Furthermore, Willis's analysis of child support incentives indicates that only between one-fifth and one-third of child support payments are actually used for the children's support. The logic of these payments is that they are used largely by the custodial parent.

Although Ellman supports a policy change to link these reciprocal obligations, he recommends that 'various noncoercive remedies' should be attempted first. However, he acknowledges that 'reductions or even suspension of the support obligation may be appropriate' in some cases that resist solution (p. 204).

The problem with an incremental approach is that it ignores the incentive effects associated with child support payments. To the extent that custodial parents directly benefit from these payments, incentive effects become more important. When a judge is specifically authorized to reduce support obligations upon finding the intentional interference of visitation, there is then a prospective cost of disruptive behaviour – and we would expect less of it.

Chapter 8 by Geoffrey Miller deals with a related issue, which is whether the original award of child support payments should be influenced by expected levels of visitation. He reviews the considerable evidence on the benefits to children from enhanced visitation, and concludes:

> Courts should presume that non-custodial parents are entitled to the most liberal visitation rights possible consistent with the best interest of the child . . . The burden [then] would be on the custodial parent to provide that the proposed schedule was not consistent with the child's best interests. (p. 223)

Once visitation levels are set, Miller considers their appropriate effects on child support awards. Here, he pays particular attention to the California rule for setting child support awards, which requires courts to adjust awards in relation to the amount of time each parent spends with the children. He argues, this 'adjustment encourages non-custodial parents to remain actively involved in the lives of their children after parental separation' (p. 229). He supports applying the California rule throughout the country.

While these two chapters are related to each other, they deal with different aspects of the same problem. While one concerns the setting of awards, the other considers whether awards should be modified in response to a failure to permit authorized levels of visitation. Despite current legal rules that emphasize the separateness of these two sets of obligations, both writers acknowledge the need to consider them in tandem.

SOME CONCLUSIONS

Child support payments are designed to immunize children from the financial consequences of divorce. The analysis provided here, and throughout the rest of this volume, suggests that this effort is unlikely to succeed. Not only can there be substantial economic costs associated with supporting two households where one existed before, but more important, the economic incentives to achieve that result are not present. It would occur, as Professor Willis points out, only if the custodial parent took the non-custodial parent's preferences fully into account when determining how her income is spent. However, there are few prospects for creating the same incentives within a single-parent household as would exist where the two parents are together. And under the revised incentive structure, we expect much lower spending levels on children.

In these circumstances, the surprising result is not that so few fathers make their child support payments, but rather that so many do. Among the largest cohort of the population – those previously married and not receiving welfare payments – nearly half of all single mothers receive these payments.

As reported in Figure 1.3, this percentage has remained fairly stable over the past 25 years. Whether to assure the living standards of his ex-spouse, accede to legal requirements, or ensure visitation rights, these payments are made despite the adverse incentives that are present.

Furthermore, as reported above, a majority of single mothers, even within this cohort, do not receive any payments. For these fathers, the incentive incompatibility between the payments and their objectives is apparently too great. As Henry points out in Chapter 5:

> This unique separation of the rights of custody and the duties of support . . . is matched nowhere else in the legal system that has prided itself upon its attention to the principle that the possessor of rights should also bear the burdens and responsibilities associated with those rights. It is this bifurcation of rights and responsibilities that is at the root of the civil disobedience portion of the child support enforcement problem. (p. 139)

A related issue follows the distinction between economic 'goods' and 'bads'. In a market economy, payments are generally made by one party to another in return for something of value. In its simplest form, a customer in the store receives an item and makes a payment in return. As a matter of economics, the item received is a 'good' such that the payer is at least as well off with a lower net income and the item as he or she was with a higher income but without the item.

At the same time, some items are economic 'bads', which means only that they place a burden on the individual who has them. A 'bad' reduces the person's well-being so that he or she is willing to make payments in order for the recipient to accept it. As in the case of rubbish, the payer must be at least equally well off with a lower net income but without the item.

Translated to the case of children and child support payments, the current support system treats children as a 'bad' rather than a 'good'. In order for absent parents willingly to make child support payments, their children must pose a burden for which they are willing to pay another to assume child-rearing responsibilities. Indeed, if children were considered an economic 'good' for both parents, payments would instead be made by the custodial parent to the non-custodial parent in order to compensate the latter for the loss of his children. Yet of course that is not what occurs.

There is considerable ambivalence in policy discussions on how children should be viewed when their parents are apart. It is this ambivalence that lies at the heart of the difficulties encountered when dealing with support issues. If children are really an economic 'good' rather than a 'bad', then the non-custodial parent who is required to make a payment that accompanies the loss of his children sees his utility twice diminished, while the custodial parent who receives both the children and the payment has her utility twice enhanced. This combination of transfers lies behind the unwillingness of many non-custodial parents to make their required payments.

There are also questions of the importance of support payments for measured levels of child performance. Is there any indication that child performance is improved along measurable dimensions when these payments are made? The final two chapters of the volume – those by Antecol and Bedard, and by Comanor and Phillips – explore these relationships. Both chapters review some of the literature on these issues but also provide new empirical evidence. On the whole, both chapters provide similar findings, which is that there is little evidence that children do better in the ways measured by these writers when child support payments are made. There is little indication here that support payments lead to enhanced child performance. Again, that result is hardly surprising, to the extent that these payments are primarily used to improve the living standards of the custodial parent.

There is growing evidence that the current system of child support collection does not work. It has imposed increasingly harsh penalties on errant fathers without expanding appreciably the proportions of single mothers actually receiving payments. What is apparent from the chapters of this book is that current policies rely on certain assumptions that are not supported by the evidence, or alternatively are so inconsistent with the interests of potential payers that they are unwilling to accept the imposed obligations. In this realm, as in many others, some level of agreement by all parties is essential.

The current system is largely an effort to create an income maintenance scheme in the name of child support. It imposes responsibilities on absent fathers that many did not see coming and seek to evade. There is also evidence that these payments have little relationship to the amounts actually spent on the children.

Major changes must be made in the current system of setting and enforcing these payments. Otherwise, we will find a continuing disparity between society's efforts to enforce these payments and the amounts actually paid.

NOTES

*   I appreciate the helpful comments and suggestions of Scott Altman, H.E. Frech and Stephen Patt on an earlier version of this chapter.
1.   While these writers acknowledge greater differences in average incomes between two-parent and female-headed households with children, they observe that 'part of the income difference across family types may exist for reasons other than difference in family structure' (p. 5). Their analysis corrects for these other factors.
2.   Argys et al. (2001), p. 228.

3. See Sorensen and Halpern (1999), pp. 6–11.
4. US HHS Report (1998), p. 46. Total assistance reimbursement in FY 2001 was $2.2 billion. US HHS Annual Data Report (2001).
5. US Department of Health and Human Services, Office of Child Support Enforcement, various annual reports.
6. Lerman and Sorensen (2001), Table 5, p. 58.
7. Ibid.
8. This purpose is clearly indicated in Grace Blumberg's proposals for the American Law Institute where she recommends adding a 'supplemental percentage' to any awards in order specifically to improve the living standards of the custodial parent.
9. See the discussion in Geoffrey Miller's chapter at pp. 210–40.
10. Where the non-custodial parent's income is two-thirds of the total, then he is responsible for only two-thirds of the children's support, assuming that the support burden is divided according to income. And if he pays one-quarter of their support directly, that proportion should be subtracted from his total obligation to reach the figure of 41.7 per cent. Another way to reach that proportion is to assume he is responsible for two-thirds of their support during the three-quarters of the year that the children are with their mother. At the same time, she is responsible for one-third of their support during the one-quarter of the year that they remain with their father. Two-thirds times three-quarters equals 50 per cent, from which is deducted one-third times one-quarter, or 8.3 per cent. This difference is 41.7 per cent.
11. The economic concept of cost pertains to these additional outlays required to reach a particular result. If housing outlays without children are a certain amount and housing outlays with a child are a greater amount, the housing cost specifically of the child is the difference between these two amounts.
12. See Chapter 3 below by Rogers and Bieniewicz, pp. 60–90.
13. At the outset of his chapter, Willis assumes that both parents have Cobb–Douglas utility functions such that these relative spending levels are set. However, this function is modified in the latter part of his chapter. In either case, the critical factor is the assumption that both parents wish to spend a certain proportion of their income on their children, and that this preference is unchanged whether the two parents live together or apart.
14. Willis reports data from the 1972–73 Consumer Expenditure Survey that the average husband had an income of $24708 while the average wife had income of $12025. The two-to-one ratio used here is generally consistent with these results. Del Boca and Ribero (1999), report similar findings for the year 1986. In their sample of non-intact families, the average income of the father is $16822 and of the mother is $7155. The ratio of their figures is somewhat higher at 2.35. See their Table 2, p. 15.
15. Where support payments are designed to replace the amounts spent originally on the children, that level of support would be considered optimal. In that case, however, it requires neutral tax effects between the parents, and also that following separation, the children spend all of their time with their mother so the father has no visitation or parenting expenses.
16. This analysis assumes that the custodial parent treats transfers from the non-custodial parent the same as income from any other source. That assumption is questioned in Del Boca and Flinn (1994), who find different propensities to spend income on a collection of child goods, including children's apparel, furniture and equipment, toys, sporting goods and recreational lessons. They report that while 1.2 cents per dollar of the average mother's income is spent on these goods, about 5.5 cents per dollar is spent from transfers including both child support and alimony. While these amounts are significantly different, their low values suggest that an overwhelming proportion of transfer income is used by the custodial parent for utility-enhancing purposes.
17. Willis writes: 'Lazear-Michael estimate that the mother will spend only about 20 cents of an additional dollar on the child. Although there may be questions about the precise numerical value of a parent's marginal propensity to spend on children, this number has some empirical basis in their analysis of consumer expenditure data and is probably not wildly off the mark' (p. 53). See also Willis's note 19. This estimate implies a five-to-one

ratio of support expenditures to increased child's consumption rather than the three-to-one ratio used in the example. And also, see Weiss and Willis (1993), p. 665.

18. Although both parents together contribute $1 to their children, the father contributes only two-thirds of that amount from his own income with the mother contributing the remaining third. In this setting, we assume joint rather than separate decision-making.

19. Del Boca and Ribero derive certain interesting implications of their model. For example, they write: 'the model implies that fathers with higher incomes transfer more [to mothers] and visit more . . . and that mothers with higher incomes allow fewer visitations' (Del Boca and Ribero, 1999, p. 11).

20. Lerman (2001), p. 459.
21. Pearson and Thoennes (1998), p. 247.
22. *Sharpe v. Sharpe*, 902 P.2d 210 (Wyo. 1995).

REFERENCES

Argys, Laura M., H. Elizabeth Peters and Donald M. Waldman (2001), 'Can the Family Support Act put some life back into Deadbeat Dads?', *Journal of Human Resources*, **36** (2), 226–52.

Beller, Andrea H. and John W. Graham (1993), *Small Change: Economics of Child Support*, Newhaven, CT: Yale University Press.

Del Boca, Daniela and Christopher J. Flinn (1994), 'Expenditure decisions on divorced mothers and income composition', *Journal of Human Resources*, **29** (3), 742–61.

Del Boca, Daniela and Rocio Ribero (1998), 'Transfers in non-intact households', *Structural Change and Economic Dynamics*, **9**, 469–78.

Del Boca, Daniela and Rocio Ribero (1999), 'Visitations and transfers in non-intact households', New York University Economic Research Reports, November.

Garfinkel, Irwin (2001), 'Child support in the new world of welfare', in Rebecca M. Blank and Ron Haskins (eds), *The New World of Welfare*, Washington, DC: Brookings Institution Press, pp. 442–56.

Garfinkel, Irwin, Sara S. McLanahan and Philip K. Robins (eds) (1994), *Child Support and Child Well-being*, Washington: Urban Institute Press.

Garfinkel, Irwin, Sara S. McLanahan, Daniel R. Meyer and Judith A. Seltzer (eds) (1998), *Fathers Under Fire: The Revolution in Child Support Enforcement*, New York: Russell Sage Foundation.

Gronau, Ruben (1991), 'The intrafamily allocation of goods: how to separate the adult from the child', *Journal of Labor Economics*, **9** (3), 207–35.

Lazear, Edward P. and Robert T. Michael (1998), *Allocation of Income Within the Household*, Chicago, IL, University of Chicago Press.

Lerman, Robert I. (2001), 'Comment', in Rebecca M. Blank and Ron Haskins (eds), *The New World of Welfare*, Washington, DC: Brookings Institution Press, pp. 456–60.

Lerman, Robert I. and Elaine Sorensen (2001), 'Child support: interactions between private and public transfers', National Bureau of Economic Research, working paper 8199, April.

Page, Marianne E. and Ann Huff Stevens (2002), 'Will you miss me when I am gone? The economic consequences of absent parents', National Bureau of Economic Research, working paper 8786, February.

Pearson, Jessica and Nancy Thoennes (1998), 'Programs to increase fathers' access to their children', in Garfinkel et al.

Peters, H. Elizabeth, Laura M. Argys, Eleanor E. Macoby and Robert Mnookin (1993), 'Enforcing divorce settlements: evidence from child support compliance and award modifications', *Demography*, **30** (4), 719–35.

Pollack, Robert A. and Terence J. Wales (1979), 'Welfare comparisons and equivalence scales', *American Economic Review*, **69** (2), 216–21.

Seltzer, Judith A. (1991), 'Relationships between fathers and children who live apart: the father's role after separation', *Journal of Marriage and the Family*, **53**, 79–101.

Sorensen, Elaine and Ariel Halpern (1999), 'Child support enforcement: how well is it doing?', *Urban Institute Discussion Papers*, December.

US Bureau of Labor Statistics, Current Population Survey, www.bls.census.gov/cps/cpsmain.htm.

US Department of Health and Human Services (1997), Office of Child Support Enforcement, 22nd Annual Report to Congress for the period ending 30 September, Washington, DC.

Van Praag, Bernard S. and Marcel F. Warnaar (1997), 'The cost of children and the use of demographic variables in consumer demand', in Mark R. Rosenzweig and Oded Stark (eds), *Handbook of Population and Family Economics*, pp. 241–73, Amsterdam, The Netherlands: Elsevier.

Veum, Jonathan R. (1992), 'Inter-relation of child support, visitation, and hours of work', *Monthly Labor Review*, June, 40–47.

Walker, Glynnis (1986), *Solomon's Children*, New York: Arbor House.

Wallerstein, Judith and Joan Kelly (1980), *Surviving the Breakup: How Children and Parents Cope with Divorce*, New York: Basic Books.

Weiss, Yoram and Robert J. Willis (1993), 'Transfers among divorced couples: evidence and interpretation', *Journal of Labor Economics*, **11** (4), 629–79.

2. Child support and the problem of economic incentives*

Robert J. Willis

1. INTRODUCTION

High divorce rates together with the growth of non-marital fertility has led to an increased proportion of children who spend a significant portion of their childhood living in female-headed households or in blended families headed by a male who is not their father. These trends have provoked considerable alarm about the demise of the traditional family and concern about potentially harmful effects on the well-being of children. Economic theories of the family, marriage and divorce have important implications for the impact of marital and living arrangements on the economic contributions that each parent makes to enhance the welfare of his or her children. In previous work Yoram Weiss and I showed that, relative to marriage, divorce reduces the incentives of both parents to devote resources to their children. In particular, divorce may lead a non-custodial father who served as an exemplary breadwinner for his wife and children during marriage to become, upon divorce, a 'deadbeat dad' who fails to pay child support (Weiss and Willis, 1985). This change in behaviour occurs even if it is assumed that the strength of the father's concern for his children's welfare remains unchanged.

The goal of this chapter is to present the reasoning behind this and other theoretical results in the economic literature in terms that can be understood by lawyers, judges, counsellors and other non-economists who deal with child support issues. The failure of non-custodial fathers to volunteer adequate support payments for their children or to comply with court-mandated child support awards is a leading source of the high risk of poverty faced by children living in female-headed households. The phenomenon of the 'deadbeat dad' presents a challenge for legislators responsible for the development of child support formulas and enforcement programmes: for lawyers, judges, divorce counsellors, social workers responsible for the implementation and enforcement of these laws and programmes, and, most of all, for the fathers, mothers and children whose welfare may be so critically affected by the outcome of this process. The existence of 'deadbeat dads' also poses a puzzle for the economic theory of the family. If the father plays the role of breadwinner within marriage, why should he fail to provide support for his children when divorce takes place? As a related puzzle, why should men who father children out of wedlock not only provide little or no economic support for their children, but also often fail to establish their legal paternity despite evidence that the vast majority of such men are concerned about their children's welfare?

2.   CHILDREN AS COLLECTIVE GOODS

The idea that children are a 'collective good' from the point of view of the mother and father is a key concept in the economic models discussed in this chapter. Collective goods, also known as 'public goods', are goods, such as national defence, which provide benefits or utility simultaneously to more than one consumer. In contrast to private goods, such as apples, one consumer of a public good is not excluded from the enjoyment of the good by the additional consumption of another consumer. Economists have long recognized that market mechanisms that work efficiently to reward producers of private goods and to allocate these goods among consumers through a price system tend to break down in the case of public goods. The reason is that a consumer's consumption of a public good is independent of whether he pays for it. Any given consumer would prefer to 'free ride', obtaining the benefit of the public good without contributing to the cost of providing it. Because of this market failure, societies develop non-market institutions, most notably governments, to facilitate effective collective action for the provision of public goods through taxation and regulation.

In what sense are children public goods? In the United States and most other societies, the parents have primary responsibility for deciding to bear children and for decisions about allocating resources to them. The resources I devote to my children, for the most part, do not benefit your children. From this viewpoint, children are private goods and their welfare is largely determined by parental resources and preferences.[1] Most people, however, do exhibit concern for the well-being of other people's children. This social concern is manifested in a variety of ways, ranging from laws about mandatory school attendance and child abuse to the institution of tax-supported public education.[2] Thus, society's interest in the education, health and welfare of children together with parents' own interest in their children means that children combine aspects of public and private goods. This, however, is not the main feature of the collective goods aspect of children emphasized in this chapter.

A concept of public goods that is related to the way in which children are treated in this chapter is 'local public goods' like public parks, police and fire services or local public schools. The benefits from these public goods have a spatial dimension that limits their benefits to those who reside in a given locality. Thus, as Tiebout (1956) showed, the fact that non-residents can be excluded from the benefits of a public good implies that markets may not fail if the community can, in effect, charge for the provision of the public good through property taxes and people can choose the bundle of local public goods they prefer by 'voting with their feet'. Household public goods, like the house itself or many items and services within it, use of which is shared by its residents, are local public goods where the locality is defined by household membership. Whether a residence contains a group of college room-mates, a childless cohabiting couple, or a husband and wife and with several children, there may be free-rider problems within the household associated with the fact that residents receive the benefits of household public goods whether or not they help pay for them. It seems likely that married couples will be better able than college room-mates to find ways to overcome free-rider problems. This issue will be discussed in more detail in the next section.

Biology and society make a child a collective good from the point of view of its parents. Beyond contributing genetic material to their child, mothers and fathers are conditioned to be concerned about the well-being of a child by their upbringing, by their families and friends, by their images of themselves, their ambitions and in many other ways. In this chapter, I assume that each parent cares about the child's welfare and hence the child's welfare is a collective good from the standpoint of the parents.

A child's welfare is in part determined by its current consumption of food, housing, health care, schooling and recreation and by the characteristics of its neighbourhood, friends and so on. A child's welfare also depends on the long-term development of its human capital, interpreted broadly to include schooling, health, religious beliefs, diligence, moral and cultural development and other factors that are expected to affect the child's success as an adult in both market and non-market activities including marriage and the production of grandchildren. The child's welfare may be viewed as the outcome of a production process which relates inputs, including time spent by parents and purchased goods, to expected child outcomes valued by the parent both in the near term and over the child's lifetime. Obviously, the 'production function' for child welfare is highly complex and multi-dimensional in both inputs and outputs. Its parameters, to the frustration of parents, teachers, doctors and psychologists, are often more a matter of guesswork than scientific knowledge, and the relationship between inputs and outputs is governed by large chance components.

In addition to uncertainty about the production process for child welfare – the relationship between means and ends – there may not be agreement about the ends themselves. Parents may disagree about the desirability of a given outcome or the weights to be attached to different outcomes. Father may want to buy hockey skates for Johnny and mother may prefer piano lessons; father may wish to raise him as a Catholic and mother as a Jew. The child, of course, may have its own preferences. Parents may defer 'altruistically' to the child's view of its own welfare or they may be 'paternalistic' (Pollak, 2003). Finally, society itself and its political representatives may have their own views, both about which specific child outcomes are desirable or undesirable, which should be the object of public policy and about the appropriate boundaries for private decision-making by parents and their children.

Economists often regard the state as the institutional entity through which market failures generated by collective goods may be resolved. However, as I wrote over 30 years ago:

> The family exists as an institution because, given altruism and the nonmarket mechanisms by which it is able to allocate commodities and welfare among its members, it has both the incentive and the capacity to resolve allocative problems involving public goods, externalities, and the like that in impersonal markets inevitably lead to market imperfections. The capacity of the family to resolve these problems efficiently provides a basis for a positive theory of family behavior . . . (Willis, 1973, p. S19).

A new branch of economics, variously called the 'economics of the family' or the 'new home economics', emerged in the aftermath of the 'Schultz volume' in which the paper that I quote above appeared, most notably in the work by Gary Becker (1991).[3] Much of the literature in the field assumes or, as in Becker's 'Rotten Kid Theorem' (Becker, 1991), offers 'proofs' of the family's ability to solve allocation problems efficiently.[4] However, the rise of divorce and the failure of many fathers to pay child support led Yoram Weiss and I (Weiss and Willis, 1985) to reconsider the view that parents will always be motivated to provide for their children in ways that the parents themselves consider to be optimal. In particular, we argued that marriage is an institution within which parental resources devoted to children can reasonably be argued to be allocated efficiently, but that divorce may dramatically decrease the incentives of both parents, particularly fathers, to provide for their children and, hence, cause a decrease in the welfare of children if divorce takes place, even if divorce has no adverse effect on the resources of the father and mother. In the remainder of this chapter, I attempt to explain our reasoning in non-technical terms, discuss some evidence of its empirical validity, and examine the implications of the theory for divorce settlements and child support policy.

3. PARENTAL EXPENDITURES ON CHILDREN AND CHILD WELFARE WITHIN MARRIAGE

Consider a family consisting of a husband, wife and one child who live together within a single household. Each parent obtains utility from his or her own consumption and from the welfare of their child. In contrast to the complex view of the relationship between inputs to children and child welfare discussed in the preceding section, we assume that child welfare is simply a function of the amount of money spent on the child. Likewise, the consumption of the mother and father depends only on their purchases of market goods. Total expenditures on the consumptions of the father, mother and child are limited by total household income which is the sum of the father's and mother's income. There are no household public goods apart from the child, so that an extra dollar's worth of goods devoted to the child means that parent's consumption must fall by a dollar. Along the way, I discuss how relaxing some of these simplifying assumptions affects the implications of the analysis, but for the most part I will stay within this extremely simple framework to make my main points.

How should this family allocate its resources? If no child were involved, allocations between the husband and wife would simply be a zero sum game: an extra dollar consumed by the husband implies that the wife must consume a dollar less. If neither partner is altruistic toward the other and they are free to allocate their incomes as they choose, each would simply consume an amount equal to his or her income. Under these circumstances, there is no gain to marriage in the sense that each partner could achieve the same level of utility by living alone.

However, the fact that each partner cares about the child's welfare implies that there are potential gains to both partners from pooling their incomes and sharing in the cost of the child. Applying the famous 'Samuelson condition' (Samuelson, 1954) for the optimal allocation of resources to a public good, child expenditures should be carried to the point at which:

$$MRS^{father} + MRS^{mother} = MC^{childwelfare} \qquad (1)$$

In other words, the equation states that marginal value to the father of another dollar spent on the child plus the marginal value to the mother of another dollar spent on the child is equal to the marginal cost of a dollar spent on the child which, of course, is $1. Marginal values are denoted by *MRS*, which stands for 'marginal rate of substitution'. In this application, the *MRS* terms measure the amount by which the father or mother would be willing to reduce his or her own consumption in order to increase child expenditure by $1. For example, if the mother and father had identical preferences and consumed at equal levels, optimal expenditures would occur at a point where, at the margin, each parent would be willing to give up 50 cents of their own consumption in order to increase expenditures on the child by $1. At the optimum, in other words, expenditures on children are carried to the point at which $MRS^{father} = MRS^{mother} = \$0.5$.

Equation (1) implies that optimal expenditures on the child reflect the preferences of both parents and that they are larger than either parent alone would choose when constrained by his or her own income. One way to see this is to suppose first that one of the parents, say the mother, undertakes to support the child out of her own income. For concreteness, let us suppose that the mother has an income of $30000 and that own consumption and child expenditures each cost $1 per unit. She may choose any combination of expenditures on the child and on her own consumption whose total cost does not exceed $30000. Suppose she considers an allocation in which she gets a very high level of consumption, say $29000, and the child receives only $1000. She could test whether this is an optimal allocation by asking herself whether she could increase her utility by reducing her own consumption by $1 in order to increase child expenditures by $1. Equivalently, she could ask whether $MRS^{mother} > \$1$.

Quite likely the answer is 'yes' if a $1000 level of expenditure puts the child at the brink of starvation and $29000 gives the mother a fairly comfortable standard of living. A caring mother might well be willing to give up $1000 or more of own consumption to increase the child's consumption by $1. As the mother continues to test successively larger allocations to the child and correspondingly lower levels of consumption for herself, MRS^{mother} will tend to fall. When child expenditures reach $10000, suppose that $MRS^{mother} = \$1$ and that the mother's level of utility is 100 utils.[5] Any further increase in child expenditures would reduce MRS^{mother} below $1 and, therefore, would reduce the mother's utility below 100 utils. Thus, an allocation of $20000 for her own consumption and $10000 to the child is optimal when the mother supports the child entirely out of her own income.

Now let us bring the father into the picture. We assume that he also cares for the child's welfare and always places positive marginal value on child welfare so that $MRS^{father} > 0$ no matter how much is spent on the child.[6] In the above scenario, he contributed nothing to the child but it is easy to show that both he and the mother can be made better off if he does contribute. At the mother's optimum, we saw above that $MRS^{mother} = \$1$. This means that the mother would be indifferent between an extra dollar spent on the child or an extra dollar spent on herself. The father could offer the mother a deal in which he would contibute a small amount, say 5 cents, to the child if the mother would contribute another $1 to the child at the sacrifice of $1 of her own consumption. This deal makes the father better off if

$MRS^{father} > \$0.05$. The mother is better off because child welfare has gone up by \$1.05 and her consumption has only fallen by \$1. Deals more favourable to the mother might also benefit both. Suppose, for instance, that $MRS^{father} = \$0.75$. Then he would be better off if the mother's contribution to the child increases by as little as \$0.26.

More generally, deals can be found which make both the mother and father better off by increasing child expenditures whenever $MRS^{father} + MRS^{mother} > \$1$. As more is contributed to the child, the MRSs of both parents decline. At the point at which $MRS^{father} + MRS^{mother} = \$1$, which is the Samuelson condition in equation (1), it is not possible to increase child expenditures any further in a way that will benefit one parent without harming the other. Thus, allocations satisfying the Samuelson condition are Pareto efficient.

In general, there are many possible efficient allocations of the couple's resources. Under a certain analytically convenient assumption, the optimal amount to spend on the collective good (children in this case) is independent of how private goods (the husband's and wife's consumptions in this case) are distributed.[7] Although there is some evidence that factors that increase the wife's share of income or power within a marriage tends to increase expenditures on children,[8] for simplicity I will make the independence assumption.

The distribution of consumption within the union interacts with the stability of the union and, as we shall see in the next section, marital stability is likely to have an effect on child welfare. For example, if the husband controls all of the couple's joint income, he might choose an allocation in which he utilizes all income not devoted to the child for his own consumption, leaving his wife with little or nothing. Such a poor outcome for the wife might be avoided because of either love or threat. If the husband loves his wife, he might wish to give her a high level of consumption even if he controls all income. Alternatively, the wife's ability to leave the marriage with both her income and the child means that even a non-altruistic husband must provide his wife with a better level of utility within marriage than she could obtain by herself. In the example at the beginning of the section, this would imply that the husband must provide the wife with a level of utility at least equal to 100 utils.

The simple model described in this section illustrates why a shared interest in the welfare of a child creates potential gains to the parents from sharing in the expense of the child. It also illustrates how the child benefits from the collaboration of its parents. Despite my rather careless use of words like 'deals' between the partners, however, I have only looked at potential allocations and have not discussed why the institution of marriage is expected to overcome free riding or other obstacles to the achievement of efficient allocations. Love between the husband and wife and mutual concern for one another's welfare reduces incentives for opportunistic behaviour. Marriage facilitates repeated mutual interactions between the spouses that allow each spouse to monitor the actions of the other to see whether or not promised contributions to the child's welfare are actually made. Monitoring reduces the scope for opportunistic behaviour and, over time, these repeated actions build trust. These considerations lend plausibility to the idea the marriage is the dominant institution within which children are best born and reared.

4.   DIVORCE AND DIVORCE SETTLEMENTS

If marriage is so good, why divorce? In their pioneering economic model of divorce, Becker et al. (1977) emphasized the role of uncertainty. A couple decides to marry based on their expectation of mutual gains. As time passes, new information accumulates about the quality of the match and about the separate prospects of the husband and wife. If the quality of the match turns out to be low, or if one of the partners discovers a better match, the couple may divorce.

If the partnership breaks, one or both partners may suffer a loss. Marriage contracts are a very old idea to deal with the risks inherent in marriage. Weiss and Willis (1993) quote from a Jewish marriage contract written in 1023 which stipulates the payments that would occur if one spouse ends up 'hating' the other, indicating that the contract would be enforced by a court. In modern marriages, the spouses need to coordinate the bearing and rearing of children with the development of the human capital and labour market careers of one or both spouses. Becker et al. (1977) emphasize the distinction between marriage-specific investments, which pay off only if the marriage endures, and general investments which pay off regardless of marriage. Because children tend to be born early in marriage and career investments tend to pay off in middle age, there is often a temporal asymmetry in the contributions to and receipt of benefits from the marriage by the husband and wife. Often the wife gives up investments, in a career in order to make match-specific investments such as bearing and rearing, developing common interests and friendship networks with her husband and so on. She makes these investments in hopes that she may enjoy their fruits throughout a married lifetime. Her loss, if the marriage goes bad, is captured by the cry, 'I gave him the best years of my life' (Cohen, 1987). A marriage contract may offer compensation to the wife against the risk of a bad marriage. If such compensation is not available, wives may be reluctant to make match-specific investments in the first place and, to the extent that this is the case, the potential gains to marriage will be reduced.

Unfortunately, marriage contracts are largely unenforceable, except in the case of prenuptial agreements between parties about the division of the financial wealth they bring to the marriage. Perhaps the most important reason is the need for third-party enforcement of contractual provisions. A contract with pay-offs triggered by an assessment of who hates whom or who did or did not wash the dishes on Tuesday night will be impossible to adjudicate because the relevant information is not available to the judge. Indeed, typically courts will only consider disputes between business partners or marital partners if the partnership is being dissolved.

An alternative view is that marriage is an implicit contract whose performance is enforced through bargaining between the spouses. In relatively small matters that do not threaten the stability of marriage, bargaining may involve temporary threats of the husband or wife to stop cooperating and retreat to their 'separate spheres' (Lundberg and Pollak, 1993). However, sufficiently large shocks may mean that there is no allocation within the marriage that can make both parties better off than under divorce, so that divorce is the efficient outcome. In this case, the welfare of the husband and wife upon divorce will be determined by the terms of the divorce settlement and the feasible allocations within marriage will depend on 'bargaining under the shadow of the law' (Mnookin and Kornhauser, 1979).

Ideally, the design of the divorce law would accomplish three ends. First, it would provide for insurance against the losses suffered by one partner relative to the other from future shocks that would cause marital disruption. For example, the division of property and spousal support orders offer some protection to a wife who specialized in marriage-specific investments early in marriage. Note, however, that it is very difficult for divorce settlements to deal with marital property embodied in the future returns to a spouse's human capital.[9] Second, divorce settlements should not create incentives that are incompatible with keeping a marriage together, which is otherwise desirable for both parties. That is, potential designs of divorce settlements that resolve efficiency and equity issues need also to consider 'incentive-compatibility constraints'. For instance, if the divorce law enforces equal property division with no provision for a prenuptial agreement, marriages between persons of unequal wealth may become infeasible. The reason is that the wealthier person may worry that his or her prospective spouse may feign love, but is really a gold-digger who will divorce soon after the marriage in order to collect a generous settlement. Prenuptial agreements are frequently designed to avoid providing such incentives. Finally, when a marriage produces children, the children remain after the marriage is dissolved and both parents retain an interest in the child's welfare. In addition, as discussed earlier, the state retains an interest in the child's welfare. In the remainder of the chapter, we consider in detail how child support, custody and other features of divorce settlements affect the welfare of the mother, the father and the child, beginning with the question of why so many fathers fail to pay child support.

5. WHY DEADBEAT DADS? DIVORCE AND CHILD SUPPORT INCENTIVES

The phenomenon of 'deadbeat dads' presents a puzzle for the economic theory of the family. If the father plays the role of breadwinner within marriage, why should he fail to provide support for his children when divorce takes place? There are several possible answers. For poor women, who qualified for AFDC welfare, the answer might be that after a $50 per month offset, there was a 100 per cent tax on transfers from the father to the mother unless the support was provided 'under the table'.[10] In effect, the state replaces the father, leaving the father with absolutely no incentive to pay child support since the child's welfare is unaffected by his payments. However, evidence that low child support awards are common and that fathers often fail to comply with their child support obligations to mothers who are ineligible for welfare programmes suggests that other forces are at work.

The collective goods aspect of children offers another possible explanation for a shift in the father's motivation to contribute to his children when divorce takes place that is not confined to the poorest segment of the population. In section 3, I argued that the interest of both the father and the mother in the child's welfare implies that it is efficient for both parents to contribute to child expenditures, and that marriage is an institution that facilitates sharing the costs of children. In short, the theory is consistent with the breadwinner role of fathers within marriage.

I now use the same simple model described in section 3 to show why fathers have an incentive to provide less child support when divorce takes place. Specifically, assume that there is one child, that each parent has an income of $30000, and that each parent has identical Cobb–Douglas preferences for own consumption and the child's welfare which each cost $1 per unit.[11] Within marriage, assume that the couple spends an efficient amount on the child so that the Samuelson condition in equation (1) is satisfied. Given the assumed symmetry between the husband and the wife, we can assume that the parents make equal contributions to the child and carry expenditures up to the point at which the marginal value to each parent of a dollar spent on the child is 50 cents. The efficient level of expenditure on the child is $20 000, or one-third of the couple's joint income of $60 000. Assume that each parent also consumes $20 000.[12]

Now suppose that the couple divorces and that the mother is awarded custody of the child. To focus on incentive effects associated with divorce, I assume that divorce itself is costless in the sense that the father and mother continue to have incomes of $30 000 and the unit costs of consumption and child welfare remain constant. If the father provides no support, leaving the mother to provide for the child on her own, she maximizes her utility, as we saw in Section 3, by carrying expenditures on the child to the point at which the marginal value of expenditure on the child to her is $1. Given her assumed utility function, this point occurs when she spends $10 000 on the child, leaving her own consumption equal to $20 000.

One way to interpret the change in the mother's behaviour between marriage and divorce without child support is that divorce caused her to lose a subsidy from the father who, within marriage, matched her child expenditures dollar for dollar. That is, imagine that the mother alone makes allocation decisions within marriage while the husband passively gives her an extra dollar for every dollar she spends on the child. Because of the matching rate within marriage, the mother behaves as if her $30 000 income can buy child welfare at 50 cents per unit and, given her Cobb–Douglas preferences, she chooses to spend one-third of her income on the child, thus obtaining 20 000 units of real goods and services for the child at 50 cents per unit. In the divorce state, she faces the full 'market price' of $1 per unit and, accordingly, devotes only 10 000 units of real goods and services to the child.

It is worth making two other observations about this example before moving on to consider the divorced father's behaviour. First, my numerical example showed that the mother dramatically decreased the resources devoted to the child in response to the increase in the effective price caused by divorce, but chose to keep her own standard of living constant. The reason for this result is that the assumed Cobb–Douglas preferences imply that the mother considers her own consumption and the child's welfare to be quite substitutable. In reality, the degree of substitutability may well be much smaller so that, as the price per unit of child welfare increases, the mother protects the child's welfare by making only a modest decrease in the resources she devotes to it. As a consequence, her total expenditure on the child would increase and, given that her income is fixed, her own consumption must fall. Second, regardless of whether the mother's own consumption remains the same or falls, being divorced without child support causes her utility to fall because of its adverse impact on the child's welfare.

In the example so far, I have assumed that the divorced father provides no child support. But, given that he continues to care for the child, it seems natural to imagine that he will wish to continue to contribute to its support. Moreover, since I assumed that divorce is costless and the couple's total resources remain intact, it would be feasible for the father, mother and child all to maintain the standard of living to which they were accustomed.

So, why doesn't the father voluntarily give his ex-wife $10000 in child support, duplicating the resources he provided for the child during marriage? Let us imagine he makes such a transfer. His ex-wife now has a total income of $40000. Given her Cobb–Douglas preferences, she will spend one-third of her income on the child and two-thirds on her own consumption. That is, while she could have replicated the marital allocation of $20000 for the child and $20000 for herself, she actually chooses only $13333 for the child and $26667 for herself. The reason she does not replicate the marital allocation is that she has no incentive to take the father's preferences into account when making her spending decisions. That is, as I showed earlier, the allocation within marriage reflects the preferences of both parents; however, if the mother no longer cares about the father and makes spending decisions that only reflect her own preferences, she will spend less on the child after divorce even if it is feasible for her to maintain the same spending on the child and herself after marriage.

Another drawback of mandating the $10000 child support transfer is that it might destabilize an otherwise viable marriage. Specifically, consider the effect of a law that compels the father to make a child support payment that allows the mother and child to maintain the same standard of living they enjoyed within marriage. As we have seen, the ex-wife could have chosen the same bundle she had within marriage, but chose not to. Thus, we can infer that her utility as a divorcee is higher when she receives the $10000 transfer than it would have been had she stayed married. Moreover, we can infer that the husband's utility, relative to marriage, would fall because his own consumption remains at $20000 while the child's welfare has fallen. Thus, this law would create an incentive for divorce by the custodial mother that, in turn, would cause an actual reduction in the welfare of the child.

The intuition underlying this implication probably needs more discussion. As I have argued repeatedly, the optimal allocation to children requires cooperative behaviour by both parents who share in the costs of the child. This allocation leads to a relatively large expenditure on the child and thus favours the child's welfare. I have also stressed that this allocation is not 'incentive-compatible'. That is, if each parent maximizes his or her own preferences without taking into account the preferences of the other party, the efficient allocation will not be attained. The preceding paragraph introduces the idea that there are also incentive-compatibility constraints for the marriage to remain intact. That is, since marriage is a voluntary institution, for the marriage to remain intact each spouse must receive at least as much utility within marriage as he or she would receive if the marriage broke up.[13] If the custodial mother had sufficient income in the divorced state to allow herself and the child to live at the same standard of living as in marriage and she actually chooses the same standard for herself and the child, her utility would be the same within marriage and divorce and she would be indifferent as to whether the marriage continues or is broken.[14] But I have shown that a divorced mother with this level of income would actually choose an alternative allocation involving a higher expenditure on her own consumption and lower expenditure on the child than was the case within marriage. Her 'revealed preference' implies, therefore, that she would be better off upon divorce, and her reduced child expenditures imply that the child would be worse off.

A corollary is that incentive compatibility constraints imply that an optimal divorce settlement must reduce the welfare of both the father and mother relative to marriage. Otherwise, the divorce settlement itself may create an incentive for divorce by one party or the other. As has been clear since the pioneering economic analysis of divorce by Becker et al. (1977), this suggests that some other factor must be invoked to understand why divorce takes place. Weiss and Willis (1985, 1993) deal with this issue by assuming that there is a random variable called the 'quality of the match' that helps determine the gains from marriage. Through courtship before marriage, couples attempt to learn as much as they can about how good a marriage they might have, but uncertainty about the quality of the match can never be fully resolved. If the match is sufficiently good, the incentive-compatibility constraint discussed above may not be binding. However, in more marginal marriages, an over-generous transfer to the custodial parent may destabilize the marriage.

Earlier, I suggested that one could imagine the efficient allocation within marriage coming about with the wife making all allocation decisions and the husband matching her expenditures on the children dollar for dollar. This might be an attractive way to resolve the incentive problem that arises upon divorce if the mother fails to take the father's preferences into account. After all, the federal government provides localities with incentives to build roads that benefit non-local drivers by matching each local dollar with nine federal dollars. Given the match rate, local decision-makers choose highways as if they cost one-tenth the true cost. In pursuing their self-interest, they act as if they are taking the interests of nonresident drivers into account.

Consider a child support law that requires matching payments by the father to the custodial mother. Two problems spring to mind immediately. First is the question about what matching rate to mandate. In the numerical example involving a mother and father with identical Cobb–Douglas preferences and identical incomes, the Samuelson condition dictated that the marginal value of expenditures on the child be 50 cents for each parent which implies a one-to-one matching rate. If other things remain the same, but we assume that the mother's income is $20000 and the father's income is $40000 a two-to-one matching rate would be required to induce the mother to purchase 20000 units of goods and services for the child. While this matching rate achieves the efficient level of expenditure on the child, the mother's consumption rises relative to marriage, indicating an incentive-compatibility problem. In order to maintain the same allocation to both the child and to adult consumption as within marriage, one might need a lump sum transfer from the custodial parent to the non-custodian and a matching payment from the non-custodian to the custodian. More generally, given heterogeneity in preferences and incomes, it would be virtually impossible to specify matching rates and lump sum transfers that would provide incentives for the custodial parent to choose an efficient allocation.[15]

Even if the correct matching rate and lump sum payments could somehow be engineered into a child support law based on matching payments, there are other potentially fatal flaws with this approach. The matching scheme requires the non-custodial father to give the mother x dollars for every dollar she spends on the child. In our simple model, dollars spent on the child are defined unambiguously – they are whatever the mother does not consume. In reality, of course, there are many jointly consumed household public goods including the house itself that benefit both the child and the mother. In theory, it would be possible to design a whole set of matching rates to give the mother the right incentives to choose the optimal mix of child-specific and jointly consumed goods. In practice, of course, these considerations only further complicate an already completely infeasible piece of social engineering.

Another important problem with the matching approach is informational asymmetries. The mother knows how she spends her money, but the father may not be able to observe her expenditures. The mother has an obvious incentive to claim large child expenditures because they trigger large transfers. Knowing this, the father has an incentive to be deeply suspicious about the mother's claims to be doing things for the child when he suspects that she is really adding to her clothes closet.

I opened this section by suggesting that the collective good aspect of children could help explain the existence of deadbeat dads even in relatively affluent groups. To show why, let us return to the numerical example with which I began. Initially, we find the divorced mother as we left her, with no child support. She has $30000 of her own income of which she spends $10000 on the child. The father is interested in the welfare of the child, but – assuming that the child is young – he can only influence the child's welfare through the agency of the mother. Assuming that he knows her preferences, he expects that if he gives her $1 she will spend one-third of it on the child and two-thirds on herself. Put another way, it will cost the father $3 to increase the welfare of his child by $1. In contrast, recall that in the marriage the marginal cost to the father of increasing the child's welfare is only 50 cents. Intuitively, a sixfold increase in the marginal cost of the child's welfare is likely to substantially reduce the father's willingness to provide support.

Weiss and Willis (1985, 1993) argue that the behaviour of the divorced father and mother can be modelled as a 'Stackelberg game'. Knowing that his ex-wife will spend one third of any transfer on the child (that is, knowing her reaction function), the father chooses a transfer level that maximizes his utility. Even though the marginal cost of child welfare is high, the father will be willing to make a positive transfer if, otherwise, the mother would be so poor that the child's welfare is extremely low. However, as the mother's income increases and she increases expenditures on the child out of her own income, the father will tend to reduce his payments until he reaches a 'corner solution' where it is optimal for him to give nothing. At such a point, we may say that he is a deadbeat dad. In this case, the father has shifted the entire cost of the child onto the mother, in effect making the economic cost of fatherhood to him zero. Willis (1999, 2000) argues that this cost-shifting is one factor that may help explain the rise of out-of-wedlock childbearing.

6.   CHRISTINA AND JOSE: EVIDENCE FROM A QUALITATIVE INTERVIEW

The theory presented in this chapter suggests that the reluctance of fathers to provide support for their children is related to their perception that money they give to the mother will not benefit the child. In this section, I provide some evidence that is in remarkable congruence with the theory from a 'qualitative interview' done in a project directed by Kathryn Edin, a sociologist at Northwestern University, to study the motivations and behaviour of a sample of young unmarried couples who have just had a baby.[16] In this section, I quote from a portion of the interview with Jose, a 19-year-old unemployed high school drop-out, who fathered a child with Christina, an 18-year-old recent high school graduate. They are of Hispanic background, live in Milwaukee, but do not live together. He lives with his mother and she with her parents. In the following quotations from the transcript 'He' refers to Jose, 'FI' is the interviewer. Words in the transcript are italicized to indicate vocal emphasis.

This segment begins with the interviewer inquiring about how Jose feels about giving money to help Christina with the baby's support. I reproduce the entire segment and make some comments at its conclusion.

He: I wish there was a way that you could *monitor* that type of thing, but you can't, you know?

Fl: *Yeah*

He: I mean like, even for instance, I wish there was a law where child support would not just be the check going to the mother. I wish they had some type of credit card for them, where you can only use this stuff for . . .

Fl: *Diapers?*

He: Diapers, food. Things that will be what babies need. Not a check where she can say, 'Well, I'll go buy their diapers and stuff, but I need this to go . . .' You know, I mean, even like . . . If you gotta fix your car, fine, cause, you know, kids will be riding in the car, you know, clothes, all that. But 'I need to get my hair done. I want a new pair of sneakers.' Even if it's, like, she's gotta job, and she's supporting her with her own money, then 'I'll use that money and then when I get the child support check, then I'll just go buy my stuff for me.' I don't feel it's right, cause I know that that check came from *me* working. You know, I'm not working for her to have good things for *her*. I'm working, I'm paying child support for my *children*.

Fl. *Right*

He: I wish they would come out with some type of, like, a *credit* card, where you can use . . .

Fl: *Right*. Like a debit card or something.

He: Yeah. You can use it at Pick-n-Save, Toys-R-Us. It has to be something to do with children, period.

Fl. *Yeah.*

He: A *lot* of money. Because a person . . . know how much you get a month but not know how much is in your account is sort of saving, you know?

Fl: *That's true.*

He: I think that would be a better way of child support, and I think more men would, a *lot* of men . . .

Fl: *Would pay it.*

He: Would file for child support themselves, you know. But a lot of men, they feel, you know 'I *know* she's not doing something for the kids.' I'm not saying that she isn't, but that's how some men think.

Fl: *Gotcha.*

He: And she probably *does* use my money for that, but it's the simple fact of not knowing for sure.

Fl: *Where your money's going.*

He: You know. Yeah. Exactly.

In this interview, Jose clearly indicates a desire to increase the amount by which he supports his child, but is frustrated by factors we have emphasized in the theory presented in this chapter. He wishes that he could monitor the actions of Christina and observe that she spends money that he gives on the baby and not on herself. While he says that he has faith that Christina will do the 'right thing', he worries that she will not. As Browning et al. (2002) argue, a non-custodial father will always prefer to make in-kind transfers to the child instead of giving fungible transfers to the mother in order to avoid leakages which implicitly raise the price per unit of child welfare to the non-custodian. Jose comes up with an ingenious public policy idea to overcome this problem by suggesting how wonderful it would be if Christina had a credit card that could only be used to purchase things that the child uses. By matching her credit card expenditures, he lowers the relative price of children's goods she faces, leading her to substitute toward these goods and away from her own consumption. If the correct matching rate is chosen, as I show in the next section, Christina will be motivated to choose an efficient level of child expenditure that reflects Jose's interest in the child's welfare.

7. QUANTIFYING THE WELFARE EFFECTS OF DIVORCE

The theory described in this chapter provides a framework within which to interpret empirical data on child support and, potentially, may offer a means of quantifying the effects of divorce settlements on the welfare of the mother, the father and their children. In this section, I discuss an attempt at quantification by Weiss and Willis (1993), referred to as 'WW' in the remainder of this section. WW investigate the effects on child support payments, expenditures on children and the consumption and utility of the mothers and fathers under alternative models of divorce settlement and post-divorce behaviour where, for simplicity, the mother is always assumed to have physical custody of the child in the event of divorce.[17] In particular, they consider how these outcomes vary across three alternative divorce regimes: (1) A 'fully efficient *ex ante* agreement' in which the divorced couple agrees to share in the costs of children and allocates resources efficiently following divorce. Based on information and expectations at the time of marriage, this agreement also stipulates divorce transfers (that is, child support, property settlement and alimony tranfers) that provide implicit 'consumption insurance' to the spouses in the event of divorce; (2) A 'quasi-efficient' regime in which the divorce settlement specifies a transfer that provides implicit consumption insurance, but the couple is unable to overcome free-rider and monitoring problems following divorce so that allocations to children result in underprovision to children following divorce; (3) An '*ex post* Stackelberg equilibrium' in which the husband has no prior commitments and may, if he chooses, make no divorce transfers at all.

WW begin by specifying a modified version of the Cobb–Douglas utility function used in examples presented earlier in this chapter. Specifically, assume that the mother and father have identical preferences given by Stone–Geary utility functions of the form:

$$u_i = (q - \gamma)^\alpha c_i^{1-\alpha}, \quad i = mother, father \qquad (2)$$

As in the standard Cobb–Douglas form, the parameter α determines a given parent's marginal propensity to spend on children. If $\alpha = 1/3$, for example, a single parent who received an extra \$100 dollars of income would spend an additional \$33 on the child. Unlike the standard Cobb–Douglas form, these preferences imply that each parent has (the same) minimum expenditure standard for children given by the parameter γ. Putting these two features together, these preferences imply that child expenditures by a single mother with income y_{mother} would be given by the linear relationship:

$$q = \gamma + \alpha y_{mother} \qquad (3)$$

Total spending on the child's welfare, q, and the amount of the divorce transfer from the father to the mother, if any, can be calculated given information on the incomes of the two parents, the values of their preference parameters, α and γ, together with an assumption about which of the three mechanisms described above governs the divorce settlement. WW use estimates of the share of children's expenditures within families by Lazear and Michael (1988) along with estimates of the magnitude of divorce transfers observed in data from the National Longitudinal Survey of Youth of the High School Class of 1972.[18] WW then calculate levels of expenditures on children, conditional on the assumed mechanism that generates the observed divorce settlement. The utility function parameters based on the Lazear–Michael data are $\alpha = 0.193$ and $\gamma = \$1181$.[19] In the NLSY72 data, the average wife had an income of \$12025 in 1986 dollars. Given these parameters, equation (3) implies that, as a single parent using only her own resources, she would spend about \$3500 on the child, which is nearly 30 per cent of her income. As her income increases, an increase of \$100 in income would lead her to increase expenditures on the child by about \$20. Note that these Stone–Geary preferences imply that the mother will protect her child at the expense of her own well-being as her income falls. Thus, as the mother's income is reduced toward $1181, she will spend almost her entire income on the child. Conversely, as her income rises, the share of income she devotes to the child falls asymptotically to 20 per cent.

I now consider the implications of the alternative models of divorce settlements, beginning with a fully efficient settlement. To fix ideas, at the beginning of marriage imagine that the couple enters into a 'marriage contract' that stipulates how their joint resources will be allocated within the marriage to the consumption of each spouse and to expenditures on the child. In the event of divorce, the contract also stipulates a divorce transfer to the custodial mother and the amount that she must spend on the child. The 'insurance' component of the divorce settlement is chosen such that the ratio of marginal utilities of consumption for the husband and wife within the divorce state is the same as it is within marriage. This implies that the husband and wife share in any gains or losses of joint income both within marriage and upon divorce. It also means that a man who promises his wife a high level of consumption within marriage, perhaps to attract her away from rivals, must also provide her with a high divorce transfer.

Given the assumed Stone–Geary utility functions, optimal expenditures on the child are independent of the magnitude of the insurance payment and depend only on the joint incomes of the two parents upon divorce. Specifically, WW show that the efficient level of child expenditure is given by:

$$q^{efficient} = (1 - \alpha)\gamma + \alpha y \qquad (4)$$

where $y = y_{father} + y_{mother}$ denotes the joint income of the parents after divorce. For the average couple in the NLSY72 data, husband's income is $24708, wife's income is $12025 and the efficient level of expenditure on the child is $8152. WW use data from the NLSY72 on divorce transfers among couples without children to infer the amount the 'insurance component' of the transfer that is needed to smooth the wife's consumption between the married and divorced states of the world. This divorce transfer of $4599 gives the divorced mother a total income of $16624 of which she spends $8152 on the child and $8472 on her own consumption.

This quantitative description of an efficient settlement may be used to illustrate diagrammatically several of the arguments made earlier in the chapter, including the potential for Jose's credit card to generate an efficient allocation by the divorced mother. Figure 2.1 presents an indifference curve diagram for the divorced mother in which child expenditures (q) are measured on the horizontal axis and mother's consumption (c^{mother}) is measured on the vertical axis. The mother's budget of $16624 under the efficient contract is given by the solid black line whose slope is -1, indicating that the mother faces a dollar-for-dollar trade-off between expenditures that benefit the child and herself. The efficient allocation, with \$8152 spent on the child, is shown at point *a*, where $MRS^{mother} = .296$ is indicated by the slope of the dashed line which is tangent to the mother's indifference curve, U^*, at point a.[20] As discussed earlier, MRS^{mother} measures the marginal value to the mother of an additional dollar spent on the child. Since the allocation at point *a* is efficient and satisfies the Samuelson condition, the corresponding marginal value for the father (not shown) is $MRS^{father} = 1 - MRS^{mother} = .704$. Thus, in the neighbourhood of the efficient contract, the mother and father value additional expenditures on the child at about 30 and 70 cents, respectively.

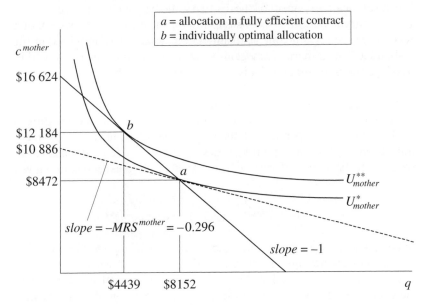

Source: Numbers in diagram based on Weiss and Willis (1993, Table 6).

Figure 2.1   Divorced mother's allocation under efficient divorce settlement

It is easy to see in Figure 2.1 why the efficient allocation is not self-enforcing and, to be feasible, would require some kind of binding agreement with third-party enforcement or a willingness by the mother to weight the father's interest in the child after the marriage breaks up. If the mother only considers her own preferences and her total budget is \$16624 (which includes a divorce transfer of \$4599), her highest attainable level of utility is U^{**}_{mother} at point *b* where her indifference curve is tangent to the solid budget line. At this point, her expenditure on the child is only \$4439 while her own consumption is $12 184. It should also be noted that mandating a divorce transfer of this size without also constraining the way in which the custodial mother spends the money could destabilize the marriage. That is, in our example, the mother's utility within marriage is U^*_{mother} whereas she could attain a higher utility of U^{**}_{mother} if she divorces and is free to choose point *b*.

It is also possible to use Figure 2.1 to illustrate the logic of Jose's suggestion that a credit card be provided to custodial mothers that could only be used to purchase goods that benefit the child. Assume that such a credit card exists and that Jose offers to match Christina's credit card expenditures with *m* dollars for every dollar she spends. Her budget is then $y^f + mq = c^f + q$ or, rearranging terms, $y^f = c^f + (1 - m)q$. Note that the effective price of *q* to Christina is now only $1 - m$ so that she has an incentive to substitute away from her own consumption toward the child. In particular, if $m = .704$ then Christina's budget line has the same slope as the dotted line passing through point *a* in Figure 2.1. However, since Christina's own income is $12 025, her actual budget is higher than the dotted line. In order for it to be individually optimal for her to choose point *a*, the settlement would need to stipulate (a) a lump sum transfer from Christina to Jose of $1139 = ($12 025 − $10 886) per year, and (b) a matching payment by Jose of 70.4 cents per dollar of child expenditure by Christina. In this case, the budget constraint faced by Christina would coincide with the dotted line passing through point *a*.

In practice, it is difficult to imagine that such an efficient contract could be written and enforced. Since carrying out the terms of the contract is not in the self-interest of custodial parent, it would require third-party enforcement through a court. Unfortunately, even if judges would be willing to oversee the expenditure patterns of custodial mothers, it is hard to see how they could get unbiased evidence on actual expenditures because each parent has an incentive to distort the data. The idea of matching payments is attractive theoretically because it creates the correct incentives for the custodial parent, but it also entails the same problem of third-party enforcement to make sure that only expenditures on the child are made by the custodian are matched and that the non-custodial parent makes the appropriate payment. Moreover, reality is of course much more complex than our simplified model in many respects. For example, many common expenditures such as housing jointly benefit both the mother and child and, ideally, the matching rate would vary accordingly.

Actual divorce awards and child support formulas, for the most part, specify a transfer of money from the non-custodial father to the custodial mother without attempting to specify how the mother can spend the money. Given this constraint, the 'quasi-efficient' settlement analysed by

WW finds the optimal divorce transfer that would be chosen by the couple to satisfy their desire for consumption insurance and their joint interest in the child's welfare. In this settlement, the wife receives a divorce transfer of $4054, giving her a total income of $16079, a slightly smaller amount than she has in the fully efficient settlement discussed above.[21] With this budget, the wife chooses an individually optimal allocation, spending $11979 on her own consumption and only $4100 on the child as compared with $8152 in the fully efficient settlement. Meanwhile, after paying this transfer the father's consumption is $20655, which is slightly higher than his consumption of $20110 in the fully efficient case.

Clearly, much of the settlement in the quasi-efficient case is, in effect, going to provide consumption insurance to the wife and is not of direct benefit to the child. Once divorce takes place, the father is assumed to have no interest in his ex-wife's welfare and is only motivated to make transfers in order to benefit the child. The '*ex post* Stackelberg equilibrium', the final case analysed by WW, addresses the question of what transfer the father will make voluntarily. Given that the father and mother have the average incomes of couples in the NLSY72 data and that they have the preference parameters WW derived from the Lazear–Michael data, the answer is simple. The father's optimal transfer is zero. The reason, intuitively, is twofold. First, given the mother's income of $12025, she will spend $3304 on the child solely out of her resources, which is quite low, but still well above the minimum expenditure given by the preference parameter $\gamma = 1176. Second, the preference parameter $\alpha = .196$ implies that a dollar transferred by the father to the mother will generate only about 20 cents' additional expenditure on the child or, equivalently, that it costs the father about $5 to increase the welfare of his child by $1. At this price, the income disparity between the mother and father would need to be considerably larger than it is for the average NLSY72 couple in order for the husband to make positive transfers voluntarily.

The quantification of the welfare effects of child support payments on the well-being of the child that we have described in this section can be summarized as follows for the average divorced couple in NLSY72. If there is no child support order or, if there is an order and it is not enforced, the child receives $3304, all provided by the mother. A child support order embodying a divorce transfer that would be chosen in an optimal marriage contract negotiated by a husband and wife at the beginning of marriage would generate total spending on the child of $4100, with the father paying $4054 as a divorce transfer. In a sense, in this simulation child support enforcement removes the father from the ranks of 'deadbeat dads' but comes dangerously close to inducing the mother to join the ranks of 'deadbeat moms'. It is important, however, to stress that child support enforcement results in a modest but significant (24 per cent) increase in expenditure received by the child. Finally, it is also important to stress that the simulation shows that the child expenditures would have been nearly twice as high, at $8052, had the marriage remained intact or had the divorced couple been able to coordinate their expenditures to achieve the efficient level.[22]

Several points of interpretation and qualification should be made about this attempt to quantify the welfare effects of divorce settlements. First, the relatively modest 24 per cent increase in the child's welfare as a result of moving from a situation in which the father pays no child support to one in which he pays the optimal level of support in the quasi-efficient case is based on the Lazear–Michael estimate that the mother will spend only about 20 cents of an additional dollar on the child. Although there may be questions about the precise numerical value of a parent's marginal propensity to spend on children, this number has some empirical basis in their analysis of consumer expenditure data and is probably not wildly off the mark.

Second, however, it is important to understand that the doubling of child expenditure in moving from the quasi-efficient to fully efficient cases, as depicted by the movement from point *b* to point *a* in Figure 2.1, depends critically on the degree to which the custodial mother (or custodial father) is willing to substitute between her own (his own) consumption and expenditures on the child. In the simulation, this effect depends on the functional form of the Stone–Geary utility function used by WW. Like its simpler Cobb–Douglas cousin used earlier in this chapter, the Stone–Geary function assumes a fairly high degree of substitutability. However, if the indifference curves depicted in Figure 2.1 had much sharper curvature, implying a lower degree of substitutability, the importance, in terms of the child's welfare, of getting parental incentives 'right' by means of Jose's credit card or in some other way would be smaller. To my knowledge, there has been little systematic empirical study of this question. An obvious suggestion is to encourage more research, although it should be emphasized that a lack of suitable data makes empirical analysis on this topic very difficult.

As a final caveat, the theory presented in this chapter should be expanded to consider the implications of such factors as housing, which jointly benefit both the child and the custodial parent, and joint physical custody which involves both joint and separate expnditures by both parents that benefit the child. Likewise, the theory should also be generalized to include parental time spent with children, both in terms of the value of that time in enhancing the child's welfare and in terms of the utility the parent receives from contact with the child. I believe that most of the factors stressed in this chapter would continue to be of importance in the expanded framework, but new issues would arise and additional aspects of the problem would need to be quantified in order to provide concrete guidance in the improvement of child support policy.

Although it is beyond the scope of this chapter to develop this expanded framework, I briefly consider joint consumption goods, focusing for concreteness on housing. Since a house is a collective good that benefits all its occupants, the household's demand for housing can be analysed using the same tools as I used earlier to analyse the demand for child quality. In particular, an efficient provision of housing for a married couple with children requires that the couple choose housing according to the Samuelson condition such that the sum of the marginal values of housing to the husband and wife equals the marginal cost of housing. The marginal value to a given parent – say the mother – is given by the sum of two terms: the marginal direct benefit to the mother plus the value she places on increment to the children's welfare from improved housing. Likewise, the marginal value of housing to the father consists of a term equal to the direct benefit of housing to him and another term reflecting the value he places on the benefit of housing to the children.

Given the couple's resources and preferences, suppose that it is optimal for them to choose a $100 000 house. Now suppose they divorce. Even if their incomes do not change, divorce now entails a reduction in the couple's real resources because the father and mother can no longer share a single home.[23] In addition, the custodial mother has an incentive to choose relatively too little housing because she does not take into account the father's valuation of housing in contributing to the child's welfare. In this sense, there is no difference from our earlier analysis of potential inefficiencies in expenditures on goods such as diapers that only benefit the child and collective goods such as housing that also benefit the mother. There is, however, an important difference between housing and other goods stemming from the ease with which the non-custodial father can observe the child's housing as compared to the difficulty he may have in monitoring other kinds of expenditures on the child. This suggests, for example, that a divorced father may be more willing to help pay to keep his children in the marital home – which was chosen to embody the preferences of both parents in terms of neighbourhood characteristics, schools and child-related amenities – than he is to give the mother money to spend in ways that he cannot observe.

Another aspect of an expanded model would take explicit account of role of parental time. As before, the fact that both parent's value the child's welfare means that the optimal amount of time that a given parent devotes to enhancing the child's welfare should reflect the preferences not only of the parent providing the time but also the preferences of the other parent. If the couple fails to reach a cooperative solution after divorce, this means that the custodial parent will tend to spend too little time as well as too little money on the child. Of course, parents may get direct utility from time spent with the child and, if so, visitation and joint custody issues need to be considered along with monetary transfers in determining divorce settlements. In addition, the custodial mother may be able to induce the father to pay child support in return for more generous visitation. The dynamics of such an exchange may be beneficent: the more the father sees his children, the better he is able to monitor the mother's expenditures of time and money, and the more willing he is to provide child support. Cooperation may break down, however, with the children becoming bargaining chips in the war between their parents.

8. CONCLUSIONS: LESSONS FOR DIVORCE SETTLEMENTS

What lessons can be drawn from the theory presented in this chapter for the design of practical child support laws and programmes? **Perhaps its major positive lesson is that the optimal allocation of resources to children requires cooperative behaviour by both parents who share in the costs of children.** Unfortunately, the theory also suggests some negative lessons. A great deal of thought and effort has been devoted to developing approaches to divorce settlements and child support formulas to protect children from the negative economic consequences of divorce and, at the same time, to provide a fair and equitable division of the economic burden of support between the custodial obligor and non-custodial obligee. **The major negative lesson of the theory presented in this chapter is that even an optimally designed and perfectly enforced child support policy will not in general hold the economic welfare of a child harmless in the event of divorce because of the adverse incentives created for both parents when they find themselves unable or unwilling to incorporate the other parent's interest in the child's welfare into their own spending decisions.**

Another contribution of the chapter is to present a theoretical framework in which the welfare of each of the affected parties to a divorce – the father, mother and children – is considered explicitly. The theory suggests that a failure to enforce child support awards may lead to a proliferation of deadbeat dads who, despite their continued concern for the welfare of their children, have incentives to shift the cost of children onto the mother. Elsewhere (Willis 1999), I have argued that a man's ability to reduce the 'cost of fatherhood' by shifting costs onto the mother may help explain the rise of out-of-wedlock childbearing. Conversely, in this chapter I have also shown that even an optimally designed and enforced child support award may have its major effect in providing 'consumption insurance' against the risk of divorce for the custodial mother with only a relatively modest effect on the welfare of the children. The theory suggests that marriage is an institution that facilitates the well-being of children by encouraging both to share in the costs of their children as they share in the utility they derive from them.

NOTES

*   An earlier version of this chapter was presented at the Conference on Law and Economics of Child Support Payments, University of California at Santa Barbara, 20 September 2002. I am grateful to conference participants, especially William Comanor, for helpful comments. I am also grateful to the MacArthur Foundation Network on the Family and the Economy for financial support and to Network members, especially Kathryn Edin, for help in developing some of the ideas in the chapter.

1.   See Willis (1973) and Becker (1991) for models of parental demand for the number and quality of children.
2.   See Becker and Murphy (1988) for a more detailed analysis of the public policy implications of society's interest in child welfare.
3.   See also Willis (1987) and chapters by Hotz et. al., Bergstrom, and Weiss in Rosenzweig and Stark (1997) for recent surveys of family economics.
4.   See, however, Bergstrom (1983) for an analysis showing the limitations of Becker's theorem.
5.   Economists assume that individuals obtain utility from their consumption of goods and services whose units are measured in 'utils'. As must no doubt seem strange to non-economists, a major triumph of twentieth-century economic theory was to show that utility need not be measurable according to any numerical scale, analogous to meters or joules, nor does it need to be measured in a way that is interpersonally comparable in order for all of the positive results of economic theory to hold. A corollary is that using a particular numerical scale for utility such as 'utils' does no harm and may make for expository convenience.
6.   The latter assumption is inessential, but makes the exposition easier.
7.   The assumption is that the husband and wife's utility functions have a particular form leading to 'transferable utility' (Bergstrom and Cornes, 1983).
8.   See, for example, Lundberg and Pollak (1993).
9.   See Borenstein and Courant (1989) for an interesting exploration of this issue in the context of a divorce involving a newly minted medical doctor.
10. See Edin (1994) for evidence that poor mothers receive more support than is recorded in official statistics.
11. To make calculations easy, the numerical examples assume that the mother and father each have Cobb–Douglas utility functions of the form $u = c^{2/3} q^{1/3}$ where c is adult consumption and q is child welfare. These preferences imply that a lone parent would always spend one-third of his or her income on the child. They also imply a unitary price elasticity of demand so that given percentage decline in the price of q leads to an equal percentage increase in demand for q. Slightly more complicated preferences will be introduced in a discussion of a quantitative analysis by Weiss and Willis (1993) that are discussed later in section 7. That analysis uses an estimate that the marginal propensity to spend on children based on data is about 0.2 (that is, a parent whose income increases by a dollar would spend an additional 20 cents on children). Note that this marginal propensity is 0.33 for the Cobb–Douglas function used in the numerical examples in the current section.

12. The distribution of adult consumption could be unequal, but the assumed utility functions imply that optimal level of child expenditure is independent of the distribution of private goods (see Bergstrom and Cornes, 1983).
13. This point is discussed again in a diagrammatic context below in section 8.
14. This argument would be qualified if there is positive 'match quality' within marriage.
15. A numerical example of this point is presented below in section 7.
16. I am grateful to Kathryn Edin for permission to use the material quoted in this section.
17. This section omits a number of the mathematical and empirical details of the analysis which can be found in Weiss and Willis (1993).
18. The NLSY72 data are based on divorces that took place before the fifth follow-up in 1986, at which time sample members were 32 years of age and their children were relatively young.
19. Lazear and Michael (1988) obtained these estimates using data on consumer expenditures. As explained in footnote 25 in Weiss and Willis (1993), Lazear and Michael estimate a function of the form $c_k/c_a = \phi(x)$ where c_k is the inferred consumption level of each child, c_a is the inferred consumption level of each adult, and x is a vector of observable characteristics, including income. The inferred consumption levels were determined from observations on the ratios of assignable adult consumption (such as alcohol) to total adult consumption among families without children. Total expenditure on children is given by $kc_k = k\phi(x)y/[a + k\phi(x)]$, where k is the number of children, a is the number of adults and y is family income. Since $\phi(x)$ depends on income, this defines a non-linear relation between child expenditure and income. To obtain the linear relation implied by (4) in the text (assuming that the allocation within marriage is efficient), Weiss and Willis proceeded as follows: to obtain the marginal propensity to spend on children, conditioned on a given k, differentiate the above expression with respect to y (see Lazear and Michael, 1988, p. 94) and substitute their sample means: $\phi(x) = 0.38$, $y = 13230$, and $\partial\phi(x)/\partial y = -0.00428$ (see Lazear and Michael, 1988, p. 86 and Tables 5.3 and 5.4). Since the marginal propensity drops rather slowly, Weiss and Willis assume that this mean value is a good approximation throughout the NLSY72 sample and set $\partial kc_k/\partial y = \alpha$. To obtain the child consumption level in the NLSY72 sample, conditioned on a given k, multiply the mean income in the NLSY72 sample by $k\phi(x)y/[a + k\phi(x)]$, setting $a = 2$, $\phi(x) = 0.38$, and using the sample mean of $k = 1.50$. Having estimated α and q, γ is obtained by solving $q = \alpha y + (1 - \alpha)\gamma$.
20. This number is calculated by evaluating the mother's *MRS* from the utility function in (2) at the fully efficient levels of child quality and mother's consumption reported in Weiss and Willis (1993).

Specifically, $MRS^{mother} = \left(\dfrac{\alpha}{1-\alpha}\right)\left(\dfrac{c_{mother}}{1-\gamma}\right) = \left(\dfrac{0.196}{1-0.196}\right)\left(\dfrac{8471}{8152-1176}\right) = 0.296$.

21. WW avoid the incentive compatibility problem within marriage discussed above by assuming that 'match quality' may be either very high or very low. In the former case, the wife would have an incentive to stay married even if she could achieve point *b* in Figure 2.1 if divorce took place; in the latter case, no possible allocation within marriage would make the parties better off than divorce. The quasi-efficient settlement discussed in this paragraph assumes that incentive compatibility constraints are not binding.
22. Argys and Peters (1993) argue that divorced couples may be able to achieve an efficient allocation of resources in the context of a 'repeated game' in which each month the father pays the efficient level of child support and the mother allocates her income efficiently, taking into account both her own and the fathers's interest in the welfare of the child. The reason this might work, according to the so-called 'Folk Theorem' of repeated game theory, is that each party knows that if he or she fails to live up to their part of the bargain in a given month, the other party will discontinue the arrangement and all future benefits of cooperation will be lost. Repeated contact between the two parents and between the non-custodial parent and the child is doubtless helpful in overcoming the monitoring problem that underlies the inefficient equilibrium discussed in this chapter.

This may well work for some couples, but for many couples the cooperative repeated game equilibrium may often break down for the very reasons that divorce occurred in the first place.

23. I am assuming that jointly consumed housing creates an economy of scale that is sacrificed when the couple separates. It is worth noting that this is not logically necessary. If each person in the household occupies a separate number of square feet within a home and the marginal cost per square foot of housing is constant, then the father and the mother and children can each be as well off at the same total cost after the divorce by choosing proportionally smaller separate homes.

REFERENCES

Argys, Laura M. and H. Elizabeth Peters (1993), 'The role of child support guidelines in the negotiation of child support awards', paper presented at the Population Association of America meetings, Cincinatti, April.

Becker, Gary S. (1991). *A Treatise on the Family*, enlarged edn, Cambridge, MA: Harvard University Press.

Becker, Gary S. and Kevin M. Murphy (1988), 'The family and the state', *Journal of Law and Economics*, **31** (1), 1–18.

Becker, Gary S., Elizabeth M. Landes and Robert T. Michael (1977), 'An economic analysis of marital instability'. *Journal of Political Economy*, **85**, 1141–87.

Bergstrom, T.C. and R.C. Cornes (1983), 'Independence of allocative efficiency from distribution in the theory of public goods', *Econometrica*, **51**, 1753–65.

Borenstein, Severin and Paul Courant (1989), 'How to carve a medical degree: human capital assets in divorce settlements', *American Economic Review*, **79**, 992–1009.

Browning, Martin, Pierre-Andre Chiappori and Yoram Weiss (2002), 'Family economics', Chapter 3 (manuscript).

Cohen, Lloyd (1987), 'Marriage, divorce, and quasi rents; or "I gave him the best years of my life"', *Journal of Legal Studies*, **16**, 267–303.

Edin, Kathryn (1994), 'Single mothers and absent fathers: the possibilities and limits of child support policy', Center for Urban Policy Research Working Paper No. 68, Rutgers University.

Lazear, Edward and Robert T. Michael (1988), *Allocation of Income within the Household*, Chicago, IL: University of Chicago Press.

Lundberg, Shelly and Robert Pollak (1993), 'Separate spheres bargaining and the marriage market', *Journal of Political Economy*, **101**, 988–1010.

Mnookin, Robert H. and Lewis Kornhauser (1979), 'Bargaining in the shadow of the law: the case of divorce', *Yale Law Journal*, **88**, 950–97.

Pollak, Robert A. (2003), 'Gary Becker's contribution to household and family economics', *Review of Economics of the Household*, **1**, 111–41.

Rosenzweig, M.R. and O. Stark (eds) (1997), *Handbook of Population Economics*, Amsterdam: Elsevier Science B.V.

Samuelson, P.A. (1954), 'The pure theory of public expenditure', *Review of Economics and Statistics*, **36**, 350–56.

Tiebout, Charles M. (1956), 'A pure theory of local expenditures', *Journal of Political Economy*, **64**, 416–24.

Weiss, Yoram (1997), 'The formation and dissolution of families: why marry? who marries whom? and what happens upon marriage and divorce?' in M.R.

Rosenzweig and O. Stark (eds), *Handbook of Population Economics*, Amsterdam: Elsevier Science B.V., pp. 81–124.

Weiss, Yoram and Robert J. Willis (1985), 'Children as collective goods and divorce settlements', *Journal of Labor Economics*, **3** (July), 268–92.

Weiss, Yoram and Robert J. Willis (1993), 'Transfers among divorced couples: evidence and interpretation', *Journal of Labor Economics*, **11** (4) (October), 629–79.

Willis, Robert J. (1973), 'A new approach to the economic theory of fertility behavior', *Journal of Political Economy*, Supplement (March/April), S14–S64.

Willis, Robert J. (1987), 'What have we learned from the economics of the family?', *American Economic Review, Papers and Proceedings*, **77** (2), 68–81.

Willis, Robert J. (1999), 'A theory of out-of-wedlock childbearing', *Journal of Political Economy*, **107** (6), S33–S64.

Willis, Robert J. (2000), 'The Economics of Fatherhood'. *American Economic Review, Papers and Proceedings*, pp. 378–82.

3. Child support guidelines: underlying methodologies, assumptions, and the impact on standards of living

R. Mark Rogers and Donald J. Bieniewicz

I. INTRODUCTION

The federal Family Support Act of 1988 required states to enact presumptive child support guidelines to address the alleged problem of too low a standard of living for custodial parents following divorce. By the end of 1989, all states had enacted guidelines that rested largely on two alternative economic models and cost tables. This chapter addresses the following questions: what child support guidelines are currently in use or considered as alternatives? What are the underlying methodologies and assumptions used for each guideline? And how does the imposition of each guideline's presumptive award affect the relative standards of living of the households of the custodial parent and the non-custodial parent? The guidelines reviewed are:

1. The simple percent-of-obligor-income guideline. This guideline is currently used by 13 states.
2. Income Shares. This guideline, developed and marketed by Policy Studies, Inc., is currently used in 33 states.
3. US Department of Agriculture (USDA) child cost table based guidelines. Currently, no state uses this guideline, but the USDA estimates have been used as a cross-check on the accuracy of existing guidelines. A guideline directly based on the USDA estimates has been introduced as proposed legislation in Minnesota (H.F. 110 in the 2003–2004 legislative session).
4. Cost Shares.[1] Currently, no state uses this guideline, but it is based on principles that were in common use and embodied in state law prior to 1988. This guideline has recently been introduced as proposed legislation in two state legislatures: Georgia (H.B. 149 in the 2003–2004 legislative session) and Minnesota (S.F. 600 and H.F. 664 in the 2003–2004 legislative session). Not reviewed are the Melson-Delaware guidelines (a combination of basic needs and standard of living adjustments),

which is used in three states, and hybrid guidelines used in Massachusetts and the District of Columbia.[2]

Child support guidelines must be economically sound and set fair and equitable awards. The courts rely heavily on these guidelines and rarely deviate from the amounts prescribed. A recent study of Ohio child support cases found that deviations from presumptive awards occurred in only 10.5 per cent of the sample cases; of these, 79 per cent were by parental agreement, not court determination.[3] A similar study conducted for the state of Arizona found that deviations occurred in only 15 per cent of the sample with 56 per cent of the deviations based on agreement of the parties.[4]

The key finding of this chapter regarding methodologies of the two key guidelines (percent-of-obligor-income and Income Shares) currently in use by most states is that these requirements have generally adverse effects in child support cases. Indeed, we find that with both percent-of-obligor-income and Income Shares guidelines, the custodial parent typically ends with a substantially higher standard of living than the non-custodial parent – even when the non-custodial parent starts with higher gross earnings. The USDA-based guideline proposed in Minnesota has similar outcomes. In contrast, the Cost Shares guideline does not lead to inequitable economic outcomes. The problems with the other guidelines are: (1) excessively high basic child cost tables due to an unrealistic standard for support and a poor methodology for estimating child costs, (2) failure to account for child-related tax benefits, and (3) failure to account for the need to support the children in both parents' households.

II. UNDERLYING METHODOLOGIES AND ASSUMPTIONS

The Percent-of-Obligor-Income (Wisconsin-style) Child Support Guideline

The simplest child support guideline is the percent-of-obligor-income guideline. It was developed for welfare case applications by the Institute for Research on Poverty at the University of Wisconsin at Madison. The Wisconsin regulatory code specifically points to the origins:

> The percentage standard established in this chapter is based on an analysis of national studies, including a study done by Jacques Van der Gaag as part of the Child Support Project of the Institute for Research on Poverty, University of Wisconsin, Madison, entitled 'On Measuring the Cost of Children', which disclose the amount of income and disposable assets that parents use to raise their children.[5]

Van der Gaag's definition of child costs is based on income equivalence concepts rather than on direct expenditures for a child. His approach considers the costs of a child as determined by how much income a one-child couple must be compensated in order to be equally well off economically as without the child.[6] He reviews various studies using this type of approach and 'averages' their results to derive a table of child costs that are expressed as a percentage of gross income. These percentages are then viewed as the basic share that children are entitled to of their parents' income.

The State of Wisconsin took Van der Gaag's estimates as baseline cost estimates and adjusted them downward slightly for the nominal visitation expenses of an 'absent' father. For welfare cases, the typical visitation was assumed to be literally a visit, such as a Saturday afternoon trip to the park. This is in sharp contrast to the extensive parenting time of many non-custodial parents today. The State of Wisconsin child support guidelines are given in Table 3.1.

Table 3.1   State of Wisconsin child support guidelines

Number of Children	% of Obligor's Gross Income
1	17%
2	25%
3	29%
4	31%
5 or more	34%

The bulk of the studies reviewed by Van der Gaag were for low-income families with average household incomes of $12000 in 1982 dollars. The low-income base would necessarily lead to high percentages for child costs since necessities would take up almost all, and in many cases more than all income, with the difference being made up by government benefits. Although some of the studies reviewed by Van der Gaag did look at direct expenditures on children, those studies calculated child costs for items such as housing and transportation on a per capita basis – leading to exaggerated child costs.

These flaws in the estimation of the child cost percentages were not seen as fatal because of their limited intended use, which was the recovery of welfare payments made to the custodial parent. Based on early papers providing the technical foundations for Wisconsin's child support guideline, the guideline was originally developed for only welfare situations. The intent was for both parents' income to be part of the formula and that there be a maximum level of support.[7]

The original concept for Wisconsin's child support plan included exemptions for obligor self-support, ceilings on income subject to the guidelines, and was based on a modest level of publicly guaranteed benefits. The state's objective was to recover as much of the costs of those benefits from both parents as was practical. It was designed to be applicable only for households with certain economic characteristics. These underlying economic characteristics of the household, and other assumptions of the original study, are:

- The household is a low-income household. For the original study, the total income of the two parents is $12000 in 1982 dollars. In 2001 dollars, this amount would be $22023. The underlying study specifically states that at higher incomes, the applicable support percentages should decline.
- The support percentages would be applied only after setting aside a self-support reserve for the payor.
- The custodial parent is assumed to care for the children and not earn any income outside the home.
- The non-custodial parent is the sole income earner, and the percentages applied to the non-custodial parent's income are based on the tax law of 1982. The non-custodial parent would receive use of all child income tax benefits.
- Because the guideline was to be applied to income earners paying little or no income tax, there was no need to take into account differences between gross income and net income.
- The children are with the custodial parent essentially 100 per cent of the time. The non-custodial parent's child costs are assumed to be negligible.
- The guideline percentages were to be applied to obligor income only up to the point of recovering welfare payments to the custodial household.

The Income Shares Child Support Guideline

There are two different Income Shares models – the original Income Shares based on the work of Thomas Espenshade and Ernst Engel (currently in use in about a dozen states) and the version based on the work of David Betson and Erwin Rothbarth, now advocated by Policy Studies, Inc. (PSI) and used in about two dozen states.[8] Each uses a different definition of child costs, but are all based on indirect income equivalence measures, rather than relying directly on parents' spending for their children.

PSI's stated reason for using indirect estimation techniques relates to data issues involving the underlying database, the Consumer Expenditure

Survey (CEX) of the US Bureau of the Census. Notably, the CEX expenditure categories do not always separate household expenditures into spending on children's goods and on adult goods. For example, there are separate categories for spending on children's clothing and adult clothing. In contrast, data on spending for housing, food and transportation are gathered only on a household basis. The issue then is one of how to allocate a portion of the food, housing and transportation costs to the children.

In order to avoid these data problems, the developers of the Income Shares method turned to income equivalence measures. These measures were originally developed more than a century ago to answer a very specific type of question: how much income is needed for different family types (varying the number of adults and children) to have the same standard of living? For example, these studies would attempt to quantify how much income a two-parent-one-child family needed to have the same standard of living as a two-adult household. While these measures were never intended to estimate child costs, that is precisely the purpose for which they are now used.

The Original Version of Income Shares: Using the Espenshade–Engel Methodology to Estimate Child Costs

The economist to first work on income equivalence measures was Ernst Engel.[9] His purpose was to measure consumption of different goods in families, and observe how outlays varied by the level of income and the number of household members. He found that the share of income allocated to food consumption declined as income rose. As income increased, spending was increasingly allocated to non-basic goods (luxury goods) and to savings. A family having children would boost its share of food consumption relative to a family without children. Engel then compared how much additional income would be needed to return the family to its earlier lower share of spending on food (boosting non-food share).[10]

The Engel methodology was used by Thomas Espenshade to estimate child costs in a 1984 US national study.[11] He defined child costs as the difference in overall consumption between a family with and without children, but with the same share of the budget spent on food. Two families of different size were assumed to be equally well off when they spent the same share of their budgets on food. PSI used data from Espenshade's study to derive the original Income Shares guideline.[12] (See Box 3.1.) States that adopted the Income Shares guideline in the late 1980s (and have not since adopted the newer Income Shares methodology) define child costs according to how food consumption changes between varying types of families according to family size. Table 3.2 shows Espenshade's child cost estimates as a percentage of net income.

BOX 3.1 PSI'S ORIGINAL DEFINITION OF CHILD COSTS FOR INCOME SHARES CHILD SUPPORT SCHEDULES:

Based on intact family data, the child cost is – when comparing two families (one with children and one without children) – the difference in expenditures between the two families when both consume equal proportions of their budget on food.

This is an 'income equivalence' definition, not a measure of actual money spent on child cost items.

Table 3.2   Child costs as estimated by Espenshade

	$0–$8499	$8500–12249	$12250–16499	$16500–19999	$20000–27999	$28000–39499	$39500+
	Percentage of Net Income Spent on Children by Income Level 1983 Net Income Dollar Levels						
One child	26.0	25.5	23.6	21.5	20.7	19.4	16.2
Two children	40.4	39.6	36.6	33.4	32.2	30.1	25.2
Three children	50.6	49.6	45.9	41.9	40.3	37.7	31.6

Equivalent 2001 Net Income Dollar Levels:*

$0–$15114	$15115–21782	$21783–29339	$29340–35562	$35563–49787	$49788–70235	$70236+

Note:
*Corresponding 2001 dollar net income ranges supplied by R. Mark Rogers, based on the ratio of the All-Urban Consumer Price Index, ratio of 2001 annual average to 1983 annual average.

The Current Version of Income Shares: Using the Betson–Rothbarth Methodology to Estimate Child Costs

PSI currently uses the Rothbarth methodology to estimate child costs and develop child cost schedules. The Rothbarth methodology compares changes in levels of household spending on purely adult goods to estimate child costs.[13] The idea is that spending levels on such goods can be used to indicate relative living standards as between households with and without children.

The version of the Rothbarth technique that is incorporated in PSI's latest Income Shares guideline was developed by David Betson. Betson uses a particular bundle of adult goods to measure a household's level of well-being – adult clothing, alcohol and tobacco. He assumes that when families both with and without an additional child spend the same amount on purely adult goods, then the two families are equally well off. In that case, any difference in total consumption expenditures must represent child costs.[14] (See Box 3.2.)

BOX 3.2   PSI'S NEW DEFINITION OF CHILD COSTS FOR INCOME SHARES CHILD SUPPORT SCHEDULES:

For intact families – one with an additional child and one with no additional child – the difference in expenditures between the two families is the child cost when both families consume equal dollar levels of adult clothing, alcohol and tobacco.

Reasons Behind the Income Shares Model's Overstatement of Child Costs

There are several reasons why PSI's methodology – using either version of Income Shares – leads to an overstatement of child costs: (1) the use of intact families to estimate child costs, (2) the use of indirect estimating techniques with household food consumption as a target definition in the old Engel estimator version and the adult goods share of consumption as a target definition in the newer version, and (3) the failure to recognize that tax benefits associated with the children offset some of these costs.

The first problem with the PSI methodology is that both the Betson–Rothbarth and the earlier Espenshade–Engel versions of the Income Shares guideline are based on studies of intact families. Yet when two households must be supported with the same income, there is clearly an increase in adult overhead such as mortgage and utilities. There is less income left for spending on all other things – including children. By using intact family data, the Income Shares guideline overestimates the ability of both parents to spend on the children and thereby the level of child costs to be shared.

The second problem with the PSI methodology is that the estimators themselves are upwardly biased. It is widely recognized by economists that the Espenshade estimates of child costs using the Engel estimator are upwardly biased. See the following statement from a recent report on these issues:

The validity of the Engel estimator is critically dependent on the assumption that the percentage of the family's expenditures on non-food items that should be attributed to the family's children is the same as the percentage of the family's food expenditures that is attributable to the family's children. There is reason to believe that this assumption is invalid; children are probably relatively 'food-intensive'. That is to say, the percentage of the family's food that is consumed by children is probably greater than the percentage of non-food items consumed by children. If this is the case, then the Engel estimator *overestimates* the true expenditures on children. Unfortunately, Deaton and Muellbauer's analysis indicates that the degree of overestimation [of child costs] may be quite substantial. This leads Deaton and Muellbauer to conclude that, 'We can construct no plausible defense for the belief that the food share correctly indicates welfare (well-being) between households of different size, and we do not believe that credence should be given to estimates based on that belief.'[15]

In the newer version of the Income Shares method, using the quantity of adult goods consumed to define income equivalence also leads to an upward bias for estimating child cost expenditures. The critical fact is that adult preferences are influenced by the structure of their families, and this approach ignores that fact. Notably, the consumption of the particular adult goods used by Betson – tobacco and alcohol – may intentionally be used less as a result of having children. A parent consumes fewer adult goods after having a child as a matter of choice. Using a standard that targets equalizing consumption shares of adult goods overstates child costs because families choose to consume fewer adult goods after having children. This standard leads to income levels that are much too high for any comparison of consumption changes that are attributed to child costs.[16]

To be sure, there are assertions that this methodology is biased downward and can be considered a 'lower bound' (floor) to estimates for child costs.[17] That position is based on the unsubstantiated belief that with the addition of children, adults choose to consume more purely adult goods and fewer goods shared by the adults and children. However, this argument lacks credibility with the consumption goods used in the Betson–Rothbarth estimator: alcohol, tobacco and adult clothing.

The Betson–Rothbarth technique uses the share of total consumption of these goods to measure overall well-being for a family. For this method to underestimate child costs, one would need to believe that when a household has an additional child, the adults decide to drink more alcohol, smoke more tobacco and spend more on adult clothes. Common sense tells us that social pressure from other family members leads to less rather than more consumption of these particular goods after having an additional child. In general, over the income levels studied, the consumption of these goods does not respond closely to changes in income and therefore require larger increases in income to restore previous levels of consumption. For this reason, the Betson–Rothbarth methodology overestimates child costs.

A third problem with the Income Shares guideline is that it ignores the offset to child costs of child-related tax benefits. These tax benefits include being able to claim the children as deductions, childcare tax credits, and the ability to file as head of household for a lower tax rate.

A fourth problem with the Income Shares guideline is that it fails to allocate child costs properly in the two parents' households. It treats all child costs as being in the custodial parent's household, even when the non-custodial parent spends considerable time caring for the children. For example, in the Income Shares guideline used by the State of Pennsylvania, there is no recognition of the child costs incurred by the non-custodial parent, and avoided by the custodial parent, until the non-custodial parent has over 40 per cent custody time with the children.

In summary, the Income Shares guideline makes the following economic assumptions:

- The household is intact, that is, parents can afford to spend as much on their children as before the divorce.
- The custodial parent cares for the children 100 per cent of the time and the non-custodial parent has no parenting time.
- Child costs are best estimated by indirect measures based on income equivalence scales, rather than direct reports of out-of-pocket spending.
- For Espenshade–Engel based Income Shares guidelines, the best method of estimating child costs is to compare household consumption percentages of food before and after having an additional child. It is assumed that children consume non-food household goods in the same proportion as food.
- For Betson–Rothbarth based Income Shares guidelines, the best method of estimating child costs is to compare household consumption levels of alcohol, tobacco and adult clothing before and after having an additional child. It is assumed that adult consumption preferences for these goods are not affected by having children or additional children. It is also assumed that for the income range studied, that these goods have an income elasticity of one.
- Tax benefits attributable to the children are not cost offsets – they are not negative costs.

The Newly Proposed USDA-based Child Support Guideline

Growing awareness of the problems with the child cost tables used in the percent-of-obligor-income and Income Shares guidelines has led several states to consider using US Department of Agriculture (USDA) child cost estimates directly as a substitute. However, the USDA estimates only partially address the flaws of current state child support guidelines.

One guideline of this type is the 'Shared Responsibility' guideline recently proposed in Minnesota (Minnesota H.F. 110, 2003–2004 Legislative Term). This guideline's cost tables are directly based on USDA estimates of parental expenditures on children.

The methodology for the Shared Responsibility guideline can be divided into two parts: (1) the estimation process used by the USDA to generate the tables in *Expenditures on Children by Families*, and (2) adjustments to the USDA expenditure tables to determine the Shared Responsibility cost tables.

The USDA explains its methodology in Box 3.3.

BOX 3.3   METHODS

Data used to estimate expenditures on children are from the 1990–92 Consumer Expenditure Survey – Interview portion (CE). Administered by the Bureau of Labor Statistics (BLS), US Department of Labor, this survey is the most comprehensive source of information on household expenditures available at the national level. The sample consists of 12 850 husband–wife households and 3395 single-parent households and was weighted to reflect the US population of interest, using BLS weighting methods.

Multivariate analysis was used to estimate household and child-specific expenditures, controlling for income level, family size and age of the younger child so estimates could be made for families with these varying characteristics (regional estimates were also derived by controlling for region). Households with two children were selected as the base since this was the average number of children in two-parent families.

Estimated household and child-specific expenditures were allocated among family members. Since the estimated expenditures for clothing, childcare, and education only apply to children (adult-related expenses for these items were excluded), allocations of these expenses were made by dividing the estimates equally among the children.

The 1994 food plans of USDA were used to allocate food expenses among family members. These plans, derived from a national food consumption survey, show the share of food expenses attributable to individual family members by age and household income level. These member food budget shares were applied to estimated 1990–92 household food expenditures to determine food expenses on a child. Similarly, health care expenses were allocated to each family member based on budget share data from the 1987 National Medical Expenditure Survey. This survey contains data on the proportion of health care expenses attributable to individual family members. These member budget shares for health care were applied to estimated 1990–92 household health care expenditures to determine expenses on a child.

Unlike food and health care, no research base exists for allocating estimated household expenditures on housing, transportation and other miscellaneous goods and services among family members. USDA uses the per capita method in allocating these expenses; the per capita method allocates expenses among household members in equal proportions. A marginal cost method, which assumes that expenditures on children may be measured as the difference in total expenses between couples with children and equivalent childless couples was not used because of limitations with this approach. The marginal cost method depends on development of an equivalency measure for which there is no established base. Various measures have been proposed, each yielding different estimates of expenditures on children. Also, some of the marginal cost approaches do not consider substitution effects. They assume, for example, that parents do not alter their expenditures on themselves after a child is added to a household.

As transportation expenses resulting from work activities are not related to expenses on children, these costs were excluded when estimating children's transportation expenses. The overall USDA methodology was repeated for families with one child and more than two children so adjustments may be made for families of different sizes.

Although based on the 1990–92 CE, the expense estimates were updated to 2001 dollars using the Consumer Price Index (CPI) (1990 and 1991 expenditure and income data were first converted to 1992 dollars; then all three years of data were updated to 2001 dollars).

Source: United States Department of Agriculture (2001), pp. i and iii.

A key issue regarding the USDA methodology is the use of per capita estimates for the three categories of housing, transportation and miscellaneous goods and services. Notably, housing and transportation costs are largely already incurred prior to having children. Children's marginal costs for housing and transportation are substantially below any costs estimated on a per capita basis. And children's costs are also lower than adults' costs in the miscellaneous goods and services category.

The Shared Responsibility guideline proposed in Minnesota uses USDA numbers, but excludes the medical, and childcare and education, components. Medical insurance, unreimbursed medical expenses, childcare, and private tuition are treated as 'add-ons' to basic child costs.

The Shared Responsibility guideline makes the following assumptions, some of which are similar to those in the Income Shares guideline:

- The household is intact. The child support award is based on combined parental incomes. The household does not have the additional overhead that is incurred by a separated family that would reduce the income available to spend on children.
- The custodial parent is assumed to care for the children 100 per cent of the time and the non-custodial parent is assumed to have no parenting time.
- Tax benefits attributable to the children are not cost offsets. They are not negative costs.
- The best method of estimating child costs for housing, transportation and 'miscellaneous' is to take household spending for these categories and give children a share of the costs equal to that for an adult.

The Cost Shares Child Support Guideline

In the mid-1990s, the Children's Rights Council (CRC) developed a prototype child support guideline based on long-established principles in state law in order to correct the evident problems with existing state child support guidelines.[18] This model guideline has since been developed into a working version called the Cost Shares child support guideline.[19] The Cost Shares guideline diverges from percent-of-obligor-income guidelines and the Income Shares guideline in several key facets. In particular, the Cost Shares guideline bases its child cost table on numbers derived directly from actual surveys of parents, rather than by using income equivalence measures.

The Cost Shares guideline relies primarily on the USDA child cost tables as the key inputs for its cost table but with specific adjustments to reduce the USDA reliance on per capita estimates for some components. The USDA child cost tables were interpolated at $50 increments using a regression-based methodology, correlating updated published data between income and expenditures. The Cost Shares guideline has child cost components for housing, food, transportation, clothing, health care and 'other'. The USDA component for 'childcare and education' is removed and these items are treated as 'add-ons'.

The Cost Shares guideline differs from other guidelines not just in its cost tables, but also by its recognition that the children will live partially in two separate households and will be supported in both. The basic model makes the following calculations:

1. Use an average of both parents' incomes to specify the standard of living of the children and the basic costs of the children living in a single-parent household. The basic table has child costs for a single-parent household according to gross income. Basic child costs exclude childcare and education expenses which are treated as 'add-ons'.
2. Add other non-basic expenses when appropriate.
3. Deduct from total child costs the tax benefit that the custodial parent receives that is solely attributable to having custody of the children.
4. Allocate the net child cost obligation (net of tax benefits) between the two parents in proportion to each parent's ability to support the children, as measured by each parent's share of combined after-tax income that is above a self-support level.[20]
5. Treat each parent as being equally entitled to reimbursement from the other parent for their share of child costs incurred while in the first parent's care.
6. The Cost Shares award is limited at a 133 per cent of poverty threshold. No award can push the obligor below this level.

The following are then the underlying facts and assumptions of the Cost Shares child support guideline:

- The family is not intact – two households are supported. The average income of the two parents is used to determine the target level of expenditures on the children.
- Child-related tax benefits of either parent are treated as cost offsets against total spending on the children.
- Day care and education are excluded from the cost tables and treated as add-ons. Medical insurance is included as part of health care expenses in the cost tables.
- The best method of estimating child costs to date is to use the USDA child cost tables, but with marginal housing costs for children substi-

tuted for the per-capita estimates of housing costs for children used by the USDA.

The key difference of the Cost Shares approach from the USDA guidelines is the economically appropriate use of the marginal cost of housing instead of per capita estimates. The housing component is derived from housing data from the US Department of the Interior's Regional Quarters Rental Survey by region. This is an extensive survey of market values of private housing for determining market values of government-furnished housing to employees. Rental costs are for owner-occupied housing. The south-east region data are used for this chapter's analysis.

For one-child costs, the Cost Shares solution is to look at the rental cost from the Department of the Interior data of a fixed square footage, constant quality house with one bedroom, and then determine the cost of the same type of house but with higher square footage to reflect the added bedroom and additional living area (a combined extra 200 square feet) associated with the addition of a child. Other housing costs – such as utilities and furnishing – are also factored onto the rental cost using cost ratios from the US Bureau of Labor Statistics. For housing costs for more than one child, the housing cost ratios from the USDA are used, which reflect ratios of two-child costs to one-child costs, and so on.

Dollar Value Differences in Presumptive Awards

Tables 3.3 to 3.5 show the awards for the various guidelines for one, two and three children for the case where the custodial parent has half the gross income of the non-custodial parent. *They demonstrate that Cost Shares awards, which more accurately reflect the post-divorce economic circumstances of the parents, the tax benefits related to the children, and the cost of supporting the children in the non-custodial household, are typically one-quarter to one-third of the presumptive awards in Incomes Shares and percent-of-obligor-income states.*

To demonstrate this result, we investigate the impact of the presumptive guidelines on relative living standards in the custodial and non-custodial households. This exercise is carried out in the following section.

III.   STANDARD OF LIVING COMPARISONS

A traditional standard-of-living comparison uses the federal poverty threshold as a benchmark. Poverty thresholds vary according to household size. Starting with the one-child case, the issue examined here is how the

Table 3.3 Dollar value of presumptive awards: One child, custodial parent's gross income 50% less than non-custodial parent's gross income

Guideline	Non-custodial parent's monthly gross income						
	$2000	$2500	$3000	$3500	$4000	$4500	$5000
Georgia (% of obligor income, gross income)	400	500	600	700	800	900	1000
Minnesota (% of obligor income, net income)	392	480	564	636	708	781	853
Rhode Island, Income Shares, Engel version	335	389	443	499	555	611	663
Pennsylvania, Income Shares, Betson–Rothbarth version	365	411	455	505	550	594	638
USDA based, Minnesota Shared Responsibility legislation	380	425	470	515	560	605	650
Cost Shares, with south-east housing, 100% sole custody	222	234	252	290	334	376	405
Cost Shares, with south-east housing, 75%/25% time split	99	103	113	144	180	214	233

Note:
All the guidelines, except Cost Shares, yield the same presumptive awards for 100% sole custody as for a 75%/25% time split with the children.

Table 3.4 Dollar value of presumptive awards: Two children, custodial parent's gross income 50% less than the non-custodial parent's gross income

Guideline	Non-custodial parent's monthly gross income						
	$2000	$2500	$3000	$3500	$4000	$4500	$5000
Georgia (% of obligor income, gross income)	500	625	750	875	1000	1125	1250
Minnesota (% of obligor income, net income)	470	576	677	763	850	937	1023
Rhode Island, Income Shares, Engel version	518	601	689	776	866	951	1031
Pennsylvania, Income Shares, Betson–Rothbarth version	518	583	650	719	787	853	911
USDA based, Minnesota Shared Responsibility legislation	612	684	757	829	901	974	1047
Cost Shares, with south-east housing, 100% sole custody	337	370	378	400	440	500	566
Cost Shares, with south-east housing, 75%/25% time split	151	171	167	176	204	213	304

Note:
All the guidelines, except Cost Shares, yield the same presumptive awards for 100% sole custody as for a 75%/25% time split with the children.

Table 3.5 Dollar value of presumptive awards: Three children, custodial parent's gross income 50% less than the non-custodial parent's gross income

Guideline	Non-custodial parent's monthly gross income						
	$2000	$2500	$3000	$3500	$4000	$4500	$5000
Georgia (% of obligor income, gross income)	570	713	855	998	1140	1283	1425
Minnesota (% of obligor income, net income)	548	672	789	890	992	1093	1194
Rhode Island, Income Shares, Engel version	649	754	863	971	1083	1189	1289
Pennsylvania, Income Shares, Betson-Rothbarth version	596	661	761	838	912	991	1061
USDA based, Minnesota Shared Responsibility legislation	707	791	874	958	1041	1125	1209
Cost Shares, with south-east housing, 100% sole custody	438	472	472	488	523	557	599
Cost Shares, with south-east housing, 75%/25% time split	226	247	231	235	256	276	303

Note:
All the guidelines, except Cost Shares, yield the same presumptive awards for 100% sole custody as for a 75%/25% time split with the children.

payment of presumptive child support awards affects the standard of living for a one-adult household of the non-custodial parent and for the one-adult and one-child household of the custodial parent. Comparisons are also made for the one-adult household versus a one-adult-and-two-children household.

The poverty thresholds established by the Bureau of the Census vary by the number of children, so that using these varying thresholds takes into account the custodial parent's higher costs from supporting the children. The relevant poverty thresholds are shown in Table 3.6.

Table 3.6 *Poverty thresholds, 2001, US Bureau of the Census Annual, current dollars*

One adult, under age 65	$9214
One adult, one child	$12207
One adult, two children	$14269

However, non-custodial parents often have significant amounts of parenting time. This increases the non-custodial parent's poverty threshold costs while reducing those of the custodial parent. We assume that the non-custodial parent has 25 per cent of total parenting time and that the children's portion of the poverty threshold shifts between the parents by that proportion. For one child, the difference between a one-adult household and a one-adult, one-child household is $2993 annually. Allocating 25 per cent of this amount to the non-custodial parent results in a one-child poverty threshold of $9962 for the non-custodial parent and $11459 for the custodial parent. This adjustment takes into account the non-custodial parent's need to provide for the children while in his or her care.

It can be argued that because of fixed costs such as housing, a straight-line allocation of the child portion of the poverty threshold is inappropriate. However, while studies indicate that custodial parent child costs go down less than proportional to parenting time, they also indicate that a non-custodial parent's child costs go up more than proportional to parenting time.[21] Therefore, straight-line allocation appears to be a conservative measure of the non-custodial parent's share of poverty threshold levels as compared to that of the custodial parent. These are provided in Table 3.7.

In the analysis below, we express living standards as multiples of the appropriate poverty threshold provided in Table 3.7. Scenarios start with custodial parent gross incomes that are 50 per cent of that of the non-custodial parent. Additional comparisons assume the ratio of 70 per cent, 100 per cent, 130 per cent and 200 per cent.

Table 3.7   Parenting time adjusted poverty thresholds, 2001, annual

	25% parenting time assumption for the NCP	
	Custodial Parent (CP)	Non-custodial Parent (NCP)
One-child case	$11459	$9962
Two-children case	$13005	$10478

What are reasonable expectations for the outcomes of these standard of living comparisons? After tax and after child support transfer, we believe that equitable outcomes would be such that where both parents have equal gross incomes, they also have equal standards of living after taking into account differences in household size and the cost of the children. However, in cases where the non-custodial parent begins with a higher gross income, one would expect that the non-custodial parent would still have the higher standard of living after paying support. One might consider it equitable that the standard of living gap be narrowed somewhat, but not eliminated, by the child support transfer when one parent has a significantly higher gross income. However, one would not expect child support transfers to increase the initial standard of living gap for the higher earning parent.

Table 3.8 shows by means of an example the basic calculations for both parents' living standards relative to the poverty threshold. The example provided in Table 3.8 starts with equal gross incomes. We believe an equitable result would be to end with equal living standards after accounting for tax differences, the child support award, and household size. However, we find a very different result. As can be seen, the custodial parent's living standard is one-third higher than that of the non-custodial parent.

Table 3.8   The standard of living impact of Pennsylvania's income shares guideline: an example

For one child, 25%/75% parenting division		
	NCP	CP
Gross income, annual	$48000	$48000
After-tax income	35207	38248
Presumptive child support	−6204	6204
After tax, after presumptive child support income	**$29003**	**$44452**
Adjusted poverty threshold	$9962	$11459
Income as multiple of threshold	2.911	3.879
Custodial parent's higher (+) or lower (−) standard of living compared to non-custodial parent		+33%

The standard of living analysis in Table 3.8 is expanded in Tables 3.9 to 3.15 for the major types of guidelines and their presumptive awards. There are scenarios for both one and two children, and for non-custodial parent monthly gross incomes ranging from $1500 to $6000. Custodial parent income is then set at different percentages of non-custodial parent income: 50 per cent, 70 per cent, 100 per cent, 130 per cent, and 200 per cent. These tables show the standard of living outcomes which are comparable to the final figure given in Table 3.8.

As can be seen in these tables, the various guidelines, except for Cost Shares, create a substantial shift in the living standards from the non-custodial to the custodial parent. When the custodial parent has moderately lower income than the non-custodial parent, the former typically ends with a higher standard of living than the latter. For situations where the custodial parent has the higher gross income, the combination of child-related tax benefits and the child support transfer boosts the custodial parent's advantage. The income sharing mechanism does not share the child cost burden in a manner to narrow any standard of living difference between higher and lower income parents in a consistent manner, regardless of whether the custodial or the non-custodial parent has the higher income. Instead, these guidelines always boost the custodial parent's standard of living – even when the custodial parent is the one with the higher income level.

With Wisconsin-style, gross income basis guidelines, as reported in Table 3.9 for situations in which the custodial parent has 50, 70 or 100 per cent of the non-custodial parent's income, the former ends up with a dramatically higher standard of living than the non-custodial parent. And when the custodial parent has a higher gross income, the custodial parent's standard of living advantage is boosted even further. For example, with the custodial parent's gross income 30 per cent higher than that of the non-custodial parent, with two children, the custodial parent achieves over a 100 per cent higher standard of living. When the custodial parent has gross income that is double that of the non-custodial parent, the custodial parent typically ends with a 160 to 200 per cent higher standard of living following the child support transfer.

For net income basis percent-of-obligor-income guidelines reported in Table 3.10, the considerable shift in the standard of living is similar to that for the gross income percentage model over the low- and middle-income ranges. Minnesota uses higher fixed percentages than Georgia to offset part of the impact of using net income. At higher incomes, the fixed net income percentages do not shift the standard of living as much as do gross income percentages. Yet, even with net income percentages, the standard of living shift is so large that the custodial parent in typical cases where the custodial parent has at least 50 per cent of the non-custodial parent's gross

Table 3.9 Custodial parent's % higher/lower standard of living compared to NCP for Wisconsin-style guideline, gross income basis, Georgia**

One child

NCP monthly gross income:	1500	2000	2500	3000	3500	4000	4500	5000	5500	6000
CP gross = 50 % < NCP gross	15	14	11	9	8	8	8	9	10	11
CP gross = 30 % < NCP gross	41	36	30	26	27	30	32	34	36	37
CP gross = NCP gross	71	61	56	58	63	67	68	68	69	69
CP gross = 30 % > NCP gross	95	89	89	91	95	97	99	99	100	103
CP gross = 100 % > NCP gross	160	164	159	157	162	168	174	178	181	184

Two children

NCP monthly gross income:	1500	2000	2500	3000	3500	4000	4500	5000	5500	6000
CP gross = 50 % < NCP gross	33	33	29	26	28	28	27	27	27	28
CP gross = 30 % < NCP gross	63	56	50	46	46	47	49	52	54	55
CP gross = NCP gross	93	85	75	74	80	84	87	88	89	89
CP gross = 30 % > NCP gross	122	108	106	108	114	117	119	120	121	123
CP gross = 100 % > NCP gross	180	183	179	177	182	188	194	199	203	207

Note: * Based on midpoints of guideline percentage ranges.

Table 3.10   Custodial parent's % higher/lower standard of living compared to NCP for Wisconsin-style guideline, net income basis, Minnesota

One child

NCP monthly gross income:	1500	2000	2500	3000	3500	4000	4500	5000	5500	6000
CP gross = 50 % < NCP gross	15	12	9	5	3	1	−1	−1	−1	−1
CP gross = 30 % < NCP gross	42	34	27	22	21	22	23	23	23	23
CP gross = NCP gross	71	59	53	53	55	57	56	55	54	54
CP gross = 30 % > NCP gross	95	87	86	86	86	85	85	84	83	84
CP gross = 100 % > NCP gross	162	160	153	149	150	153	156	157	158	159

Two children

NCP monthly gross income:	1500	2000	2500	3000	3500	4000	4500	5000	5500	6000
CP gross = 50 % < NCP gross	29	27	22	17	15	13	11	9	7	7
CP gross = 30 % < NCP gross	59	49	42	36	33	31	31	31	32	32
CP gross = NCP gross	89	77	66	63	64	66	65	64	63	62
CP gross = 30 % > NCP gross	117	100	96	96	96	95	94	93	92	92
CP gross = 100 % > NCP gross	175	172	165	160	160	161	163	164	165	166

Table 3.11 Custodial parent's % higher/lower standard of living compared to NCP for income shares guideline, Espenshade–Engel estimator version, Rhode Island

One child

NCP monthly gross income:	1500	2000	2500	3000	3500	4000	4500	5000	5500	6000
CP gross = 50 % < NCP gross	7	1	−5	−9	−11	−12	−14	−15	−14	−15
CP gross = 30 % < NCP gross	31	21	12	6	5	6	7	7	7	6
CP gross = NCP gross	57	42	33	32	35	37	36	34	32	30
CP gross = 30 % > NCP gross	77	65	62	61	62	61	59	56	54	53
CP gross = 100 % > NCP gross	133	130	120	114	113	114	114	113	110	107

Two children

NCP monthly gross income:	1500	2000	2500	3000	3500	4000	4500	5000	5500	6000
CP gross = 50 % < NCP gross	43	34	22	16	15	14	11	8	16	6
CP gross = 30 % < NCP gross	71	52	40	34	30	28	29	29	28	26
CP gross = NCP gross	96	77	61	56	58	60	59	56	52	49
CP gross = 30 % > NCP gross	120	95	87	85	87	85	81	77	73	69
CP gross = 100 % > NCP gross	166	159	147	139	136	133	131	128	122	117

Table 3.12   Custodial parent's % higher/lower standard of living compared to NCP for income shares guideline, Betson–Rothbarth estimator version, Pennsylvania

One child

NCP monthly gross income:	1500	2000	2500	3000	3500	4000	4500	5000	5500	6000
CP gross = 50 % < NCP gross	11	6	−2	−10	−13	−16	−18	−19	−20	−20
CP gross = 30 % < NCP gross	36	24	11	5	3	2	2	2	1	0
CP gross = NCP gross	62	44	35	33	33	33	31	30	27	26
CP gross = 30 % > NCP gross	84	68	64	62	61	59	57	54	54	54
CP gross = 100 % > NCP gross	140	135	125	119	117	118	120	121	120	119

Two children

NCP monthly gross income:	1500	2000	2500	3000	3500	4000	4500	5000	5500	6000
CP gross = 50 % < NCP gross	41	34	20	11	7	3	−2	−5	−7	−8
CP gross = 30 % < NCP gross	71	52	37	27	20	17	16	15	14	12
CP gross = NCP gross	101	74	56	50	49	48	46	43	39	38
CP gross = 30 % > NCP gross	125	91	83	79	77	74	70	67	67	66
CP gross = 100 % > NCP gross	167	157	145	137	132	131	133	133	130	128

Table 3.13 Custodial parent's % higher/lower standard of living compared to NCP for USDA child cost table based guideline, 'shared responsibility' legislation, Minnesota

One child

NCP monthly gross income:	1500	2000	2500	3000	3500	4000	4500	5000	5500	6000
CP gross = 50 % < NCP gross	66	10	1	−5	−9	−11	−14	−15	−15	−15
CP gross = 30 % < NCP gross	44	28	16	9	7	6	6	6	6	5
CP gross = NCP gross	66	47	37	34	35	36	35	33	32	31
CP gross = 30 % > NCP gross	85	69	64	62	61	60	59	58	57	58
CP gross = 100 % > NCP gross	138	130	120	115	115	117	119	120	117	114

Two children

NCP monthly gross income:	1500	2000	2500	3000	3500	4000	4500	5000	5500	6000
CP gross = 50 % < NCP gross	85	58	39	28	23	19	14	11	8	7
CP gross = 30 % < NCP gross	106	73	54	42	36	33	31	30	29	29
CP gross = NCP gross	124	93	71	63	63	62	61	58	56	55
CP gross = 30 % > NCP gross	142	108	95	90	89	87	85	83	82	81
CP gross = 100 % > NCP gross	182	166	152	143	142	143	144	145	137	131

Table 3.14   Custodial parent's % higher/lower standard of living compared to NCP for cost shares guideline, without tax benefits as cost offsets nor NCP 25% share of child costs considered

One child

NCP monthly gross income:	1500	2000	2500	3000	3500	4000	4500	5000	5500	6000
CP gross = 50 % < NCP gross	58	31	14	−4	−13	−18	−22	−24	−26	−27
CP gross = 30 % < NCP gross	94	41	14	2	−3	−5	−6	−7	−7	−8
CP gross = NCP gross	56	36	25	21	21	21	19	18	16	15
CP gross = 30 % > NCP gross	51	48	46	45	44	43	41	40	39	39
CP gross = 100 % > NCP gross	90	100	96	93	93	95	97	97	98	99

Two children

NCP monthly gross income:	1500	2000	2500	3000	3500	4000	4500	5000	5500	6000
CP gross = 50 % < NCP gross	166	98	60	24	10	1	−6	−11	−15	−17
CP gross = 30 % < NCP gross	230	91	44	25	14	8	5	3	2	1
CP gross = NCP gross	93	63	43	34	32	31	29	27	25	23
CP gross = 30 % > NCP gross	71	63	58	55	54	52	49	48	46	45
CP gross = 100 % > NCP gross	92	106	104	100	99	99	99	100	100	100

Table 3.15 Custodial parent's % higher/lower presumptive standard of living compared to NCP for cost shares guideline, with tax benefits as cost offsets and NCP 25% share of child costs considered

One child

NCP monthly gross income:	1500	2000	2500	3000	3500	4000	4500	5000	5500	6000
CP gross = 50 % < NCP gross	−18	−28	−32	−36	−37	−37	−38	−38	−39	−39
CP gross = 30 % < NCP gross	−5	−14	−19	−21	−21	−21	−23	−24	−25	−25
CP gross = NCP gross	5	2	1	−1	−1	−2	−3	−3	−3	−3
CP gross = 30 % > NCP gross	17	20	19	17	18	18	18	18	18	19
CP gross = 100 % > NCP gross	56	62	61	60	62	65	67	69	70	71

Two children

NCP monthly gross income:	1500	2000	2500	3000	3500	4000	4500	5000	5500	6000
CP gross = 50 % < NCP gross	−4	−20	−25	−31	−34	−35	−35	−36	−37	−37
CP gross = 30 % < NCP gross	5	−9	−17	−20	−20	−20	−22	−23	−24	−25
CP gross = NCP gross	5	2	0	−2	−3	−4	−4	−5	−5	−6
CP gross = 30 % > NCP gross	13	16	15	14	14	14	14	14	14	14
CP gross = 100 % > NCP gross	43	51	51	51	53	55	57	59	60	61

income ends up with a higher standard of living than the non-custodial parent.

The Income Shares guidelines in Tables 3.11 and 3.12 show little difference from the Wisconsin-style guidelines at low- and middle-income ranges, except when the custodial parent makes significantly higher gross income. At higher income levels, however, Income Shares awards do not create as high an advantage for custodial parents as do the Wisconsin-style guidelines. Yet, the Income Shares methodology is still so upwardly biased as to give the custodial parent the higher standard of living in typical cases even when the custodial parent has significantly lower gross income. Furthermore, when the custodial parent has the higher gross income, Income Shares awards widen the custodial parent's standard of living advantage rather than narrowing it.

The pure USDA guideline provided in Table 3.13 has standard-of-living outcomes that are similar to the Espenshade–Engel version of Income Shares. The pure USDA guideline provides large gains to custodial parents – even when custodial parents have the higher gross income.

The Cost Shares guideline awards provide very different results, as shown in Tables 3.14 and 3.15. Table 3.14 shows the results of using the Cost Shares approach without including the appropriate adjustments in the awards for the child tax benefits and the parenting time of the non-custodial parent. This table shows that without these adjustments, even Cost Shares awards generally give the custodial parent a higher standard of living profit, although not to the same extent as other guidelines. Note that for equal gross incomes, the custodial parent has approximately a 20 per cent advantage at moderate income levels with one child and a 30 per cent advantage with two children. In Table 3.15, however, where the full Cost Shares guideline is implemented, the standard of living effects are more equal. For example, in this case, when both parents have equal gross incomes, after the award both parents still have generally equal standards of living. Also, when gross incomes differ, the Cost Shares award somewhat narrows the standard of living difference regardless of which parent is the higher earner. The Cost Shares guideline's standard of living impact is closer to what is expected of an equitable guideline.

IV. SUMMARY

The child support guidelines currently in use typically generate awards that are much higher than would be the case if based on economically sound cost concepts and with an equal duty of support for both parents. These guidelines do not conform to equitable standard of living outcomes. They

88 *The law and economics of child support payments*

include Wisconsin-style guidelines (gross and net income basis) and Income Shares (Espenshade–Engel and Betson–Rothbarth basis) as well as a recently proposed USDA child cost table that has sparked legislation in Minnesota.

Specifically, all of these guidelines have presumptive awards that exceed child costs to such an extent that:

1. In many cases where the custodial parent has significantly lower gross income than the non-custodial parent, the custodial parent still receives a significantly higher standard of living than the non-custodial parent.
2. In other cases where the custodial parent has significantly higher gross income than the non-custodial parent, the presumptive award boosts the custodial parent's relative standard of living rather than narrowing it.

Only the Cost Shares guideline conforms to expected standards of equity. These outcomes include:

1. In typical cases in which the custodial and non-custodial parents have equal gross incomes, the child-support award results in essentially equal standards of living on an after-tax, after-child support basis.
2. In typical cases, the higher income parent (whether custodial or non-custodial) retains a higher standard of living than the other, but the child support award narrows the standard of living gap.

Both of the two standard guidelines in use are severely flawed. Continued use of these guidelines generally results in inequitable child support awards. Furthermore, simple USDA child cost table based guidelines have similar flaws. States undergoing guideline reviews should consider adopting the Cost Shares methodology in order to achieve more equitable presumptive awards.

NOTES

1. Rogers and Bieniewicz (2002), pp. 333–80.
2. Venohr and Williams (1999), p. 11.
3. Guidubaldi (2000).
4. Venohr (1999).
5. Wisconsin, State of (1999).
6. Van der Gaag (1982), p. 18.
7. Institute for Research on Poverty, University of Wisconsin-Madison (1982), pp. 143–4 and (1981), p. 51.
8. Venohr et al. (2000).
9. Houthakker (1957), p. 532.

10. Lewin/ICF (1990), Section 2, p. 13.
11. Espenshade (1984).
12. Williams (1986), Section I, p. 8.
13. Lewin/ICF (1990).
14. Betson (1990).
15. Lewin/ICF (1990), Section 2, pp. 28–9.
16. Rogers (1999), pp. 135–56.
17. Lewin/ICF (1990), Section 2, p. 29.
18. Bieniewicz (1994), pp. 104–25.
19. For more detail, see Rogers and Bieniewicz (2002), pp. 333–80.
20. A self-support reserve of 133 per cent of the poverty threshold is the recommendation of an appointed panel on medical child support reporting to the US Department of Health and Human Services and US Department of Labor. See US Department of Health and Human Services (2000), p. 70. The poverty threshold for a one-adult only household in 2000 is $8959 annually or $747 monthly.
21. Henman and Mitchell (2001).

REFERENCES

Betson, David M. (1990), *Alternative Estimates of the Cost of Children from the 1980–86 Consumer Expenditure Survey*, Institute for Research on Poverty, University of Wisconsin-Madison.

Bieniewicz, Donald J. (1994), 'Child support guideline developed by Children's Rights Council', in US Department of Health and Human Services, *Child Support Guidelines: the Next Generation*, pp. 104–25.

Espenshade, Thomas J. (1984), *Investing in Children: New Estimates of Parental Expenditures*, Washington, DC: Urban Institute Press.

Guidubaldi, John (2000), *Ohio Child Support Deviation Study: April 1996 to August 2000 Final Report*, Ohio Department of Human Services.

Henman, Paul and Kyle Mitchell (2001), 'Estimating the costs of contact for non-resident parents: a budget standards approach', *Journal of Social Policy*, **30** (July), 495–520.

Houthakker, H.S. (1957), 'An international comparison of household expenditure patterns, commemorating the centenary of Engel's Law', *Econometrica*, **25** (October), 532–51.

Institute for Research on Poverty, University of Wisconsin-Madison (1981), *Child Support: A Demonstration of the Wisconsin Child Support Reform Program and Issue Papers*, Volume II, SR32B, Special Report Series, p. 51.

Institute for Research on Poverty, University of Wisconsin-Madison (1982), 'Documentation of the methodology underlying the cost estimates of the Wisconsin Child Support Program', Child Support: Technical Papers, Volume III, SR32C, Special Report Series, pp. 143–4.

Lewin/ICF, Washington DC (1990), 'Estimates of expenditures on children and child support guidelines', submitted to Office of the Assistant Secretary for Planning and Evaluation, US Department of Health and Human Services.

Rogers, R. Mark (1999), 'Wisconsin-style and income shares child support guidelines: excessive burdens and flawed economic foundation', *Family Law Quarterly*, Spring, pp. 135–56.

Rogers, R. Mark and Donald J. Bieniewicz (2002), 'Child cost economics and litigation issues: an introduction to applying cost shares child support guidelines', in Thomas R. Ireland and John O. Ward (eds), *Assessing Damages in Injuries and Deaths of Minor Children*, Tucson, AZ: Lawyers & Judges Publishing Co.

United States Department of Agriculture (2001), Center for Nutrition Policy and Promotion, Miscellaneous Publication Number 1528–2001, *Expenditures on Children by Families, 2001 Annual Report*.

US Department of the Interior (2001), *Regional Quarters Rental Survey, Southeast, July 2001*.

US Department of Health and Human Services (2000), '21 million children's health: our shared responsibility, the Medical Child Support Working Group's report, full report', p. 70.

Van der Gaag, Jacques (1982), 'On measuring the cost of children', Child Support: Technical Papers, Volume III, SR32C, Institute for Research on Poverty, Special Report Series, University of Wisconsin, p. 18.

Venohr, Jane (1999), *Arizona Child Support Guidelines: Findings from a Case File Review*, submitted to Supreme Court, State of Arizona.

Venohr, Jane and Robert G. Williams (1999), 'The implementation and periodic review of state child support guidelines', *Family Law Quarterly*, **33** (1), Spring, Table 1, 11.

Venohr, Jane, Robert G. Williams and David A. Price (2000), *Economic Basis for Updated Child Support Schedule, Commonwealth of Kentucky*, Denver, CO: Policy Studies, Inc.

Williams, Robert G. (1986), 'Child support guidelines: economic basis and analysis of alternative approaches', *Improving Child Support Practice, Volume One*, American Bar Association, Section I, p. 8.

Wisconsin, State of (1999), *Register*, No. 523, July, Chapter DWD 40, 51.

4. Child support guidelines and equal living standards

Sanford L. Braver and David Stockburger

In 1984, the Child Support Enforcement Amendments enacted by Congress mandated that states make numeric child support guidelines available to decision-makers in every jurisdiction. In the Family Support Act of 1988, amendments to the original act required that rebuttably presumptive child support guidelines be enacted by state statute (Venohr and Williams, 1999). Thus, unless a judge decides otherwise, ordered child support amounts since the 1990s are calculated by precise formulas. Interestingly, however, the Act did not specify any given type of formula the states needed to specify nor even at what goals states' guidelines should aim (Venohr and Williams). Most states appear to have adopted the 'continuity of expenditure' goal, wherein the guideline amounts attempt to assure that the children receive the same overall percentage of parental income as they would if the parents were still together (Garrison, 1999). Both the 'income shares' approach and the 'percent-of-obligor-income' standard supposedly attempt, by different means, to achieve this goal (Garrison).

Despite the reasonableness of such a goal, many advocates (for example Garrison, 1999; Cassetty and Sprinkle, 1987; Eden et al, 1987), have urged that equalization of the living standards of the two households be the preferred goal instead. So far, no states have explicitly endorsed such a goal, much to their advocate's chagrin. In fact, clearly such a goal is incompatible with the fundamental notion of child support, which is to support the child. Willis (Chapter 2 this volume) has shown that child support inevitably benefits the custodial parent even though intended solely for the child, thus only a share of joint costs is appropriately attributable to the child. If greater equalization of living standards is desired by decision- or policy-makers, there is another mechanism of income transfer for divorced or separated families designed precisely for this purpose: alimony. However, alimony or spousal maintenance appears less politically acceptable at present (with both spouses so often being employed full-time) than it was historically. Indeed, it appears to be ordered relatively rarely, in less than 15 per cent of divorce cases (Braver and O'Connell, 1998; Maccoby and

Mnookin, 1992). Ellman has written several essays intended to set better guidelines for ordering alimony or 'compensatory spousal payments' (Ellman, 1989, 1991; Ellman et al., 1998; ALI 2002).

While alimony is apparently politically less acceptable, child support is widely regarded as necessary and appropriate. As a result, some advocates are attempting to accomplish their goal of equalization of living standards by the more circuitous, and less direct means of disguising it within complicated and opaque child support calculations. Thus, for example, Grace Blumberg (1999), in drafting the American Law Institute's recommended formula (ALI, 2002), calculates a base award to achieve continuity of expenditures using familiar principles, but then adds a 'supplement percentage' intended to bring the two households' standards of living (SOL) into closer agreement. The supplemental percentage can increase the award by 70 per cent. Moreover, to the degree that any guideline amount exceeds the (proportionate) cost of the actual costs of raising the child, the guideline automatically contains hidden alimony. Roger Gay (1995) has produced demonstrations that many guidelines do so.

While equalization of living standards can hardly be regarded as a legitimate goal of child support guidelines, suppose it were. It is widely assumed by its advocates that applying this goal will lead to much higher child support awards. What has not been widely recognized, however, is that child support guidelines could conceivably be generous enough that equality of outcomes has already been achieved. In fact, it is at least theoretically possible that guidelines have already become too generous; that the living standards advantage generally believed to be enjoyed by the non-custodial parent (NCP) may already be overcorrected. Thus, by inept income transferring through child support, we might inadvertently be making custodial households more well off than non-custodial ones. An important goal of this chapter is to provide the concepts and calculations to properly compare post-divorce living standards, which requires the analyst to take into account a large number of factors.

Most frequently overlooked are two factors: (1) differential taxation of the two households; and (2) that an appreciable portion of expenses due to children may be borne directly by the non-custodial household. With respect to taxation, Braver (1999) and Braver and O'Connell (1998, Chapter 3) showed that a large number of tax advantages are available to the custodial parent (CP), but not similarly available to the NCP. These include the claiming of the children as 'exemptions'; the Child Tax Credit; a lower tax rate for 'head of household' filing status; the availability of the Earned Income Credit; and the fact that child support income is tax-free.[1] When the CP receives the child support, she[2] does not have to pay any taxes on it, unlike most other income. In contrast, when a NCP pays child support to his ex-spouse, he must pay federal income tax, social security or FICA tax, state, and local taxes on this amount. (Alimony has the opposite tax status.) Consequently, NCPs pay all the taxes on the child support amounts while CPs get to keep the full amount. For example, assume both parents gross $2000/month and live in Oklahoma, and there are three children who live with the CP who claims them on her taxes. According to calculations we will detail below, assuming they both take the standard deduction, he will pay $43 more per month in state taxes; he will also pay $179 per month in federal taxes, while she will not only pay no federal tax, she will actually receive $250 per month in total from the Earned Income Credit and the Child Tax Credit that he will not qualify for. Then he will pay her $400 per month in after-tax dollars for child support and she will receive these as tax-free dollars. After this transfer, she will have more than twice his spendable (that is, after tax, after child support) income.

With regard to the second point concerning who pays the expenses for the children, virtually all comparisons (other than mine) of post-divorce standard of living (SOL) make what we call the 'sacrosanct household' assumption. That is, they assume that all the family units' income and only the family units' income goes to support only that household's members. Put another way, it assumes that a single person spends all after-tax income to support only him- or herself, and that a family pays for all its members' needs out of only its own after-tax income. This is an entirely reasonable assumption for unrelated households, for which the analyses were originally designed. However, when applied to a divorced family, the assumption is commonly inappropriate. It would be valid only if child support and alimony were the only monetary transfer of income and expense between the households. In actuality, however, child support and alimony paid may well represent only a portion of the expenses for the children assumed by NCPs. If they pay for the child's food or transportation while the child is with them during visitation or access, if they buy clothes for the child, if they pay out of pocket for medical and dental expenses, and so on, the model is ill-applied, and the sacrosanct household assumption is violated. Instead, means need to be sought to take into account these direct payments for child's needs when comparing SOL.

We will describe in detail below an analytic method of incorporating these transfers and defrayals of children's expenses in financial comparisons. A variant was used in Braver (1999) and Braver and O'Connell (1998), when analysing a matched sample of households getting divorced in 1986. It was found there that when appropriate corrections for the two factors above are applied, the living standards of the two households were approximately equal. However, the comparisons are probably now outdated since the divorces analysed all occurred before guidelines were enacted in 1988.

Guidelines increased child support substantially (Thoennes et al., 1991; Bay et al., 1988; Garrison, 1994). Moreover, some of the tax advantages to the custodial household have been expanded. In particular, the Child Tax Credit was not part of the tax code in the prior analyses. As a result of these factors, there is a basis to hypothesize that cases in which the CP has a substantially higher SOL than the NCP may now have become the majority.

In the current analysis, we assess more current situations, using the 2001 child support guidelines of seven representative states that have various formulas and approaches and are from different parts of the country. Rather than analyse actual family income data, we examine multiple hypothetical but plausible scenarios. In each state, for each of the scenarios, we compute what gross income the CP would need to have in order that, after taxes and child support, the two households have the identical SOL.

The goal in this chapter is thus to determine what gross income a CP or obligee would need in order that her SOL would be exactly equal to the NCP's or obligor's. Once this gross income figure is identified, its implication is that any CP who earns more than this amount has a higher SOL than her matched NCP, while any CP who earns less has a lower SOL.

Any such calculations necessarily contain a large number of assumptions, which may or may not be accurate or may or may not apply to a particular case. An advantage of the present approach, however, is that developing financial estimates requires making these assumptions explicit and transparent. To the degree that they are in contention, at least a critic knows exactly what assumptions are being made. A second advantage is that one can evaluate to what degree the final calculations depend upon making these assumptions. Sensitivity analyses may be conducted which evaluate the dependence of the estimates on the exact assumptions by inserting alternative plausible values into the calculations. If the resultant estimates vary dramatically, especially if they vary in one direction, then we say the estimates are 'sensitive' to the assumptions. A happier outcome is when varying the assumptions does not result in substantially different conclusions, in which case one concludes that the calculations are insensitive or 'robust'. Sensitivity analyses are included here for most or all of the assumptions made.

DEFINING SOL, NET INCOME AND THE MATTER OF TAXES

In order to perform this calculation, we need to operationally define SOL. In our definition, consistent with the basic approach of Duncan and Hoffman (1985), Weitzman (1985), Peterson (1996) and Braver (1999), SOL is spendable income (by our definition, net income, after both taxes and child support and other transfers) divided by an index of the family's need.

The numerator of this fraction, spendable income, is defined as gross income minus taxes plus (for the recipient) or minus (for the payer) child support, alimony and any other transfers between the households. The taxes we incorporate here are of the three nearly universal types: federal income tax, state income tax and payroll taxes (FICA and Medicare). In the scenario calculations to follow, we estimate the exact amount of taxes CPs and NCPs would pay under the scenario's specifications.[3] After taxes are subtracted from gross income, child support is subtracted from the obligor's and added to the obligee's net income.[4] As in other similar investigations, we assume that the amount ordered is actually paid. The child support calculations need to be specific to the state in which the order originates, since different states have entirely different schemes.

There may also be other monetary transfers to consider (that is, to subtract from NCP's after-tax income and add to CP's) besides child support and alimony. Any amounts that NCP pays to CP (or vice versa, for that matter) should also be included. The most obvious recurring example is payment for medical expenses that insurance does not cover. This sort of transfer is included in the estimates we develop below if the state requires that each parent pay a portion of such expenses over and above child support.

The states we selected for analysis are Arizona, Kentucky, Massachusetts, Missouri, Oklahoma, Washington State and Wisconsin. These states were selected because they cover most of the major US geographic regions, as well as having representative child support schemes. For example, Wisconsin and Massachusetts are percent-of-obligor income states, while the others use the income shares approach (Venohr and Williams, 1999).[5] They also vary in terms of how large the child support burden is that they impose (Dodson and Entmacher, 1994; Morgan and Lino, 1999; Pirog et al., 1998). For example, Massachusetts often is found to have one of the highest child support guideline regimens, while Missouri has one of the lowest. Some have adjustments for NCP's visitation expenses, while others do not. They also have different state income tax schemes. For example, Washington has no state income tax, while Kentucky does not have a head of household distinction and taxes low incomes at a relatively high level.

Because the various states used such a variety of challenging calculation schemes for child support and state tax that we tried to replicate here, the chance for inadvertent error was high. Accordingly, we have verified our calculations of taxes and child support with independent calculators available on the Web.[6]

AN INDEX OF FAMILY NEED BASED ON HOUSEHOLD SIZE AND COMPOSITION

Next we consider the denominator of the SOL definition, an index of the family's need, which reflects the different size and composition of the two households. We need to divide by a number reflecting family size because it is inappropriate – and unfair to CPs – to simply compare after-tax/after-child-support incomes. After all, in the CP's household, the income must go to support more family members, the children and the parent. Because the marginal financial burdens attributed to additional family members are clearly diminishing (there are 'economies of scale'; for example, the third child does not generally add as much cost to the household as the first did) the method most economists recommend is a 'needs-adjusted income' technique. This divides income by a value that is related to – but not equal to – family size and composition, but is adjusted to take into account marginal living costs. At least two different such 'equivalence factors' have been used by different analysts comparing SOL for divorced families, including the Bureau of Labor Statistics '1977 Lower Standard Budget' (Duncan and Hoffman, 1985; Weitzman, 1985; Peterson, 1996; Blumberg, 1999), which was phased out as obsolete after the report of an Expert Panel (Watts, 1980) in 1980, and Federal Poverty Thresholds (Rogers and Bieniewicz, Chapter 3, this volume; Braver, 1999), which replaced it (for a history and explanation of the issues surrounding choice of equivalence scale, see Johnson et al., 2001).

In the present analysis, we use a third index of need or household composition, one developed by the Panel on Poverty and Federal Assistance in response to a directive from the Joint Economic Committee of Congress in 1992. We prefer this index endorsed by the National Research Council for three reasons. (1) it is the most recent – and official – consensus technique for accounting for family size; (2) it lends itself most readily to incorporating the variations we propose here to account for divorced family households; (3) it is expressed in units that are commensurable with family size, albeit fractional (they may be called 'first adult equivalents'). It should also be noted that results using it may not be materially different from those using the older outdated methods (Braver, 1999), and that, in any event, the other two methods will be compared in the sensitivity analyses.

According the Panel's report (Citro and Michael, 1995) family size should be expressed according to the following expression:

$$FSF = (A + CCM^*K)^F \tag{1}$$

where *FSF* stands for family size factor, *A* represents the number of adults in the family, *CCM* represents the child cost multiplier, *K* represents the number of children, and F represents an economy of scale factor. If $K=0$, and $F=1$, FSF would reduce simply to the number of adults, A. Thus dividing net income by it would essentially be to find per capita income. If CCM were set at 1.0, this would indicate that we could simply add together the number of adults plus children. However, the Panel indicated that CCM should be set at .7, rather than 1.0, in reflection of the fact that children typically cost somewhat less than adults to maintain. In addition, the Panel recommended that F be set at values somewhat lower than 1.0, to reflect the economy of scale. The consensus of the Panel is that F should be set between .65 and .75. We shall commonly use the midpoint of those two values, .7; thus, in what follows, both F and CCM in (1) will both be set to .7 as in (2) except for the sensitivity analyses.

$$FSF = (A + .7*K)^{.7} \qquad (2)$$

Suppose there were two adults and no children; then $A=2$ and $K=0$, and according to (2), $FSF=1.62$. This indicates that the two adults' needs constitute 1.62 times that of one adult (note that it is less than 2 times, as a per capita index would yield). A household composed of two adults and two children would have $FSF=2.36$, implying it would require 2.36 times the net income of one adult to support the family at the same SOL. If we added one additional child, we would get an FSF of 2.69, 14% greater than the 2.36.

In what follows, we divide spendable income by FSF, yielding (3), our fundamental definition of SOL.

$$SOL_{NEEDS\ ADJUSTED} =$$

$$\frac{AFTER\ TAX\ INCOME \pm CHILD\ SUPPORT \pm OTHER\ TRANSFERS}{FSF}$$

$$(3)$$

To assess the SOL of a divorced parent, we assume each parent is the sole adult in their respective household, meaning we preclude consideration of situations such as remarriage, cohabitation, roommates, or moving in with parents, which complicate matters beyond the capability of the present analysis to deal with them. Thus for A in (2), we always use 1.

We also add to formula (2) an adjustment to capture the possibility that some proportion of the child's expenses may be directly borne by each parent. This results in (4):

$$FSF = (1 + .7*PCE*K)^{.7} \qquad (4)$$

In (4), *PCE* represents the proportion of the child's expenses the parent expends directly on behalf of the child. In the divorce scenario, we would have an *FSF* for the CP and another for the NCP, (designated with subscripts *C* and *N*, respectively). Thus, we would have:

$$FSF_C = (1 + .7*PCE_C*K)^{.7} \qquad (5)$$

$$FSF_N = (1 + .7*PCE_N*K)^{.7} \qquad (6)$$

The sacrosanct household assumption, within this formulation, implies that we assume that, *other than child support*, the CP bears all (or 100 per cent) of the child's expenses ($PCE_C = 1.0$) and the NCP bears none (or 0 per cent) of them ($PCE_N = 0$). In this case, the formulas would reduce:

$$FSF_C = (1 + .7*K)^{.7} \qquad (7)$$

$$FSF_N = 1^{.7} = 1 \qquad (8)$$

However, we wish here to be able to relax this simplifying assumption implicitly made by previous analysts (Blumberg, 1999; Duncan and Hoffman, 1985; Peterson, 1996; Weitzman, 1985) to account for what is probably the far more common instance where the CP directly spends less than 100 per cent and/or the NCP directly expends more than 0 per cent on children's expenses, yielding more general solutions for PCE_C and PCE_N.

OBTAINING EXPRESSIONS FOR PCE

The *PCE* for *N* and *C* represent respectively the proportion of the total child expenses (*TCE*; the denominator of the *PCE* expression), paid for directly by the NCP and CP, respectively. Thus, the numerator of each *PCE* expression is the total amount paid by that parent. Thus:

$$PCE_P = CEP_P/TCE \qquad (9)$$

where CEP_P represents the Child Expenses Paid for directly by Parent P. However, determining CEP_P generally is difficult; it becomes a far more tractable problem if we abandon (9) and instead attempt to break overall expenditures required on behalf of children down into various types of expenses, such as that estimated by the US Department of Agriculture (Lino, 1998) or the Consumer Expenditure Survey (Morgan and Lino, 1999). The list should include amounts for the following expenses: housing, utilities, food, transportation, clothing, health care (both insurance and non-covered or unreimbursed expenses), childcare, baby-sitting (distinguishable from childcare because the childcare is work-related or occurs during working hours, whereas the latter does not; the IRS makes a similar distinction for the Child Care Credit), education expenses, recreation, toys and games, personal care items, uniforms and equipment, and lessons and memberships. For older children, we might include allowance, and expenses concerning cars, such as insurance, car purchase, fuel and oil, and car maintenance expenses.

For purposes of determining and comparing the SOL of the two parents, we propose to divide these myriad expenses into four categories described in more detail below, because each of the categories likely has a different pattern for the potential sharing of expenses across the two households: variable expenses (denoted V), fixed unduplicated expenses (denoted U), fixed duplicable expenses (D) and ordered allocation expenses (which we denote O). (The first three categories were specified by Judge Vaughn of New Jersey; see discussion in Venohr and Williams, 1999.) Thus, the total child expenses (TCE) is the sum of these four categories of expense, so that:

$$TCE = V + U + D + O \tag{10}$$

An expression alternate to (9) may be found for PCE that does not require direct determination of the CEP_P values. This alternative and more tractable formula for PCE is

$$PCE_P = p_{PV}*P(V) + p_{PU}*P(U) + p_{PD}*P(D) + p_{PO}*P(O) = \Sigma p_{Pi} P(i) \tag{11}$$

where the p_{Pi} represent the proportion of expense category i paid directly by parent P, and the $P(i)$ (that is, the $P(V)$, $P(U)$, $P(D)$ and $P(O)$, respectively) represent that category's relative proportion of total expense TCE. ($\Sigma P(i) = P(V) + P(U) + P(D) + P(O) = 1$). Since we want a PCE expression for each parent, we really have two equations:

$$PCE_C = p_{CV}*P(V) + p_{CU}*P(U) + p_{CD}*P(D) + p_{CO}*P(O) \tag{12}$$

$$PCE_N = p_{NV}*P(V) + p_{NU}*P(U) + p_{ND}*P(D) + p_{NO}*P(O)^7 \tag{13}$$

V, U, D and O expenses

The distinguishing feature of variable (V) expenses is that they are regarded as borne entirely by the parent with whom the child is residing at the moment the expense is incurred. Thus, they are zero-sum (what one parent pays subtracts from what the other needs to) and are directly related to the amount of time the child spends with the parent. The V expenses we include from the earlier list include food, recreational expenses (for example, the cinema), any extra utilities needed when the child is in the home, transportation expenses, and baby-sitting. We denote with t the proportion of time the child is in the NCP's care; thus the child is in the CP's care $1 - t$. As discussed above, we assume the parents divide the V expenses in exact accordance with the amount of time spent in each household. Thus, we assume $p_{NV} = t$, and $p_{CV} = 1-t$.

The two 'fixed' expenses are either of the duplicable or unduplicated variety. Fixed unduplicated (U) expenses are of the sort that only one parent pays them, regardless of where the child is at any given moment; from the original list, U expenses include uniforms, memberships and lessons (for example, piano or karate), car expenses for teenagers, and allowance. We assume, as did Judge Vaughn (Venohr and Williams, 1999) that the CP pays all of these expenses, directly out-of-pocket.[8] Thus, $p_{CU} = 1.0$, and $p_{NU} = 0$.

Fixed duplicable (D) expenses are items that may or may not be duplicated in each parent's home. The best example is housing; the child may or may not have a bedroom in each parent's house; clothing, toys, games, equipment and personal care items are also in this category. We assume $p_{CD} = 1$, meaning that we assume the CP pays 100 per cent of such expenses. However, we assume that the NCP may also pay some of these (after all, they are duplicable expenses). In particular, we assume p_{ND} phases in with t; there is a lower value of t below which the NCP spends nothing on this category (we will denote this lower threshold t_L),[9] and a high value of t, above which the NCP pays just as much as the *CP*; that is, $p_{ND} = 1$. This higher, fully phased-in value is denoted t_F. In between these two values, we assume a linear increase of p_{ND} with t. In other words,

$$
\begin{aligned}
p_{ND} &= 0, & \text{if } t \leq t_L \\
&= \frac{t - t_L}{t_F - t_L}, & \text{if } t_L < t < t_F \qquad (14) \\
&= 1, & \text{if } t \geq t_F.
\end{aligned}
$$

For example, if t_L is set to .15 and t_F is set to .45, we imply that NCPs who have the child less than 15 per cent of the time expend \$0 on expenses such as housing, clothes, and toys; NCPs who have the child 45 per cent of the time or more are as well equipped and spend as much in terms of these items as CPs, but those who see the child 25 per cent of the time have $(.25-.15)/(.45-.15) = .33$ of the expenses for housing, clothes, toys, personal items, and so on as would be the case in an intact household.

Finally, the ordered allocation expenses (O) are expenses whose allocation between the parents is directly addressed in the child support order, either as an integral part of the calculation or as 'side payments' (for example, when the NCP writes an additional cheque to the CP to reimburse for a portion of doctor's bills). According to Elrod (1994), 'the *basic* child support guideline chart amount does not include the costs of child care or health insurance'. Nonetheless, she notes, by recommendation of the US Commission on Interstate Child Support, these expenses need to be taken into account in the child support order. Generally, then, O expenses include the following from the above list: health care items (both insurance itself and non-reimbursed expenses), childcare expenses (during working hours) and some educational expenses, such as for special educational needs. Most child support orders and divorce decrees specify, for example, which parent is to pay for medical and dental insurance, how non-covered medical expenses are to be shared between the parents, and whether the NCP should directly pay, over and above any child support, a proportion of special educational needs or childcare. Most states' guidelines incorporate this expense directly into the child support order by adding (or subtracting in some cases) to the 'basic award' (which is supposed to provide for every other non-O expense on the list), an amount based on the O expenses.[10] The most common rule for allocating O expenses between the two parents is proportional to gross income, although there are other rules as well.

For example, if the CP is the one paying for health insurance for the child of $150 per month and childcare of $175, and the CP earns 40 per cent of the couples' combined gross income (this would be the case, for example, if NCP's monthly gross income was $3000, while CP's was $2000), the NCP's child support ('basic award') will probably be augmented by $195 (60 per cent of $150 + $175). However, imagine instead that better health insurance is available to the NCP. Then he might pay the $150 health insurance directly, as a payroll deduction. CP would then 'owe' him 40 per cent of that $150, but NCP would owe her 60 per cent of the $175 for childcare, for a net debt to her of $45. His child support order would be increased by $45, but this would be in addition to the $150 he pays directly for the insurance. Thus in either event, his payment for the child is increased by $195. It simplifies the analysis considerably that the net effect is the same regardless of who directly pays the O expense. Thus, for simplification purposes, we may assume that CP is the one who actually pays the insurance and childcare costs and that NCP pays his share through a child support add-on, recognizing that it comes out the same way under different arrangements. Since the amount for ordered expenses is then considered added directly to the child support order, we don't need to further account for it in the PCE calculations. Instead, we may assume that, like U expenses, the CP pays all (or 100 per cent) of the actual expenses and the NCP pays none (after the child support is augmented as described above), so that $p_{CO} = 1.0$, and $p_{NO} = 0$.[11]

OBTAINING VALUES FOR THE $P(I)$

Morgan and Lino (1999) published a table of annual expenses in each of several categories by age of children and income level, estimated from Consumer Expenditure Survey data. Table 4.1 breaks their table down into percentages by assuming food and transportation are V, miscellaneous (which a footnote describes as including personal care items, entertainment and reading materials) are U, housing and clothing are considered D, and health care and child care/education are considered O. Based upon Table 4.1, we initially set the $P(i)$ to the values for the 'average' 'middle income' family; in other words, we set $P(V) = .3243$, $P(U) = .1130$, $P(D) = .4012$, and $P(O) = .16146$. When we use the latter $P(O)$ value to calculate the add-in portion of child support, we need to calculate what additional percentage of the remaining (that is, V, U and D) expenses it is, so we actually divide it by the sum of the remaining expenses (see the Arizona example below). Later, when we conduct sensitivity analyses, we insert other plausible values from Table 4.1 instead.

OBTAINING VALUES FOR PCE_C AND PCE_N

Putting the expressions discussed above together with (12) for CP, we have:

$$
\begin{aligned}
PCE_C &= p_{CV}*P(V) + p_{CU}*P(U) + p_{CD}*P(D) + p_{CO}*P(O) \\
&= (1-t)*P(V) + 1*P(U) + 1*P(D) + 1*P(O) \\
&= 1 - P(V)t \\
&= 1 - .3243t
\end{aligned}
\tag{15}
$$

while, for NCP, putting the expressions together with (13), we have:

$$
\begin{aligned}
PCE_N &= p_{NV}*P(V) + p_{NU}*P(U) + p_{ND}*P(D) + p_{NO}*P(O) \\
&= tP(V) + 0*P(U) + 0*P(D) + 0*P(O), \quad \text{if } t \le t_L \\
&= .3243t \quad \text{if } t \le t_L
\end{aligned}
\tag{16}
$$

$$
= t*P(V) + 0*P(U) + \frac{t - t_L}{t_F - t_L}*P(D) + 0*P(O), \quad \text{if } t_L < t < t_F
$$

$$
= tP(V) + P(D)\left(\frac{t - t_L}{t_F - t_L}\right), \quad \text{if } t_L < t < t_F
$$

$$
= .3243t + .4012\left(\frac{t - t_L}{t_F - t_L}\right), \quad \text{if } t_L < t < t_F
\tag{17}
$$

and

Table 4.1   *Percentages of child expenses in Variable (V), Unduplicated fixed (U), Duplicable fixed (D) categories, and Ordered (O) categories, by income level and age of child*

Age of Child	Low Income (%)				Medium Income (%)				High Income			
	V	U	D	O	V	U	D	O	V	U	D	O
0–2	26.8	10.0	44.5	18.7	**25.8**	**11.0**	**42.7**	**20.5**	23.6	12.5	44.6	19.3
3–5	27.4	10.0	43.1	19.6	**26.6**	**11.0**	**41.1**	**21.3**	24.3	12.3	43.4	20.0
6–8	33.1	10.4	41.7	14.8	**31.6**	**11.4**	**40.5**	**16.5**	27.9	12.7	43.4	15.9
9–11	37.9	10.8	38.8	12.5	**35.6**	**11.8**	**38.8**	**13.8**	31.1	13.1	42.6	13.2
12–14	36.2	11.9	42.0	9.9	**34.1**	**12.6**	**42.1**	**11.2**	30.7	13.5	44.9	10.8
15–17	43.6	8.8	35.2	12.4	**39.7**	**10.0**	**35.9**	**14.4**	33.8	11.5	39.9	14.8
Average	34.5	10.3	40.8	14.5	**32.4**	**11.3**	**40.1**	**16.1**	28.7	12.6	43.1	15.6

$$= t*P(V) + 0*P(U) + 1*P(D) + 0*P(O), \text{ if } t \geq t_F.$$
$$= tP(V) + P(D)$$
$$= .3243t + .4012, \text{ if } t \geq t_F. \tag{18}$$

It should be noted that PCE_C and PCE_N often sum to more than 1.0 (whenever $t > t_F$). This is because of the duplicated expenses, D. In cases where $t \geq t_F$, the sum is 1.4012, implying that in such shared custody families, the child is costing the parents 140 per cent of what the same child would cost in an intact household, or any family in which the child remains exclusively in one household. Williams (1987) has made a slightly higher assumption of 150 per cent, the figure that has now been adopted by most states with a 'duplicable expense multiplier' (Venohr and Williams, 1999).

To gauge relative SOL, we replace the value of PCE_C in (5) with (15), and replace the values of PCE_N in (6) with either (16), (17) or (18), as appropriate depending on the value of t relative to t_L and t_F. Then, the obtained values for *FSF* are inserted in (3) to get the values for CP and NCP of $SOL_{needs\ adjusted}$. These two SOL values are then compared.

COMPREHENSIVE EXAMPLE

Table 4.2 provides one particular detailed example for the scenario involving the state of Arizona, with NCP's gross income set at $3000 monthly, with two young children spending 30 per cent of their time with the NCP. The calculations were generated by an Excel spreadsheet.[12] The results were obtained iteratively with a specially written macro. That is, once the scenario involving a particular state, a particular NCP income, a particular number of children and a particular percentage of time with NCP was selected, an arbitrary starting value for CP's gross was selected. Taxes were calculated[13] and subtracted from each parent's gross, then child support was calculated, subtracted from NCP's net and added to CP's. Then the *PCE*s were calculated based on the percentage time in each household, using (15) for CP, and either (16), (17) or (18) for NCP; then the *FSF*s were calculated. We in turn divided the spendable net income by *FSF* to produce $SOL_{needs\ adjusted}$. It was observed whether the ratio of NCP's to CP's $SOL_{needs\ adjusted}$ was greater than or less than 1.0. If less than 1.0, the macro inserted a lower value for CP's gross income, while if greater than 1.0 a higher value was inserted and the process continued, 'homing in' on the CP gross income value that gave a ratio of exactly 1.0. The final value that gave a ratio of exactly 1.0, that is, that equated the two parents' SOLs, was inserted in Table 4.2 as CP's gross income.

Table 4.2   *Example calculation for Arizona, with NCP earning a gross monthly income of $3000, two children spending 30% time with NCP*

2 children in Arizona, 30% time with NCP	NCP	CP	CP's % of NCP Gross
Monthly gross income	$3000	$1578	52.59%
Federal tax	$332	$0	
State tax	$79	$5	
FICA (payroll tax)	$230	$121	
Federal tax credits (income)	$0	$306	
Net after tax	$2359	$1758	
Child support transfer	−$635	$635	
Net after tax and child support (spendable)	$1724	$2393	
Family size multiple ('needs factor')*	1.276	1.772	
Monthly income per unit adult	$1351	$1351	

Notes:
*Poverty Panel formula: each child costs .7 of an adult; .70 is the 'economy of scale' factor. Because of V, U, D and O child expenses, NCP bears 42% of child's costs, CP bears 78%.

It can be seen that the gross income the CP would need under these assumptions to have the same SOL as the NCP as found by the macro is $1578 (which is 53 per cent of the NCP's $3000 gross, nearly $1500 per month less than NCP's gross). With these gross incomes, NCP would have $332 deducted monthly in federal income tax ($3987 annual tax), while CP would pay $0; the Arizona state income tax would be $79 monthly for NCP ($948 total annual state tax), while CP would pay $5 monthly ($58 annual); and the respective payroll (FICA) tax would be $230 monthly for NCP, $121 monthly for CP. CP would also qualify both for $2780 of Earned Income Credit ($232 monthly) and $893 of 'additional child tax credit' ($74 monthly), which in essence is extra income. These taxes bring the net incomes to $2359 for NCP and $1758 for CP, more than halving the difference in their gross income. Under the Arizona child support guidelines, which use the income shares method, the 'basic obligation' would be $1024, the amount the guidelines presume would be spent monthly on non-O expenses for the two children in a married household when the parents' combined gross income was $4578. Since the NCP's percent of combined annual gross income is 66 per cent, the income shares approach requires him to pay 66 per cent of the basic obligation, or $671 monthly.

Arizona is one of only a few states that have a visitation credit that spans a wide range of visitation scenarios. In the example, visitation is at

30 per cent, or 110 days, which the Arizona guidelines turn into a .161 credit or $165, which subtracts from the 'basic award', reducing it to $506. Then we assume there will be another $197 of O expenses spent on the children (19.26 per cent of the basic obligation),[14] of which the NCP's portion is .66 for another $129 monthly. This brings the combined child support award to $635. This amount is then subtracted from NCP's net income and added to CP's, giving them spendable incomes of $1724 and of $2393, respectively.

We wish to divide these amounts by their respective Family Size Factors (*FSF*s), which means we first need to compute PCE_N and PCE_C, the respective proportions of child expenses NCP and CP pay directly. With t being above t_L, PCE_N, according to (17), is $.3243(.3) + .4012$ $(.3 - .15/.45 - .15) = .2979$ (meaning NCP pays 29.79 per cent of the total children's expenses directly out of pocket), while according to (15), PCE_C is $1 - .3243t$, or $1 - .3243(.30) = .9027$. Note that since t is greater than the threshold t_L, the sum of PCE_N and PCE_C exceeds 1.0, meaning duplication of some of the D expenses is occurring. When these PCE amounts are inserted into (6) and (5), we get FSF_N of 1.276 and FSF_C of 1.772. These may be interpreted as suggesting that, given the visitation situation, NCP's Family Size Factor is 1.276 (that is, his expenses run about 28 per cent more to maintain the same SOL as if he were truly single) while CP's expenses run about 77 per cent greater to maintain the same SOL as if she were truly in a one-person household. When these two *FSF*'s divide the respective parent's spendable monthly incomes, they each have $1351 per month per first adult equivalent, exactly equal, so their $SOL_{\text{needs adjusted}}$ are identical, as sought by the macro. Thus if the CP brings in more than $1578, the CP gross income calculation identified as the equalization of living standards gross income, the CP will have a higher living standard than the NCP in this scenario. Only if the CP earned less than $1578 would her SOL be less than NCP's.

MAIN RESULTS

Table 4.3 provides the results of similar calculations for each of 198 scenarios in Arizona, where each scenario represents a unique combination of number of children (1–3), percentage of time the children typically spend with the NCP (0 per cent to 50 per cent, in 5 per cent increments), and NCP gross monthly income ($2000–$7000, in $1000 increments). The determined value from Table 4.2 is placed in a box. Table 4.4 then converts each of those results into percentage of NCP's gross income (by dividing the solved-for CP's gross income by the NCP's income); for example, in place

Table 4.3 CP's gross income amounts required for CP's SOL to equal NCP's SOL

Arizona	% Time With NCP										
NCP gross	.00	.05	.10	.15	.20	.25	.30	.35	.40	.45	.50
1 child											
$2000	$1044	$1034	$1040	$1048	$1045	$1050	$976	$946	$1044	$1126	$1095
$3000	$2526	$2504	$2511	$2515	$2476	$2462	$2206	$2112	$2373	$2647	$2576
$4000	$3434	$3418	$3418	$3418	$3377	$3357	$3167	$3090	$3270	$3461	$3407
$5000	$4290	$4257	$4255	$4254	$4192	$4162	$3930	$3846	$4039	$4276	$4194
$6000	$5348	$5304	$5299	$5295	$5222	$5169	$4830	$4696	$4970	$5272	$5176
$7000	$6376	$6326	$6315	$6308	$6208	$6136	$5775	$5617	$5906	$6226	$6126
2 children											
$2000	**$941**	**$926**	**$926**	**$926**	**$884**	**$876**	**$769**	**$726**	**$826**	**$995**	**$959**
$3000	**$2586**	**$2491**	**$2476**	**$2451**	**$2226**	**$2076**	**$1578**	**$1471**	**$1776**	**$2218**	**$2078**
$4000	**$3589**	**$3526**	**$3508**	**$3479**	**$3326**	**$3225**	**$2842**	**$2681**	**$2941**	**$3229**	**$3134**
$5000	**$4527**	**$4445**	**$4420**	**$4383**	**$4193**	**$4059**	**$3626**	**$3433**	**$3711**	**$4026**	**$3924**
$6000	**$5774**	**$5650**	**$5605**	**$5561**	**$5260**	**$5032**	**$4402**	**$4176**	**$4476**	**$4928**	**$4773**
$7000	**$6945**	**$6781**	**$6726**	**$6676**	**$6326**	**$6076**	**$5371**	**$5044**	**$5431**	**$5907**	**$5726**
3 children											
$2000	$957	$926	$925	$903	$826	$785	$671	$626	$726	$876	$826
$3000	$2833	$2754	$2694	$2626	$2111	$1863	$1531	$1323	$1575	$1852	$1748
$4000	$3922	$3798	$3738	$3691	$3376	$3152	$2568	$2226	$2645	$3006	$2883
$5000	$5026	$4863	$4776	$4689	$4308	$4026	$3420	$3129	$3434	$3808	$3672
$6000	$6472	$6226	$6126	$6026	$5426	$5001	$4201	$3868	$4203	$4607	$4443
$7000	$8282	$7870	$7651	$7462	$6545	$6076	$5076	$4600	$5041	$5576	$5351

Table 4.4   CP's % of NCP's gross income required for CP's SOL to equal NCP's SOL

Arizona NCP gross	% Time with NCP										
	.00	.05	.10	.15	.20	.25	.30	.35	.40	.45	.50
1 child											
$2000	52	52	52	52	52	52	49	47	52	56	55
$3000	84	83	84	84	83	82	74	70	79	88	86
$4000	86	85	85	85	84	84	79	77	82	87	85
$5000	86	85	85	85	84	83	79	77	81	86	84
$6000	89	88	88	88	87	86	81	78	83	88	86
$7000	91	90	90	90	89	88	83	80	84	89	88
2 children											
$2000	**47**	**46**	**46**	**46**	**44**	**44**	**38**	**36**	**41**	**50**	**48**
$3000	**86**	**83**	**83**	**82**	**74**	**69**	**53**	**49**	**59**	**74**	**69**
$4000	**90**	**88**	**88**	**87**	**83**	**81**	**71**	**67**	**74**	**81**	**78**
$5000	**91**	**89**	**88**	**88**	**84**	**81**	**73**	**69**	**74**	**81**	**78**
$6000	**96**	**94**	**93**	**93**	**88**	**84**	**73**	**70**	**75**	**82**	**80**
$7000	**99**	**97**	**96**	**95**	**90**	**87**	**77**	**72**	**78**	**84**	**82**
3 children											
$2000	48	46	46	45	41	39	34	31	36	44	41
$3000	94	92	90	88	70	62	51	44	52	62	58
$4000	98	95	93	92	84	79	64	56	66	75	72
$5000	101	97	96	94	86	81	68	63	69	76	73
$6000	108	104	102	100	90	83	70	64	70	77	74
$7000	118	112	109	107	93	87	73	66	72	80	76

of reporting $1578 as CP's gross income for the example scenario, we report that it is 53 per cent of NCP's $3000 gross. We term this E%N, implying the *E*qualization of living standards percentage of *N*CP's gross income. **Thus an E%N of .65 would only mean that the gross income of the CP would need to be 65 per cent of that of the NCP's in order to equate their SOLs.** An E%N of greater than 1.00 means that the CP must have a higher gross income than the NCP in order to share the same SOL, while one less than 1.00 indicates the CP needs less gross income than the NCP to maintain the same SOL. It can be seen that for the NCPs with only $2000 gross, the E%N varies from 31 per cent to 56 per cent. For higher income NCPs, the E%N is generally in the 80s and 90s and exceeds 1.0 for the highest income NCPs.

We use three main ways to reduce this information for AZ and the remaining states. First, we report the E%N for three representative scenarios, in terms of number of children, time spent with NCP, and NCP's gross monthly income, as well as the mean E%N, averaged over all 198 scenarios, in Table 4.5. The table discloses that average E%N over all 198 scenarios for Arizona was .76. For the remaining states it is: Kentucky, 61 per cent; Massachusetts, 40 per cent; Missouri, 92 per cent; Oklahoma, 74 per cent; Washington, 73 per cent;[15] Wisconsin, 49 per cent.

Second, we report the relationship between E%N, NCP gross monthly income, and number of children, averaged over all of the values of time spent with NCP. For the values in Table 4.4, these results can be seen in Figure 4.1a. As can be seen, for Arizona, the E%N is smallest for NCP gross incomes of $2000 per month, increasing at $3000, and leveling off at $4000 per month.

The remaining states are presented in this fashion in Figures 4.1b–g. Oklahoma has a similar pattern, as does Missouri, but the latter's level is higher. The remaining states have a variety of different patterns. Since there is no justifiable basis to discriminate against either CPs or NCPs based on either NCP gross income or on number of children, what should be desired is a pattern that is flat (E%N should be a relatively constant percentage whatever NCP's gross income) and tight (E%N should not vary by number of children). The only state that has the desired relatively flat and tight pattern is Massachusetts, however, as noted, its overall level is very low.

Finally, we present the relationship between E%N, and time spent with the NCP, for each of the various numbers of children, averaged over all of the values of NCP gross income. For the values for Arizona in Table 4.4, these results are presented in Figure 4.2a. As can be seen, the E%N shows a dip beginning at about 15 per cent time, reaching its minimum at 35 per cent time, then leveling back off. The results for one child are sometimes highest and sometimes lowest.

The remaining states are presented in this fashion in Figures 4.2b–g.

Table 4.5   Percentage of NCP's income necessary for CP to maintain standard of living equal to NCP's, for three representative scenarios in terms of number of children, % time child spends with NCP, and NCP's gross monthly income, and averaged over all scenarios

Scenario	Arizona	Kentucky	Massachusetts	Missouri	Oklahoma	Washington	Wisconsin
1 child, 20% time, $5000/month	84%	81%	32%	95%	78%	87%	53%
2 children, 0% time, $3000/month	88%	87%	95%	93%	94%	99%	59%
3 children, 40% time, $7000/month	72%	34%	3%	91%	76%	53%	59%
Average over all scenarios	76%	61%	40%	92%	74%	73%	49%

110

Oklahoma has a pattern very similar to Arizona's, despite a visitation adjustment scheme in its guidelines that is somewhat different (see note 5). Kentucky and Washington, neither of which adjust for visitation, demonstrate patterns very similar to one another, but very different from Oklahoma and Arizona. Massachusetts, which does not adjust for visitation and which has a hybrid child support model, has a pattern which is the most widespread, with E%N ranging from a low of 15 per cent to a high of 115 per cent.

Again, the most desirable system would be one resulting in a flat, tight pattern; otherwise the regime unjustifiably discriminates against either CPs or NCPs based either on how much time the child spends with NCP or on number of children. The state that comes closest to this ideal is probably Missouri, but, as noted, its overall level of E%N is very high.

MAIN RESULTS SUMMARY

The results showed enormous variability from state to state. The overall average E%N ranged from 40 per cent (Massachusetts) to 92 per cent (Washington). In Massachusetts, for example, most CPs who make more than only 40 per cent of their NCP's gross income have higher standards of living (SOLs) than their ex-spouses.

In all of the income shares states (that is, all but Massachusetts and Wisconsin), the E%N undesirably decreased as NCP income decreased. This means, for our very poorest NCPs, their counterpart CP had the greatest chance of enjoying a higher SOL than they did. Likely this is due to the large tax advantages given to low-income CPs and not available to NCPs. Alternatively, it may be due to the income shares states assumption that the larger the income, the smaller the percentage necessary for child support. Our basic model assumes that this proportion is constant.

States that include NCP parenting time as part of the formula in computing presumptive child support generally showed a relatively constant E%N for differing amounts of NCP parenting time, which is desirable. Based on our analysis, it would seem difficult to justify a criterion or cutoff amount for time spent with NCP. Using the E%N as a criterion, it also appeared that many states overcompensated for the number of children, by having too much spread in their graphs. This was especially apparent in Kentucky and Wisconsin.

A desirable pattern would be tight and flat, so that unjustifiable discrepancies due to number of children, percentage time with NCP, or income level might be avoided. None of the states analysed achieved such a pattern, but overall, Arizona and Oklahoma were closest.

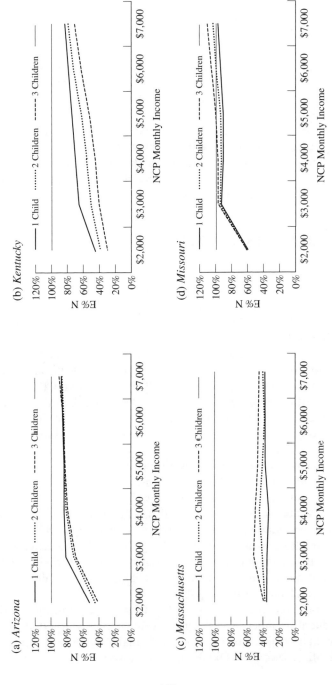

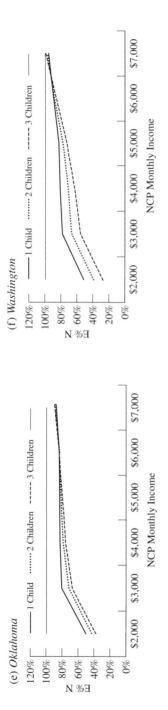

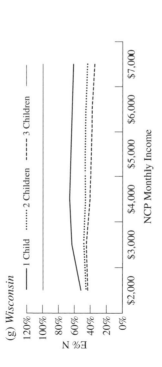

Figure 4.1   Relations between E%N and NCP monthly income

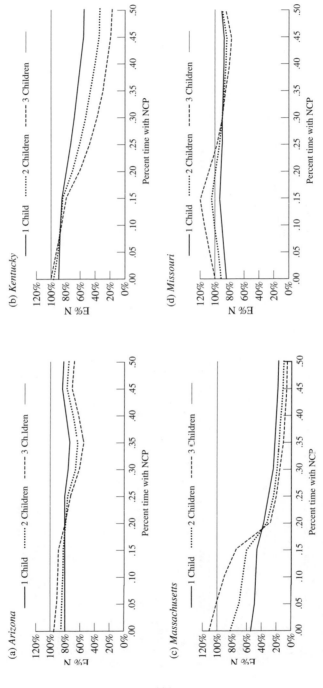

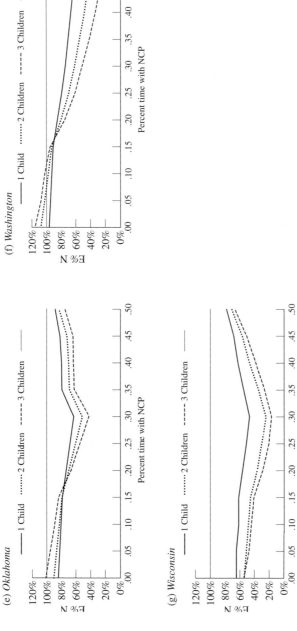

Figure 4.2   Relations between E%N and time spent with NCP

115

SENSITIVITY ANALYSIS

As indicated above, there were many assumptions made to yield the above set of results. It is certainly possible that any particular assumption is invalid, debatable, or does not apply in a specific family. Accordingly, we wished to test the sensitivity of the results to the various assumptions made, as is considered good practice in economic analyses with assumption-laden estimates (but too often overlooked in the child support arena). To conduct the sensitivity analysis, we repeated our calculations numerous times, each time inserting other realistic values for many of the variables required for the estimates and re-solving for E%N. The variables we evaluated for sensitivity, and the other realistic values inserted were:

A.   *CCM*, the Child Cost Multiplier

As noted earlier, based on Citro and Michael's NRC (1995) recommendations, we used a value of .7 for *CCM* in (1) and later formulae and the base analysis of Tables 4.2–5, and Figures 4.1 and 4.2, implying that children cost exactly .7 of an adult. Other plausible values were inserted instead in the sensitivity analyses; we used values of .6, .65, .7, .75 and .8. When .8 was inserted in the example of Table 4.2, for example, it moved E%N from 53 per cent to 59 per cent; inserting .6 lowered E%N to 49 per cent.

B.   Age of Children

A few states have different ordered payment amounts depending upon whether the children are older (more than 12 years old) or younger. In the 'base' estimates of Tables 4.2–5, and Figures 4.1 and 4.2, we assumed no children were older. In the sensitivity analyses, we let the number of older children range from none to all. In the case of the analysis in Table 4.2, if both children were older (and simultaneously raising CCM from .7 to .77, since older children are reported to cost about 10 per cent more than younger children, according to Lino and Morgan's 1999 USDA figures), the E%N would drop from 53 per cent to 43 per cent.

C. $P(V)$, $P(U)$, $P(D)$ and $P(O)$

In the base analysis, as noted earlier, we used $P(V)=.32$, $P(U)=.11$, $P(D)$ $=.40$, and $P(O)=.16$. In the sensitivity analyses, we substituted instead the most extreme sets of values from Table 4.1: if the oldest child was young, $P(V)=.26$, $P(U)=.09$, $P(D)=.43$, $P(O)=.21$; if the oldest child was 'old' (older than 12; see 'B. Age of Children', above), $P(V)=.45$, $P(U)=.09$,

$P(D) = .36$, $P(O) = .10$. This variable is called *VUDO* in Table 4.6, below. The 'young' values lowered E%N in Table 4.2 to 44 per cent; the 'older' values left it unchanged at 53 per cent.

D. *F*, the Economy of Scale Factor in (1)

As noted earlier, we used a value of .7 for *F* in (1) and later formulae. Other plausible values were inserted instead in the sensitivity analyses.

We used both .65 and .75, recommended as alternatives by Citro and Michael (1995). These values changed E%N in Table 4.2 from 53 per cent to 49 per cent and 59 per cent, respectively. In addition, we used values for *F* derived in two different alternate ways. According to the Betson (1990) data, widely used in the development of the income shares approach, two-parent families' expenditures on children as a percent of total net income decreases as the income level increases. A chart depicting these percentages is available in Venohr and Williams (1999, p. 14). In the first method we used this chart to solve for *F* in the formula below, where *B* represents the Betson percentage:

$$\frac{(A)^F}{(A + .7K)^F} = (1 - B) \tag{19}$$

In (19), the denominator represents the needs of the entire family and is identical to (2), while the numerator represents the needs of only the adults, expressed in the same fashion. The resulting ratio is the percentage of the family's needs attributable to the adults in the family; which should be the complement of the percentage of the families' needs attributable to the children. Since the Betson chart is based on two-parent families, we substituted 2 for *A*, then solved for *F* (using logs),[16] using *B* as found from the families' combined net income and number of children in Betson's chart. The maximum *F* found for any family was .9675, while the minimum was .4791. In the second method, a least squares solution was used to estimate the Morgan and Lino (1999, p. 202) data. The value of *F* was estimated as a linear function of the inverse of annual family income with $F = .24 + 27103/Income$.[17] Within the ranges of income used in this chapter, the values of *F* ranged from .32 to 99. Inserting the latter values into Table 4.2 changed E%N from 53 per cent to 32 per cent and 90 per cent, respectively. These alternative values are termed 'Type of exponent' in Table 4.6.

E. t_L and t_F

In the base calculations we used .15 for t_L and .45 for t_F. In the sensitivity analyses, we let t_L vary from 0 to .3 (by .10 increments) and let t_F vary from .30 to .50 (by .10 increments). However, we never allowed both t_L and t_F to

Table 4.6 Sensitivity analysis for three scenarios

State and scenario	Our value in base analysis	Mean	s.d.	VUDO	F	Type of exponent	Older kids	t_L	t_F	Kids mult	Index	CP tax correction	NCP tax correction	CP tax deduction	NCP tax deduction
AZ-1	.841	.832	.106	.026	.038	.026	.039	.198	.028	.06	.193	.033	.156	.016	.187
AZ-2	.875	.791	.201	.199	.12	.006	.076	0	0	.163	.256	.002	.127	0	.022
AZ-3	.718	.708	.14	.029	.011	.052	.05	.055	.228	.007	.05	.018	.163	.023	.26
KY-1	.809	.824	.112	.019	.036	.025	0	.192	.027	.057	.187	.047	.195	.016	.197
KY-2	.867	.87	.159	.183	.122	.01	0	0	0	.164	.309	.01	.167	0	.024
KY-3	.341	.395	.134	.072	.01	.029	0	.036	.174	.006	.031	.002	.294	0	.36
MA-1	.323	.399	.208	.049	.019	.008	.154	.131	.017	.031	.107	.003	.176	0	.191
MA-2	.948	.711	.343	.096	.107	.008	.116	0	0	.145	.228	.005	.141	0	.02
MA-3	.033	.027	.039	.092	.004	.005	.25	.021	.068	.003	.017	0	.12	0	.174
MO-1	.947	.947	.128	.018	.039	.03	0	.199	.028	.062	.185	.055	.195	.042	.172
MO-2	.933	.929	.153	.158	.124	.014	0	0	0	.166	.361	.01	.138	0	.02
MO-3	.906	.922	.186	.012	.013	.052	0	.055	.218	.007	.045	.048	.144	.071	.211
OK-1	.78	.788	.098	.024	.035	.024	0	.187	.027	.056	.193	.04	.21	.01	.202
OK-2	.94	.923	.161	.152	.124	.014	0	0	0	.167	.327	.011	.171	0	.023
OK-3	.761	.799	.201	.018	.013	.051	0	.052	.23	.007	.042	.037	.191	.045	.258
WA-1	.873	.825	.11	.017	.039	.026	.216	.201	.028	.061	.185	.018	.075	.01	.119
WA-2	.987	.872	.157	.136	.094	.01	.358	0	0	.126	.236	.003	.023	0	.005
WA-3	.533	.439	.159	.04	.01	.034	.378	.04	.182	.006	.036	.001	.075	0	.165
WI-1	.592	.607	.098	.029	.031	.016	0	.167	.026	.049	.203	.022	.238	0	.228
WI-2	.588	.628	.141	.141	.13	0	0	0	0	.173	.283	0	.223	.002	.029
WI-3	.387	.42	.099	.02	.011	.033	0	.038	.186	.006	.033	.004	.275	0	.368
Mean	.7134	.698	.149	.073	.054	.023	.078	.075	.070	.072	.167	.018	.167	.011	.154

be the same value, .30. Using $t_L = 0$ and $t_F = .3$ changed E%N in the example of Table 4.2 from 53 per cent to 38 per cent, while inserting instead .3 and .5, respectively, raised it all the way to 94 per cent.

F. Alternate Equivalence Factors

While we used the Citro and Michael (1995) *FSF* formulation in the base analysis, we inserted instead the two main alternative indices in the sensitivity analysis, the outdated Bureau of Labor Standards' Lower Standard Budget (BLS-LSB) approach and the Poverty Threshold approach. For the BLS-LSB approach, we used its 'equivalence scale' that expresses the cost of each type of household in a ratio to that of the 'base family' household: a two-adult-two-child household with an over-35-year-old householder. For example, according to this approach, a one-adult-two-child family with an over-35-year-old householder requires 76 per cent of the income of the base family and a one-adult-no-children household with an over-35-year-old householder requires 36 per cent to be at the same SOL.[18] To calculate a BLS-LSB equivalence factor that took into account sharing of child expenses, each household was deemed to be one with the children their respective *PCE* proportion of the time, and a single adult-no-children household the remaining time. In the example of Table 4.2, as noted in the Comprehensive Example section, the value of *PCE* was .2979 for NCP and .9027 for CP, meaning that NCP paid nearly 30 per cent of the direct expenses of the children, while CP paid about 90 per cent of the direct expenses of the children. To calculate the BLS-LSB equivalence value for NCP for that scenario, for example, we assumed NCP's household had the expenses of a one-adult-two-children household (which has 76 per cent of the expenses of the base family) .2979 of the time, and a one-adult-no-children household (having 36 per cent of the expenses of the base family) the remainder or .7021 of the time (76*.2979 + 36*.7021 = 47.92). This adjusted equivalence scale then was used as the divisor for that parent's spendable income. Using the over-35-year-old householder BLS values in the example of Table 4.2 raised the E%N from 53 per cent to 73 per cent, while using the under-35 values raised it to 61 per cent.

For the Poverty Threshold approach, we used the 2001 poverty levels[19] in an analogous fashion. For example, for a one-adult household the poverty level is $9214, while for one adult with two children, it is $14269. The adjusted poverty level for the example of Table 4.2 is found by assuming the NCP's household had the poverty threshold of a one-adult-two-children household .2979 of the time, and that of a one-adult-no-children household the remainder or .7021 of the time (14269*.2979 + 9214*.7021 = 10,720). This was used as the divisor for NCP's spendable income with an analogously calculated divisor for CP's spendable income. This method is a slight adaptation of what was used in Braver (1999) and Braver and O'Connell (1998). Using poverty thresholds instead of *FSF* in the example of Table 4.2 lowered the E%N from 53 per cent to 44 per cent. Thus the *FSF* approach is intermediate between the two alternatives.

G.   Taxes

In the base analysis, we assumed the standard deduction was taken by both parents. In fact, however, those who own their own home, as well as some others, typically take the higher itemized deduction, which lowers their taxes. In addition, any individual's actual taxes depend on a variety of other factors. In the sensitivity analyses, we allowed each parent's taxes to be one of six possibilities: (1) standard deduction; (2) standard deduction plus 10 per cent additional tax for any factors not considered; (3) standard deduction, but a credit (subtraction) of 10 per cent of their final tax for factors we could not consider (the 10 per cent 'fudge factor' was ample enough to account for Child Care Expense tax credit); (4)–(6) each of the above combined with an itemized deduction. We chose a total itemized deduction of 30 per cent of gross income to account for mortgage interest expense and real estate tax deduction; 30 per cent was chosen since it is the maximum percentage of gross income that mortgage lenders will commonly consider. The highest E%N for any combination of tax specifications for the Table 4.2 example was 70 per cent.

RESULTS OF THE FULL FACTORIAL SENSITIVITY ANALYSES

We reported above the effects of varying each of the assumptions on the example of Table 4.2, but still to be determined was the sensitivity to these assumptions in other scenarios, as well as the effects of altering the various assumptions in combinations. To assess this sensitivity, the E%N values for all unique combinations of the variants for the above variables were computed (the 'full factorial' analysis) for the same three representative scenarios as used in Table 4.5 (one child, 20 per cent time, $5000/month NCP income; two children, 0 per cent time, $3000/month NCP income; and three children, 40 per cent time, $7000/month NCP income) for each state. In states without corrections for older children, 26136 combinations were found. In states with corrections for older children, the numbers of values computed were 52272, 78408 and 98799 for the three scenarios, respectively.

The mean and standard deviation of all E%N values were computed over all these combinations for each of the three scenarios for each state and compared with the value that was found in the base analysis. The results are presented in the third and fourth columns, respectively, of Table 4.6. With one exception (MA-2) the means were quite close to the value computed in the base analysis for that scenario (in Table 4.5 and repeated in column 2 of Table 4.6). More importantly, the standard deviations were generally not too large (again with the exception of MA-2), suggesting that for the most part the analyses were substantially insensitive to or robust against the assumptions. While it is certainly true that a number of assumptions needed to be made to generate exact values in Tables 4.2–5 and Figures 4.1 and 4.2, as a general statement, altering these assumptions in other plausible and reasonable ways did not change the overall conclusions greatly.

We also wished to detect whether certain assumptions were more critical than others. In order to establish which of the various assumptions made the biggest overall difference in the results, multiple correlation/regression analysis was conducted. In subsequent columns of Table 4.6, the E%N values were regressed on each of the realistic values variables and the value of eta-squared computed. Eta-squared is a common index which represents the proportion of the variance in E%N that is due to or accounted by a given assumption (that is, predictor) variable.

Examining the values in these remaining columns in Table 4.6 shows most of these eta-squared values are small, under .1. This shows that few of the assumptions had much of an effect, but exceptions were notable. The two variables or assumptions with the biggest effect were which index of needs was used and NCP's tax situation. This suggests that caution should be used when interpreting the results if a different needs index is used besides Citro and Michael's *FSF* (1995). However, as noted above for the Table 4.2 example, the *FSF* index's result was intermediate between the other two indexes. Using poverty thresholds yields somewhat smaller E%Ns and using BLS-LBS values (especially for over-35-year-old householders, see note 18) yields substantially larger ones. Caution is also necessary if NCP's tax situation is other than the base analysis assumes. When NCP itemized deductions, E%N were noticeably higher than in the base analysis. One additional assumption, how many older children there are in the family, also had a big impact but only for one state – Washington.

CONCLUSIONS AND IMPLICATIONS FOR CHILD SUPPORT POLICY

Since we studied hypothetical scenarios, the question arises as to whether, in general, given the child support regimes currently in place, CPs actually do have higher SOLs than their matched NCPs. The answer to this question depends on how many CPs actually have gross incomes in excess of the E%Ns we obtained. Published empirical literature provides some answers to that question. In California, Maccoby and Mnookin (1992) estimated that CPs earned on average only 46 per cent of what NCPs did shortly after divorce, while I found the ratio in Arizona was 63 per cent one year after divorce (Braver, 1999). This latter estimate is very close to the 66 per cent value found in an analysis of 400 randomly selected new filings in the state of Arizona in 2002 (Venohr and Griffith, 2003).[20] However, there is clear evidence that CP's earning capacity grows substantially and disproportionately as time accrues after divorce (Duncan and Hoffman, 1985), undoubtedly due to a combination of working more hours, upgrading job skills and education, and remarriage. Thus the best comparison is not one that is confined to the early post-divorce years, as in each of the previous citations, but is more comprehensive in terms of how long it is after the divorce when comparative income is assessed, so that it covers the entire span of time over which the children are still minors and subject to the child support order. Fabricius et al. (2003) found that among college students whose parents had divorced (who typically would have been covered by a child support order in the preceding year), the average reported mother's household income was fully 86 per cent of the father's. The most definitive estimates are probably those of the Census Bureau. According to 1999 US Census data, the median income of the closest category to male NCP's, 'non-family households with a male householder' is $30753, while for the category closest to divorced female CP's, 'family households with a female householder, no husband present' the median is $26164, 85 per cent of the NCP's (Current Population Studies, 1999). Thus, in comparing the values in the last row of Table 4.5 with this 85 per cent standard, we believe **our results suggest that under current child support guidelines, the majority of CPs currently have higher SOLs than their matched NCPs,** dramatically so in Massachusetts and Wisconsin, to a lesser extent in Kentucky. On the other hand, in Missouri, it can be assumed that NCPs often had higher SOLs than CPs, but this was the only state studied where that conclusion is probably warranted.

Assuming the foregoing is correct, what are the implications of the analysis for child support policy? We believe the results show that many of the guidelines in place (especially Massachusetts, Wisconsin and Kentucky, but probably not in Missouri) result in the majority of NCPs who are worse off after divorce than their CP counterparts. Thus, those who advocate using child support guidelines to equalize SOLs (Garrison, 1999; Blumberg, 1999) should recognize that doing so with an accurate analysis will probably result in lower overall child support awards.[21] The states with the flattest and tightest patterns in Figures 4.1 and 4.2 (and therefore least discriminatory) were those using the income shares (rather than percent-of-obligor income) approach and those with the most continuous and generous adjustments for time with NCP. If equalization of living standards is one of the goals, states that do not incorporate such features should give them serious consideration.

Because taxes figured prominently in the analyses, two other possibilities for tax reform should be considered: (1) routinely give the tax advantages due to the children to the NCP rather than the CP (as Arizona does; see note 13), since there will probably be greater impact this way; and (2) make child support (like alimony and almost every other form of income) taxable to the obligee and tax-free to the obligor.

Alternatively, policy-makers could systematically disregard the comparative living standards of the two households. We argued earlier that equalization of living standards of the two households was **not** the rationale for child support; instead, it's the basis for alimony. Child support, as the name suggests, is simply to support to the child. If policy makers aim only at that simple goal, and don't attempt to equate the two households, many of the complexities apparent in the present analysis disappear.

NOTES

1. The parties can negotiate who receives the first two of the preceding tax benefits, but the federal tax code by default gives them to the CP unless the CP signs a special form (Form 8332). The remaining tax benefits referred to are not negotiable.
2. For expository convenience, but with some loss of accuracy, we use the feminine gender for CP, the masculine gender for NCP.
3. To estimate the federal income tax, we use the following assumptions: only the CP gets to take the children as exemptions, for the earned income credit and for the child tax credit. As a result, the filing status of the former is 'head of household', while the NCP's is 'single'. We also assume initially that both parties take the standard (not itemized) deductions. Initially we assume $0 in deductible childcare expenses. When the earned income credit is available because of CP's low gross income, we assume the entire income is 'earned income' rather than investment income. We assume any interest, dividends, capital gains, IRA distributions, pensions and annuity income, unemployment compensation, social security income is included in gross income, and any student loan interest deductions are already subtracted from gross income
4. It is appropriate to compute this transfer after taxes because, as mentioned above, under the US (as well as every state's) tax code, child support is a transfer of NCP's after-tax dollars to the CP, who has no tax obligations on this income. Alimony, however, should be incorporated before any taxes are calculated. In this investigation, $0 in alimony is assumed. This was the assumption in order to compare the SOLs of the two households under a scenario in which SOL-equating was not taken as a goal, as it is with alimony, and because it is relatively rare in any event. However, if it is desirable to incorporate it into the calculations, it can be done in principle by assuming NCP's and CP's gross incomes are at the values they assume after alimony.

5. Arizona is an income shares state with an adjustment for time the child spends with the NCP that is continuous, though non-linear. It also has a 'proportion of total gross income' method of dividing Ordered childcare and health insurance. Kentucky is an incomes shares state with no adjustment for time spent with NCP. It also uses 'proportion of total gross income' to allocate Ordered expenses. Massachusetts uses a hybrid income shares and income percentage with a custodial reserve to assess child support. Massachusetts has no presumptive allowance for visitation frequency or shared custody. The guidelines correct for health insurance but not other extraordinary or childcare expenses. Missouri uses the income shares method with 'proportion of total gross income' to allocate Ordered expenses. Time spent with NCP is deducted proportionally. Oklahoma uses an income shares approach in assessing child support with an NCP time 'cliff' that kicks in at about 32 per cent time or greater. Washington assesses child support on an income shares basis imposed on net income with no consideration for NCP visiting time in the presumptive amount. The child support table stops at a combined net income of $7000. When combined monthly net income exceeds that amount, the court uses its discretion. Wisconsin assesses child support as a straight percentage of NCP's gross income. Parenting time kicks in at 35 per cent and more. No adjustment is made for health insurance or extraordinary expenses.
6. For federal tax, we used www.quicken.com/freedom.
7. To aid the reader in recognizing that (9) and (13) yield identical results, consider an example, which uses the expense amounts that Morgan and Lino (1999) estimate are paid on average by a high-income family for its only child, a ten-year-old, when broken down into our categories as described subsequently. These costs are $3760, $1580, $5150 and $1600 for V, U, D and O respectively, totalling $12090 ($TCE$ = 12090). Suppose the NCP pays directly $1128 of the $3760 V expenses (p_{NV} = 30% or .3), $158 of the $1580 U expenses (p_{NU} = .10), $2060 of the $5150 D expenses (p_{ND} = .40) and $80 of the $1600 O expenses (p_{NO} = .05). Then he pays $3426 altogether (so CEP_N = 3428 = 1128 + 158 + 2060 + 80). Thus, according to (9), he pays 28.3 per cent of the TCE total expenses, since PCE_N = CEP_N/TCE = 3429/12090 = .283. This identical value for PCE_N can also be obtained by application of (13) if one notices that $P(V)$ = 3760/12090 = .311, $P(U)$ = 1580/12090 = .131, $P(D)$ = 5150/12090 = .426, and $P(O)$ = 1600/12090 = .132, respectively (the preceding percentages are shown in Table 4.1): PCE_N = $p_{NV}*P(V) + p_{NU}*P(U) + p_{ND}*P(D) + p_{NO}*P(O)$ = .3*.311 + .1*.131 + .4*.426*.05*.132 = .283.
8. However, it should be noted that, in contrast to the assumption, we have found many decrees that specify other breakdowns for which parents will pay for lessons, and so on.
9. We (Fabricius and Braver, 2003) have recently completed an analysis of such expenses as reported by children of divorce who are now college students, finding that such expenses indeed vary with the amount of time the child spends in the NCP household, but are more appreciable than believed (according to the now-young-adult child's report) even for low levels of contact. For example, 49 per cent of children who spent only 20 per cent or less of their time with the NCP nonetheless had their own room in the NCP household (perhaps shared with siblings); 30 per cent of children spending 30 per cent or less time with NCP nonetheless had their own bicycle at the NCP's home.
10. While this is true in most states, some (for example, Washington and Wisconsin) do not add a share of such costs to child support. The computations to follow do so only when that particular state's rules to do so.
11. We also need to consider non-covered items, such as health care costs for the children that insurance does not pay for, and 'copayments'. Any such costs incurred are hardly ever included as add-ons to the monthly child support amounts, since they are irregular and unpredictable. Instead, such expenses are usually paid for by one parent out-of-pocket. However, most states and decrees order ultimate division between the parents of such costs by the same 'proportional to gross income' rule. Thus, even if we assume it is the CP that directly pays all of them, we should also assume the NCP will reimburse CP for his proportionate share. Accordingly, these non-covered items should adjust the PCE expenses. However, such costs are highly variable from family to family, and it is virtually impossible to get any sort of reliable estimates of typical amounts. Therefore, they

have been left out of subsequent calculations with the ultimate result being that the NCP's *PCE* is slightly to somewhat underestimated.

12. The spreadsheet is available upon request from the first author.

13. Arizona is perhaps the only state in the US (and certainly the only state in the current study) in which the guidelines specify that the NCP can sometimes claim the child as an exemption on tax returns and reap the tax benefits thereof. If the NCP has two-thirds of the combined gross income, for example, the Arizona guideline specifies that he should claim the child two out of every three years. This rule, however, would not entitle him to the head-of-household designations, nor to the EIC, and so on. For present purposes, we did not treat Arizona uniquely in this respect. The reader may assume, instead, that this was one of the years that the CP was entitled to the benefit.

14. The basic award of $1024 in the example is assumed by the guideline to represent *V*, *U* and *D* expenses only, which together comprise 83.85 per cent of children's expenses according to Table 4.1. We need to solve for what additional proportion *O* is. The algebra reduces to: if 1024 is 83.85 per cent of the total, what (*O*) amount is 16.15 per cent? The solution is $197. In general, we solve for the *O* amount to add in to child support by the expression .1615/.8385 = .1926.

15. As observed in Note 5, Washington's guidelines do not cover all of our scenarios, since the tables stop at a combined total net income of $7000. Our study used the $7000 child support amounts when these income limits were exceeded. Health insurance and extraordinary expenses in Washington are treated slightly differently, with corrections for health insurance only if it exceeds a certain dollar amount. Our study split extraordinary expenses equally between health insurance and other.

16. Since (19) can also be stated (inserting 2 for *F*) as $\left(\dfrac{2}{2+.7K}\right)^F = (1 - B)$, taking logs of both sides yielded $F = \dfrac{\log(1 - B)}{\log(2/(2 + .7K))}$.

17. The percentage of family income *i* spent on child(ren) was estimate by a least-squares estimate where % on Child $= ((2 + .7 K)^{a+b(1/i)} - (2)^{a+b(1/i)})/(2 + .7 K)^{a+b(1/i)})$, where *K* is the number of children and *a* and *b* are estimated parameters. The Morgan and Lino (1999) data were for two adult families.

18. Lower values arise in the BLS-LSB approach and tables if the householder is younger than 35. For example, the values for such younger families that correspond to the 36 and 76 of the main text are 35 and 67 for younger families. Even though the median age of divorcing parents is near the critical 35-year-old age mark (Venohr and Griffith, 2003), we used the over-35 values in most of the sensitivity analyses.

19. From the Census Bureau's web-page: http://www.census.gov/hhes/poverty/threshld/thresh01.html. For a one-adult household with one and three children, respectively, the poverty levels are $12207, and $18566.

20. The figure reported is the ratio of the obligee's mean income to the obligor's mean income. Using medians instead, the ratio is 64 per cent (Venohr, personal communication, 8 April 2003.)

21. One justification proffered for the idea that child support guidelines should be set at an amount that helps to equalize living standards is that to do otherwise means the child may disproportionately bear the adverse economic consequences of the parental divorce (Blumberg, 1999; Garrison, 1999). We have shown here that this probably happens far less frequently than believed. Even in cases where the obligor's SOL is substantially higher than the obligee's, however, the adverse economic impact to the child is mitigated to the degree that the NCP makes substantial non-child support voluntary outlays on behalf of the child (as found in Fabricius et al. 2003, and Fabricius and Braver, 2003) and/or the child spends substantial time with each parent (according to Venohr and Griffith, 2003 data, 65 per cent spend 25 per cent or more time with NCP) and therefore shares in the SOL of each.

REFERENCES

American Law Institute (2002), *Principles of the Law of Family Dissolution: Analysis and Recommendations*, Dayton: Lexis-Nexis.

Bay, C., S.L. Braver, B.S. Fogas, P. Fitzpatrick and S.A. Wolchik (1988), 'New child support guidelines: changes and perceived fairness', presented at Western Psychological Association, Burlingame, CA.

Betson, D.M. (1990), 'Alternative estimates of the cost of children from the 1980–86 Consumer Expenditure Survey', report to the US Dept. of Health and Human Services.

Blumberg, G.G. (1999), 'Balancing the interests: the American Law Institute's treatment of child support', *Family Law Quarterly*, **33**, 39–110.

Braver, S.L. (1999), 'The gender gap in standard of living after divorce: vanishingly small?' *Family Law Quarterly*, **33**, 111–34.

Braver, S.L. and D. O'Connell (1998), *Divorced Dads: Shattering the Myths. The Surprising Truth about Fathers, Children and Divorce*, New York: Tarcher/ Putnam.

Cassetty, J. and G.K. Sprinkle (1987), 'The ELS (Equal Living Standards) model for child support awards', in Women's Legal Defense Fund, *Essentials of child support guidelines development: Economic issues and policy considerations*, Washington: Women's Legal Defense Fund.

Citro, C.F. and R.T. Michael (1995), *Measuring Poverty: A New Approach*, Washington, DC: National Academy Press.

Current Population Studies (1999), 'Money income in the United States. Consumer income', (Document P60–209), Washington, DC: US Bureau of the Census.

Dodson, D. and J. Entmacher (1994), *Report card on state child support guidelines*, Washington: Women's Legal Defense Fund.

Duncan, G.J. and S.D. Hoffman (1985), 'Economic consequences of marital instability', in M. David and T. Smeeding (eds), *Horizontal Equity, Uncertainty, and Economic Well-Being*, Chicago, IL: University of Chicago Press, pp. 427–71.

Eden, P., et al. (1987), 'In the best interests of children: A simplified model for equalizing the living standards of parental households', in Women's Legal Defense Fund, *Essentials of child support guidelines development: Economic issues and policy considerations*, Washington: Women's Legal Defense Fund.

Ellman, I.M. (1989) 'The theory of alimony', *California Law Review*, **77**, 1–88.

Ellman, I.M. (1991) 'Should non-financial losses and motivations be included in the theory of alimony?' *B.Y.U. Law Review*, **259** (Symposium Issue).

Ellman, I.M., P.M. Kurtz and E.S. Scott (1998), *Family Law: Cases, Text, Problems.*

Elrod, L.H. (1994), 'Adding to the basic child support award', in *Child Support Guidelines: The Next Generation*, US Dept. of Health and Human Services, Office of Child Support Enforcement.

Fabricius, W.V. and S.L. Braver (2003), 'Non-child support expenditures on children by nonresidential divorced fathers: results of a study', *Family Court Review*, **41** (3), 321–36.

Fabricius, W.V., S.L. Braver and K. Deneau (2003), 'Divorced parents' financial support of their children's college expenses', *Family Court Review*, **41** (2), 224–41.

Garrison, M. (1994), 'Child support and children's poverty: a review of Small Change: The economics of child support and America's children: Resources from family, government and the economy', *Family Law Quarterly*, **28**, 489–90.

Garrison, M. (1999), 'Child support policy: guidelines and goals', *Family Law Quarterly*, **33**, 157–89.

Gay, R. (1995), 'The alimony hidden in child support, new scientific proof that many child support awards are too high', *Children's Advocate*, **7** (5).

Johnson, D.S., J.M. Rogers and L. Tan (2001), 'A century of family budgets in the United States', *Monthly Labor Review*, May, 28–45.

Lino, M.C. (1998), *Expenditures on Children by Families: 1997 Annual Report*, Washington: US Department of Agriculture.

Maccoby, E.E. and R.H. Mnookin (1992), *Dividing the Child: Social and Legal Dilemmas of Custody*, Cambridge, MA: Harvard University Press.

Morgan L.W. and M.C. Lino (1999), 'A comparison of child support awards calculated under states' child support guidelines with expenditures on children calculated by the US Department of Agriculture', *Family Law Quarterly*, **33**, 191–218.

Peterson, R.R. (1996), 'A re-evaluation of the economic consequences of divorce', *American Sociological Review*, **61**, 528–36

Pirog, M.A., Klotz, M.E. and K.V. Byers (1998), 'Interstate comparisons of child support orders using state guidelines', *Family Relations*, **47**, 289.

Thoennes, N. et al. (1991), 'The impact of child support guidelines on award adequacy, award variability, and case processing efficiency', *Family Law Quarterly*, **25**, 339–40.

Venohr, J.C. and T.E. Griffith (2003), *Arizona Child Support Guidelines: Findings from a Case File Review*, Denver, CO: Policy Studies, Inc.

Venohr, J.C. and R.G. Williams (1999), 'The implementation and periodic review of state child support guidelines', *Family Law Quarterly*, **33**, 7–37.

Watts, H.W. (1980), 'Special panel suggests changes in BLS Family Budget Program', *Monthly Labor Review*, **103** (12), 1–10.

Weitzman, L. (1985), *The Divorce Revolution: The Unexpected Social and Economic Consequences of Divorce for Women and Children in America*, New York: Free Press.

Williams, R.G. (1987), *Development of Guidelines for Child Support Orders, Part II, Final Report*, report to the US Office of Child Support Enforcement, Policy Studies Inc.

5. Child support policy and the unintended consequences of good intentions

Ronald K. Henry

INTRODUCTION: THE GROWTH OF CHILD SUPPORT ENFORCEMENT

Over the course of the past two decades, Congress has taken an increasingly interventionist approach to child support enforcement. Formerly a matter reserved exclusively to the states, child support enforcement has become heavily federalized. The Office of Child Support Enforcement (OCSE), a unit within the Administration for Children and Families at the United States Department of Health and Human Services, publishes and posts on its website detailed statistics about the Child Support Enforcement Program from which much can be learned.[1] From OCSE data, we learn that the federal government spent $3.0 billion and, largely as a result of federal mandates, the states spent an additional $1.5 billion for a total of a little over $4.5 billion in child support enforcement expenditures in fiscal year 2000. This is, undeniably, a big programme and big programmes need big justifications which OCSE is quick to provide.

According to the OCSE data, the Child Support Enforcement Program had a 'cost-effectiveness' of 3.95, meaning that $3.95 of child support was collected for each dollar of programme expense. As described to congressional appropriators, the programme is, thus, highly effective and continues to grow year by year. In this post-Enron era of accounting disclosures, however, it is worthwhile to look more closely at the numbers.

The federal role in child support enforcement came about as a means to recoup welfare expenditures. Congress was told that the taxpayers were supporting children on welfare because 'deadbeat dads' were running away from their responsibilities. Congress passed legislation requiring welfare mothers to assign to the federal government the right to receive child support as a means for the government to recoup its welfare expenditures. Congress then began the effort of collecting this assigned child support. It sounded like a good idea but, in the OCSE data, we find that Uncle Sam lost $2 038 123 863 on his expenditure of $3 006 361 184 in fiscal year 2000. Let's say that again. Uncle Sam's own data show that he spent over $3 billion on child support enforcement in fiscal year 2000 and recouped less than $1 billion ($968 237 321) for a loss of $2 038 123 863. The cost-effectiveness ratio is only 0.32, not 3.95, meaning that Uncle Sam recouped only $0.32 for each dollar spent on child support enforcement.

Actually, the stated loss of $2 038 123 863 grossly understates the total loss since all revenue is counted but the costs of law enforcement (court costs, police costs, prosecutor costs, jail costs and so on) and sanctions (license revocations, tax refund intercepts, denial of passports and so on) which are not directly imposed and administered by the child support bureaucracy are omitted from the OCSE calculation. If all expenditures were fully considered, the true cost-effectiveness of the program would likely be in the range of 0.2.

How could such a disparity between actual and reported cost-effectiveness arise? The simple answer is Enron. To build its numbers, OCSE counts all money that passes through the Child Support Enforcement bureaucracy rather than only the money that is retained to recoup federal welfare payments. Pursuant to 42 U.S.C. '666 (a)(8) and (b)(3), all new and modified child support orders must contain a provision requiring automatic garnishment and payment through the child support enforcement bureaucracy even in non-welfare cases unless a waiver is obtained on an individual case basis. Except for the small amount of money that is retained to recoup welfare expenditures, the great bulk of the money simply passes through the bureaucracy on its way from the non-custodial parent to the custodial parent. As a result, the federal government claims total collections of $17 854 271 521 even though the net federal share is only $968 237 321. In other words, the government builds its statistics by forcing approximately $20 of child support to flow through the government for each $1 of child support that is retained by the government as recoupment of welfare expenditures. Even Enron did not build its house of cards nearly so high as this.

There are multiple consequences from the pass-through gimmick, none of which represents good public policy. First, there is delay. A custodial parent who once received cash or a check directly from the non-custodian now must wait through a multi-step administrative process that is fraught with delay and error. Everyone who has any familiarity with child support enforcement has heard more stories than can be counted of lost, delayed and erroneous administrative payments. Some of the state processing bureaucracies are better or worse than others but not one state claims that it is even close to correctly processing the vast sums that are required to pour through it.

Second, the mandate for pass-through creates enormous, unnecessary expense. Every state is required to maintain a bureaucracy that does nothing but process (and frequently lose) child support payments that were never in dispute and that had been paid regularly before interposition of the administrative pass-through mandate. The cost-effectiveness claim of $3.95 is an obvious sham unless the reader blindly accepts the assumption that not one cent of the $17854271521 in child support collected would have been paid in the absence of the newly created administrative pass-through mandate. To the author's knowledge, the federal government has never attempted to measure the differences between child support payments actually made with and without the intervention of the pass through mechanism. One older study conducted prior to the imposition of mandatory withholding, contained the following modest projection:

> These findings suggest that a successful system of mandatory withholding, coupled with greater efforts to establish obligations, could recover somewhat between 15 and 20 percent of AFDC benefits.[2]

Rather than continuing to pour more money into an ever-enlarging programme, Congress should require a serious and independent programme review to determine what the taxpayers are actually receiving for their yearly investment in child support enforcement.

Third, the administrative pass-through will continue to distort public policy. As old, informal child support payments expire and as more new cases are forced through the administrative pass-through, 'total collections' will inevitably increase. This does not mean that more child support is being paid, it only means that a greater portion of the child support is passing through the bureaucracy with its attendant delays and errors. As more money passes through the bureaucracy, its self-proclaimed 'cost-effectiveness ratio' will continue to grow with absolutely no change in effort or the amounts actually paid by non-custodians. With a stroke of its legislative pen, Congress has created a programme manager's Nirvana: a programme whose self-proclaimed results get better year by year regardless of who steers the ship or what direction they turn. Year after year, Congress votes more taxpayer money for this 'cost-effective' programme despite having no idea of the true human costs of lost or delayed payments, of erroneously imposed garnishments, of erroneously revoked drivers' licenses and professional licenses and of the misery caused by the criminalization of a civil debt.

According to OCSE, total programme costs (federal and state) were $4525771150 but only $1354080032 was collected in cases involving current welfare recipients. The largest, most aggressive collection effort the world has ever known is still limited in what it can obtain from 'dead broke dads'. The original premise that welfare expenditures could be recouped from non-custodial parents was simply wrong. The simple truth is that low-income women tend to have children with low-income men and the invention of new coercions to squeeze harder will not bring more blood from these very dry stones. It is time for a new approach.

As we move into a new round of child support reform, social science researchers continue to confirm what societal tradition and intuition have told us all along – children need the active physical and emotional involvement of two parents, a father and a mother. For every social problem that we experience – teenage pregnancy, drug abuse, poor school performance, low self-esteem, depression, suicide, or any other item on our list of social ills – research confirms that family breakdown and, particularly, father loss are primary causal factors. From the conservative American Legislative Exchange Council to the liberal Progressive Policy Institute to the National Commission on Children, a political consensus has emerged to acknowledge the reality that public policy must begin to focus on issues of family formation, family preservation and demilitarization of the divorce process where parental separation cannot be avoided.

Unfortunately for children, public policy initiatives too often consist of bandages and tonics designed to cover or suppress individual symptoms while failing to diagnose or cure the underlying disease. Sometimes, the tonics have unintended consequences and side-effects which exacerbate the original disease or stimulate new ones.

In the 1970s, we had a smug, stereotypical caricature of the 'welfare queen' who was the alleged source of all our problems. When accumulating empirical evidence would no longer allow the complex lives of low-income families to be dismissed by invocation of the 'welfare queen' caricature, we didn't get any smarter or more sophisticated, we simply switched to a new caricature, the 'deadbeat dad'.

Like its predecessor, the phrase 'deadbeat dad' is catchy, supported by anecdotes of extreme behavior, and wildly overused. Also like its predecessor, the truth is beginning to catch up and the phrase has not much longer to live.

LESSONS FROM THE 'MOST WANTED' LISTS

The stereotype of the 'deadbeat dad' is the wealthy surgeon who abandoned his children in poverty to squire his new trophy wife around in a shiny red Porsche. If the stereotype were true, we should be able to see it in the 'Most Wanted' lists put out by the various states. These are the 'Public Enemy Number One' lists of the biggest evaders and worst lawbreakers that each state has been encouraged to create to capture the horrid miscreants.

As this paragraph was being written, for example, the first five names on Georgia's 'Most Wanted' list were:[3]

Name	Amount of Arrearage	Occupation
Robert E. Hartley	$93 670	Bricklayer
John Rickey Garrett	$77 900	Pipefitter
Michael Edward Neary	$61 013	Carpenter
Bobby Jefferson Stokes	$60 450	Mechanic
Lucas J. Mumper	$50 304	Unknown

In another part of the country, Wyoming's first five names were:[4]

Name	Amount of Arrearage	Occupation
James E. Frier	$18 893	Truck driver
Richard H. Brockmeier	$104 062	Unknown
Jeffrey C. Peterson	$21 618	Taxi driver
Marvin Michael Hoshow	$34 814	Labourer
Brian Wayne Preuninger	$29 660	Labourer

In still another part of the country, Kentucky's first five consisted of the following:[5]

Name	Amount of Arrearage	Occupation	Status
Eric C. Brown	over $13 000	Carpenter	Found
Alexandar West, III	over $22 000	Sales	Found
James R. Cooper	over $10 000	Electrician	Found
Kupsammy Tandrian	over $17 000	Home depot	
Michael Price	over $30 000	Construction	

Three states from three very different parts of the country with very similar lists. Where are the doctors, the lawyers and the investment bankers? Space limitations prevent reproduction of the full lists here but you can follow the links given in the endnotes. Every name on these lists is an economically marginal blue-collar or occasional worker. We cannot know from the 'Most Wanted' lists alone whether these were good people or bad people, but a few things are clear. It is most unlikely that any of them was ever able to afford the services of a lawyer in establishing or modifying their child support obligation. All have hopelessly high arrearages in relation to their economic circumstances and, at least in Kentucky, the majority of them cannot even be said to be 'Wanted' because that state acknowledges that three of the five have been found.

What happens after one of these 'Most Wanted' blue-collar workers is found? Only on rare occasions does the bureaucracy (in this case, Virginia) report upon the limits of its success in shaking such towering money trees as these:

> Frankie L. Adams: Mr. Adams is out of jail and making payments; however, he is unemployed.

> Robert Mountcastle Flannery: The judge ordered a wage witholding for $100 a month on Mr. Flannery's SSA benefits. The first $100 payment was received in August.

> Ferman LaMont Peyton: Mr. Peyton was located in Dublin, Virginia, after making application to receive food stamps.[6]

Regardless of the form of coercion attempted, we are never going to pull large amounts of money out of the unemployed, the disabled and food stamp recipients. The question is whether these are anomalous cases or part of a systemic problem of imposing unsustainable burdens on child support obligors.

The names on these three 'Most Wanted' lists are in no way anomalous. All of the other state lists are similarly loaded with low-income obligors – see: http://www.IN.gov/fssa/children/support/related.html. This site displays a list with hotlinks to the 'Most Wanted' list websites for the various states.

The available evidence indicates that there is a systemic problem in which existing child support guidelines overburden obligors. For example, the state of Florida found that traditional means of collection were unsuccessful and hired two private contractors, Lockheed Martin IMS and Maximus, Inc., to pursue approximately 200 000 difficult cases. Lockheed was assigned 101 325 cases of which it closed 37 270. Over 14 months, Lockheed was paid $2.2 million and 'managed to collect $137 839 in child support payments'. Maximus was assigned 89 560 cases of which it closed 46 692. Maximus was paid $2.25 million and 'got 12 deadbeats to cough up $5867'.[7] According to the story in the *Orlando Sentinel*:

> What Maximus and Lockheed Martin learned in the process of tracking down non-paying parents is that most who don't make child support payments are, in a word, broke. You can't give what you don't have.[8]

Similarly, when the state of Maryland decided to get tough with 'deadbeat dads' by suspending 9000 drivers' licenses, only about 800 were able to make sufficient progress on their arrearages to get their licenses restored.[9] In modern America, the ability to drive a car to work, to the grocery store, to just about anywhere, is an indispensable part of simple survival. There were not many trophy wives or shiny red Porsches among the 91 per cent who were unable to make sufficient payments simply to regain the freedom to drive.

Also lost in the hunt for 'deadbeats' is any hint of the humanity of these parents. We have to demonize them lest someone might start to think that some of them are just working stiffs who cannot carry the burdens the courts have imposed upon them. Go to the Wyoming website and look at the picture of Brian Wayne Preuninger which is severely cropped but cannot quite block out the fact that he is seated and smiling with a child on his lap. Consider also the impossibility of the situation in which these individuals find themselves. Does anyone really believe that Robert E. Hartley, the Georgia bricklayer, has a secret, offshore bank account worth \$93 670 hidden away somewhere? In a legal system where the Bradley Amendment prohibits the modification of arrearages and even the most illiterate obligors are required to provide their own attorneys or go unrepresented, can anyone be surprised that these people have gone underground? As Bruce Walker, a former Oklahoma district attorney who has jailed hundreds of obligors for non-payment, recently acknowledged:

> [These obligors are] seldom the mythic monsters described by politicians. Many times I prosecuted impoverished men. I prosecuted one deadbeat dad who had been hospitalized for malnutrition and another who lived in the bed of a pick up truck.[10]

As horror stories pour in from the field, professional research into the status of child support obligors is beginning to receive funding. For example, the team of Laura Lein (University of Texas) and Katherine Edin (Rutgers University) recently found that:

> Many of the absent fathers who state leaders want to track down and force to pay child support are so destitute that their lives focus on finding the next job, next meal or next night's shelter . . . . The initial findings are sobering, filled with descriptions of life in the streets or cheap motels, rummaging for food as restaurants are closing and seeking shelter, often a week or a day at a time.[11]

According to Professor Lein:

> One of the things that really surprised me was how short a job was. People really talked about good jobs as jobs that lasted five or six days, or two weeks was really terrific . . . But economically and emotionally marginal as many of these fathers are, they still represent a large portion of low-income fathers who continue to make contributions to their children's households and to maintain at least some level of relationship with those children . . . What's most valuable (in the study)

is the total texture of people's lives. What we are finding with the men is that in lots of different areas, there are pressures, in terms of their housing, in terms of their job stability, in terms of trying to be a father, in terms of education and health. There are problems in every domain.[12]

Evidence has been building over the past decade that the obligations imposed on non-custodial parents are unsustainable but, for many of those years, little notice was paid. For example, in 1991, the United States Department of Health and Human Services touted a programme under which obligors were rounded up and told that they could either go to jail or charge their arrearages on their credit cards. The description of the programme made no mention of the constitutionality of debtors' prison or the morality of driving people into 18 per cent revolving credit card debt to pay obligations that supposedly had been established on the basis of ability to pay. The description merely noted that the success of the programme in pilot studies was limited because 'the majority of obligors . . . most of them from non-AFDC families' – were already so poor that they 'had neither charge cards nor checking accounts'.[13]

In a 1992 study, the General Accounting Office reported that, when custodial mothers were asked the reasons why they had not received expected child support payments, 66 per cent of the mothers themselves (in both in-state and interstate cases) gave the reason as 'father unable to pay'.[14]

Whenever the exaggerations of the child support lobby are exposed, the ready response is that critics must surely admit that at least some child support is not paid. True enough, but this response invariably begs the question of why some child support payments are not made. Senior officials of the Office of Child Support Enforcement of the United States Department of Health and Human Services acknowledge that very little data exists on why child support payments are not made and that even this small body of data is not publicized. The federal and state agencies now spend over $4.5 billion annually on child support enforcement, yet the government has had no meaningful understanding of how many non-paying obligors are unemployed, disabled, supporting second families, or engaged in civil disobedience because they have been unable to see their children.

The enforcement of child support is already the most onerous form of debt collection practiced in the United States. Tax returns are intercepted, credit reporting services are notified, multibillion dollar bureaucracies are fed, and obligors are even jailed. If compliance is still inadequate despite the efforts of this massive enforcement apparatus, society must begin looking at the question of 'Why?'

The demonization of non-custodial parents is used to justify all manner of inhumane treatment. Sylvia Folk, a non-custodial mother, testified before Congress that she was incarcerated for 72 days for non-payment.

The judge in her case candidly acknowledged from the bench his knowledge that she lacked the money to pay but vowed to and did hold her until
the ransom was paid by her church.[15] Ms Folk's treatment is by no means
uncommon. Writing in the Charleston, South Carolina, *Post and Courier*,
Family Court Judge L. Mendel Rivers, Jr. explained:

> The problem is, chronic non-supporters do not have dependable jobs, nor tax
> refunds, nor seizeable property. That's why they are chronic.
>   As cruel as it sounds, the one remedy that almost always works is incarcera-
> tion. We family court judges call it 'the magic fountain.' . . .
>   Of course, there is no magic. The money is paid by his mother, or by the
> second wife, or by some other innocent who perhaps had to liquidate her life's
> savings.[16]

The theory is that child support is supposed to be set to meet the child's
needs within the limits of the obligor's ability to pay. When the difference
between theory and reality is so great that the required revenue can only be
generated through medieval kidnappings for ransom in the style of Judge
Rivers, the system must ultimately collapse of its own weight. This is
exactly what is happening.

Every year, the federal and state governments spend more money on
child support enforcement only to report larger caseloads, backlogs and
arrearages. The collection tactics tolerated for child support debt are tolerated for no other form of debt in American society yet, after every round
of new coercions, we find that the problem has only worsened. The lack of
research and programme evaluation has delayed the realization that child
support obligations imposed on low-income obligors are not sustainable
but truth cannot be suppressed forever.

Front-line enforcement workers who begin with zeal their crusade
against deadbeats end up reporting that:

> I just couldn't stand what they were doing to people. I got a call from a homeless
> shelter and was told that I had put a man and . . . his four children out on the
> street because I had put an enforcement order . . . for 50 percent of his income. I
> was devastated. That was the beginning of the end for me, because I think that
> was the first time I was in touch with the ramifications of what I was doing.[17]

CHILD SUPPORT GUIDELINES: THE POWER TO
TAX IS THE POWER TO DESTROY

Consider the operation of a typical guideline. Assume a family with two
children in which the non-custodial parent has a modest gross income of
$20000 per year:

- If the custodial parent is voluntarily unemployed, the non-custodial parent's support order under the guideline will be set at 25 per cent of gross income.
- If the custodial parent takes employment and achieves the same $20 000 per year gross income, the non-custodial parent's child support obligation is not reduced by one penny.
- If the custodial parent remarries and now has a high household income, say $100 000, the non-custodial parent's child support obligation is still not reduced by one penny.
- If, alternatively, the non-custodial parent remarries and now has a second family to support, the non-custodial parent's child support obligation is still not reduced by one penny, unless the second family has fallen below the poverty level regardless of the standard of living achieved by the first family.[18]

All of these results are presumed to be equally fair and valid under the guideline. Only the non-custodial parent has burdens. Only the custodial parent has choices.

In a study conducted for the Urban Institute, Laura Wheaton and Elaine Sorensen calculated the effect of child support transfers and income tax effects for families collectively described as the 'working poor'. Where mother and father each work in the range between $9000 and $18 000 per year, Wheaton and Sorensen calculated that the non-custodial parent would have to earn between 50 per cent more (one child) and 100 per cent more (two children) than the custodian to have an equal standard of living on an after-child-support/after-tax basis.[19] Under existing guidelines, the non-custodian frequently is reduced to a standard of living substantially below that of the household he has been indentured to support. The situation is actually even worse than it appears because the non-custodial parent does not really constitute a one-member household. The non-custodial parent also must somehow find resources to provide for the children while they are in his care. Even old-style 'standard visitation orders' place the children with the non-custodian between 20 per cent and 25 per cent of the time. Where is the non-custodian supposed to find money to feed, house, entertain and otherwise care for his children when we have already dragged him down to a level insufficient to support a single person at the custodial household's level? Before we criticize 'runaway' fathers who see their children too little after divorce, we need to examine the extent to which the economic burdens we have imposed upon those fathers have made them driven-away or thrown-away. Are they deadbeats or dead broke?

HOW DID WE GET INTO THIS MESS?

Throughout most of our nation's history and in much of the world today, the law contained a strong or conclusive presumption that sole custody would be awarded to the father in the event of family dissolution. The early feminist meeting in Seneca Falls, New York, in 1848, for example, included the fact that fathers automatically received custody as a principal complaint in its Declaration of Sentiments.

Prior to the Industrial Revolution, most parents worked side by side with the children on the family farm or in the family trade. Children were nurtured and educated through almost continuous contact with both parents and child-rearing books through the eighteenth and mid-nineteenth century emphasized the father's centrality in raising the children and preparing them for the adult world. As the Industrial Revolution accelerated through the nineteenth century by pushing more fathers out of the family enterprise and into the factories, social theorists began to exalt rigid sexual separations with Father as external wage-earner and Mother as home-bound nurturer. Still, the pendulum swung slowly and the pro-feminist philosopher John Stewart Mill observed that, while the idea was interesting, the public was insufficiently prepared to discuss mother custody.

Continued industrialization coupled with the then-perceived virtue of getting women out of the paid workforce in order to create jobs for returning servicemen at the end of the First World War culminated in a full-blown 'cult of motherhood' and the establishment of the 'tender years doctrine' in most states. The pendulum of public prejudice, having swung from one extreme to the other, then enforced automatic mother custody with the same rigidity as the earlier enforcement of automatic father custody.

Today, that rigidity is eroding and the most recent report of the United States Census Bureau is that fathers constitute approximately 18 per cent of all single parents, with their numbers having grown 25 per cent in the past three years alone.[20] Still, old prejudices die slowly and the Gender Bias Commissions of each state which have addressed the issue have found continuing gender bias against fathers in custody determinations.

Against the backdrop of changing custody standards, child support policy has evolved. In the past 20 years, public involvement in child support has grown to such a large scale (the federal government spends over $3 billion per year) that it is sometimes forgotten that the entire concept of child support transfer payments is a recent invention.

Historically, a parent's duty was to support the child in the parent's own home and to keep the door open for the child to enter. Transfer payments arose only in the highly uncommon situation of a parent who had rejected his or her own children and thereby created a burden for the state or third parties. Child support transfer payments were thus rare during the era of father custody and remained rare during the early years of the mother custody era. As the pendulum of prejudice shifted to sole mother custody during a time in which women generally did not work outside the home, the courts began to recognize the consequences of ordering the placement of children in the least economically viable fragment of the former family. The 1920s to 1940s then saw a large-scale transformation in the fundamental structure of child support.

Under the new formulation, the parent who 'lost' custody was both deprived of the companionship of the child and ordered to pay the other parent for services that the 'loser' had historically provided with love and without charge in his or her own home. This unique separation of the rights of custody and the duties of support became a consequence of the 'tender years' doctrine that is matched nowhere else in a legal system that has prided itself upon its attention to the principle that the possessor of rights should also bear the burdens and responsibilities associated with those rights. It is this bifurcation of rights and responsibilities that is at the root of the civil disobedience portion of the child support enforcement problem. Current policy makes the simplistic assumption that all non-custodians are 'runaway' parents when, in fact, many non-custodians view themselves as 'thrown-away' parents who are victims of a court order that assumed children needed only 'a custodian and a check'.[21]

What has been left out of the equation is our understanding of human nature and, particularly, our understanding that parents support children because of their relationships with those children. We do not have a problem with large numbers of parents who refuse to provide for their children during an intact marriage, yet those same responsible parents become 'deadbeats' upon divorce. It is time to examine the role of government policy in the post-divorce behaviour of the non-custodial parents. When we say to non-custodial parents that we care nothing about their relationships with their children, that we will offer no protection against the custodial parent's interference with that relationship, and that we will devote government resources only to extracting financial payments, we should not be surprised by the result. Parents support children when they are permitted to be parents; slaves run away.

The link between emotional relationship and financial relationship could not be more plain. The Census Bureau has reported that:

- child support compliance was 90.2 per cent in cases of joint custody;
- child support compliance was 79.1 per cent where access to the child was protected by a visitation order; and

- child support compliance was only 44.5 per cent where neither joint custody nor access were protected by an order.[22]

Like any other artificial bifurcation, the separation of emotional support from financial support has created distortions. By deluding themselves into believing that only financial support was relevant for policy-makers, it became easy to meet all objections with simple chants of 'more is better' and 'it's for the children'.

The 'more is better' movement was fuelled by advocacy research, particularly that of Lenore Weitzman whose 1985 book, *The Divorce Revolution*, claimed that, after divorce, women's standard of living declined 73 per cent while men's standard of living increased 42 per cent. Weitzman's figures were repeatedly debunked[23] even though Weitzman refused to make her data available for peer review and were further debunked when the data finally became available in 1996:

> Weitzman, a professor of sociology and law at George Mason University in Fairfax, VA, now acknowledges her figures were wrong. She blames the loss of her original computer data file, a weighting error, or a mistake in the computer calculations performed by a Stanford University research assistant. But 'I'm responsible – I reported it', she says.[24]

Despite being massively wrong, Lenore Weitzman's figures have been convenient for advocates and have become ingrained in both the popular culture and in academic circles. It is hard to find a text on the subjects of divorce, custody or child support that does not repeat Weitzman's erroneous figures. For advocates, truth is secondary to the mission and Weitzman's erroneous figures continue to be quoted.

While advocates copied to tmeister Melvin Belli's quest for 'the adequate award and the more adequate award', both the state and federal governments played a role in advancing the 'more is better' philosophy. Government was paying a huge amount of money in welfare benefits and wanted to get that money back from somebody. Never mind that the government established the levels and conditions for welfare eligibility and, until recently, actively discouraged work among welfare recipients. Never mind that the government was making payments to one household and wanted to recoup its payments from a second household without ever asking whether the second household was prepared to assume custody and provide directly for the needs of the child. Never mind that the welfare programme had 'man in the house' rules that drove economically marginal couples apart. The government wanted its money back and saw child support enforcement as a profit center.

The federal government further clogged the child support enforcement rolls with the Bradley Amendment, 42 U.S.C. ' 666(a)(9)(c), which provides that, once accrued, child support arrearages cannot be modified. Originally intended as a response to anecdotes that judges were forgiving arrearages too freely, the Bradley Amendment became a classic example of the unintended consequences of federal overkill. If an obligor loses his job, we want him to spend his time in employment offices looking for a new job. Under the Bradley Amendment, he needs to spend his time in court seeking a modification because any arrearage that accrues while he is unemployed is not modifiable. Since the unemployed worker cannot afford a lawyer, of course, his support order is not modified, the arrearage accrues, and he ends up on a 'Most Wanted' poster.

WHAT NEEDS TO BE DONE

No one on any side of the issue would disagree that child support enforcement is a current disaster, characterized by huge caseloads, huge arrearages and huge administrative paralysis. Despite spending over $3 billion in federal funds alone each year, child support enforcement is more chaotic and overwhelmed than ever. Among the many items reported in the media are the following:

- Virginia sent 2300 erroneous license revocation notices to non-deadbeats.[25]
- After spending $20 million on a computer system for child support enforcement, a state legislative audit found that 'almost one-third of the West Virginia Child Support Enforcement Division's files contained incorrect data. Those errors led the agency to wrongly collect about $1.7 million from 3788 parents.'[26]
- An audit in the District of Columbia determined that 3500 cheques (or more than 10 per cent of the total) were not forwarded to custodial parents despite payments by the non-custodians.[27]
- In Los Angeles County, an average of 350 men per month are assigned child support orders despite the fact that they are not the fathers of the supported children.[28]
- A child support enforcement employee in Indiana diverted at least $680000 in child support payments to himself and his girlfriends.[29]

Solving the problems of child support enforcement requires attention to four distinct areas: (1) administrative procedures reform, (2) child support guideline reform, (3) custody reform, and (4) research to understand the lives of real people.

ADMINISTRATIVE REFORMS ON THE STATE LEVEL

We know that new cases are coming into the system faster than we can handle them. Rather than devoting all of our resources to the pathologies already in the pipeline, the child support enforcement community must begin to look at mechanisms for reducing the number of new cases that require servicing. Each unwed couple that marries is a child support success story. Each married couple that avoids divorce is a child support success story. Each shared parenting agreement that keeps both parents involved physically and emotionally in the child's life is a child support success story.

Downward adjustment of an unfair order is enforcement. Job training is enforcement. Mediation of access disputes is enforcement. Encouraging family formation is enforcement. Marriage counseling is enforcement. Reducing the need for income transfer and the sense of estrangement after divorce through thoughtfully developed plans for shared parenting is enforcement.

Child support advocates often lobby state legislatures and agencies with arguments that particular actions are required by federal law. While federal law does contain many procedural requirements, the sources of failure and paralysis within the enforcement apparatus are not mandated by federal requirements. In the following paragraphs, a number of innovative programs, some already adopted by one or more states, are described. Information on implementation of each of these programs is available from organizations such as the Children's Rights Council[30] or the Men's Health Network.[31]

1. Parentage Establishment

The typical in-hospital paternity establishment form instructs the father that signing the form will create liability for child support, but that he will have to separately petition the court if he wants visitation or custody of the child. In other words, the father is instructed that signing the form will create burdens and no benefits. Not surprisingly, many fathers refuse to sign the form.

The solution is to utilize in-hospital parentage establishment forms that address both the establishment of custody and child support. While still in the hospital, the unwed mother and father can establish parentage and develop their initial plans for both the physical and financial needs of the child. Such a programme is already in effect in the state of New Hampshire. By protecting the father's interest in access to the child, the willingness to acknowledge paternity and accept the burdens of child support is increased.

2. Administrative Support Modifications

All states have procedures for initiating child support modifications. Many states, however, are in violation of federal law because they will only process upward modifications or requests made by custodial parents. Federal law requires that child support services be made available, without discrimination, to both custodial and non-custodial parents. Section 103 of the Family Support Act of 1988 (PL 100–485) requires states to have procedures for review and adjustment of orders upon the request of either parent.

Some states have refused to provide services to non-custodial parents by contending that they have an attorney–client relationship with the custodial parent. This is not correct. The child support bureaucracy represents the interest of the state in ensuring fair support of the child and does not stand in the position of private attorney to either parent. As the Department of Health and Human Services has explained:

> Our agency has taken the position that the Family Support Act provides that each party to the support order has a right to request a review and, if appropriate, the state agency must adjust/modify the order in accordance with the state's child support guidelines . . . The child support agency does not provide legal services per se and the traditional attorney–client relationship does not exist between the recipient of child support services and the agency attorney handling the case.[32]

The failure or refusal to process requests for downward modifications both violates federal law and creates uncollectible arrearages which adversely affect the state's enforcement performance. By beginning to follow the federal law with respect to downward modifications, the state will improve compliance and reduce enforcement costs.

3. Temporary Suspensions of Support Obligations

Because of the Bradley Amendment, a child support arrearage is unmodifiable even if it is utterly uncollectible because of the obligor's poverty. Accordingly, states have an interest in identifying the circumstances under which child support obligations should be suspended or modified prior to the accrual of an arrearage. If an obligor becomes temporarily disabled or is laid off from his job and has no income for a period, it does no good to pretend that an income exists since any child support accrual will simply become another uncollectible arrearage on the state's books.

Many different solutions are possible. For example, a child support order could specify that child support will cease to accrue upon the happening of certain events such as job loss, disability or incarceration. The simplest solution is to put a 'stop loss' into the order to ensure that obligations do not accrue beyond a sustainable level while avoiding the need for micro-management by the court as follows:

> Mr. Jones shall pay _____ dollars per week child support provided that child support shall not exceed ____ percent of income.

If Mr Jones stops earning the overtime that made the initial award level possible or is temporarily disabled, the above language avoids the need for the parties to return to court, avoids the accumulation of uncollectible arrearages, increases fairness, and simplifies enforcement.

4.   Temporary Assistance to Needy Family (TANF)

The 1996 welfare reform legislation created a revolution that is, as yet, only partially understood. In addition to the well-known provisions for time-limited benefits and work participation, the legislation specified that the block grants could be used to support programmes which advance any one or more of the four following purposes:

a.   provide assistance to needy families so the children may be cared for in their own homes or in the homes of relatives;
b.   end the dependence of needy parents on government benefits by promoting job preparation, work and marriage;
c.   prevent and reduce the incidence of out-of-wedlock pregnancies and establish annual numerical goals for preventing and reducing the incidence of these pregnancies, and
d.   encourage the formation and maintenance of two-parent families.[33]

This revolution cannot be overstated. In the past, the federal government made a devil's bargain with our poorest citizens, offering benefits on the condition that the recipients must neither work nor marry. We then claimed to be surprised when people took us up on the deal. For low-income fathers, we had 'man in the house' rules which made those fathers less than useless by ordering them to stay away upon pain of their children's loss of benefits. The consequence was family disruption and an economic incentive for the separation of low-income parents.

The new law has recognized the anti-family fallacy of prior policies. Rather than drive fathers away, the block grants can now be used for 'promoting marriage' and to 'encourage the formation and maintenance of two-parent families'. The consequences of the new law for child support enforcement are profound. Instead of struggling to collect child support from people who can barely manage to support two marginal households, we can now help those people get together or stay together as a two-parent family. We can provide marriage counselling, we can provide mediation, we can provide parenting training, we can provide conflict resolution assistance, we can provide any service that will help them get together or stay together.

The problem with child support enforcement is that new cases have been coming in through the front door faster than we can process them through the building and out the back door. The new TANF programme allows us, for the first time, to address ourselves to reducing the number of cases that come in through the front door. Every couple that gets together or stays together avoids the need for a paternity establishment, avoids the need for a custody determination, avoids the need for a support determination, and avoids the need for support enforcement. Two-parent households are the best child support enforcement programme because all of the resources of both parents are present and focused on the household where the children reside. We have long known that marriage is the best welfare prevention programme. We must now also act upon the knowledge that two-parent families are the best child support enforcement programme.

5. Demilitarization of Divorce

Congress has long known that child support and visitation are 'inextricably intertwined'. In many cases, one parent is withholding access because support is unpaid and the other parent is withholding support because access is denied. A programme similar to Michigan's Friend of the Court system can deal with and resolve these reciprocal problems on a unified basis. Other court services can reduce the need for child support enforcement. Divorce education classes before the divorce can help parents to understand the impact of the divorce upon their children and help them plan to avoid some of the worst consequences. The use of parenting plans as a step toward the determination of custody helps parents understand the magnitude of the task of rearing children and allocate the tasks reasonably between themselves. Mediation and alternate dispute resolution can avoid the need for judicial intervention.

6. Child Dependent Tax Exemption

In the absence of a court order to the contrary, the child dependent tax exemption is allocated to the custodial parent. Since the custodial parent most often has the lower taxable income and the lower tax bracket, this is a wasteful allocation of the exemption which unnecessarily increases the combined taxes of the family and reduces the overall funds available for child support and other living expenses. Each state should have legislation or a statewide judicial procedure specifying that the child dependent tax exemption must be addressed in domestic relations orders and allocated to the parent who provides more than 50 per cent of the support.

Similarly, state law should provide that domestic relations orders will allocate the child tax credit and the childcare tax credit to the parent providing more than 50 percent of the support or childcare expense.

7. Employment Reporting

Each state is required by federal law to compel new-hire reporting by employers. New-hire reporting, however, only tells half the story and leads to erroneous child support collection databases. State law should require reporting of terminations of employment as well, for at least two reasons:

a.   Failure to report terminations results in child support database information showing multiple employments and creates confusion about available income which leads to erroneous administrative actions.
b.   Reporting of termination of employment provides important corroboration in cases where a downward modification is sought by an obligor.

8. *Pro Se* Procedures

The great bulk of all domestic relations litigants and virtually all low-income litigants lack representation by counsel. Every court system should have *pro se* procedures written in language that is understandable to the educational level of typical litigants. To be effective, *pro se* procedures must be gender-neutral and avoid presumptions about the outcomes that are available to litigants. For example, some older forms still in use assume that the mother will be the custodian or assume that sole custody will be utilized even though more recent legislation has created an option or even a presumption of joint custody.

9. Proof of Custody

Prior to the entry of a court order restricting custody, each child is in the joint custody of both parents under the law of most states. In joint custody, each parent is entitled to unlimited, unrestricted access to the child and neither parent can have a support obligation to the other. Nevertheless, some states are imposing 'temporary' child support orders prior to a determination of 'temporary' custody. This is, of course, a *non sequitur*. There cannot logically be an order to support a custodial household until there has been a determination of which household is the custodial household. State law or statewide judicial procedure should provide that the first issue to be addressed and resolved in any domestic relations proceeding involving children is the determination of temporary custody.

10. Due Process

In a typical child support proceeding, the custodial parent is represented by a government-provided attorney while the non-custodian appears *pro se* or does not appear at all. Default judgments and judgments entered against unrepresented individuals are sources of tremendous error and create uncollectible arrearages from low-income obligors. Service of process 'at the last known address' results in tens of thousands of men who accrue years of unmodifiable arrearages before they even learn that they have been named as fathers.[34] Many of these men, in fact, are not fathers, as is established through subsequent DNA testing, but most states allow the default judgment to stand and even victims of wilful paternity fraud get no relief.

State law should provide that default paternity and child support orders are interim or contingent orders that shall not be entered as unmodifiable final orders until the court receives proof that the obligor has received actual service and an opportunity to appear. Most particularly, the courts need to aggressively punish the practice of 'sewer service' in which the process is discarded and a false declaration is filed. Similarly, paternity fraud should never be condoned by the court. If, at any time, it is learned that a fraud upon the court has been committed through a false paternity identification, the victim must be freed and the perpetrator punished. It is never in the 'best interests of the child' to knowingly enslave one human being for the benefit of another. A child has a right to support from his parents but not from an innocent bystander. The wrongly convicted must be freed.

The monumental consequences of child support establishment and enforcement require the assistance of counsel, at least, at the sanctions stage. Recently, the ACLU has begun to notice that child support obligors are being rounded up and jailed without access to counsel and often without a hearing.[35]

CHILD SUPPORT GUIDELINE REFORM

There are two fundamental principles that must necessarily be the foundation of any fair establishment of child support:

- the marginal cost of a child's presence in the household; and
- the after-tax income of the obligor.

The marginal cost of the child's presence in the household is simply a way of asking what expenses are added to a household by the addition of a child. A single adult may have the need for a one-bedroom apartment. Adding a child may create the need for a second bedroom (marginal or incremental cost) but does not create the need for a second apartment (per capita cost). Marginal cost is important not only because it is the only rational starting point for assessing the needs of the child but also because it is the only substantive requirement imposed by the federal government upon the states in the development of their guidelines. Federal law provides:

> (h) As part of the review of a state's guidelines required under paragraph (e) of this section [every four years], a State must consider economic data on the costs of raising children.[36]

Although the concept of marginal cost is well understood and is broadly given lip service, there is no current guideline in the United States which fully implements a marginal cost analysis. In the first phase of child support guideline development, certain gaps in data existed which made it difficult to compute marginal cost for some elements of child support. Accordingly, the economic assumptions in each child support guideline are a melange of marginal cost, per capita cost, and 'intact family patterns of expenditure' factors. For example, in many guidelines, the cost of transportation is calculated on a per capita basis. That is, in a single parent, two-child household, two-thirds of the cost of the family car is attributed to the children. Everyone knows that this is not true. The single parent would need a car in the absence of the children and the presence of the children merely increases the usage of the car (marginal cost) beyond the adult's personal use. The use of per capita cost where marginal cost is clearly required distorts child support guidelines.

Some proposed guidelines utilize data provided by the United States Department of Agriculture in a publication entitled *Expenditures on Children by Families* issued annually and authored by Mark Lino of the US Department of Agriculture, Center for Nutrition Policy and Promotion. On its face, however, this report explains why it should not be used for child support guideline development:

> U.S.D.A. uses the per capita method in allocating these [housing, transportation, and other miscellaneous goods and services] expenses; the per capita method allocates expenses among household members in equal proportions. A

marginal cost method, which assumes that expenditures on children may be measured as the difference in total expenses between couples with children and equivalent childless couples, was not used.[37]

'Intact family patterns of expenditure' factors also distort child support guidelines. These factors purport to measure the portion of intact family income that was spent on certain activities before the divorce, in order to require a similar level of spending after divorce. The obvious flaw in these intact family patterns of expenditure factors is that the divorced family no longer has the economies of scale found in the intact family and must now support two separate households rather than one. A finding that the average intact family has certain patterns of expenditure is meaningless to divorced parents who have to devote the bulk of their resources simply to maintaining two separate households. Only by looking at marginal cost can a rational guideline be developed. We need to know – what does it reasonably cost Mom during the time the children are with her and what does it reasonably cost Dad during the time the children are with him? The sum of these two figures represents the needs of the children and can be fairly apportioned between Mom and Dad.

The US Department of Health and Human Services has presented a model marginal cost child support guideline in its publication *Child Support Guidelines: The Next Generation*, edited by Margaret Campbell Haynes. In addition to utilizing marginal cost, the model guideline clearly discloses all assumptions to eliminate the 'black box' effect found in many guidelines, acknowledges and measures the costs incurred by both parents, and avoids the 'cliff effect' of large swings in child support at certain thresholds of extended visitation. The guideline is authored by Donald J. Bieniewicz, co-author of Chapter 3.[38]

The second indispensable element for development of a fair child support guideline is the use of after-tax income. The United States tax code and the tax codes of the various states contain numerous provisions which substantially alter tax liability and after-tax income on the basis of the number of children, childcare and custodial arrangements. Among these are the head of household tax rates, the dependency exemption, the child tax credit, and the childcare credit. Collectively, these tax effects can make a difference of many thousands of dollars in after-tax income. Most fundamentally, it is necessary to use after-tax income because it is after-tax income that determines how much money people actually have available to meet their living expenses.

Child support guidelines based on pre-tax income create numerous distortions and inequities among people of similar gross incomes. For example, among obligors with $30000 of gross income, some are self-employed, others are corporate employees. The self-employed must pay combined FICA and Medicare taxes of 15.3 per cent and have less income available to pay child support than the corporate employees who pay only 7.65 per cent combined FICA and Medicare.[39] Similarly, taxpayers with equal gross incomes differ substantially in the availability of deductions, credits and other adjustments which significantly affect tax liability and after-tax income.

Advocates of a gross income approach argue that net income is too complicated and too subject to manipulation. This can hardly be true since taxpayers must file tax returns annually under penalty of perjury. Further, both gross income and net income child support guidelines must make assumptions about future income from a review of data on past income. In gross income models, the last payslip stub is used. In net income models, the last tax return is used. Use of net income is not more difficult, it is just more fair.

In addition to the importance of marginal cost analysis and utilization of after-tax income, there are a number of other considerations to guideline development including the following.

1.   Avoidance of Hidden Assumptions

Many guidelines are presented as an obligation for the payment of a certain percentage of income by the obligor. The model by which the percentage was developed and the economic assumptions that went into the model are undisclosed. The result is that a guideline which on its face purports to be rebuttable becomes irrebuttable because neither parent can explain to the court the ways in which their particular circumstances differ from the undisclosed model. As the court wrote in striking down the original District of Columbia guideline:

> Since the guideline is presumptively fair, any party opposing its application would have a higher burden of proof than it might have without the guideline. . . . The guideline report offers no economic basis for the Child Support Guideline Committee's determinations. Consequently, the party trying to argue against application of the Guideline faces a monumental obstacle in attempting to demonstrate a case is 'exceptional' without knowing what 'unexceptional' is. The existence of the Guideline alone has coercive power through the rigidity of its calculations and the ease of its application. Rather than deciding each case individually, decision-makers may be tempted to plug in numbers that explain themselves without making further findings.[40]

The model guideline published by the US Department of Health and Human Services avoids this flaw.

2. Costs Incurred by Both Parents

The first generation of child support guidelines, currently in effect in most states, made a simplifying but highly distorting assumption. The assumption was that 100 per cent of all child-related expenses were incurred by the custodial household and that all income needed to support the child should be transferred to that household. Even in cases of minimal visitation, this assumption is obviously untrue and becomes increasingly untrue with the growing trend toward extended visitation which approaches joint custody. Robert G. Williams, President of Policy Studies, Inc., is acknowledged as the father of child support guidelines. As a consultant to most of the first-generation state guidelines, Dr Williams developed and implemented the income shares and percentage-of-income methodologies utilized around the country. In response to an inquiry about the extent to which visitation expenses had been incorporated into the Virginia guideline and others, Dr Williams wrote:

> The answer to this question is 'none.' To my knowledge, there are no data that would allow us to include in the schedule of support obligations an adjustment for visitation costs. Our review of other states' guidelines indicates that most states have not made adjustments for what might be considered normal visitation.[41]

While certain costs are more heavily incurred in one household (for example, payment of school fees or other fees), other costs tend to be proportional with the time spent in each household (for example, meals). Some costs tend to be 'lumpy' (for example, although overnights may be split 75:25, both households need to provide a bedroom). Finally, some costs are incurred primarily by the non-custodial parent (for example, transportation between residences). A rational guideline must consider the expenses of both parents.

The model guideline published by the Department of Health and Human Services does contain a mechanism for crediting the costs incurred by both parents.

3. Avoidance of Primogeniture

Some guidelines discriminate against subsequent children. Sometimes known as the 'second family problem', these guidelines penalize second-family children. These guidelines specify that a child support obligation must be calculated as if the subsequent children did not exist and then relegate these children to whatever dregs are left of the non-custodial parent's income. There is no moral basis to this discrimination and the state has no interest in disadvantaging one group of children in relation to their half-siblings. The proper resolution is to determine the total number of children to be supported in all families, find the guideline amount for that number of children, and distribute the child support to the households being supported based on the number of children supported in each household. Recently, two Tennessee appellate courts have held that the primogeniture risk in that state's guideline was an unconstitutional violation of the subsequent children's right to equal protection.[42] The issue is now on appeal to the Tennessee Supreme Court.

4.   Anti-Joint Custody Bias

Some guidelines were written with an eye toward discouraging the utilization of joint custody. In these guidelines, an arbitrary factor (such as 150 per cent) is imposed to increase the child support obligation and discourage joint custody. There is no economic basis for this surtax.

Every custody order appears on a continuum in which the child's time is divided between two households. Usually, the range is between 75/25 (standard visitation) and 50/50 (equal joint physical custody). At any point in the range between 75/25 and 50/50, both households are incurring expenses on behalf of the children. Many of these expenses are duplicative such as the need to provide space, clothes, toys and so on in both houses. There is no point on the continuum at which a substantial joint custody surtax can logically be imposed. The rational course is to determine the point on the continuum occupied by the particular couple, determine the expenses incurred in each household, find the sum of the expenses in the two households and establish a child support amount that allocates obligation for the expenses between the two parents. The model child support guideline published by the Department of Health and Human Services avoids the 'cliff effect' or joint custody penalty which appears in many first-generation guidelines.

PROFESSOR BLUMBERG'S PROJECT FOR THE AMERICAN LAW INSTITUTE

Grace Blumberg, under commission from the American Law Institute, has developed another version of a model guideline. While Prof. Blumberg has identified and attempted to correct some of the flaws in existing guidelines, her document is largely a backward-looking recapitulation of old practices that should have little impact.

On the positive side, Blumberg's model correctly recognizes the need to utilize net income as the starting point for child support calculations because, as we all know, families must live upon their after-tax income, not their pre-tax income. Use of after-tax (net) income eliminates many of the distortions and absurdities which have crept into the existing child support guidelines of some states.

Further, the Blumberg model correctly states that child support should involve a calculation of the marginal expenditures resulting from the presence of the child in a household. This is basic economics. An adult has certain expenses in maintaining a household. Adding a child to that household adds certain new expenses. These 'marginal expenditures' caused by the addition of a child are the proper subject of a child support guideline. The use of per capita expenditures creates an artificial transfer of costs from the adult to the child and thereby creates a disguised alimony which is utterly inappropriate as a matter of child support enforcement.

While the Blumberg model recognizes the centrality of marginal cost, Blumberg does not know when to stop. Under the Blumberg model, a rule-maker is supposed to calculate a 'base' child support obligation and then add a 'supplement' obligation (Section 3.05). As defined, however, the 'base' obligation represents the full marginal cost. That is, the 'base' calculation asks the rule-maker to assume that the two households have equal pre-transfer incomes (that is, equal standards of living without children) and then to make a transfer to the residential household sufficient to maintain equal standards of living after the addition of the child to that household (marginal cost). This is a cumbersome way of calculating marginal cost but, if the Blumberg draft had stopped here, there would be no substantive problem because the marginal costs of placing the child into the custodial house would have been fully accounted for. As Blumberg herself explains:

> Readers familiar with the concept of marginal child expenditure may wish to use it in lieu of the *base*, as defined by these Principles. They are substantially equivalent measures.[43]

The 'base' or 'marginal cost' fully captures the costs associated with placing the child into one of the households. The problem is that Blumberg then proceeds to seek a 'supplement' to raise the standard of living of the custodial parent. All of this supplement is disguised alimony. If the custodial parent is entitled to an enhanced standard of living, it is properly treated in the court's handling of alimony issues. There should not be a concealed alimony component built into the child support guideline.

As for the rest, the Blumberg model largely copies from the District of Columbia Child Support Guideline. The ill wisdom of that approach can be seen in the fact that, since the 1988 adoption of this model by the District of Columbia and Massachusetts, no other state has moved in this direction.

The District of Columbia Guideline was full of bad ideas ten years ago and a new dust cover makes it no better now.[44]

The schizophrenia inherent in the ALI project is unavoidably transparent when the various chapters of the overall project are seen together. Ira Ellman was commissioned to write a chapter on alimony. Grace Blumberg was commissioned to write a chapter on child support in which she seeks a disguised alimony 'supplement' because having access to more money is in the best interests of children. Kate Bartlett was commissioned to write a chapter on child custody in which she forbids the fact-finder from considering the parents' income during the determination of the child's best interests. Collectively, these proposed rules mean that the court cannot consider income to determine the child's best interests (custody) but, subsequently, must transfer income to advance the child's best interests (child support).

Unintentionally, Blumberg provides a powerful treatise in support of the case for shared custody and father custody. Page after page argues for the centrality of more money in the best interests of the children. Blumberg argues that it was a mistake to bifurcate the issues of custody and support. A simple return to the historical rule that each parent has the obligation to support his or her child in his or her own home would eliminate the considerable attention directed to how to make one household bear the costs of elevating a different household.

As stated by Eloise Anderson, former Director of California's Department of Social Services:

> Child support issues probably need to be rethought in light of more than just middle-class women and their children . . . What is it that we expect out of fathers vs. mothers? We say fatherhood is a check and that men are not expected to nurture their children. Surely we won't let him have custody of his child . . . The woman, we base her value to the family on nurturing, not financial responsibility . . . . Therefore he bears all the financial burden. I think that is an unfair policy, which means that we have to rethink custody. *If a father has a lot of resources and mom has very few resources, and we want the child to continue to live in the comfort the father provided, maybe the father ought to have custody.* [emphasis added][45]

CUSTODY REFORM

Gender bias in custody determinations is slowly dying but acceleration of the movement for custody reform has implications for child support enforcement. Federal data show that child support compliance is 90.2 per cent in cases of joint custody, 79.1 per cent in cases where visitation is protected, and 44.6 per cent in cases with neither joint custody nor protection of visitation.[46] This data confirms the intuitive point that parents increase their support of children as they are permitted to be involved with them. Joint custody both increases willingness to pay and decreases the amount of income that needs to be transferred because a substantial portion of the child's needs will be provided in each of the joint custodial homes. It requires no great insight to understand that parents more willingly spend to support children in their own home than to support them in someone else's home.

Beyond joint custody, if the goal of child support policy is improved well-being for children, we must join Eloise Anderson in a serious reconsideration of the value of father custody. The world is changing; we are starting to recognize that fathers are more than the sum of their paycheques.

THE NEED FOR RESEARCH

Everyone is familiar with the Census Bureau figures on child support non-compliance, but no one has investigated the reasons for the non-compliance. How many of these obligors are unemployed, disabled, supporting second families, engaged in civil disobedience because they have been denied access to their children, imprisoned, or even dead? Incredibly, all of these categories, even the dead (the ultimate 'deadbeats'), were lumped together as 'non-compliant' by the Census Bureau. This occurred despite the fact that other government data showed that 66 per cent of custodial mothers reported the reason for non-compliance as 'father unable to pay'.[47]

The Fragile Families Coalition coordinated by the Ford Foundation estimates that there are over 3 million non-custodial fathers who are eligible for food stamps. If these obligors are so poor that they need assistance simply to put food on the table for themselves, it is unfair to characterize them as 'deadbeats' when we find that they do not have resources to transfer to another household. We need more research on the real-world consequences of child support guidelines. We know that, at lower income levels, existing child support guidelines create unsustainable burdens. We also know that, at higher income levels, existing child support guidelines create disguised alimony. We know that there is gender bias in custody determinations. Until there has been a fair establishment of child custody, visitation and the level of the support obligation, there is no moral authority for enforcement of the support obligation.

CONCLUSION

Child support reform is needed but that reform must recognize obligors as citizens and as parents, not as anonymous beasts to be herded more efficiently. We know that the three best predictors of child support compliance are: (1) the fairness of the order; (2) the obligor's access to the child; and (3) the obligor's work stability. Improvement in child support compliance must be addressed to these factors and not to old myths and stereotypes.

NOTES

1. United States Department of Health and Human Services (1999, 2000).
2. Robbins (1986).
3. www.cse.dhr.state.ga.us/mostwanted/wmain.asp.
4. dfsweb.state.wy.us/csehome/wywantez.
5. www.law.state.ky.us/childsupport/wanted.
6. Virginia Department of Social Services (1991) p. 4.
7. Parker (1999).
8. Ibid.
9. Valentine (1997).
10. Walker (2002).
11. Hughes (1998).
12. Ibid.
13. US Department of Health and Human Services (1991) p. 6.
14. General Accounting Office (1992), p. 19.
15. Folk (1992).
16. Rivers (1992).
17. Former Deputy District Attorney Elisa Baker, quoted in Riccardi and Krikorian (1998).
18. Twenty-five per cent of gross income is used as an average child support guideline amount for two children. In my part of the country, the guidelines are all somewhat higher – 30.4 per cent in Virginia (4A Va. Code Annot. '20-108.2 (Michie 1998 Supp.)); 30.7 per cent in Maryland (Md. Code Annot., Family Law '12-204 (Michie 1999); 26, 28.6 or 29.9 per cent in the District of Columbia depending upon the ages of the children (5 D.C. Code Annot. '16-916.1 (Michie 1998 Supp.))
19. Wheaton and Sorensen (1998).
20. Cohn (1998). The population has risen from 1.7 million single fathers in 1995 to 2.1 million single fathers in 1998 compared to 9.8 single mothers in 1998.
21. Note that the roles are sometimes reversed. When mothers are ordered to pay child support, their compliance rate is lower than that of fathers. See, for example, Office of Child Support Recovery, State of Georgia (1991), Meyer and Garasky (1991).
22. Bureau of the Census (1991), 7. These figures have held relatively constant over time. Bureau of the Census (1995) found 85 per cent compliance in joint custody cases, 79 per cent compliance where visitation was protected, and 56 per cent compliance where neither joint custody nor visitation was protected.
23. See, for example, Abraham (1989); Jacob (1989); McIssac (1986); Faludi (1991).
24. Associated Press (1996).
25. Melton (1998).
26. Breed (1998).
27. Harris (1998).
28. Riccardi and Krikorian (1998). The multi-part series in the *Los Angeles Times* goes on to describe an enforcement bureaucracy that 'uses hardball legal tactics and has imposed insurmountable financial burdens on fathers, many of whom are poor and unable to hire attorneys to seek judicial redress'.
29. Booker (1999).

30. The Children's Rights Council may be reached at:

    Children's Rights Council
    6200 Editors Park Drive
    Suite 103
    Hyattsville, MD 20782
    Telephone (301) 559–3120

31. The Men's Health Network may be reached at:

    Men's Health Network
    316 F Street, N.E.
    Suite 200
    Washington, DC 20002
    Telephone (202) 543–6461

32. Letter from Leon R. McCowan, Regional Administrator, Department of Health and Human Services, to Hon. Richard Armey, United States House of Representatives (20 February 1992).
33. Personal Responsibility and Work Opportunity Reconciliation Act of 1996, Section 401(a), 8 U.S.C.A. 1611 (1998 West Supp.).
34. The *Los Angeles Times* reports that 53 per cent of the cases in Los Angeles County do not provide personal service and that 70 per cent of non-custodial parents are not present in court when their child support obligation is set (Riccardi and Krikorien, 1998).
35. Associated Press (2002).
36. 45 C.F.R. '302.56(h).
37. United States Department of Agriculture (1995).
38. The guideline is available from:

    United States Department of Health and Human Services Administration for Children and Families
    Office of Child Support Enforcement and National Training Center
    Mail Stop 0CSC/TC
    370 L'Enfant Promenade, S.W.
    Washington, DC 20447
    Telephone (202) 401–9383
    (or from Mr Bieniewicz directly at (703) 255–0837)

39. Under federal income tax law, the other half of FICA and Medicare (7.65 per cent) is paid by the employer without reduction of the employee's gross income.
40. *Fitzgerald v. Fitzgerald*, 566 A.2d 719, 731 (D.C. App. 1989).
41. Letter from Robert G. Williams, PhD, President, Policy Studies, Inc., to Paul M. Robinson, Virginia Child Support Study Commission, 28 August 1992.
42. Mansfield (2002).
43. Blumberg (2000).
44. When the District of Columbia model was adopted by court rule, it was overturned by the court of highest jurisdiction. *Fitzgerald v. Fitzgerald*, 566 A.2d 719 (D.C. App. 1989). When the bulk of the guideline was readopted by legislation the following year, it could not be deemed unconstitutional, but the flaws remained. The mere fact that the Constitution does not prohibit a particular approach does not make that approach a good idea.
45. Lynch (1997).
46. See note 24.
47. See note 16.

REFERENCES

Abraham, Jed H. (1989), *The Divorce Revolution Revisited: A Counter-Revolutionary Critique*, 9 N. Ill. Rev. 251.

Associated Press (1996), 'Study goofed on gap in post-divorce standard of living', *Manchester Union*, 17 May.

Associated Press (2002), 'ACLU challenges Lawrence County jailings', *Pittsburgh Post-Gazette*, 6 September.

Blumberg, Grace (2000), *Principles of the Law of Family Dissolution: Analysis and Recommendations*, Section 3.05, Comment D, 16 May, American Law Institute.

Booker, William J. (1999), 'State charges former staffer in $700000 fraud case', *Indianapolis Star*, 28 January.

Breed, Allen G. (1998), 'Woman uses homemade software to take on state's system and wins', Associated Press, 2 May.

Bureau of the Census (1991), 'Child support and alimony: 1989', *Current Population Reports*, Series P-60, No. 173, September.

Bureau of the Census (1995), 'Child support for custodial mothers and fathers', *Current Population Reports*, Consumer Income, Series P60, No. 187, August.

Bureau of the Census (various), *Current Population Reports*.

Cohn, D'Vera (1998), 'Single father household on rise', *Washington Post*, 11 December.

Downey-Hyde Child Support Enforcement and Assurance Proposal: Hearing before the Human Resources Subcommittee, Committee on Ways and Means, United House of Representatives, 102 Cong. 126 (1992) (Statement of Sylvia D. Folk).

Faludi, Susan (1991), 'Don't be happy, worry', *Washington Post Magazine*, 20 October.

Fitzgerald v. Fitzgerald, 566 A.2d 719, 731 (D.C. App. 1989).

General Accounting Office (1992), 'Interstate child support: mothers report receiving less support from out-of-state fathers', January, GAO/HRD-92-39FS.

Harris, Hamil R. (1998), 'Parents fighting bugs in DC support', *Washington Post*, 18 July.

Hughes, Polly Ross (1998), 'Many dads who don't pay child support are destitute', *Houston Chronicle*, 18 December.

Jacob, Herbert (1989), 'Another look at no-fault divorce and the post-divorce finances of women', *Law and Society Review*, **23** (1).

Lynch, Michael W. (1997), 'Hints from Eloise', *Reason*, June.

Mansfield, Duncan (2002), 'Guide to figure child support is ruled unconstitutional', *Tennessean*, 10 August.

McCowan, Leon R., Regional Administrator, Department of Health and Human Services (2002), Letter to Hon. Richard Armey, United States House of Representatives, 20 February.

McIssac, Hugh (1986), 'The divorce revolution by Lenore Weitzman', *Transitions*, July.

Melton, R.H. (1998), 'Va. falsely threatens 2300 in mistakes on child support', *Washington Post*, 29 January.

Meyer, Danielle R. and Garasky, Steven (1991), 'Custodial fathers: myths, realities and child support policy', *Technical Analysis Paper*, no. 42, Office of Human services Policy, Office of the Assistant Secretary for Planning and Evaluation, US Department of Health and Human Services, July.

Newark Star Ledger, New Jersey (2002), 6 September.

Office of Child Support Recovery, State of Georgia (1991), *Statistics of Child Support Compliance*.

Parker, Kathleen (1999), 'Deadbeat Dads more myth than reality', *Orlando Sentinel*, 24 January; www.orlandosentinel.com/features/0124park.

Personal Responsibility and Work Opportunity Reconciliation Act of 1996, Section 401(a), 8 U.S.C.A. 1611 (1998 West Supp.).

Pittsburgh Post-Gazette (2002), 'ACLU challenges, Lawrence County jailings', 6 September.

Riccardi, Nicholas and Greg Krikorian (1998), 'LA county, state, both get blame', *Los Angeles Times*, 11 October.

Rivers, L. Mendel, Jr (1992), 'The magic fountain', *Post and Courier*, Charleston, SC, 27 June.

Robbins, Philip K. (1986), 'Child support, welfare dependency and poverty', *American Economic Review*, **76**, September, 768–88.

US Department of Agriculture (1995), *Expenditures on Children by Families*, Annual Report, Executive Summary, Misc. Pub. No. 1528–1995.

US Department of Health and Human Services (1991), 'Charge it please', *Child Support Report*.

US Department of Health and Human Services (1999, 2000), Administration for Children and Families, Office of Child Support Enforcement, Amended Statistical Report for Fiscal Years 1999 and 2000 Financial Overview 1999 and 2000.

Valentine, Paul (1997), 'Md. cleans up on child support', *The Washington Times*, 9 June.

Virginia Department of Social Services (1991), Division of Child Support Enforcement, 'Previous most wanted lists yield results', *The Support Report*, October.

Weitzman, Lenore (1985), *The Divorce Revolution: The Unexpected Social and Economic Consequences For Women and Children in America*, New York: The Free Press.

Wheaton, Laura and Elaine Sorensen (1998), *Tax Relief for Low-Income Fathers who Pay Child Support*, The Urban Institute, January.

Williams, Robert G., Ph.D., President, Policy Studies, Inc. (1992), Letter to Paul M. Robinson, Virginia Child Support Study Commission, 28 August.

6. Hopelessly defective: an examination of the assumptions underlying current child support guidelines

Robert A. McNeely and Cynthia A. McNeely

No one meant for it to turn out this way. When the US Congress in 1984 required states to create child support guidelines, the goals were reasonably laudable: to increase the adequacy, consistency and predictability of child support awards that had previously developed into a patchwork of inconsistent awards under the common law; to make administration of child support cases easier; and to increase compliance through 'perceived fairness' of these awards.[1] Nineteen years later, the system is a mess: a massive child support industrial complex has developed,[2] countless numbers of parents – almost exclusively fathers – have been jailed for non-payment, and there is no evidence that outcomes for children have improved. A 1996 survey of Florida judges, hearing officers and special masters that heard child support cases found that one half of those charged with ordering guideline child support thought the guidelines were unfair.[3] Of that half, 79 per cent felt the guidelines treated non-custodial parents unfairly.[4]

How did this happen? This chapter seeks to answer that question by examining the principles and assumptions that guided the creation of child support guidelines. Some principles were expressly stated when the guidelines were created; these will be examined for their success or failure. Others, however, became apparent only after the guidelines were implemented.

Ultimately, however, the conclusion is inescapable: the child support guidelines suffer from irreparably weak foundations. If the constant litigation, legislation and incarceration related to child support is to ever have any hope of ending, if the nation's children with unmarried parents residing in separate households are to ever have any hope of thriving, then the process of creating child support awards must be rebuilt. A new model is needed.

There are two caveats to this chapter. First, we do not propose solutions or new models; instead, we examine and critique the policies and assumptions upon which the current guidelines rest. Our goal is to create a consensus in America that the current child support guidelines are so defective that they must be scrapped and recreated. The first step in this effort is to acknowledge the existing problems.

Second, we do not advocate either higher or lower child support awards. We advocate fairness. The higher goal of 'perceived fairness' has never been achieved. We believe American citizens follow laws they perceive to be fair and with which they have the ability to comply. In many cases, child support laws are not perceived to be fair, and bear little relationship to an obligor's ability to comply. At other times, child support guidelines are perceived to let irresponsible but well-to-do parents escape with paying far less than they could afford to help raise their children. Neither conclusion implies, however, that guidelines should result *ipso facto* in lower or higher child support awards.

A new analysis is required but one that is not results-oriented. For too long, child support guidelines have been fuelled by results-oriented analyses seeking higher or lower awards, as the following story demonstrates. Instead, we believe child support guidelines must be developed, determined, applied and enforced in a way that not only is fair, but that the public will accurately perceive to be fair. When parents who find themselves in the child support system believe they are in a system that is fair, we believe litigation will decrease, family conflict will decrease, collections will increase and, most importantly, children will thrive.

A WEIRD SCENE FROM INSIDE THE GOLD MINE

In April 2000, the House Committee on Family Law and Children of the Florida state legislature was meeting. The committee was considering amendments to Florida's child support guidelines schedule, which determines presumptive awards of child support.[5] Committee staff explained that the bill before the committee updated the guidelines schedule for the first time since 1993. The staff advised, 'The proposed table is based on more current economic research and more recent economic data on household expenditures than the existing schedule. *These changes are designed to make the guidelines more equitable and more consistent with economic changes that have occurred since the existing schedule was developed.*'[6] In other words, the existing schedule which governed all child support awards in Florida was using outdated economic research and old economic data, was inequitable, and had failed to recognize economic changes in the intervening seven years.

The committee members, Democrats and Republicans, listened to staff and reviewed the new, more accurate table. A committee member asked staff about the ultimate impact of the new table: would child support awards go up, down, or stay the same? They would go down, staff replied, almost across the board, because the data used to support the 1993 schedule was flawed and outdated. With this information, the committee acted with swift and unanimous resolve. Its members promptly amended the bill to delete the new, more accurate guidelines schedule and replaced it with the existing, outdated, flawed schedule. Their world existed in black and white: higher guidelines were good, lower guidelines were bad.

FIRST INTERLUDE: A BRIEF HISTORY OF THE DEVELOPMENT OF CHILD SUPPORT GUIDELINES

Prior to congressional involvement, child support awards varied in the discretion of the trial judge.[7] Generally, courts considered the obligor's ability to pay child support and the child's needs.[8] Faced with inconsistent orders that generally seemed inadequate, Congress passed in 1974 the Family Support Act, Title IV-D of the Social Security Act.[9] The Act required states to establish and enforce child support obligations.[10]

In 1984, Congress approved the Child Support Enforcement Amendments of 1984.[11] These amendments required states 'to establish numeric guidelines to determine appropriate amounts of child support' by 1 October 1987.[12] The application of the guidelines, however, remained discretionary.[13] In 1988, Congress required the states' guidelines to be rebuttably presumptive.[14]

SECOND INTERLUDE: GIVING CAESAR HIS DUE

The current child support guidelines are, by and large, the offspring of Robert G. Williams. Dr Williams, the author of an influential advisory report to Congress, is, for all intents and purposes, the Father of Child Support Guidelines in the United States. In 1983, Dr Williams consulted with the Department of Health and Human Services Office of Child Support Enforcement, and for the next seven years directed research and technical assistance for the federally funded Child Support Guidelines Project. In 1984, Dr Williams created a private company to handle and coordinate this new child support consulting work, Policy Studies, Inc., of Boulder, Colorado. In 1987, through his work on the Advisory Panel, Dr Williams led the charge to create the Income Shares model of child support guidelines, used in 34 states. Dr. Williams and PSI have consulted with most if not all of those states throughout their child support process.

The application of the Income Shares model led to the establishment of child support awards significantly beyond an obligor's ability to pay. As a survey of Florida judges, hearing officers, and special masters indicated, the application of the Income Shares model has led to support awards that are unfairly high.[15] One result is that many awards were not paid. In 1991, moreover, PSI was awarded the first federal contract for private child support collection. Thus, Dr Williams and PSI financially benefited from the breakdown of the very system they helped create. He created a formula that guaranteed substantial non-compliance, and then founded a business to earn money by pursuing non-compliant obligors.

When PSI was created in 1984, it had three employees. In mid-1997, PSI boasted 500 employees and revenues exceeding $21 million. In 2002, the company described itself on its website as a '$93 million company'. In April 2002, the *Denver Business Journal* named PSI 'the ninth fastest growing large private company in Colorado based on revenue growth over the past three years'. The *Journal* also noted the company, for the first time, ranked among the largest 25 Colorado companies based on revenue volume.[16]

THE STATED PRINCIPLES UNDERLYING THE GUIDELINES

The advisory panel created by the 1984 legislation delineated eight principles for states to follow in creating their guidelines:

1. Both parents should share legal responsibility for support of their children, with the economic responsibility divided between the parents in proportion to their income.
2. The subsistence needs of each parent should be taken into consideration in setting child support, but in virtually no event should the child support obligation be set at zero.
3. Child support must cover a child's basic needs as a first priority, but, to the extent either parent enjoys a higher than subsistence-level standard of living, the child is entitled to share in the benefit of that improved standard.
4. Each child of a given parent has an equal right to share in that parent's income, subject to factors such as age of the child, income of the parent, income of a current spouse and the presence of other dependents.
5. Each child is entitled to determination of support without respect to the marital status of the parents at the time of the child's birth. Consequently, the guidelines should be used equally in cases of paternity, separation and divorce.
6. Application of the guidelines should be sexually non-discriminatory.

7. A guideline should not create extraneous negative effects on the major life decisions of either parent. In particular, the guidelines should avoid creating economic disincentives for remarriage or labour force participation.
8. A guideline should encourage the involvement of both parents in the child's upbringing. A guideline should take into consideration the financial support provided by parents in shared physical custody and extended visitation arrangements.[17]

For the most part, the states adopted the Advisory Panel's principles. For example, in Florida, seven of the eight principles were offered to guide the work of a Child Support Study Commission charged with making recommendations for Florida's new guidelines, and the one that was not shortly found its way into statute.[18]

The foregoing principles have often been lost in contemporary debates and discussions about child support. We believe, however, that any meaningful discussion of child support reform must begin with an examination and re-evaluation of the founding principles. Before examining them in detail, it is necessary to review how those principles ultimately looked when the guidelines were actually created.

THE ECONOMIC FOUNDATION AND ASSUMPTIONS UNDERLYING CHILD SUPPORT GUIDELINES

1. From Espenshade to Asking the Wrong Question

In 1973, Thomas J. Espenshade, a senior research assistant in the Women and Family Policy Program at the Urban Institute, published the results of a study intended to provide 'reliable estimates of the costs parents face in raising their children'.[19] Although not intended as such, Espenshade's research would form the economic basis for child support guidelines.

One reason these 'reliable estimates' were needed was to assist courts setting child support awards and to provide them with 'a valid basis on which to make those decisions'.[20] Examining data collected from intact families in the urban United States by the US Bureau of Labor Statistics in 1960–61, Espenshade reached several conclusions relevant to the creation of child support guidelines a decade and a half later: (1) expenditures on children increase as family income increases; (2) the first child in a family is likely to be more expensive than subsequent children (perhaps twice as expensive as a second child); and (3) costs increase with the age of the child, with a child age 12 to 17 costing approximately three times as much as an infant to a five-year-old.[21]

Importantly, although the impetus for the study was to provide 'reliable estimates' of the costs of raising a child, Espenshade's study, and a subsequent study in 1984, distinguished between 'cost' and 'expenditure'.[22] Accordingly, by 1984, Espenshade announced his research was 'estimating parental *expenditures* on children, not the cost of raising them'.[23] This point bears repeating: the economic assumptions underlying the development of child support guidelines expressly disregarded the costs of raising a child and did not attempt to determine what fair, objective or appropriate costs were. Instead, they focused on intact families' reports of what they spent on their kids. Accordingly, the development of the guidelines was skewed from its inception toward answering the question, 'What should be spent on children?' This skewed beginning led to the complete disregard of two fundamentally critical questions that should have guided the creation of child support guidelines: (1) 'What do children of unmarried parents need, financially, from their parents?' and (2) 'What are the limits of the state's interest in ensuring that need is met by parents?'

Moreover, by relying on data only from intact families to answer the question of 'What should be spent on children?', the question begged an answer that required split families to support their children as though they were intact.[24]

In his defence, Espenshade never proposed – at least in his written studies – that his research should play such an important role in the development of child support guidelines. Indeed, today even Espenshade himself does not advocate the use of his rather outdated data in child support guidelines.[25] Nevertheless, the use of his data remains the foundation of the guidelines, placed there originally by Dr Williams and the Advisory Panel.

2.   A Pause for the Flaws

Throughout the years, various defences of these fundamental flaws in the economic assumptions underlying the development of child support guidelines have been advanced. For example, one study defended the inclusion of using Espenshade's data on expenditures rather than costs as follows:

> Researchers felt that when individuals inquired about the 'cost of raising children', it invited not only a response directed toward a minimum level required for subsistence, but also carried the implication that a single answer could be provided when in actuality a broad range of responses is theoretically possible.[26]

Examining each reason in detail, the first reason concludes, in other words, that focusing on expenditures rather than costs invites a result that will avoid child support awards at 'a minimum level required for subsistence'. One should not miss the irony: guideline formulation rejected an economic analysis that could have resulted in child support awards at only a minimum subsistence level when a fundamental reason to create guidelines was to replace minimum subsistence level welfare awards with child support payments.

History supports this point: in 1935, Congress created the Aid to Families with Dependent Children (AFDC) programme.[27] This programme was designed to 'provide a minimum monthly subsistence payment to families'.[28] Then, in 1974, Congress passed the Family Support Act requiring states receiving AFDC funds to establish and enforce child support obligations with the 'primary goal' of reducing 'the federal cost of the AFDC program by sharpening enforcement of support obligations'.[29] The means of achieving this goal was expanded by Congress with the Child Support Enforcement Amendments of 1984 which required states to create numeric child support guidelines.[30] Thus, child support awards based on numeric guidelines were designed to replace welfare funds that provided a 'minimum monthly subsistence payment'.

Espenshade's 1984 study formed the economic foundation for the creation of numeric child support guidelines. That study, however, expressly rejected any analysis that would provide data showing 'minimum subsistence' levels of costs of raising children. The study therefore assumed data on minimum subsistence levels of child rearing were undesirable. It focused on the significantly higher levels of expenditures on children. In so doing, a critical economic assumption underlying the creation of the child support guidelines suffered from a fundamental and fatal flaw: it created guidelines that ignored 'minimum subsistence' data when the primary purpose of guidelines was to remove families from 'minimum subsistence' welfare.[31] Accordingly, the guidelines that resulted from this flawed economic assumption bore no rational relationship to the primary purpose for which guidelines were originally intended.[32]

The second reason provided to avoid an analysis of the cost of raising children was that such an analysis erroneously implied 'that a single answer could be provided when in actuality a broad range of responses is theoretically possible'.[33] This reason lacks persuasiveness, however, when one considers that the guideline schedules created for the Income Shares model used by 34 states and based on expenditures, rather than costs, include hundreds of responses to the question, 'What should be spent on children?'[34] The Florida guidelines, based on the Income Shares model, for example, provide for 528 different basic child support awards depending on the combined net monthly income of the parents and the number of children.[35] Thus, providing 'a broad range of responses' is no reason for research to have been avoided.

Other fundamental flaws exist in using Espenshade's analysis to create guidelines. The most obvious was that it relied on data from intact families to apply only to situations where families were not intact. The justification for using this flawed data was provided by Dr Williams. He argued there was 'no credible or current data for single-parent households' when the guidelines were created, and further argued that 'the data concerning intact households was believed to *generate higher support levels* than in a single-parent household because the parties to a divorce usually experience an overall reduction in their standard of living following their divorce'.[36] The former justification is suspect, given that Espenshade's 1984 study was based on data from 1972–73.[37] Even if the former justification were meritorious, the purported problem should have long since been resolved by subsequent data collection and, even if it were not, a lack of valid data cannot stand as a rational reason to compel American citizens to part with their earnings under threat of incarceration. The latter justification merely perpetuates a results-driven analysis to create artificially high guidelines.

Years later, in a 1997 report for the Florida Legislature, Dr Williams was still defending the use of intact family expenditures to determine child support guidelines. He noted that a 1990 report by Dr David Betson, then an economist at the University of Notre Dame, examined expenditure patterns of both intact and single-parent families, but he argued Dr Betson's samples of single parents were 'much smaller' than for two parents.[38] 'Unfortunately,' Dr Williams continued, 'even if valid data exist on expenditure patterns in one-parent households, such data do not provide meaningful guidance for setting child support awards.'[39] Why? Because, he argued, in 'economic terms, the "costs" of child-rearing are defined by what parents actually spend on their children'.[40] Translation: Espenshade determined 'costs of raising a child' could not be determined, but expenditure patterns could be; thus, to Dr Williams and the promulgators of child support guidelines, the inherent flaw in their research became not a cause for caution or concern, but a *cause célèbre*. They simply avoided the difficult issue of determining 'costs of raising a child' by redefining what that phrase meant: it now meant 'expenditure patterns'.

Dr Williams gave the following example to support his conclusion that, 'in economic terms, "costs" of child-rearing are defined by what parents actually spend on their children':

> For a middle class child, for example, the only way of determining whether part of that child's costs should include a new bicycle, Nintendo game, or own bedroom is by observing how other parents at that same income level divide their income between their own needs and those of their children. All economic studies on child rearing costs have found that parents spend more on children as

they have more income available. The relevant question is, *how much of that additional income do they spend on children?*[41]

With all due respect, that question is irrelevant unless two social policy assumptions are taken for granted: (1) unmarried parents – but *only* unmarried parents – should be required by the state to 'keep up with the Joneses', at least insofar as providing material goods for their children; and (2) children of unmarried parents – but *only* children of unmarried parents – are entitled, as a matter of state policy, to the necessary share of their parents' income so that they can keep up with the Joneses' children. Both assumptions were promulgated with little apparent recognition of the breadth of their reach.

We submit there is no compelling, legitimate or even rational state interest in ensuring a certain standard of living for only certain children. An example illustrates the irrationality of such a state policy.

Imagine one family, living in Florida, a married husband and wife with two children. The husband earns $60000 per year, the wife $37000 per year. The husband, however, has a gambling problem, and spends 50 weekends a year on a river boat in Biloxi, Mississippi, gambling away all his earnings and half of his wife's. Unless the neglect in the family has dropped below a level such as to deprive the children of their basic needs, the State of Florida professes no interest in the standard of living enjoyed, or suffered, by the children. The 2002 federal poverty level for a family of four was $18100 a year in gross income;[42] after the husband's squandering of assets, the family still had $18500 a year in gross income to live off. As far as Florida would have been concerned – or any other state for that matter – the state had no interest in this family.[43]

Now change one fact about the family: divorce the parents. All other facts remain the same but the parents' marital status has changed. Under the flawed assumptions underlying the child support guidelines, the State of Florida suddenly has a substantial, perhaps even compelling, interest in the children's standard of living. Why? Because the state has determined that children of unmarried parents should enjoy a standard of living not necessarily equal to or even similar to the one enjoyed during a marriage, but one closely equal to the mythical Jones family. Accordingly, solely by virtue of a change in the parents' marital status, the state will require the father (in this case) to pay a substantial portion of his earnings to support the children, when the state would have imposed no such requirement had the parents remained married.

The reason supporting that conclusion is stated in the second assumption above, the state entitlement by children of unmarried parents to a percentage share of their parents' income.

3. A Historical Entitlement for Some

The concept of a child of unmarried parents having a state entitlement to a percentage share of his or her parents' income first appeared in two of the guiding principles for the development of child support guidelines, the relevant parts of which stated:

> 1. Both parents should share legal responsibility for support of their children, with the economic responsibility divided between the parents *in proportion to their income*;
>
> 4. Each child of a given parent has an equal *right* to share in that parent's income . . . [44]

These principles created, for the first time in American history, a right of children to a mathematical proportion of their parents' income, with said proportion determined by the government based on how average parents with similar incomes spent money on their children. Thus, for the first time ever, *some* American children (those whose parents were not married) had a government-determined entitlement to a proportionate share of income earned by their parents.

This new, statutory right to a percentage share of a parent's income must be distinguished from parents' common law duties to support their children. When America was a group of British colonies, Blackstone both observed this duty and placed a cap on it:

> The duty of parents to provide for the maintenance of their children, is a principle of natural law . . . . By begetting them, therefore, they have entered into a voluntary obligation, to endeavor, as far as in them lies, that the life which they have bestowed shall be supported and preserved. And thus the children will have a perfect right of receiving maintenance from their parents.[45]

However, Blackstone also observed:

> [T]he policy of our laws, which are ever watchful to promote industry, did not mean to compel a father to maintain his idle and lazy children in ease and indolence; but thought it unjust to oblige the parent, against his will, to provide them with superfluities, and other indulgences of fortune; imagining they might trust to the impulse of nature, if the children were deserving of such favors.[46]

Thus, Blackstone's world did not concern itself with whether a child 'should' have a new bicycle or Nintendo game. Those concerns were the creation of the modern child support guidelines, and never more prevalent than in the assumption that children have a right to share in the income of their parents.

We submit that this fundamental assumption underlying contemporary child support guidelines – that children of unmarried parents have a state entitlement to a percentage share of their parents' income – is a socially destructive, socially indefensible assumption that must be discarded in any meaningful child support reform. We believe that this recent entitlement of children, sought and enforced, as it is, almost exclusively by custodial parents and the IV-D agencies that assist them, has led to:

- the destruction of families by creating financial incentives to divorce;
- the prevention of families by creating financial incentives not to marry upon conceiving a child out of wedlock;
- the alienation of non-custodial parents, most of whom are fathers, by placing financial burdens on them that they never voluntarily assumed in the first place, and that even exceed the financial burdens voluntarily assumed by their married counterparts; and
- the creation of a child-support-as-entitlement lottery, whereby custodial parents buy in to the assumption and internally and emotionally conclude they are entitled to child support based on a percentage of income, without any relationship between the support and the child's reasonable – or even subsistence-level – needs.[47]

This 'entitlement' assumption crept in to the law of child support with little examination of both its scope and its impact. This assumption is social engineering devoid of any substantial, legitimate, or even rational state interest and, as such, it should be stricken down and abandoned. Moreover, this basic assumption lies at the very deepest and strongest root of the current child support guidelines. That means the guidelines cannot be adjusted to achieve fairness unless and until this flawed assumption is removed.

FLAWS IN THE IMPLEMENTATION OF OTHER GUIDING PRINCIPLES

While the other guiding principles appeared to have had the best of intentions, many of them collapsed in implementation. For example, the second principle stated, 'The subsistence needs of each parent should be taken into consideration in setting child support, but in virtually no event should the child support obligation be set at zero.' To this end, guidelines such as Florida's and the 33 other states using the Income Shares model, provided obligors with a 'self-support reserve' based on the federal poverty guideline. The flaw in implementation appears in Dr Williams' own 1997 description of the self-support reserve:

The inclusion of a self-support reserve ensures that obligors have sufficient income to maintain a minimum standard of living. Below that minimum, a support obligation is not computed. The Schedule . . . includes a reserve of $645 net per month. This latter amount is equivalent to the 1996 federal poverty guideline for one person.[48]

One person? In the most simplest of child support circumstances, each household should be set up to accommodate two persons: the adult and the child. Yet the guidelines assume no non-custodial parent involvement. If the non-custodial parent is involved, as most are, then he or she is automatically financially penalized because the 'self-support reserve' assumes he or she has a household alone with no children.

It is interesting to consider how this guideline-based assumption of completely absent non-custodial parents has worked its way into policy literature. For example, note how the Florida House of Representatives Committee on Family Law and Children has treated the non-custodial father in the first of two comprehensive reports on child support guidelines since 1997.[49] The relevant portion of the report illustrated the application of the guidelines by creating two parents, John and Mary, with two children; giving primary residential responsibility to Mary; establishing the parents' net hypothetical incomes, combined monthly net, and arriving at a child support figure.[50] It then reaches the following conclusion that offends every non-custodial parent who loved and was involved with his or her children: 'Assuming that neither party has other dependents in the household, this would leave John with a monthly net income of [his amount] for a family of *one*. Mary would have a monthly net income of [her amount] for a family of *three*.'[51] Sadly, the guidelines were designed not only to strip some parents of income for highly questionable purposes, but also to strip all children of some parents. According to the guidelines and their interpretation by policy-makers, a father who does not live with his children's mother and who has only visitation or court-ordered access with the children has no family.

Another flaw appears in the fourth guiding principle, which stated, 'Child support must cover a child's basic needs as a first priority, but, to the extent either parent enjoys a higher than subsistence-level standard of living, the child is entitled to share in the benefit of that improved standard.' Aside from the obvious problems of yet another state-mandated entitlement for children, this principle failed upon implementation because the entitlement 'to share in the benefit' is not enforced; only the entitlement to receive higher child support is enforced. Thus, while a custodial parent can and will receive an increase in child support upon the good financial fortune of a non-custodial parent, there is no assurance made to the court – or even required to be made to the court – that the increased revenue will be used to benefit the child. Thus, this principle suffers from another flawed assumption: child support sent to the custodial parent is spent on the children. In other words, what is good for the gander is good for the goslings.

In Florida law, the flaw in this principle is highlighted by a little-known and apparently rarely, if ever, used criminal statute. A close reading of the statute compels the conclusion that a child support recipient can use child support money however he or she sees fit – even if it never benefits the children – so long as certain basic needs of the children are met. The statute provides that the wilful misapplication of child support funds is a first-degree misdemeanor on a first offence, and a second-degree misdemeanor on a second offence. A 'wilful misapplication' occurs when child support funds 'are spent for any purpose other than for necessary and proper home, food, clothing, and the necessities of life, which expenditure results in depriving the child of the above named necessities'. Thus, as expressed through criminal law, the state's interest in child support fund transfers is only in ensuring the funds are not so misused by the recipient as to deprive the child of 'necessities of life'. Beyond meeting those needs, the rest of the money is gravy.

The glaring inconsistency between the stated principle – 'Child support must cover a child's basic needs as a first priority, but, to the extent either parent enjoys a higher than subsistence-level standard of living, the child is entitled to share in the benefit of that improved standard' – and the above-referenced criminal statute is offensive and demeaning. It offends public policy for such inconsistencies to exist and to go uncorrected; it demeans child support obligors who for years have complained their funds were not being used to support their children, but to support their former spouses or spouses' lovers. The truth is no child support law requires that funds received for the purpose of benefiting a child actually go to benefit that child.

For reasons previously discussed, the seventh principle has broken down entirely in application. It stated, 'A guideline should not create extraneous negative effects on the major life decisions of either parent. In particular, the guidelines should avoid creating economic disincentives for remarriage or labor force participation.' In truth, the guidelines dramatically impact upon major life decisions. For example, a recent article queried whether the recent decline in the marriage rate reflected men engaging in an informal strike against marriage, in part because of fears of becoming victims of child support guidelines should the marriage fail.[52] Additionally, the guidelines routinely include 'overtime' income when computing support obligations, thereby creating economic disincentives, and their income-based approach continues to create significant incentives not to realize full labour market potential.

For example, assume a $50000 a year gross income obligor with two children and an obligee who earns $15000 a year working part time. Under the Florida Income Shares model and adjusting for taxes, the obligor's estimated basic monthly child support obligation would be $1068. Assuming an 18 per cent marginal tax rate for the obligor, his monthly gross income of $4167 has been reduced by 44 per cent by taxes and child support. If the obligor is a father alienated from the children,[53] then he 'feels' he is earning only 56 cents for every dollar he earns. An opportunity for career advancement for an extra $10000 a year only puts $5600 more in his pocket. Accordingly, his financial incentive to accept better-paying employment is only a little more than half of what it should be. That result creates a significant 'negative effect' on his major life decisions.

The final guiding principle has become so flawed in its application as to be unrecognizable: 'A guideline should encourage the involvement of both parents in the child's upbringing. A guideline should take into consideration the financial support provided by parents in shared physical custody and extended visitation arrangements.'[54] As noted above, the guidelines actively discourage joint parental involvement in a child's upbringing. Furthermore, the guidelines were designed to assure such lack of involvement.

First, as noted, the guidelines set the self-support reserve for the non-custodial parent as though he or she were a family of one. Second, the guidelines assume the non-custodial parent has no visitation or access costs. Why? Dr Williams provides an answer:

> Since the Schedule is based on expenditures for children in intact households, there is *no consideration given for visitation costs*. Taking such costs into account would be further complicated by the variability in actual visitation patterns and the duplicative nature of many costs incurred for visitation (e.g. housing, home furnishings).[55]

In other words, we collected expenditure data from a marginally relevant database (intact households) to apply the data to a completely different data group (split households), and we expressly chose not to adjust for actual expenditures affecting half of the data group (non-custodial housing, home furnishings) or even make recommendations for adjustments based on different visitation patterns. It was easier to assume no involvement by the non-custodial parent, than to try to create guidelines that encouraged non-custodial parental involvement. Or, put another way, it was easier to put the burden of demonstrating parental involvement on the non-custodial parent, thereby creating yet another direct financial incentive for custodial parents to restrict such involvement and yet another barrier for non-custodial parents to overcome.

CONCLUSION

Child support guidelines suffer from irreparably flawed economic and policy principles and assumptions. Some of these flaws arose in the actual principles that guided the development of child support guidelines. Others arose only after these principles were implemented, exposing fatally flawed assumptions contained within the principles. The result compels the conclusion that the current child support guideline system is not broken, because that conclusion would imply that it can be fixed. Instead, it suffers irreparable structural design flaws and, as such, cannot be fixed in anything resembling its current form. Instead, a new analysis – focusing on fairness and with a complete understanding of the social implications of the underlying policies, and not focusing on higher or lower child support awards – must begin. America's policy-makers at the state and federal levels must clearly define the exact nature of the state interest in child support awards and then carefully craft guidelines to achieve those interests.

NOTES

1. Morgan (2001).
2. One commentator, writing thirteen years ago, called it a 'multibillion dollar, government-assisted child support enforcement industry' (Harry D. Krause, 1990).
3. Florida House of Representatives Committee on Family Law and Children (1997). A fair question for policy-makers would ask how average citizens should be expected to perceive child support guidelines as fair when only one out of two of those who ordered guideline-based awards considered them to be fair.
4. Ibid.
5. See Proposed Committee Bill 4 (introduced as HB 2421 on April 19, 2000). Florida uses the Income Shares model of child support guidelines, as do 33 other states. See Florida House of Representatives Committee on Family Law and Children (1997), note 7, at 6. This model is 'based on the assumption that children of parents not living together should receive the same portion of their parents' income that they would have received had the parents stayed together' (ibid.). The model essentially adds the incomes of both parents, applies the combined monthly income against a 'tax table'-type chart, multiplies the figure from the chart by each parent's percentage share of the combined income total, and then requires the non-custodial parent to pay his or her share to the custodial parent each month. See, for example, Fla. Stat. § 61.30(6). The examples and case law discussed in this chapter will be drawn from Florida's Income Shares guidelines.
6. Bill Research and Economic Impact Statement, Proposed Committee Bill 98–02, Committee on Family Law and Children (18 September 1997). The language from this staff analysis was substantially similar to that provided to the Committee considering the same amendments in April 2000.
7. Morgan (2001), 1–3.
8. Ibid.
9. See generally ibid., 1–3 – 1–5. See also Social Security Amendments of 1974, Pub. L. 93–647, 88 Stat. 2337, at 42 U.S.C. §§ 651–665.
10. *Id.*, 1–5. This legislation marked the origin of the still-existent federal and state policy directly linking welfare payments and child support awards. In passing the Family

Support Act of 1974, amending the 1935 legislation establishing the Aid to Families with Dependent Children programme (commonly called 'welfare'), Congress made the continued receipt of federal welfare funds by states dependent upon the creation of a state agency – known as a 'IV-D agency' – to establish and enforce child support obligations. Morgan (2001), 1–5. This relationship between welfare and child support was not beyond reproach. While some, such as Morgan, argue for a direct link between federal welfare payments and child support (for example, if non-payment of child support could be rectified, then the federal government would save taxpayer money because the welfare rolls would be reduced), others described this alleged link to be 'incredible' and debunked by research showing, among other things, 'the most prevalent reported cause of non-payment of court ordered child support is unemployment' which no draconian child support enforcement measure can cure. See Gay (2002a).

11. Pub. L. 98–378, 98 Stat. 1305, amending 42 U.S.C. §§ 657–662.
12. See generally Florida House of Representatives Committee on Family Law and Children (2000).
13. Pub. L. 98–378, 98 Stat. 1321, § 18.
14. Pub. L. 100–485, 102 Stat. 2343, codified at 42 U.S.C. § 667(b)(2).
15. See note 3 above.
16. Sources for the preceding discussion of Dr Williams and PSI: (1) Johnston (1998); (2) http://www.policy-studies.com/about/about_intro.htm; (3) http://www.policy-studies.com/whatnew/new_dbj.htm.
17. Williams (1987).
18. See Slater (1986). For reasons not reflected in the record, Florida did not include Advisory Panel principle number five, requiring guidelines to apply regardless of marital status and to paternity, separation, and divorce cases. Ultimately, all three scenarios were included in guideline law. See generally Fla. Stat. § 61.30.

    Additionally, in an apparent attempt to clarify that equal parental involvement with children did not necessarily mean no child support would be ordered, the Florida Commission added language to the final Advisory Panel principle (encouraging parental involvement and accounting for varying custody arrangements) that 'even a fifty percent sharing of physical custody does not necessarily obviate the child support obligation'.
19. See Florida House of Representatives Committee on Family Law and Children (2000), note 16, at 35.
20. Ibid.
21. *Idem*, at 78.
22. *Idem*, note 16, at 36 (citing Espenshade, 1984).
23. Espenshade (1984). This 1984 study relied upon the 1972–73 Consumer Expenditures Survey ('CES') administered by the US Bureau of Labor Statistics and the Bureau of the Census, surveying both rural and urban intact families nationwide.

    The CES is not an objective measure of consumer expenditures. It uses two subjective measuring tools, a quarterly Interview Survey and a weekly Diary Survey wherein families self-report their expenditures. See Florida House of Representatives Committee on Family Law and Children (2000), note 16, at 39.
24. Indeed, in describing the most popular child support guideline formula, the Income Shares model, Dr Williams explained: 'The Income Shares model is based on the concept that the child should receive the same proportion of parental income that he or she would have received if the parents lived together.' See Williams (1994).
25. Morgan and Lino (1999) (citing Bergmann and Wetchler, 1995).
26. Florida House of Representatives (2000), note 16, at 36.
27. Codified at 42 U.S.C. § 601 *et seq.*
28. Morgan (2001), note 5, at 1–5.
29. *Idem*, at 1–6 (citing M. Dobbs, et al., *Enforcing Child and Spousal Support* § 4.04 (1995), for the proposition, 'AFDC benefits are in a direct sense child support paid by the taxpayer').
30. Pub. L. 98–378, 98 Stat. 1305, amending 42 U.S.C. §§ 657–62.

31. This conclusion is not meant to suggest that Espenshade intended this result. The analytical sleight of hand was made by those who used Espenshade's data to create flawed guideline models.
32. Whether this lack of a rational relationship to a legitimate state interest violates due process guarantees is beyond the scope of this chapter.
33. Florida House of Representatives (2000), note 16, at 36.
34. See, for example, Fla. Stat. § 61.30(6) (2002).
35. See ibid.
36. Sasser and Holz (1999) (internal quotation marks omitted) (emphasis added) (citing Williams 1987), at II-iii and 36–38).
37. Ibid.
38. Williams et al. (1997). Others have criticized Dr Betson's work, noting that his estimates 'were consistently higher than more established estimates'. See Gay (2002b).
39. Williams et al. (1997), note 40, at 13.
40. Ibid.
41. Ibid.
42. See <http://www.aegis.com/factshts/network/access/poverty.html> (visited 9 September 2002).
43. See also Krause (1990), note 6, at 20: 'Married parents . . . do not legally owe their children a lifestyle that is consistent with their income and station in life. They may choose to rear their children in any reasonable way they see fit.'
44. Williams et al. (1997), note 19 (emphasis added).
45. I. W. Blackstone, *Commentaries on the Laws of England* 447–48 (1765) (as quoted in Krause (1990), note 6, at 6.
46. I. W. Blackstone, *Commentaries on the Laws of England* 437 (1765) (as quoted in Krause (1990), note 6, at 19.
47. See, for example *Carr v. Blake*, 2000 WL 192138 (Ohio App. 1 Dist. Feb. 18, 2000) (unpublished opinion) (custodial unwed mother of 18-month-old child sought $240 000 per year in 'child support' for child of professional football player); *Finley v. Scott*, 707 So.2d 1112 (Fla. 1998) (custodial unwed mother sought in excess of $120 000 per year 'child support' to raise two-year-old child of professional basketball player).
48. Williams et al. (1997), note 40, at 27.
49. Florida House of Representatives (1997), note 7, at 8.
50. Ibid.
51. Ibid. (emphasis added).
52. Thompson and Sacks (2002).
53. See, for example, Krause (1990), note 6: '[T]he typical custody adjudication on divorce terminates the father's parental status, at least in any meaningful sense. This de facto termination of parental status comes at the very time we impose on the absent parent a child support obligation that typically is far larger than what he might have shouldered, or was legally obligated to provide, in the ongoing family.' [citations omitted].
54. Williams (1987), note 19.
55. Williams (1997), note 40, at 40 (emphasis added).

REFERENCES

Bergmann, Barbara R. and Sherry Wetchler (1995), 'Child support awards: state guidelines vs. public opinion', *Fam. L.Q.*, **483**.
Carr v. Blake (2000), WL 192138 (Ohio App. 1 Dist., 18 February (unpublished opinion).
Espenshade, Thomas J. (1984), *Investing in Children: New Estimates of Parental Expenditures*, 2.

Florida House of Representatives Committee on Family Law and Children (1997), 'Child support guidelines, interim project report 20', 12 March.

Florida House of Representatives Committee on Family Law and Children (2000), 'Child support guidelines, interim project report', 4–9 March.

Gay, Roger (2002a), 'A brief history of prevailing child support doctrine', www.lectlaw.com/files/famll.htm.

Gay, Roger (2002b), 'History of current child support doctrine', www.lectlaw.com/files/famll.htm.

Johnston, James R. (1998), 'The father of today's child support public policy, his personal exploitation of the system, and the fallacy of his "Incomes Shares" model', August, www.fathermag.com/907/childsupport/.

Krause, Harry D. (1990), 'Child support reassessed: limits of private responsibility and the public interest', 24 *Fam. L.Q.*, **1** (2) (Spring).

Morgan, Laura W. (2001), *Child Support Guidelines: Interpretation and Application*, 1–10, Aspen Law & Business.

Morgan, Laura and Mark C. Lino (1999), 'A comparison of child support awards calculated under states' child support guidelines with expenditures on children calculated by the US Department of Agriculture', 33 *Fam. L.Q.* 191.

Sasser, Thomas J. and Rana Holz (1999), 'Child support myths and truths: exploring the assumptions underlying Florida's statutory guidelines', *Fla. Bar. J*, **58** (October).

Slater, Phyllis (1986), Memorandum to Robert Lester (22 December), Child Support Study Commission Meeting, 19 December, Orlando, Florida.

Social Security Amendments of 1974, Pub. L. 93–647, 88 Stat. 2337, at 42 U.S.C. §§ 651–665.

Thompson, Dianna and Glenn Sacks (2002), 'A "marriage strike" emerges as men decide not to risk loss', 5 July, www.mensnewsdaily.com/stories/Thompsonsacks070502.

Williams, Robert G. (1987), 'Development of guidelines for child support orders: advisory panel recommendations and final report', US Department of Health and Human Services, Office of Child Support Enforcement.

Williams, Robert G. (1994), 'Child support guidelines: the next generation', US Department of Health and Human Services, Office of Child Support Enforcement, ed. M.C. Haynes.

Williams, Robert G., David A. Price and Jane Venohr (1997), 'Economic basis for updated child support schedule 13', submitted to Florida Joint Legislative Management Committee, 30 January.

7. Should visitation denial affect the obligation to pay support?

Ira Mark Ellman

The imposition of an unjustified obligation is not as bad if it is not enforced, and failing to impose a justified obligation is not nearly as consequential if it would not have been enforced anyway. The government's increasing determination to collect child support obligations over the past few decades has therefore made the substantive law of child support more interesting: the rules and procedures for identifying support obligors, and setting the size of their obligation, now matter much more. One context in which they now matter is the focus of this chapter: should the non-custodial parent's obligation to contribute to the child's support be affected by actions of the custodial parent that impair the support obligor's access to the child? Before the age of enforcement, most support obligors who believed the other parent had thwarted their access to their child could simply stop making support payments. No effective effort to enforce them was likely to follow, regardless of whether the non-payment was in principle legally defensible. That is of course no longer true.

And the law's treatment of the relationship between support and visitation is important in a lot of cases. Studies from the late 1980s and early 1990s found that only a sixth of non-residential parents see their child an average of once a week, and about half had not seen their child at all for at least a year (Pearson and Thoennes, 1998).[1] A variety of factors contribute to this result, but tension between the parents is one of them. These same studies found that a fifth of custodial parents concede that they have denied the other parent access to the child. A third of non-custodial parents claim such denial (Pearson and Thoennes, 1998).[2] Studies have long shown an association between the frequency with which divorced fathers see their children and the level of their compliance with support orders, although the nature of the causal relationship is contested. But even divorced fathers who see their children fairly regularly report feeling cut out from their children's life,[3] and it seems certain that the reduced emotional connections between children and their divorced fathers is one important reason for the historically low level of voluntary compliance with support orders.

Certainly, both mothers and fathers typically see the issues of visitation and support as connected. Strong majorities of both believe that the two issues should be considered together.[4] Fathers who believe that their access to their child has been impaired are more likely to resist providing support; mothers see fathers' complaints about access as reflecting discontent with the support order (Pearson and Anhalt, 1994).[5]

While mothers and fathers are thus clear in seeing visitation and support as reciprocal obligations, the law is more confused. At the most fundamental level, the legal rule is consistent with the social norm, because the obligation of support and the right of access are both regarded as essential characteristics of parental status. The Supreme Court has confirmed the Constitutional status of parents' pre-eminent right to decide who has access to their children,[6] and as a general matter only parents have a legal duty of support. These fundamental principles mean that the legal right of access and the legal obligation of support typically arise and recede together, even if the law is not framed as establishing their reciprocal nature. For example, a divorce court cannot normally deny visitation rights to a non-custodial parent who reliably complies with the support order,[7] because meeting his support obligations is normally sufficient to maintain the obligor's parental status, and even parents who are poor candidates for primary custody are presumptively entitled to visitation. Conversely, when the state terminates a parent's 'rights', the obligation of support normally ends as well,[8] and a parent who chronically fails to comply with a support order may on that ground have his parental rights, and thus his legal right of access to his child, terminated.[9]

But despite both these familiar principles and prevailing social norms, most (although not all) courts routinely hold that the support and visitation provisions of a divorce decree state independent, not reciprocal obligations. That means that each parent is obliged to comply without regard for the other's non-compliance. Visitation denial is therefore rejected as a defence to an action for failure to pay support, and courts may decline to relieve the support obligor of his prospective support obligations as a remedy for the other's parent's interference with his access to the child. Courts will in principle take the same position in responding to the custodial parent who wishes to deny visitation because of the obligor's spotty payment record. So in the context of resolving the common disputes over support and visitation, the social norms and the legal rules are thus in tension.

Why then do courts often follow this legal rule? In brief, the answer is their assumption that support payments are necessary for the child's welfare, and that terminating or suspending the obligation to make them would therefore be harmful to children. Courts make similar assumptions about the beneficial impact of visitation, in denying the custodial parent's request to suspend it as a remedy for unreliable support. Most courts thus take the position that while remedies ought to be available for either parent's non-compliance with the outstanding decree, excusing the complaining parties' compliance is not an appropriate remedy because it would further impair the child's interests. The Wyoming Supreme Court offers a typical statement of this rule and its rationale:

> Visitation is primarily for the benefit of the child, and ordinarily a support order must be paid even if the custodial parent wrongfully denies the non-custodial parent's right to visitation. The custodial parent's misconduct cannot destroy the child's right to support, nor may child support payments be used as a weapon to force a child's visitation with a non-custodial parent. The duty to support one's minor child is a continuing obligation. Entitlement to child support is not contingent upon visitation rights . . . *The welfare of the child is a primary concern, and the duty of a noncustodial parent to support his or her child cannot depend on that parent's opportunity to exercise visitation rights.*[10]

This chapter asks whether the assumption underlying this rule, that support payments are essential to protect child welfare, is in fact true in the full range of cases to which the rule is typically applied. It concludes that it is not. It considers other reasons (in addition to child welfare) for enforcing the support obligation, and finds them usually inapplicable to some of the same cases. It also concludes that the rationale underlying the legal duty to pay support may be compromised by visitation denial. For all these reasons, the chapter therefore finds that the usual rule treating the support obligation as independent of the other parent's duty to facilitate visitation with the child should probably be applied in a narrower range of cases than it currently is. One should make a parallel inquiry with respect to the converse question: is protection of the obligor's visitation rights in fact essential to the child's welfare in all the cases in which courts decline to limit the non-compliant support obligor's visitation? Unfortunately, space limitations preclude an examination of that question in this chapter.

'Visitation-denial' disputes, as I shall call them, can be classified along two different dimensions. Substantively, they vary in the severity of the disruption to the non-custodial parent's relationship with the child. Procedurally, they vary as to timing: does the support obligor raise the disruption as the basis for altering his support obligation in the future, or as a defence to his failure to pay it in the past? For ease of exposition, I will for the most part conflate this potential four-cell matrix into two cells. The obligor raising a visitation denial defence is in the weakest position, procedurally, if he first stops paying support and then raises the defence later in response to an action to collect support arrearages. The first section below looks at these arrearage defence cases. In doing so it focuses on those in which the arrearages arose during a period in which the custodial parent entirely concealed the child from the support obligor, without justification, thus preventing any contact whatsoever between non-custodial parent and child.[11] These are the cases in which the interference with visitation is most severe and clear cut; if this form of visitation-denial is not accepted as a defence in arrearage cases, then no form of visitation-denial will be. I conclude, however, that concealment should defeat many arrearage claims, even though defences alleging less severe disruption in the parent–child relationship do not. The second section below addresses prospective support defences, cases in which the support obligor seeks a reduction or elimination of his future support obligation on account of the custodial parent's continuing pattern of denying him access to their child. This section focuses on visitation denial short of concealment, such as claims that visitation has been regularly frustrated or prevented by the custodial parent's conduct. Concealment cases need not be discussed in this section because the prior conclusion that concealment should often defeat claims for arrearages necessarily suggests that it is also sufficient grounds for adjusting current support obligations.

A.　ARREARAGE DEFENCES

May a support obligor stop paying when he discovers that the mother and child have disappeared, leaving him with no means to contact them? Or perhaps better put, if she and the child reappear, is he then liable for the support payments accruing but unpaid during their absence? Courts often say he is. As a Pennsylvania court explained when it required the father to pay the arrearages that had accrued during the mother's concealment, 'the misconduct of the mother does not affect a father's duty to support his child. Indeed, this duty is well nigh absolute, and a support order must ordinarily be complied with even if the actions of the wife place her in contempt of court . . . [W]e are loath to deprive the child of support payments because of the improvident actions of the mother.'[12] Is the child's welfare really dependent upon the collection of arrearages in such concealment cases? Does the father's duty to support his child survive such concealment? Neither question is often examined with care in these cases, but we pursue them below.

1.　Pre-decree Concealment

The legal obligation to support one's children of course exists in the law apart from particular court orders enforcing it, and it is therefore possible for courts to provide remedies for non-support during a period preceding the commencement of any legal action. In cases involving unmarried fathers, however, legal parentage, and thus also the support duty, may not be clear at the outset of the child's life, even though it is later established. The question that arises is whether courts should impose a retroactive support obligation on the newly established legal father, for the period between the child's birth and the establishment of paternity. Jurisdictions give varying answers to this question, but some allow an assessment of arrearages against such a man for an amount equal to the support payments that would have been ordered if paternity had been established earlier. We consider here the cases that do this even when the child's very existence, much less location, were previously concealed from the newly established support obligor.

A Wisconsin case, *Brad v. Lee*,[13] provides an example. Brad was born to Catherine in 1977; she was unmarried and never sought to establish Brad's paternity. She changed her mind in 1992 when Brad was 15 and wrote to Lee, who did not reply. All agreed that Lee never knew of Brad's existence before receiving Catherine's 1992 letter. But at Catherine's request the county child support enforcement office obtained blood tests confirming Lee's biological paternity, and the court then ordered him to pay retroactive support – arrearages – for the past 15 years, as well as current support during the next three. During his 15 years of ignorance, Lee had married, fathered two children, and ran a farm and logging business with his wife. Perhaps he had been setting aside college money for his two marital children, perhaps he would have made some life decisions differently during the past 15 years if he had known he was responsible for a third child. But while expressing some sympathy for these concerns, the court concluded that Brad was nonetheless entitled to the money, for 'the child cannot be held responsible . . . simply because the father was not aware of his child's birth'.[14] The court explained that Lee was always liable for Brad's support, though he could not have known that he was. It never considered whether biological paternity alone is an adequate basis for requiring such retroactive payments from a man denied any opportunity to become the child's social father.

While not all the cases may seem as extreme as *Brad*,[15] some are arguably more so, and the explanation they offer is no more persuasive. In *Salazar v. Roybal*[16] the parents' brief relationship led to the birth of son in 1976. The mother concealed the son's existence from the father until after he turned 18 in 1994. The son himself initiated a support claim in 1996, when he was 20, which the mother declined to join. The trial court ordered the father to pay the son $23760 in support arrearages. Although noting that it did not 'condone Mother's actions' or 'wish to minimize the impact on Father of being deprived of parenting Son', the appeals court affirmed. In doing so it conceded that 'Son had been provided for in Father's absence [by] Mother and her family'. The father argued that the support order could therefore have no purpose other than funding the son's college tuition, a purpose which was not valid in New Mexico, where the case arose, because like many states it does not permit courts to require unwilling support obligors to pay for their adult child's college education.

Implicitly conceding the point about college, the appeals court held that the order's real purpose was not the payment of tuition but the 'Son's retroactive support which was Father's accrued obligation . . . [T]he overriding policy consideration . . . is ensuring support for children based upon the parental responsibility that goes with sexual activity . . . [Son's] interests are not judged by what may have been mother's wrongful conduct [in concealing his existence from the father].'[17] The same court had the opportunity to comment further in *Tedford v. Gregory*[18] when it considered an adult daughter's claim. Jeanne's mother had divorced when Jeanne was 14 months, and her former husband had paid child support for Jeanne throughout her minority in the belief he was Jeanne's father. But when Jeanne was 16, her mother told her that her real father was actually another man named Gregory. When she was 20 Jeanne sought 18 years' support arrearages from Gregory. The court ordered him to pay after genetic tests confirmed he was her biological father. It left open the possibility that the mother's former husband could get reimbursement from Jeanne, in whatever amount she collected from Gregory.

These cases show courts acting reflexively rather than thoughtfully, perhaps a particular danger when the subject is collection of child support. The problem is not their assumption that children need support and that their parents are morally obliged to provide it, but their failure to consider whether these two propositions are sufficient to explain their decision in these cases. It is a mistake, for example, for the court in *Tedford* to assume without discussion that Gregory was Jeanne's father, although that view seems consistent with the same court's comment in *Salazar* that parental obligations should arise inevitably from sexual activity. But in fact biological paternity has never been the exclusive basis upon which legal or moral parenthood can or should be based. Under the *Tedford* facts many courts would treat the mother's former husband, not Gregory, as Jeanne's legal father, and I have elsewhere argued that they would be correct (Ellman, 2002). *Salazar*, unlike *Tedford*, presents facts that suggest no nominee for legal father other than biological father who is mentioned, and the court seems content to treat the child support obligation as a price of sexual activity. Again, I have elsewhere argued that a biological father's support obligations necessarily rest on his also having an opportunity to be the child's social father – that the man who is denied that chance, through no fault of his own, should not usually be liable for the child's support, and perhaps is not appropriately treated as the child's legal father at all, except as he might volunteer to undertake its responsibilities (Ellman, 2002). While that argument has obvious application to cases like these, I wish here to focus on a different question that I did not address in that earlier paper: can these decisions be defended as serving the policy interests of protecting child welfare, as that interest has been defined by the governing child support law that these decisions purport to implement? And if they cannot, is there some other important public policy that explains them?

The collection of child support years after it is due seems unlikely to contribute much to child welfare, simply because it comes too late. A toddler's pangs of hunger are not calmed by eating double portions as a teenager. And perhaps there were no hunger pangs (or other deprivations). Custodial mothers who choose (without justification, in the cases we consider) to conceal themselves from the father may be more likely than most to believe that they will have access to other resources to replace the support the father might otherwise have provided.[19] In such cases it may be hard to identify any damage to the child from the support shortfall, much less any damage that could be addressed by the payment of arrearages years later.

The three cases we have looked at are examples. In *Salazar* the court conceded that the son had been provided for during his minority, and it never explained how the required arrearage payments would serve any child welfare purpose for which support could be ordered under the governing law. In *Tedford*, the payments went directly to the adult daughter who had been supported during her minority by the man who then believed himself her father – and who may have an action against her for reimbursement anyway. Even in *Brad*, where the arrearages might be thought to offer some benefit to the son who was not yet 18, it is unlikely that the benefit would be one contemplated by the support law. A 17-year-old may realize true benefit from a sudden infusion of funds that allow him to buy a car, for example, but no court would order an ordinary middle-class father to make payments for that purpose in addition to the current support he is obliged to pay. Some states would order additional support for college, of course – but if *Brad* arose in such a state, then that award could be made directly, as part of the current support obligation, not through the subterfuge of collecting arrearages. In short, there appears to be no child welfare interest recognized by the child support law which is furthered by the collection of arrearages in these cases.

This point of course applies to the collection of arrearages generally, not just to those arising in concealment cases: child support payments made on time are more likely than past-due payments to confer the intended benefits upon the child whose welfare is the order's primary rationale. But that does not mean there is no reason ever to collect arrearages; in the ordinary case there is, even if some or all of the child welfare benefit has been irreversibly lost. The problem, as explained below, is that these additional reasons (beyond child welfare) may not apply in the concealment context either, and especially not when the concealment occurred prior to the establishment of any legal obligation to pay support.

What are the reasons for collecting arrearages even when they are unlikely to yield the child welfare benefits that were the order's original purpose? There are three points to note. First, the enforcement of arrearage claims is necessary to achieve fairness as between the parents. The obligor should have been paying, and if the custodial parent managed to scrape by and make up for his defalcation, then she should have a claim against him in her own right. The delayed collection allows her to realize now the savings that her earlier frugality would have yielded, had he paid her in a timely fashion. But it is apparent that no such fairness rationale could support any arrearage claims on behalf of the custodial mothers in *Brad*, *Roybal* or *Salazar*. These mothers' violation of the norm of reciprocity is fatal to any fairness-based claim they might otherwise have made on their own behalf against an obligor whose children they concealed. While there is no way for the law to require her to make him whole for the parental loss she caused him, it must at least bar her from making such reimbursement claims against him, as some courts do appreciate.[20]

A second reason for enforcing the ordinary arrearage claim arises from the obligor's failure to make payments that a court has already ordered. A rule excusing payments by obligors who are able to elude the claimant's enforcement efforts over a long-enough period would obviously create problematic incentives. But this point simply does not apply to cases like *Brad*, *Salazar* and *Roybal*. No programme of incentives or deterrence can improve voluntary compliance with support obligations that the purported obligor never knew he had. The custodial parent's failure for so many years to even establish the purported obligor's paternity brings one to the third point: these claims are brought too late. Both statutes of limitation and the legal doctrine of *laches* assure that private law claims between adults are lost when the claimant allows too much time to pass before bringing them. The reasons are both institutional (the difficulties of gathering reliable evidence concerning long-past disputes) and substantive (the perceived unfairness in allowing a party to resurrect a long-dormant claim). There is no reason to make an exception to the timeliness requirement for support claims whose substantive rationale is fairness as between the parents, even if we appropriately make exceptions for claims necessary to serve the child's interests.[21] A parent may lose her own claims from her neglect or tardiness, even if she cannot lose her child's.

In sum, cases like *Brad*, *Salazar* and *Roybal* impose on a man with questionable moral responsibility an obligation for support payments that neither child welfare concerns nor parental fairness claims can justify, and which are, in any event, brought too late. It is therefore not surprising that many jurisdictions reject them. Some states address the matter through legislation. Ohio's targeted provisions, newly enacted, bar courts from ordering pre-decree arrearages when paternity is first established after the child's third birthday and the father 'had no knowledge and had no reason to have knowledge of his alleged paternity of the child' before that initial paternity filing.[22] Other states limit the pre-decree time period for which arrearages may be ordered, although they may then apply the limit to all cases, not just those in which the father had no knowledge of the child.[23] California bars pre-decree arrearages in their entirety in nearly all paternity cases.[24] California's rule may reflect legislative doubts of a man's moral responsibility to provide support for a child before his paternity is established, but the rule's sweep is too broad to rest on that rationale alone, because it also applies to unmarried fathers who *do* know of their child's existence and location, so long as there has not yet been any judicial decision recognizing their paternity.[25] Among other things, then, the California rule must also reflect a sense that the pressing child welfare concerns that fuel a general public determination to collect child support do not apply with the same force to arrearages.

California's position may seem particularly interesting, because it contrasts with the position that state's highest court has taken with respect to arrearages arising during the custodial parent's post-decree concealment of the child. The next section considers whether those California decisions, which echo the decisions of courts in most other states, are correct in treating post-decree concealment so differently from pre-decree concealment. The opinions explaining the court's decisions are worth examining because, unlike the decisions we have just examined, they ask directly whether enforcement of arrearages will confer a benefit on the child, and claim to state a rule that requires their enforcement only in those cases in which it will.

2.   Post-decree Concealment

The question of collecting support arrearages that accrue during a period of post-decree concealment is addressed in a trio of recent California cases, beginning with the state supreme court's decision in *Damico v. Damico*.[26] California provides by statute that the 'existence or enforcement of a duty of support owed by a noncustodial parent for the support of a minor child shall not be affected by a failure or refusal by the custodial parent to implement any rights as to custody or visitation granted by a court to the non-custodial parent'.[27] But *Damico* held that despite this provision a custodial mother who had concealed the child from the father could be equitably estopped[28] from later claiming support arrearages against him. The mother had been awarded primary custody of the couple's infant son in their 1960 divorce, and apparently the father had no contact with the child after that year. As he explained it, the mother told him at his last 1960 visit that she would never allow him to see his son again, and he fled when her brother attacked him with a knife. Despite his efforts he could not find the mother and child after that. His troubles continued in 1979 when an action for 18 years' support arrearages, plus interest, was decided against him by default because his attorney, unbeknownst to him, did not appear at the hearing. The case that finally came to the California Supreme Court was the mother's 1991 action to enforce that 1979 default judgment. By 1991 his son would have been about 30 years old.

The California Supreme Court held the mother's claim barred if the father's story were true; it sent the case back to the trial court to decide the facts. In doing so it distinguished between simple frustration of visitation rights, which fall within the statutory rule,[29] and the custodial parent's active concealment of the child, which, the court held, did not. The lower court, which had also ruled for the father, said that it 'declined to permit a custodial parent to undermine the parent–child relationship by active concealment of the child – which we view as an implicit election to raise the child without financial assistance from the noncustodial parent – with no disruption of the corollary right to reimbursement for child support arrearages'.[30] But the California Supreme Court chose to rest its affirmance on different grounds, because it viewed the mother's concealment of the child from the father as 'a species' of the custodial behaviour addressed by the applicable statute.[31] It therefore emphasized instead that concealment renders useless any of the other remedies for visitation-denial which the court had in an earlier case directed frustrated obligors to seek: 'contempt proceedings, terminating or reducing spousal support, modifying custody or child support orders, and requiring a bond to assure compliance with the visitation order'. And it observed that concealment

> . . . *precludes the very child support payments that the custodial parent later seeks to collect.* One cannot make child support payments to a person who cannot be located. Concealment thus defeats the entire purpose of the order, which is to provide support to a third party, the child. In finding an estoppel defense under these facts, we rely on the unfairness of enforcing a judgment against a person who had no clear way of paying the monthly obligation because the custodial parent had gone into hiding. It is unfair to let the parent hide during the term of the obligation – usually a lengthy term – and then reappear and demand

payment of arrearages in full after he or she has defeated the purpose of the judgment.[32]

It turned out that the key language of the court's decision was the final quoted phrase, 'defeat the purpose of the judgment'. That defeated purpose, as the court explained two years later in *Comer v. Comer*,[33] was child welfare – and if that purpose could be served by a judgment for arrearages that arose during concealment, then the judgment ought to be awarded. The Comers' two sons were born in 1980 and 1983, when the family lived in Florida. In 1985 financial difficulties prompted their move to Arizona, where the wife's parents lived. He stayed behind to complete some business, but before he could join the family later that year, she obtained an Arizona default divorce decree that included both custody and support provisions. She did not give him her address and also told her Arizona family to keep it from him. In 1988, after he moved to California, he arranged with her parents to spend a weekend at their residence to visit the children. But the children never appeared. Father–son contact was finally re-established in 1992 when the older boy called him. In that conversation he learned for the first time that his former wife had remarried and taken her new husband's name.

The father had made no support payments between 1985 and 1992. At some point during these seven years the mother received assistance from AFDC, and the county later initiated this support action against him. The lower courts, applying *Damico*, held both the mother and the county estopped from seeking arrearages for the seven-year period during which the mother had concealed herself and the children.

The California Supreme Court reversed, holding *Damico* inapplicable for two reasons. We can put aside the second (that the county's claim should not be affected by the mother's behaviour) because it is tangential to our concerns. More central to the decision's logic, as well as for us, was the court's primary rationale, based upon the fact that the Comer children, at 16 and 12 years old, were still minors when the case was decided. The court reasoned that they, unlike the *Damico* child, would therefore benefit as children from any payment of arrearages. It was also 'unpersuaded that requiring father to pay his child support arrearages would be unjust' because the father 'had the use of the money in the past, but his child[ren]'s needs are in the present and surely exceed the amount of the current order for support'.[34] In other words, the delayed collection is not unjust because it will benefit the children in the present, when the father does have access to them, and can thus be justified on the same basis as any other child support payment.

Our earlier discussion suggests we should question the court's assumption that arrearages collected at a child's seventeenth birthday will further a child welfare interest contemplated by the support law. But even accepting *Comer* at face value, we might still expect California to bar the collection of arrearages accumulating during a period of concealment if the enforcement action is not brought until after the child becomes an adult, even if the concealment itself ended beforehand, because the adult child's current needs cannot normally justify a support order. But the final case of this California trio, an appeals court decision, reached the opposite conclusion. The father in *Marriage of Vroenen*[35] paid no support during the four years the mother concealed their sons from him; he began paying current support when contact was re-established after one of the boys called him. Both sons were over 18 when an action was brought in 1999 to collect the arrearages arising during the four-year concealment. *Vroenen* construed *Comer* as allowing this arrearage claim because the concealment ended before the children reached majority, even though the arrearage claim was not brought until afterward.

Vroenen seems to be in tension with *Comer*'s rationale; even if the concealment ended before the children were 18, the *Vroenen* order will not serve the purpose of assisting minor children, and child support is not available in California (and many other states) to assist young adults (with their education or otherwise). That tension is evident in the *Vroenen* opinion itself when it concedes that it cannot order the mother to apply the funds to her children's benefit, because the children are adults. So the court instead expressed 'hope' that she would use the funds for her children. Yet how could the court compel the father to make the payments in the first place, if it could not require the mother to apply them to benefit the children whose interest was their ostensible justification?[36] Nor, of course, could parental fairness justify an arrearage order for this mother, any more than for the mothers in the pre-decree concealment cases we earlier reviewed. Perhaps thus sensing its inability to explain its decision on either child-welfare or parental fairness grounds, the court ultimately relied instead on the impact it thought that its rule would have on children in general:

> [T]he reasoning in *Comer* leads us to conclude that regardless of the . . . equities between the parents, we must formulate a rule that leads to the greatest benefit for children . . . Children do not benefit from the defense of equitable estoppel when concealment ends during the child's minority. Allowing the noncustodial parent to avoid payment by waiting for the custodial parent to take legal action to collect the arrearages, if anything, harms the child by encouraging delay in payment of arrearages.[37]

This explanation assumes that the prompt, voluntary payment of arrearages will be encouraged by a rule allowing obligees to delay enforcing them. But if the potential of legal enforcement is responsible for at least some voluntary payment by otherwise recalcitrant debtors, then surely prompt voluntary payment is more likely under rules that move creditors to prompt action. Indeed, it might seem particularly implausible to think that child support obligors with arrearages accrued during the other parents' concealment would volunteer their prompt payment to newly resurfaced custodial parents who make no enforcement effort – which is precisely what the *Vroenen* rule allows them. If the interests of children in general is the rule's *raison d'être*, it ought to be fashioned so as to encourage obligees to move promptly, rather than let them delay enforcement efforts until after their children are grown.

So while *Comer* and *Vroenen* limit *Damico*, they do not explain why the interests of children require a different result in *Comer* and *Vroenen* than in *Damico*. The interests of children are a poor explanation for collecting arrearages in most cases, and none of these cases present an exception. Nor do they present facts that would justify the award on parental fairness grounds, or to preserve payment incentives. As *Damico* initially observed, it is the obligee, not the obligor, who has disappeared and thereby made payment, as well as visitation, impossible. All that said, there does remain an important difference between the pre-decree and post-decree cases which one would expect courts to take account of, and which may offer the best explanation for the results in *Comer* and *Vroenen*. Litigants are supposed to obey court orders until they are modified or reversed. This general principle applies to child support orders, even when the other parent's concealment renders it impossible to get current payments to her. The responsible obligor cannot ignore the court's order, but must ask the court to modify or suspend it. Understood that way, these cases are not about children and parents at all, but about the need to enforce respect for courts by parties subject to their orders. Of course, this rationale for *Comer* would also apply to *Damico*, suggesting that it was wrongly decided, or was perhaps a sport case whose result is dependent upon exceptional facts.

This rationale also suggests, however, that the support order in all three of these California cases should have been suspended, prospectively, had the obligor promptly sought this remedy after the obligee's disappearance. Indeed, this result could be achieved automatically if initial support orders were framed differently as a general practice. They could provide for their automatic suspension whenever the obligee moves and fails, within some reasonable time, to provide the obligor, or the state agency forwarding the obligor's payments, with her current address or contact information. That change would prevent arrearages from accumulating in the first place. It would not deprive the child of any current support that would otherwise have been available, because the obligee's failure to provide contact information would in any event prevent the obligor or the applicable state agency from forwarding funds to her. The obligee who flees and conceals herself for good reason, such as to avoid physical abuse, could seek an amendment to the existing custody decree barring contact on that basis; those cases must be dealt with individually in any event.[38] But it is reasonable to require the concealed obligee to take the initiative: the obligor cannot initiate any action that could meaningfully adjudicate such a claim because he would have no reliable method by which to give the obligee actual notice of an action. Perhaps he could obtain a default judgment based on substitute service to relieve him of the danger of accumulating arrearages, but that alternative offers no advantage over an automatic suspension.

If failure to give notice to the state's support enforcement agency is to trigger the obligation's suspension, one would of course need to be sure that such notification is simple and easy to provide, and that once provided it will be recorded accurately and promptly. The obligee's failure to notify the appropriate agency cannot serve as an objective and accurate indicator of likely concealment if the agency routinely loses such notifications or enters them months late, or if obligees who move often give no notice to the agency because the support system routinely permits parties to avoid reliance on it for collecting and forwarding support payments. An alternative is to rely on the obligee's failure to give notice to the obligor himself. The required notice ought to be given with sufficient formality (for example, certified mail) to avoid disputes over whether it was given. It might seem unduly burdensome to require obligees to provide such formal notice of every move, but in fact many states already have statutory provisions requiring custodial parents who relocate to give the other parent such notice, often in advance of their actual move. The provisions are intended to allow the other parent the opportunity, prior to any move, to seek appropriate modifications in the custodial provisions to reflect it. But the notice provisions can also be relied upon to establish a conveniently available, objective indicator of concealment giving rise to a suspension of the support obligation, as herein suggested.[39]

Disputes between obligee and obligor over the visitation schedule or the obligee's facilitation of it are a different matter. An obligor who believes that the obligee is undermining his access to their child may or may not have a valid complaint on the facts, and only a court or other appropriate factfinder can hear evidence and resolve the likely factual dispute. Therefore no rule setting an automatic suspension could work in such cases, as it would create too great an incentive for the reluctant obligor to generate selfserving complaints about the obligee's non-compliance. Moreover, in these cases, unlike the relocation cases, an automatic suspension would deprive the child of current support payments which could otherwise be made. In these cases, then, there is no alternative to case-by-case factfinding. But what should a court do when it in fact finds that the custodial parent has frustrated the obligor's access to the child? That is the question addressed in the next section.

B. PROSPECTIVE SUPPORT DEFENCES

Cases in which the parents do not cooperate effectively, or which involve estrangement between non-custodial parent and child, are undoubtedly more common than the concealment cases already considered. It is thus particularly problematic if we cannot identify any effective legal strategy for dealing with them. Some of the possibilities were listed by the California Supreme Court in *Damico*: 'contempt proceedings, terminating or reducing spousal support, modifying custody or child support orders, and requiring a bond to assure compliance with the visitation order'.[40] Contempt is not a coercive sanction itself, but a process which may lead to a sanction. An individual found in civil contempt for defying a court order may be fined or imprisoned, and either sanction may continue until the defendant complies with the order. Fines are but one species of financial sanction; bond forfeitures, and adjustments in spousal support or child support, are other variations.

These various versions of financial sanction are largely indistinguishable for policy purposes. One certainly cannot assume that the portion of a custodial parent's income labelled 'child support' confers benefits only on her children, while income with other labels (such as spousal support) confers no benefits upon them. The custodial household is a single economic unit. Money in the hands of the custodial parent is money. There are necessarily many items of joint consumption in the custodial household. If the child has heat, so does the parent, and the television and telephone are available to both. Even when dedicated uses are conceptually possible they are usually impractical. No one expects the custodial parent to feed her child steak while she eats macaroni. There is the occasional arrangement in which child support is applied to a particular child activity, such as summer camp or music lessons, which the custodial parent would not otherwise purchase, but such arrangements do not account for most ordered child support. So there is normally no difference between a dollar's reduction in the custodial parent's spousal support or in child support. Bond forfeitures or fines of course also have the same impact on the custodial household as dollar-equivalent reduction in support.[41]

The real question presented by these cases is whether coercive remedies – jail or financial penalties – are useful at all as a tool through which to maintain or re-establish a parent–child relationship that has suffered from lack of contact. They are called coercive remedies because their purpose is to coerce an offending party – perhaps the custodial parent, perhaps the child – into complying with the order. Coercive remedies cannot be applied until a court identifies the blameworthy party, who must be coerced into altering his or her behaviour. They can be contrasted with non-coercive remedies, of which there are two principal possibilities: counselling, and a change in custody. The first seeks a change in the parties' relationship, but not through the device of imposing a continuing penalty on the party or parties deemed at fault for its unsatisfactory state. The second accepts the existing visitation arrangements as unworkable, and replaces them with a new custodial plan that the decision-maker believes is more consistent with the child's interests. Let us look first at these non-coercive alternatives.

Therapeutic intervention can be employed by a judge who simply orders the parties to attempt to work out their difficulties with the assistance of counsellors employed by the court or a cooperating agency. In many states, however, visitation enforcement programmes have been specifically set up to respond to the problem of visitation. The most common technique employed by these visitation enforcement programmes is a change in the language of the custody decree to make the details of the visitation arrangement more explicit, but the next most common is referral of the parents to a counselling programme.[42] One study found that half of both the mothers and the fathers referred to such a programme reported after their participation that their visitation problems were solved, although these results may overstate the programmes' effectiveness because there was no control group of non-participants against whom they could be compared. On the other hand, one might hope that further experience and study could promise even more effectiveness from counselling interventions. Certainly, more detailed decrees and the provision of counselling are simple and easy enough to implement that they are worth doing if they help in very many cases. Nonetheless, it appears that something like half the cases are resistant to these solutions.

Perhaps a change in the custodial arrangement would work in some of these remaining cases. Of course, no change would be appropriate if the court suspects that visitation problems arise from the non-custodial parent's own negligent behaviour. So some inquiry into the sources and consequences of the visitation difficulties is unavoidable when considering a custodial change. On the other hand, a change in primary custody need not necessarily require a finding that the current custodian has acted in a culpable manner to frustrate the other parent's access to the child. The conclusion that a change in primary custody is likely to produce better relations with both parents, and that this is in the child's interests, may be sufficient to justify the order. A difficult inquiry into blame might thus be avoided.

Indeed, many states include, among the factors courts are instructed to consider in making an initial custody determination, the parent's willingness to foster a continuing relationship with the other parent.[43] But despite these advantages, it is apparent that in many cases changing primary custody is impractical or ill-advised. The non-custodial parent seeking relief, motivated to maintain his relationship with his children, may nonetheless be unable, because of his employment, to assume the responsibilities of primary custodian (which may be why he did not assume that role in the first place). Nor would it be appropriate to switch primary custody to a parent who has a poor relationship with the child, no matter the reason for the poor relationship. And finally, even where the relationship of child and non-custodial parent is less strained, a transfer of primary custody might in any event cause the child disruption and dislocation if it means moving her from the home of her historic primary caretaker. So one might assume that changing primary custody will not be a practical alternative in many of the difficult cases that we are left to consider.

Some states employ temporary custodial changes as a penalty intended to deter non-compliance, rather than make permanent changes in the child's arrangements. A Florida statute requires a court, if it concludes that a custodial parent has '[refused] to honor a noncustodial parent's . . . visitation rights without proper cause', to 'award the noncustodial parent . . . a sufficient amount of extra visitation to compensate the noncustodial parent . . . which visitation shall be ordered as expeditiously as possible in a manner consistent with the best interests of the child and scheduled in a manner that is convenient for the person deprived of visitation'.[44] This remedy may seem practical in some cases in which a complete change in primary custody would not, and its realistic threat may deter some non-compliance. It certainly seems worth trying. But there will be some cases in which even this modest custodial change would be difficult to implement expeditiously in a way that works for both child and non-custodial parent, and others in which its implementation does not induce compliance. We are then left with jail and financial penalties as the only remaining alternatives for dealing with the more difficult cases resistant to non-coercive sanctions. Yet both these choices also seem problematic.

It is hardly plausible to suggest that we protect a child's interests by imprisoning the custodial parent, particularly given that we are necessarily dealing with cases in which we have already decided that a change in primary custody is inappropriate. It is thus not surprising that it is difficult to find any reported decision affirming a parent's imprisonment for contempt of a court-ordered visitation schedule. The difficult cases in which one might feel pushed to consider such a possibility often involve such strained relations between the parties that it may not be clear who to imprison, or whether jail would have the desired effect of restoring relations between child and non-custodial parent. The few cases that flirt with the possibility of jail illustrate these concerns.

Shellhouse v. Bentley, decided by an Alabama appeals court in 1997, is an example.[45] The trial court had earlier suspended the non-custodial mother's support obligation when her daughter would not see her, but was reversed on appeal because 'parental support is a fundamental right' and that, therefore, 'the waiver of rights of visitation in exchange for release from the duty of child support is a legal impossibility'. So on remand the trial court instead ordered the parties to comply with the visitation schedule, which meant that non-compliance could now constitute contempt. And that is what the mother argued when visits still did not take place. But in fact the father faithfully brought their 14-year-old daughter to the appointed meeting place; the problem was that she refused to leave his car to see her mother. The trial court nonetheless sentenced him to 36 days in jail at hard labour for contempt, with a chance for early release after ten days if the daughter visited with the mother. The trial court later relented, at the daughter's request, by suspending the father's remaining sentence after just one day in jail. But it conditioned the suspension on the daughter's continuing visitation with the mother. Some might thus regard the trial court's approach as a success, since it resulted in visits between mother and daughter. It was nonetheless reversed on the dad's appeal.

The father, the appeals court said, could not be held in contempt because of the child's refusal to visit. Moreover, because of the daughter's age the court believed that her wishes bore importantly on any assessment of her best interests, suggesting, in effect, that visitation over her objection might be inappropriate to order in any event. Finally, the appeals court concluded that in no event could the child be held in contempt of court, even if she refused to participate in seeing her mother as provided under the custody order. In a similar case, an Illinois trial court was bolder about in its approach to the children. It held both daughters in contempt of court when they refused to visit their father, who lived in another state. It ordered the mother to ground the younger daughter, and the older one placed in juvenile detention, until they agreed to see him. One is not surprised to learn that the appeals court reversed here as well.[46] What is surprising, perhaps, is that the appeals court agreed the children could be placed in contempt, while cautioning that they should not be subject to sanctions unless no other remedy could work. What other remedy should the trial court first try? The appeals court's only suggestion was placing sanctions on the custodial mother – precisely the remedy that the Alabama court found inappropriate in such a case. A court contemplating the failing of custodial parent or child usually concludes that a different order is preferable.

The Florida statute quoted earlier also attempts to provide an alternative to jail that might be more palatable for courts to consider in dealing with recalcitrant custodians. It allows the court to order, instead of jail, that such a parent 'do community service if the order will not interfere with the welfare of the child'.[47] Coerced community service is reminiscent of jail because it deprives the custodial parent of choice in how she spends her time, but might in some cases perhaps have the advantage of imposing no corresponding detriment on the child. Whether the concept works in practice is not clear. The provision is relatively new, and one cannot tell how often it is used. For custodial parents who work, the problems are evident: such an order must either create the same disruption in the work schedule, and thus the same risk of income loss, as would jail, or it must take the parent away from the child during the relatively limited periods each week in which the custodial parent does not work. For the custodial parent who does not work the approach might have more promise, at least if the children are of school age.[48] Yet custodial mothers of school-age children who do not work are relatively uncommon, so that this choice will be of limited utility if applied only to them.

Consider as well that there are multiple reasons why courts are reluctant to place children or custodial parents in jail, and some may apply to the Florida provision as well. One of the reasons, undoubtedly, is our particular aversion to mistakenly depriving people of their liberty: unlike mistaken fines, there can be no reimbursement to repair such errors. In this context, avoiding that mistake requires courts to sort out why a parent and child have no relationship, so that they can assign blame and jail the blameworthy party. Who is the guilty party in *Shellhouse*? The daughter, or her father for shaping her view of the mother she refuses to see, or her mother for acting unreasonably so as to alienate her daughter? Finding these facts may be more than the court can do, or even more than is conceptually possible to do. People in close family relationships sometimes develop great hostility to one another even when no one is to blame, in the sense of having acted immorally; something about their situation, or incompatibilities in their perceptions and expectations, may bring out the worst in them all. This difficulty in making the fundamental findings of blameworthiness necessary to the imposition of a jail sentence is exacerbated by the nature of the contempt remedy, which inherently assumes the court's ongoing scrutiny to ensure continued compliance with its orders. So even if visits take place after they are coerced, but then stop, or do not go well, the court would have to determine why: who if anyone is to blame for the latest difficulty, and thus liable anew to be jailed for contempt? Other legal remedies are not of this nature. When a court grants P compensation for D's misconduct, the case is over; there is no occasion to maintain ongoing scrutiny over

D's behaviour to determine whether he has reformed. But in visitation enforcement the difficult task of assigning blame is potentially continuing.

Another central problem with jail is efficacy. Jail, or coerced community service, should be tried only in cases that have resisted less problematic solutions, given the other problems associated with it. But because we reserve jail for consideration in only the most difficult cases, we may be concerned it too will not work. There is some evidence for the efficacy of jail in the historic use of the contempt power in child support enforcement,[49] although it is used sparingly today because wage assignment, which collects more support with fewer problems, is now available. But while garnishment or jail may work to collect support whether or not the obligor is himself inclined to comply, a social obligation to one's parent or child is another matter. One may doubt that the *Shellhouse* court's threat to imprison the father would really help heal the relationship of mother and daughter, even if it resulted in their spending some time in one another's physical presence.

So if counselling, and tinkering with the custody order, leave a core of hard cases unresolved, and if jail or its substitutes also seem unlikely to work, do financial remedies, including the reduction or elimination of the child support obligation, offer more promise? On first impression financial remedies would seem to share two of jail's problems: it requires assigning blame, and may not coerce meaningful compliance. Yet while many courts resist reductions in child support, their resistance is less than their resistance to imposing jail. Courts, at least, see financial penalties as buying useful results at an acceptable cost more often than they see incarceration doing so, even if not very often. And consider that the *Principles of the Law of Family Dissolution* recently adopted by the American Law Institute provide that '[i]f a parent persistently interferes with a support obligor's access to the child, the court may modify the child-support obligation'.[50]

But the states vary. California's statutory provisions bar modification of child support as a remedy for visitation denial.[51] On the other hand, there are other states, such as New York, which explicitly provide for it,[52] and cases can be found which do it. For example, in the New York case of *Kershaw v. Kershaw*[53] the court suspended the father's support obligation for his 13-year-old daughter after finding that since the parties' separation two years earlier, his efforts to maintain a relationship with her had failed because of the mother's influence. In reaching this result, the court noted that there was no evidence that the suspension would result in the child becoming a public charge. But is the financial penalty in *Kershaw* any more likely than jail in *Shellhouse* to restore the parent–child relationship? It is hard to see why it would. Indeed, the court's understandable concern that the child not be left a public charge serves to emphasize one particular weakness of the financial remedy: the less dependent is the custodial household upon the child support payments, the less powerful is their suspension as a coercive tool. So in just those cases in which courts are most comfortable suspending the support obligation – where the custodial household can sustain a reasonable living standard on its own – we might expect the suspension to have the least coercive punch. One might thus expect that terminating or reducing support offers little advantage over alternative remedies in dealing with the difficult cases that are resistant to soft interventions like counseling or clarifying the order, unless we were willing to apply it even when a reduction in the custodial household income would have maximum coercive power because it would put the household members in real financial jeopardy. The dilemma posed by that observation is obvious.

Consider, however, a different rationale for the order in *Kershaw*. Perhaps suspension or termination of the support obligation is appropriate even if ineffective in achieving the key goal of restoring the parent–child relationship, because in that case the duty to support may be absent. Support is of course widely regarded as a parental obligation. On the other hand, the definition of 'parent' for this purpose need not necessarily follow the parties' genes. I have written elsewhere about how the law traditionally vindicated social relationships more than biology as the basis of parental status, and I have urged that this orientation be maintained even in the face of technological advances that now permit far more reliable identifications of a child's biological father (Ellman, 2002). I also argued that in the case of biological fathers who enjoy no social relationship with their children, their status as parents ought to depend upon *why*. Distinction ought therefore be drawn, I suggested, between men who make no effort to take social responsibility for children they beget, and men who never have the opportunity to make such effort because the child's location, parentage or even existence has been concealed from them. I argued that social policies require imposing support obligations on the first group but not the second. The same arguments would suggest that there is no policy basis for imposing a support obligation upon a parent who is prevented from seeing his or her child by the other parent, and who in consequence has no relationship with the child despite his conscientious efforts to establish or maintain one. Indeed, these duty arguments apply on their face even to the case in which termination of the support obligation would impose substantial burdens on the child; the fact that the child is needy is obviously insufficient, of itself, to explain why any particular person is obligated to meet that need. Of course, in the absence of any social safety net to ensure such a child's financial security in these cases, it is unlikely courts would terminate the support obligation in them.

The idea that the duty to provide support might end when the relationship ends is not entirely foreign to existing child support law, and may lie behind New York's rule even though it is not articulated in this way. The idea also seems to underlie at least some applications of the widespread if somewhat confused legal doctrine of emancipation. At common law, the minor child's marriage or entry into the military service terminated or suspended the parental support obligation.[54] Living apart from one's parents could have the same effect.[55] There are today statutes in many states that establish procedures for judicial emancipation at the behest of the child or, in some cases, the parent. They vary widely on the standard for declaring emancipation and the scope of an emancipation.[56] Although a child seeking to escape parental authority can bring an emancipation action, the doctrine has more typically been raised by a parent who seeks to avoid paying a third party who provided services to the child.[57] Courts have on occasion found a child emancipated as a consequence of having left the parental home and rejected parental control.[58] Other courts have rejected the doctrine's application to such facts.[59] Some make the decision turn on their evaluation of whether the parent or the child is to blame for their estrangement.[60] Declaring a child 'emancipated' on the petition of a support obligor who shows that the estrangement was not his fault is quite similar to recognizing visitation denial as a valid basis upon which to terminate prospective support obligations. One important respect in which the two are similar to one another is that both are reversible: emancipation can be rescinded and the child returned to a dependant status when the facts that gave rise to the emancipation change.[61] By contrast, the alternative of terminating parental status is permanent; the status can be restored only through a formal adoption.

In sum, if one asks whether reduced visitation has an impact upon the duty to provide support, rather than whether reducing support can effectively coerce increased visitation, one may be more likely to conclude that the remedy should be granted. This conclusion may seem to fly in the face of rules often found in statutes and cases concerning the independence of the two, but those rules are not universal. They are also in tension with the social norms of reciprocity instinctively assumed by most parents, with some other family law rules, and with fundamental ideas about the nature of parenthood that conceive of it as including both a duty to support and a right to access. That said, the problem of assigning blame for the parent–child estrangement seems to remain. Even if we explain the reduction in support as following from the obligor's diminished duty, rather than from its efficacy in deterring visitation-denial, we still need to establish that the impairments in the child's relationship with the support obligor are not the obligor's own responsibility. But perhaps the task of blame assignment is easier in this context because some questions might not be necessary to answer. Perhaps, unlike the case of jail, we need only decide that the obligor is not to blame, without deciding who is.

Consider the example of a difficult case like *Shellhouse*. In deciding whether jail was an appropriate remedy, the court was understandably concerned with whether it was the 14-year-old daughter or her custodial father who sabotaged the visitation; apart from whether one wants to incarcerate children, one does not want to incarcerate one actor for the another's offence. Financial penalties present a somewhat different picture, however. Although some formulations appear to distinguish between child support and spousal support, we have already noted that fluctuations in the income of the custodial household are as a general matter economically equivalent no matter the label put on any particular source of income that is enlarged or diminished. A dollar's reduction in spousal support affects custodial parent and child both, and in the same way, as a dollar's reduction in child support. It is thus a matter of bookkeeping more than social justice as to which pot the penalty is paid from. Perhaps the shared fate of the members of the custodial household is a reason for concern about financial penalties altogether. But what is clear is that there would be little point in requiring a court, before imposing a financial penalty, to probe the dynamics of the *Shellhouse* family so as to decide whether daughter or custodial father was more to blame, because nothing of practical consequence would turn on it. A financial penalty cannot be shaped to target one household member alone.

Moreover, we may also decide that the duty of support is compromised even when neither the child nor the custodial parent are blameworthy, so long as we believe the obligor also is not. Consider, for example, one common pattern in which the issue arises: the custodial mother remarries with a child from her first marriage who is still relatively young. She has additional children with her second husband. The mother naturally wishes all her children to see one another as siblings and members of the same family; she does not distinguish among them according to their paternity. Her new husband, with her encouragement, develops a paternal relationship with her child from her first marriage. Perhaps the mother moves with her new family to another community, for any number of perfectly understandable reasons: convenience to employment, better housing options for the enlarged family, or better choices of school. Or perhaps the non-custodial father moves for similarly understandable reasons, such as job opportunities, or the preferences of his new spouse. The moves need not be far; divorced men who live more than 75 miles from their children see them much less than those who live closer because that distance makes day trips much less convenient (Hetherington and Kelly, 2002, p. 134). The mother may not be hostile to the idea of maintaining a relationship between her first child and the child's father, but maintaining it involves intrusions into her new family that are increasingly inconvenient. The child herself might come to see visits with her father as increasingly irrelevant to her 'real' family, none of the rest of whom treat him as a family member. And facing these hurdles of emotional and possibly geographical distance, the father gradually presses less to overcome them, especially if he also acquires new children in a second marriage, in whom he must invest time and emotional energy.

Asking who is to blame for the absence of father–child contact in this situation is not likely to be helpful. As difficult as it is to show causation in human affairs, it gets one only part way because causation alone is not sufficient to establish blame. Blame cannot be based, for example, on the simple conclusion that the mother's remarriage, or move to a distant location, caused the father–child estrangement. Blame is a moral concept requiring the additional finding that the behaviour which caused the undesirable result was itself wrong. That is why estrangement can arise when no one is to blame: both the parents' and child's behaviour may be non-wrongful adaptations to a shift in family arrangements. In such a case the reconstituted family arrangements may also be a good outcome for the child who has become integrated into his new family. Of course, that happy picture, even if true, does not mean that there will be no visitation or support disputes between the parents.

Nor does the conclusion that no one is to blame mean the parties will feel content with their situation. For example, a non-custodial father whose former spouse has moved far away may recognize the consequences of this reality for his visitation rights, and the inevitability of acquiescing to them, but still be unwilling to agree to legal severance of his paternity and adoption of the child by the mother's new husband. But even if he wants to retain the status of legal parent, and the right to see the child at least some times (perhaps in the hope that things will one day improve), he may also understandably resent paying the full amount of child support when his access to and relationship with the child has been so substantially diminished. At one time, the divorced parents might have developed an informal understanding in this circumstance: in recognition of the diminished relationship between the father and the child, and the mother's diminished financial needs in light of her remarriage, he would reduce his support payments, or perhaps even cease them altogether. Today such an arrangement is difficult and perhaps impossible to establish. If the father's income is subject to a wage assignment order, as most today are, that assignment will continue unless the parties obtain a formal modification of the order. Indeed, under procedures required by recent federal mandates, the assignment will typically follow the father to a new employer without further action by mother or father, although perhaps with a few months' delay. If there is no wage assignment order, the father could perhaps simply stop paying. But in doing so he would incur a substantial risk of liability for arrearages should the mother later decide to seek them: more than one court has enforced such arrearages despite the parents' informal agreement to depart from the formal support order, when the custodial mother later changes her mind.[62]

What should the court do if the parents come to it seeking a formal modification to reflect their understanding, or if the father alone seeks a reduction or suspension of his support obligation in recognition of the new reality in which his role in the child's life has been circumscribed substantially? Most courts would today reject the modification, on the grounds that the parties cannot waive the father's support obligation, which belongs to the child, and that the lack of visitation is not ground for its reduction, at least where the father has not shown the mother guilty of having 'wrongfully interfered with or withheld visitation rights', to use the language of the New York statute quoted above.[63] And in the case I am positing, he probably could not make that showing. I am suggesting that this is the wrong standard to use in such a case. The question is not whether the mother is blameworthy, but whether the father's duty has become diminished. In this case there is good reason to think it has, because circumstances for which he has no moral blame have enlarged the already substantial barriers that most non-custodial parents face in maintaining a meaningful relationship with their child – enlarged them to the point that he cannot reasonably be assumed able to overcome them. The issue, in other words, is whether he has been involuntarily estranged or separated from his child, not necessarily whether that separation was caused by the mother's wrongful conduct. There is nothing wrongful, for example, about the mother's desire to move 3000 miles away to remain with her second husband who has taken new employment, or in her taking the child with her pursuant to a court order that allows it. But that should not necessarily render irremediable the serious impairment in father–child relations that result.

Custodial parents often remarry, and in some cases the other parent's relationship with the child continues unimpaired. But in others it does not. My hypothetical case is but one version of that story; there are many others. I suggest that courts *consider* the non-custodial parent's claim that his child support obligation should be reduced to take account of the resulting impairment in his relationship with his child; I do not suggest that such reductions always follow. Reductions should be available only if the factfinder decides two key points. First, the relationship's impairment must arise in the absence of any culpable behaviour on the obligor's part. Second, the remarriage must render the support obligor's payments less important to the child's welfare. As previously noted, the impact on the child of changes in the custodial household's income are not dependent upon the label put on the dollars, whether child support, spousal support or a new spouse's income. Continuing contributions from the non-custodial parent may be helpful in maintaining harmony between the custodial parent and her new spouse, and may be particularly useful when earmarked for special expenditures that confer benefit upon the child exclusively. But these purposes can typically be served even if the total support obligation is reduced. Yet many states decline to consider the new spouse's income in calculating child support obligations. While that rule can in many circumstances be explained and justified, it ignores the economic reality that income in the custodial household is largely fungible regardless of source. Even apart from any general reconsideration of this rule, it should be reconsidered where the remarriage is, at least over time, accompanied by an estrangement in the relationship of the child and non-custodial parent. That parent might prefer a full relationship and full payment, and most observers would probably say he should. But if the law cannot protect the relationship, it should at least reduce the obligation.

CONCLUSION

Existing law seems a confused combination of statements affirming the independence of the support and visitation portions of any divorce decree, and of rules that are not always consistent with those statements; of proper concern with the welfare of the children subject to those decrees, and of inattention to the question of whether protection of children's welfare can really explain the orders issued on their behalf. The first part of this chapter examined cases involving claims for arrearages arising during periods of visitation denial. It concludes that child-welfare purposes often cannot justify the collection of arrearages arising during a period of concealment, particularly if the arrearages will not be collected until the child is beyond or near the age of majority. Nor, if concealment has taken place, can collection of the arrearages be justified on the alternative ground of fairly allocating the burden of support. I therefore suggest that divorce decrees make suspension of the support obligation the default result during such concealment periods, subject to the obligee's demonstrating to the court a justification for the concealment. Suspending it is consistent with the social norms and expectations of the parties themselves. Allowing the collection of arrearages accrued during periods of concealment is therefore more likely than suspension to surprise the parties, and thus also to pose a heightened risk of injustice.

In contrast, we must require continued payments from the non-custodial parent who believes the other parent has interfered with his access to or relationship with their child, at least until that parent persuades a court of facts that justify a different result. A court confronted with such claims is best advised to seek various non-coercive remedies, such as counselling and decree clarification, or even a change in primary custody, before imposing jail or financial penalties upon a parent or child it believes responsible for the visitation problems. Some cases will inevitably resist solution through these non-coercive remedies, but even then jail remains a problematic choice. Reductions or even suspension of the support obligation may be appropriate in some of them. In considering such financial remedies, courts must be cautious to avoid creating undesirable incentives that could reward the non-custodial parent who is more concerned with avoiding payment than seeing his child. But once satisfied that the lack of contact between the obligor and his children is not the result of inappropriate, uncaring or wrongful behaviour on his part, it should consider financial sanctions. Such sanctions may be unlikely to yield an improvement in the amount of contact or in the relationship of the child and the support obligor in the difficult cases for which this remedy is reserved. But when an obligor's opportunity to maintain a meaningful relationship with his child is impaired, through no fault of his own, then so is his duty to support that child.

In some of these cases the reduction or termination of the support obligation may put the child in serious financial jeopardy. That may not undermine the argument for the obligor's impaired duty, but in the absence of any social safety net to replace his support, courts cannot be expected to compromise it. Without anyone to pass his support duty to, the obligor may not be able to shed it; better he than the child be left without a chair when the music stops. In many cases, however, reduction or suspension of the current support obligation will not place the child in serious financial jeopardy. In some the custodial parent has other resources, such assistance from family, that is not normally counted in the calculation of child support obligations but which are a reality. Indeed, a custodial parent willing to risk the loss or impairment of the support obligation through actions that impair the other parent's access to the child may be more likely than custodial parents in general to have such 'off the books' resources available to them. Even more numerous may be the cases in which the custodial parent has remarried, to someone with reasonable income, and thereby becomes less dependent upon receipt of child support. Although states typically do not count a new spouse's income in calculating child support, it is reasonable to consider it when deciding whether to suspend or reduce it as a consequence of an impairment in the obligor's access to or relationship with the child that did not result from wrongful, negligent or uncaring behaviour of the obligor himself.

NOTES

1. Pearson and Thoennes cite studies by Seltzer and by Cherlin and Furstenberg. See also Hetherington and Kelly (2002).
2. Pearson and Thoennes (1998).
3. Pearson and Thoennes found that even among fathers who saw their children 'fairly' regularly, 65 per cent felt cut out of their children's lives, as did 38 per cent of those who saw their children nine days a month or more. Pearson and Thoennes (1998) at 237–8.
4. See also Pearson and Anhalt (1994).
5. For clarity of exposition I shall in most cases employ the male pronoun for the parent with the support obligation and the female pronoun for the parent with primary custody; while this relationship is hardly universal it still remains far more common than its converse.
6. *Troxel v. Granville*, 530 US 57 (2000).
7. For example, Ill. Comp. Stat. Ann. Ch. 750, para. 5/607(a) (1997) (parent not granted custody 'is entitled to reasonable visitation rights unless the court finds . . . that visitation would endanger seriously the child's physical, mental, moral or emotional health'); Calif. Fam.Code § 3100 (a) (2001) (visitation may be denied only if it is shown to be 'detrimental to the best interests of the child'); *Smith v. Smith*, 869 S.W.2d 55 (Ky. 1994) (trial court reversed for denying visitation to a father incarcerated for murder, kidnapping and robbery, without first finding, on the basis of a hearing, that visitation would endanger the child).
8. For example, *Cty. of Orange v. Rosales*, 121 Cal.Rptr.2d 788 (App. 2002); *Ventura Cty v. Gonzales*, 106 Cal.Rptr.2d 461 (App. 2001), (termination of unwed father's rights also terminated his support obligation, so county cannot collect from him).
9. Although chronic nonsupport might be a ground for termination in any case, it appears to be relied upon primarily where the question is whether to allow adoption by a stepfather over the father's objection. In these cases, of course, termination allows the law to substitute a new legal father whose support may be more reliable. For example, Cal.Family Code § 8604 (1997) (non-custodial parent's failure to provide support for one year is grounds for terminating his rights by allowing adoption by stepparent without his consent); *Dusseau v. Martyn*, 411 N.W.2d 743 (Mich.App. 1987) (stepfather may adopt over father's objection where father had not paid support).
10. *Sharpe v. Sharpe*, 902 P.2d 210 (Wyo. 1995), quoting earlier authorities, including its own prior decision in *Broyles v. Broyles*, 711 P.2d 1119 (Wyo. 1985).
11. The qualification 'without justification' is important. For example, we might well take a different approach to concealment if the mother was hiding herself and the child from a physically abusive father. We might have a different view in that case for a variety of reasons, one of which could be our belief that such a father is himself responsible for his lack of contact with the child by having forced the mother to take such self-defensive actions. Clearly such cases exist; I exclude them from this part of the analysis because I want to examine a particular conceptual question: is there, as many courts seem to believe, a good justification for requiring support payments even for a period during which the mother was in hiding without justification.
12. *Kramer v. Kelly*, 401 A.2d 799 (Pa. Super. 1979).
13. *Brad Mitchell v. Lee D.*, 564 N.W.2d 354 (Wisc.App. 1997).
14. *Idem* at 360. Wisconsin later decided that in such cases a court could order less support than specified by the applicable guidelines. See *Brenton T.C. v. Patrick G.B.*, 2001 WL 101588 (Wis.App.).
15. The cases are collected at Anno, *Liability of Father for Retroactive Child Support On Judicial Determination of Paternity*, 87 A.L.R.5th 361 (2001).
16. 963 P.2d 548 (N.M.App. 1998).
17. 963 P.2d at 550.
18. 959 P.2d 540 (N.M.App. 1998).
19. Obviously, one might have a different intuition about the likely financial circumstances

of custodial mothers who conceal themselves with justification, as in a desperate effort to avoid physical abuse.

20. See, for example, *In re Loomis*, 587 N.W.2d 427, 430 (S.D. 1998).

21. Federal law enacted in 1984 requires the states to allow the establishment of paternity at any time up to the child's eighteenth birthday, overriding provisions then in effect in some states which established shorter limitation periods for paternity actions. 42 U.S.C. § 666(a)(5). But this provision does not require the enforcement of retroactive support obligations for periods preceding the action.

22. Ohio R.C. § 3111.13(F)(3)(c), enacted in 2000.

23. Maine, for example, limits all arrearages to six years back from the date on which paternity was established. This provision was applied in *Dept of Human Services v. Bell*, 711 A.2d 1292 (Me. 1998).

24. More specifically, the statutes bar orders enforcing child support arrearages covering any period preceding the filing (or sometimes the service) of the initial pleading establishing the support obligation. California Family Code § 4009 (Westlaw 2002). See *Marriage of Goosmann*, 31 Cal.Rptr.2d 613 (App. 1994) and *Cty. of Santa Clara v. Perry*, 956 P.2d 1191 (Cal. 1998) (§ 4009 held to also apply to paternity actions brought by the district attorney).

25. Consider, for example, that California's bar on pre-decree arrearages would apply to the case of a custodial mother who initially depends upon the father's voluntary contributions, but then brings a support claim when they cease. She can obtain an order for prospective support but cannot claim arrearages for any dollar gap between the voluntary payments she previously received and the amounts that would have ordered for that earlier time had enforcement then been sought. While denying this arrearage claim may be the right result, one could not explain its denial by doubts about this father's moral responsibility to support the child.

26. 7 Cal.4th 673, 872 P.2d 126, 29 Cal.Rptr.2d 787 (1994).

27. This provision survives today as California Family Code § 3556 (2001).

28. Equitable estoppel is a doctrine that arises in many areas of the law, under which an individual is barred from asserting an otherwise established legal right. A judge-made rule, it is employed when the claimant's own conduct has so compromised the position of the persons against whom the right would be asserted that it is inequitable to permit him to assert it.

29. For a California case holding that the father must pay despite such frustration by the mother, see *Moffat v. Moffat*, 165 Cal.Rptr. 877, 612 P.2d 967 (Cal. 1980), which was distinguished by *Damico*. As the Court explained: 'Mrs. Moffat has systematically endeavored to circumvent the visitation order through an unrelenting variety of legal proceedings. These include a petition to give up her children and to have them declared wards of the juvenile court, a proceeding in which she reasserted the molestation accusation previously found to be untrue; a motion to terminate the July visitation order; and criminal charges against Mr. Moffat for failure to provide . . . To this day Mrs. Moffat has obdurately refused to comply with the visitation order and has thus denied the children their right to know and to be with their father . . . In seeking to avoid the plain meaning of the statute, Mr. Moffat frames the following issue: "Where the father has consistently performed his duty of support, can a mother leave California, quit her job, go on relief in another state, for the express purpose of depriving him of visitation with his children and still use RURESA, and not be subject to [the] defense of estoppel because of [the statutory language]?" Despite our sympathy for a noncustodial parent thrust into that predicament, our reply, in short, is affirmative.' 612 P.2d at 969–970.

30. As quoted in *Damico*, 872 P.2d at 790, 29 Cal.Rptr.2d at 129.

31. *Idem* at 131 and 793.

32. 872 P.2d 131, 29 Cal.Rptr.2d 792.

33. 14 Cal.4th 504, 927 P.2d 265, 59 Cal.Rptr.2d 155 (1996).

34. 59 Cal.Rptr.2d at 161 (in part quoting earlier lower court opinion).

35. 114 Cal. Rptr.2d 860 (App. 2001).

36. One might also argue that the payments can be justified as some form of compensation

to the children for the support they were wrongfully denied as minors. The problem with that rationale is that the child support law does not allow the court to direct that the funds be spent on the children who are not minors. State law sometimes allows support for adult children if they are disabled, but never allows support orders to benefit a healthy adult simply because that adult had a childhood that fell short of what it should have been. Perhaps it should.

37. 114 Cal. Rptr.2d at 863–64. The court also suggested that claims brought years after children become adults, for periods of concealment that ended during their minority, might still be barred under the equitable doctrine of *laches*, thus avoiding truly egregious cases.

38. They must be dealt with individually because the claims of abuse may be contested and because even when true the nature of any abuse may vary considerably among cases. A court must fashion an order appropriate to the facts of the particular case; it can, if necessary, protect the confidentiality of the obligee's whereabouts as one aspect of a protective order.

39. For an example of such a notice provision, see Ariz. Rev. Stat. § 25–408.

40. The court's mention of child support is perhaps puzzling given its construction of the California statute barring the visitation-denial defence as applicable in all but concealment cases.

41. While bond forfeitures are ordinarily thought of as single events, they would presumably have to be reimposed regularly so long as the offender remained in contempt. In some cases the proceeds of a bond forfeiture, like a fine, might be paid to the court rather than to the other party. There being no obvious reason why the court rather than the non-custodial parent should receive the financial benefit of the remedy for visitation denial, this distinction just makes them less attractive than reductions in child support as sanctions for visitation denial.

42. Pearson and Anhalt (1994).

43. For example, Ill. Stat. Ann. Sect. 750 para. 5/602(a)(8) (Smith-Hurd 1993); Colo.Rev.Stat. § 14–10–124 (1.5)(f) (court must consider the 'ability of the custodian to encourage the sharing love, affection, and contact between the child and the noncustodial party'. See *Morehouse v. Morehouse*, 452 S.E.2d 632 (S.C. App. 1995) (father awarded custody because he encouraged good relationship between child and mother, though mother claimed he had engaged in 'almost every kind of misconduct'); *Garrett v. Garrett*, 527 N.W.2d 213 (Neb. 1995) (Jehovah's Witness mother awarded custody despite depression, because father tried to alienate children); *In re Marriage of Quirk-Edwards*, 509 N.W.2d 476 (Iowa 1993) (refusal of one parent to provide opportunity for other parent to have meaningful contact with child without just cause shall be considered harmful to the child's interest).

44. Fla. Stat. § 61.13(4) (Lexis 2002).

45. *Shellhouse v. Bentley*, 690 So.2d 401 (Ala.App. 1997).

46. *Marriage of Marshall*, 663 N.E.2d 1113 (Ill.App. 1996).

47. Fla. Stat. § 61.13(4) (Lexis 2002),

48. For children of pre-school age the cost of childcare to make the mother available for community service might be substantial, and the disruption in the child's routine might present the very kind of risk of detriment to the child that this alternative to jail is surely meant to avoid.

49. That was shown in the classic study by David Chambers, *Making Fathers Pay*.

50. American Law Institute, *Principles of the Law of Family Dissolution* (Lexis-Nexis 2002), § 3.21 (3), page 554.

51. California Family Code § 3556 (2001) states that the 'existence or enforcement of a duty of support owed by a noncustodial parent for the support of a minor child shall not be affected by a failure or refusal by the custodial parent to implement any rights as to custody or visitation granted by a court to the noncustodial parent'.

52. See New York Domestic Relations Law § 241 and the explanatory material contained in the McKinney annotations. Oregon is more explicit. Or. Rev. Stat. § 107.431 allows a court to 'terminate or modify that part of the order or decree requiring payment of money for the support of the minor child' when there has been a 'showing that the parent

or other person having custody of the child or a person acting in that parent or other person's behalf has interfered with or denied without good cause the exercise of the [other] parent's parenting time rights'. Note that all states have adopted some form of the Revised Uniform Enforcement of Support Act, which has long provided that claims of visitation denial cannot be raised as a defense in a Uniform Act enforcement action.

53.   701 N.Y.S.2d 739 (App.Div. 2000). For another recent New York example, see *Tibaldi v. Meehan*, 676 N.Y.S.2d 607 (App.Div. 1998).

54.   See *Meyer v. Meyer*, 493 S.W.2d 42 (Mo. App. 1973) (marriage); *LaVoice v. LaVoice*, 214 A.2d 53 (Vt. 1965) (military service); *Bishop v. Bishop*, 671 A.2d 644 (N.J. Super. Ch. Div. 1995) (child enrolled at United States Military Academy is, by definition, emancipated); *Porath v. McVey*, 884 S.W.2d 692 (Mo. App. 1994)(same); Katz et al. (1973).

55.   For example, *Town v. Anonymous*, 467 A.2d 687 (Conn. Super. Ct. 1983) (16-year-old daughter who had voluntarily left parents' home to live with putative father of her baby was emancipated); *Holt v. Holt*, 633 S.W.2d 171 (Mo. App. 1982) (19-year-old son who had left home to live with others, retaining his monthly earnings of $900 emancipated); but see *In re Marriage of Robinson*, 601 P.2d 358 (Colo. App. 1979) (parents' financial obligations continue during child's temporary employment away from home)

56.   Such emancipation provisions include Cal. Fam. Code §§7001–7003 (West 1997); Conn. Gen. Stat. Ann. §§46b-150b, 46b-150d, 46b-150e (West 1996); Or. Rev. Stat. Ann. §§419 B.552, 419 B.558 (1995).

57.   See Annot., Parent's Obligation to Support Unmarried Minor Child Who Refuses to Live with Parent, 98 A.L.R.3d 334 (1980).

58.   Roe v. Doe, 29 N.Y.2d 188, 324 N.Y.S.2d 71, 272 N.E.2d 567 (1971) (duty of support terminated by daughter's actions in voluntarily abandoning father's home to avoid parental control); *Debra R. v. Sidney R.*, 85 Misc. 2d 914, 380 N.Y.S.2d 579 (Fam. Ct. 1976) (dismissing petition for support where minor on public assistance had emancipated herself by voluntarily leaving parent's home without justification), as described and relied upon by R.R. v. C.R., 797 P.2d 459 (Utah App. 1990).

59.   *Carroll v. Carroll*, 593 So. 2d 1131 (Fla. App. 1992) (no termination of support even where child had successfully petitioned for termination of obligor's visitation rights); In re Brown, 597 N.E.2d 1297 (Ind. App. 1992) (17-year-old's refusal to visit non-custodial parent does not justify finding of emancipation); *Doerrfeld v. Konz*, 524 So. 2d 1115 (Fla. App. 1988) (refusing to terminate father's support duty where daughter gave birth to non-marital child while living with mother).

60.   See, for example, *Allison C. v. Susan C.*, 598 N.Y.S.2d 970 (App. Div. 1993) (lack of parent–child contact was obligor's fault); *Trosky v. Mann*, 581 A.2d 177 (Pa. Super. 1990) (imposing obligation where 16-year-old said he 'wanted absolutely nothing' from his parents after leaving home; court found child incapable of self-support and he was made unwelcome in his parents' home).

61.   See, for example, *Berks County Children and Youth Services v. Rowan*, 631 A.2d 615 (Pa. Super. Ct. 1993) in which a 15-year-old girl married with her parents' permission but later separated from her husband. The court found that she was no longer emancipated, and her parents were once again legally responsible for her support. Also, see *Wulff v. Wulff*, 500 N.W.2d 845 (Neb. 1993) (emancipation rescinded where child who had left home and given birth returned to the parental home); *Eyerman v. Thias*, 760 S.W.2d 187 (Mo. App. 1988) (reinstating child support obligation after annulment of daughter's marriage).

62.   Indeed, there are cases in which the parties agreed that the child would change residence and live with father, but neglected to formally change either the custody or the support order, with the result that the mother was later able to collect arrearages from the father for the period during which the child lived with him. *Price v. Price*, 912 S.W.2d 44 (Ky. 1995); *Houser v. Houser*, 535 N.W.2d 882 (S.D. 1995).

63.   For discussion of the judicial reluctance to accept agreements waiving child support obligations in exchange for a waiver of visitation rights, see Ellman et al. (1998), 866–872.

REFERENCES

Annotation (1980), 'Parent's obligation to support unmarried minor child who refuses to live with parent', *American Law Reports 3d*, **98**, 334–42.

Annotation (2001), 'Liability of father for retroactive child support on judicial determination of paternity', *American Law Reports 5th*, **87**, 361–472.

Chambers, David L. (1979), *Making Fathers Pay: the Enforcement of Child Support*, Chicago: U. of Chicago Press.

Ellman, Ira (2002), 'Ambiguous father families', in Stephen Sugarman, Mary Ann Mason and Arlene Skolnick, *All Our Families*, New York: Oxford University Press; reprinted as 'Thinking about custody and support in ambiguous-father families', *Family Law Quarterly*, **36** (1), 49–78.

Ellman, Ira, Paul Kurtz and Elizabeth Scott (1998), *Family Law: Cases, Text, Problems*, 3rd edn, Charlottesville, VA: Lexis Law Publishing.

Hetherington, Mavis and John Kelly (2002), *For Better or for Worse: Divorce Reconsidered*, New York: W.W. Norton.

Katz, Sanford N., William A. Schroeder and Lawrence R. Sidman (1973), 'Emancipating our children – coming of legal age in America', *Family Law Quarterly*, **7**, 211–41.

Pearson, Jessica and Jean Anhalt (1994), 'Examining the connection between child access and child support', *Family and Conciliation Courts Review*, **32**, 93–109.

Pearson, Jessica and Nancy Thoennes (1998), 'Programs to increase fathers' access to their children', in Irwin Garfinkel, Sara McLanahan, Daniel Meyer and Judith Seltzer (eds), *Fathers Under Fire*, New York: Russell Sage Foundation, pp. 220–52.

Phear, W.P.C., J.C. Beck, B.B. Hauser, S.C. Clark and R.A. Whilney (1983), 'An empirical study of custody agreements: joint versus sole legal custody', *Journal of Psychiatry and Law*, **11**, 419–41.

Principles of the Law of Family Dissolution § 3.21(3) (2002), Philadelphia: American Law Institute, p. 1051.

Sanger and Willemson (1992), 'Minor changes: emancipating children in modern times', *University of Michigan Journal of Law Reform*, **25**, 239–355.

Sugarman, Stephen, Mary Ann Mason and Arlene Skolnick (2002), *All Our Families*, New York: Oxford University Press.

8. Parental bonding and the design of child support obligations

Geoffrey P. Miller[1]

To what extent, in awarding child support, should courts take account of the level of the non-custodial parent's visitation? Possible options range from taking no account of visitation in setting support obligations, to including visitation as part of the basic support calculation. If the latter option were chosen, non-custodial parents who commit to a strong and continuing interaction with their children, as measured by days of visitation, could receive a credit against their child support obligations. Non-custodial parents who were not willing to undertake to be actively present in their children's lives could pay a surcharge over the support that would otherwise be awarded. California – long a leader in family law innovations – already requires courts to adjust child support awards based on the amount of time each parent spends with the children. This chapter analyses the pros and cons of the California approach.

I. THE GROWING CRISIS OF PARENTAL ABSENCE

Present parents – both mothers and fathers – are important for healthy child development.[2] Yet missing parents – especially fathers – are ubiquitous in American society. Many children born out of wedlock never meet their biological fathers. These children may experience fatherhood as a series of emotionally distant men who become involved for a time with their mothers and disappear. Even when children are born to a married couple, divorce often separates fathers and children. Divorced fathers, who rarely obtain physical custody, are all too prone to drift away and, over time, to neglect the children of their former marriage. And when fathers are missing, children suffer: absent fathers have been associated with depression, emotional insecurity, substance abuse, impoverishment, crime, delinquency, premature sexuality, teen pregnancy, unemployment and poor educational achievement. These problems are just as bad – if not worse – when the missing parent is a mother. Although the discussion that follows focuses on problems with absent fathers, this is in no way meant to diminish the catastrophic effects on children that can follow from the loss of a present mother.

Although now a fixture in American society, the disappearance of fathers has largely occurred only over the past few generations. Between 1980 and 1998, single-parent households increased from 6.9 million to 11.9 million, of which over 9.8 million – 82.4 per cent – were headed by women (US Bureau of the Census, 1999, p. 64).[3] About half of children recently born in the United States will spend at least part of childhood in a father-absent household (McLanahan and Bumpass, 1988, pp. 130–52).

The growth of fatherlessness does not appear to reflect significant increases in the percentage of single-parent households headed by women. That proportion has remained surprisingly stable over the past century. In 1900, for example, among children living in a single-parent household, 71 per cent were with their mothers (Gordon and McLanahan, 1991). This ratio has increased, but not dramatically. The principal cause for the increase in fatherlessness is not a change in the percentage of single-parent homes headed by women, but rather a massive increase in single-parent homes overall. In 1900, approximately 14 per cent of children were living apart from one or both parents. That ratio remained fairly constant through the first six decades of the twentieth century; in 1960 the comparable figure was 12.3 per cent (Gordon and McLanahan, 1991). Beginning in about 1960, however, family structure changed dramatically in the United States. Two parallel developments contributed to the change: increases in out-of-wedlock births, and increases in divorce.[4]

The percentage of out-of-wedlock births increased 600 per cent in the roughly three decades between 1960, when it stood at 5 per cent of all births, and 1993, when it had reached 31 per cent (Coney and MacKey, 1998). Among some groups, such as African-Americans, the rate is much higher: 67 per cent overall and, according to some estimates, 80 per cent in the poorest communities (Smith, 1994, p. 81). The overwhelming majority of children born out of wedlock live with their mothers. Fathers rarely seek custody or visitation, and may not acknowledge (or even know of) paternity.

Divorce rates inched upwards in the United States for most of the twentieth century and then skyrocketed between the early 1960s and the early 1980s.[5] Rates have since levelled off (Goldstein, 1999), but they remain high by historical standards and are unlikely to plummet soon.[6] Divorce is predicted for as many as two-thirds of first marriages contracted during the 1980s (Castro-Martin and Bumpass, 1989) and more than half of first marriages overall (Furstenberg, 1990, p. 382). When divorce occurs, the children of the union overwhelmingly stay with their mothers.[7] Fathers move out and see their children through visitation.

Divorce itself is, often, merely a step in a process of gradual separation of the father from the life of his children – one that may often end with him completely disappearing from the child's life, notwithstanding visitation rights. Indeed, it has become nearly the norm for biological fathers to play no continuing role in their children's life (Furstenberg and Cherlin, 1991). Furstenberg and Nord found that in a typical month, 64 per cent of children of non-custodial fathers did not see their fathers, 80 per cent did not sleep at their father's house,[8] 55 per cent did not speak with their fathers over the telephone, and 93 per cent did not receive letters from their fathers (Furstenberg and Nord, 1985). More than a third had not seen their fathers in over five years and 58 per cent had never been in their father's house. Seltzer and Bianchi found that 35.2 per cent of children living with their mothers in single-parent households never have contact with their fathers, and a 24.4 per cent have contact with their fathers less than once a month (Seltzer and Bianchi, 1988, p. 670). Not all studies report these levels of disengagement (for example, Maccoby et al., 1993, p. 29). Overall, however, the evidence is overwhelming that non-custodial fathers often play little or no role in their children's lives.

The pattern for non-resident fathers, moreover, tends to be one of increasing distancing over time. Seltzer and Bianchi found that children who had only recently (within one year) started living apart from a biological parent were more likely to have frequent contact with the absent parent than were children who had been separated for longer periods (Seltzer and Bianchi, 1988, p. 670). Furstenberg and Nord, similarly, found that 69 per cent of non-custodial parents saw their children in a typical month during the first two years after separation; 46 per cent of non-custodial parents saw their children in a typical month during years two to nine; and only 26 per cent of non-custodial parents saw their children during a typical month in years ten and beyond (Furstenberg and Nord, 1985).

Fathers, rather than mothers, are principally responsible for the observed distancing over time.[9] Why do many fathers drift away from their children when they are not connected by continuing involvement in a marital relationship? The leading explanation is that men and women experience marriage and parenthood differently: for women, the two functions are separated, so they can remain responsible and involved parents after the dissolution of the marriage, whereas for men, marriage and parenthood are linked, so that after divorce they disengage from their biological children (Seltzer, 1994; Furstenberg and Cherlin, 1991). This explanation might be criticized as primarily descriptive. It is not clear that the hypothesized linkage between marriage and parenthood does much more than restate the fact that men separate from their parenting responsibilities after divorce – much like saying that opium causes sleep because of its 'dormative properties'.

Another explanation for the father's propensity to distance from his children after divorce is the difficulty many men feel at managing feelings, especially if they are emotionally fragile (Cohen, 1998). Men often experience loss, grief, anger and guilt during the separation period – feelings that, if not resolved, can interfere with the ability to establish a regular schedule of visitation after the separation (Kruk, 1994; Lund, 1987, p. 215; Fox, 1985, p. 407). Seeing the children may stir up feelings left over from a failed marriage or a painful divorce (Warshak, 1992, p. 78). Fathers may find it difficult to cope with their children's stress when separating after visitation (ibid.) and may dread contact with a hostile ex-spouse (Fox, 1985, p. 407; Greif, 1995). Even fathers in 'intact' households reduce their involvement with children in the presence of marital conflict (Harris et al., 1998). Fathers' inability to deal constructively with feelings may interact poorly with the emotional turmoil that the early episodes of visitation are likely to create for all family members, and especially children. Rather than deal with these emotions, fathers check out.

Another possible reason for the male propensity to distance themselves is that fathers do not feel secure as parents outside the context of marriage (Biller, 1993, p. 2). This sense of insecurity is not assuaged, but rather reinforced, by the many social institutions that take for granted the mother's primary role in childcare and upbringing. For example, a divorced father may wish to remain involved with his children's school performance, yet find it difficult to attend parent–teacher conferences that are scheduled during workdays and on short notice (Lamb et al., 1983, p. 253). Report cards are likely to be sent only to the mother. Social service professionals may be unresponsive (Kruk, 1994, p. 16), and may harbour prejudice against fathers as being irresponsible or irrelevant (Lamb et al., 1983, p. 255). Fathers may be excluded from social activities organized by mothers of their children's friends. Fathers who live in a different town may have trouble finding venues where they can take their children during visitation.

Fathers may also feel obliged to provide endless fun and excitement to make up for the lack of day-to-day contact. Because endless fun and excitement are impossible, fathers may give up trying. Other practical problems can also interfere. For example, if either parent moves away, the father may experience the need to travel for visitation as a serious impediment (Stephen et al., 1993, p. 184).

Fathers may distance themselves from the children of a prior relationship once they have established a new household. Although merely forming another relationship may not predict reduced paternal contact, the presence of new children in the father's life – especially the birth of a baby – appears to decrease contact with the children of the previous union (Manning and Smock, 1999). Similarly, if the mother remarries, the presence of a stepfather may reduce contact between children and their biological fathers (Furstenberg et al., 1983; Furstenberg and Nord, 1985; Seltzer and Bianchi, 1988).

Men may also experience their ex-wives as interfering with visitation (Fox, 1985, p. 407; Lund, 1987, p. 217; Turkat, 1995). An ex-wife may schedule the children for educational or recreational activities during the father's visitation; the father may then be placed in the position of having to choose between his time with the children and an activity which is good for them (Warshak, 1992, p. 78). Mothers may resist attempts by social service providers to include fathers in therapy or problem-solving over children's issues (Kruk, 1994, p. 23). The mother may simply forbid the father to visit (Warshak, 1992, p. 79).[10]

Paternal absence may be self-reinforcing (Becker, 1991, p. 329). Fathers who drift away from their children begin to feel less altruistic towards them. Because they are less altruistic, they are less likely to want time with the children, since time with children is an opportunity cost (the father could be doing other pleasurable things or earning money). So fathers reduce their level of visitation, which further reduces altruism. Left unchecked, the process could end with the father abandoning visitation altogether.

II. COSTS OF PARENTAL ABSENCE

It has long been an article of faith in our culture that children do better with mothers present. Over the past few decades, a substantial body of social science evidence has suggested that children also benefit from present fathers and suffer when fathers are absent (Blankenhorn, 1995; Coney and MacKey, 1998, p. 146; Popenoe, 1996, p. 12). As will be seen, this evidence is not sufficiently strong to constitute proof of the proposition, largely due to the presence of confounding factors such as socio-economic variables or the problem of testing how children would have done if their parents had not separated. Many of the studies involve small numbers of observations, use incompletely specified variables, or lack control groups. And results are not always consistent. Despite these difficulties, the large number of studies and their fairly high, although not unanimous, agreement about the direction if not the magnitude of effects suggests that they are reporting something valid about the importance of fathers.

This proposition was not always a mainstream view in the social sciences. Until recently, many authorities thought that – aside from their role as breadwinners – fathers were largely dispensable (Biller, 1993, p. 12). The important relationship was between children and their mothers, a nearly mystical bond in which the father had no part.[11] Because of their secondary role in child development, it was not crucial that fathers remain involved after divorce (Goldstein et al., 1973).

This concept of the minimal father is no longer widely accepted. Far from being disinterested or uninvolved, fathers have a well-developed capacity to connect with their offspring – one that begins before the child is born (Miller, 2000). Research in a variety of fronts suggests that fathers count in the lives of his children.

Fathers and mothers interact differently with children. In dealing with infants and toddlers, women tend to be more soothing and emotionally comforting, while men tend to be more active and arousing, emphasizing physical dexterity and autonomy (Biller, 1993, p. 13). Fathers are more inclined to be playful whereas mothers spend more time caretaking (Lamb, 1982, p. 14). For older children, too, fathers adopt different parenting styles: they emphasize rough-and-tumble play, competition and achievement, whereas mothers place more stress on security and relationships (Popenoe, 1996, p. 12). Although these studies do not establish that the father's different parenting style is beneficial for children,[12] they at least suggest that fathers bring something valuable to the table.[13]

Positive effects of father presence have been described even for infants and toddlers. Pre-school-aged children with involved fathers have been found to display superior cognitive skills, enhanced empathy, a lower level of stereotyping in sex role beliefs and greater self-control (Lamb, 1982, pp. 16–17); greater tolerance of frustration and lower stranger anxiety (Kotelchuck, 1975); greater skills in crawling, climbing and manipulating objects (Biller, 1993, p. 15); greater curiosity (Pedersen and Robson, 1969; Pedersen et al., 1979); and greater problem-solving competence (Easterbrooks and Goldberg, 1984).

If a father's presence is beneficial, his absence can be harmful, and appears to be more damaging when the separation occurred early in a child's life (Woodward et al., 2000). Father-absence has been found to have adverse effects on school performance (Krein and Beller, 1988),[14] school completion (McLanahan, 1985; McLanahan, 1988), and grades on standardized tests (Angel and Angel, 1993, p. 119; Blanchard and Biller, 1971; Furr, 1998). These effects seem most pronounced for boys (Radin and Russell, 1983, p. 198), but are observable in girls as well (Biller and Salter, 1989, p. 347). Present fathers also appear to enhance capacities for healthy emotional development (Simons et al., 1999),[15] especially in the case of very young children (Biller, 1982; Japel et al., 1999). The adverse effects of father absence on emotional development are more severe for boys than for girls (Hetherington et al., 1985). Yet girls too reap emotional benefits from present fathers: involved fathers contribute to a girl's ability to develop security and maturity (Biller and Salter, 1989).

Fathers appear to exert a positive influence on their children's ability to develop competence in their social interactions (Biller and Salter, 1989, p. 347; Radin and Russell, 1983). Again, the effects appear more pronounced for boys than for girls. Close relations with fathers are correlated with the development in boys of positive feelings of acceptance by others and the ability to make and retain friends, while unaffectionate or distant relationships with fathers are associated with feelings of rejection and poor capacities at intimate relationships (Radin and Russell, 1983, p. 198).

Children with present fathers appear to develop a firmer concept of right and wrong and to do so earlier than children with absent fathers (Hoffman, 1971a; Hoffman, 1971b; Santrock, 1975). Children whose fathers are actively involved in their care during early childhood are more likely to display empathy towards others in later life (Koestner et al., 1990). Father-absent children are more likely to become delinquents (Lamb 1982, p. 28; Warshak, 1992, p. 49),[16] commit crimes (Biller, 1974), or use drugs (Jenkins and Zunguze, 1998). Although the effect appears most salient among boys (Hetherington et al., 1985), some studies have found that girls in father-absent homes are more likely to engage in early sexual behavior (Wu and Thomson, 1998), to marry and bear children early, and to have children out of wedlock (McLanahan and Bumpass, 1988).

Father absence may inhibit, to an extent, a child's development of a secure sense of his or her sexual role. For boys, father absence has been linked both to lower-than-average masculinity and to compensatory displays of hyper-masculinity (Lamb 1982, p. 27). These effects appear to be more pronounced when the father's absence occurred early in the child's development (Biller, 1981; Lamb, 1982). Father-absent girls may not to be as strongly affected, but at puberty they have been found to be more interested in and dependent on males as compared with daughters of two-parent families (Hetherington, 1972). These studies may be criticized for applying outmoded or subjective criteria for what constitutes 'masculinity' or 'femininity', but they do suggest possible disruption in sex role identity as compared with prevailing social norms.

The evidence that fathers contribute to the healthy development of their children, and that children suffer when the father is absent, does not necessarily mean that children would be better off if absent fathers had greater continuing involvement in their lives. The damage to children in single-mother families may be due to emotional factors other than the absence of the father, including the presence of tension and discord in the family prior to the breakup (Hetherington et al., 1982), the emotional disruption incident to the breakup (Lamb, 1986; Peterson and Zill, 1986), or the stress from social isolation and public disapproval of the single mother afterwards (Hetherington et al., 1982). Some have argued that divorce and disturbance in children afterwards are mostly a function of an inherited predisposition on the part of parents and children to experience depression and other emotional problems (Harris, 1998).

The damage to children in single-parent families may also be due to the economic stress that the break-up causes for the custodial parent. Women experience reduced income after divorce (Bianchi et al., 1999; Furstenberg, 1990, p. 386). The financially related stresses of divorce can account for some of the reduced performance, impaired emotional functioning, and lower skill levels observed in children of divorce.[17] However, economic stress alone probably cannot account for all of the damage that children experience from father absence.

The damage to children in single-mother families might be alleviated if, as often happens, the mother's remarriage brings a stepfather on the scene (Furstenberg, 1990; Mott, 1990). Stepfathers can offer substitute caretaking and provide income that enhances the mother's economic situation. However, evidence on this question generally does not support the hypothesis that the mother's remarriage remediates the problems. Girls show few benefits from remarriage of the custodial mother, and may even experience an increase in behaviour problems (Hetherington et al., 1985; McLanahan and Bumpass, 1988, pp. 146–7). As for boys, there is some evidence that the mother's remarriage can have a positive effect, perhaps because it introduces a male role model into a fatherless home, but such children are still unlikely to be as well-adjusted as boys in intact families (Hetherington et al., 1985). Moreover, even if a child has developed positive feelings for his or her stepfather, there is no reason to suppose that he or she cannot also benefit from close contact with the biological father (Furstenberg, 1988).

The empirical evidence on the effects of paternal visitation is inconclusive (Amato and Rezac, 1994). However, since children generally have good relationships with visiting fathers (Munsch et al., 1995; Seltzer and Brandreth, 1994, p. 67), there is reason to suppose that many of the benefits of paternal presence can be provided through visitation, at least to some extent. Children themselves testify that they want to spend more time with their non-custodial fathers after divorce (Clingempeel and Reppucci, 1982; Kelly, 1993), and there appears to be little reason to doubt the sincerity or accuracy of these views. Several studies support the hypothesis that frequent visitation is desirable, finding that interaction with non-custodial fathers is good for children (Bronstein et al., 1994; Hanson, 1985, p. 383; Hess and Camara, 1979; Hetherington et al., 1978; Seltzer and Bianchi, 1988; Tschann et al., 1989; Wallerstein and Kelly, 1976), and that the advantages do not vary significantly by race, mother's education, or whether the child was born within or outside of marriage (King, 1994). The clinical literature also tends to endorse the value of maintaining close contact with both parents after divorce (Kruk, 1994, p. 16). These studies finding significant benefits from continuing contact with non-resident fathers are sometimes based on relatively subjective observations and small sample sizes, however. Other studies have found no significant effects from regular visits by non-custodial parents (Amato and Gilbreth, 1999; Furstenberg et al., 1987; Kurdek et al., 1981; Simons et al., 1994).

The potential benefits of frequent paternal visitation may be a function of more subtle factors that are not picked up in general demographic data. If the parents remain hostile after divorce, a high level of paternal involvement may not be beneficial (Hetherington et al., 1978). The value of paternal visitition would then be determined by trading off the benefit of contact with fathers against the costs of exposure to parental conflict (Maccoby et al., 1993, p. 25). Visitation by fathers may also be better for boys than for girls (Simons et al., 1999; Amato and Rezac, 1994). If the non-custodial parent is emotionally disturbed, extensive visitations may harm more than they help (Dudley, 1991). And frequency or regularity of visitation may be less important than the quality of contact (Amato and Gilbreth, 1999; Easterbrooks and Goldberg, 1984; Kurdek and Berg, 1983; Furr, 1998; Simons et al., 1999). If fathers maintain close ties with their children or demonstrate firmness in setting behavioural limits, the effects are likely to be beneficial (Amato and Gilbreth, 1999).

III. LEGAL TREATMENT OF VISITATION AND SUPPORT

The law's approach to the problem of absent fathers is found, most importantly, in the policies a state adopts towards visitation.[18] All states have adopted guidelines that tie support levels to factors such as parental income and number of children.[19] The key issue for present purposes is whether the guidelines take explicit account of the degree to which the noncustodial parent engages in visitation. The statutes fall into four categories along this dimension.

Little or No Adjustment

In some states, virtually no adjustment is made for the degree of the non-custodial parent's involvement post-divorce. In Illinois, for example, the non-custodial parent's support obligation is set at a percentage of net income, which increases with the number of children from 20 per cent for one child to 50 per cent for six or more children.[20] The statute provides that these guidelines 'shall be applied' unless the court makes a finding that application of the guidelines would be inappropriate, after considering the best interests of the child in light of a number of factors such as the financial resources and needs of the child, the financial resources and needs of the custodial parent, the standard of living the child would have enjoyed had the marriage not been dissolved, the physical and emotional condition of the child, his or her educational needs, and the financial resources and needs of the non-custodial parent.[21] Notably, no mention is made of the amount of visitation time with the non-custodial parent.

In *Marriage of Demattia*,[22] the divorce agreement provided the father with visitation from 6 a.m. to 2 p.m. four days each week during the mother's work shift, every other weekend, Saturdays when the mother worked, and half of all vacations and holidays. The father, in effect, spent as much time with the children as the mother, although the children slept at the mother's home most evenings. Nevertheless, the court rejected the father's argument that his child support obligations should be adjusted downward to reflect his visitation obligations. The court observed that the child support guidelines did not recognize extended visitation as a factor potentially justifying a modification of the calculation. While the trial court was free to consider the father's extended visitation in setting an award of child support, it was not required to do so, and even if the court had considered the father's visitation obligation, it could not deviate from the guidelines in the absence of 'compelling evidence'. Under Illinois law, accordingly, there appears to be little chance that even extended visitation by the non-custodial parent will result in an adjustment of support.

Adjustment for Significantly Greater-than-Average Visitation

A second approach takes account of the non-custodial parent's involvement when it reaches a sufficiently large magnitude – usually the amount of visitation necessary to qualify as shared or joint physical custody. In Oregon, for example, special guidelines apply when the parties have 'shared custody', defined to mean cases where one parent has physical custody not more than 65 per cent of the time and the other has physical custody not less than 35 per cent of the time. In shared custody cases, the guidelines require that the parties' respective obligations be calculated with reference to the number of overnights each have with the children.[23] In Virginia, time spent with a parent counts as a credit towards child support if the arrangement is characterized as a shared custody arrangement, defined to mean cases where each spouse has the children more than 90 days of the year.[24] New Mexico, to like effect, provides a special, 'shared responsibility' calculation for cases where each parent has the children at least 35 per cent of the time; this calculation, unlike the ordinary one, takes account of time spent with each parent.[25] Pennsylvania's guidelines, likewise, provide that when the obligor spends 40 per cent or more time with the children, his or her percentage share of the combined basic support obligation is reduced by the percentage of time spent over and above the routine partial custody or visitation arrangement.[26]

States vary in the degree of discretion courts are allowed to adjust support levels. Some include an adjustment as part of the support calculations once visitation reaches a defined threshold and allow deviations from the adjusted amount only if courts conclude that there are reasons to vary the award. Others specify that adjustments are within the court's discretion. Florida's guidelines, for example, permit but do not require courts to adjust the minimum child support award if the non-custodial parent spends more than 28 days with the children.[27] Washington, similarly, permits but does not require deviation when the child 'spends a significant amount of time' with the non-custodial parent.[28] Louisiana requires courts in joint custody cases to consider 'the period of time spent by the child with the non-domiciliary party' as a basis for adjustment to the amount of child support,[29] but courts of that state are not obligated to adjust the awards after undertaking this inquiry, and are likely to refuse an adjustment if the expenses of the custodial parents remain constant.[30]

Across-the-Board Adjustment

A third approach is one in which the courts are given discretion to adjust support to reflect visitation commitments in all cases, not just shared or joint custody arrangements. This pattern may overlap the previous one: a state may permit or require adjustments for time with children in joint or shared custody cases, but may also permit discretionary adjustments in ordinary custody situations.[31] However, the presence of an express adjustment for joint or shared custody may suggest the lack of any authority on the part of courts to adjust support obligations in the more typical case of sole physical custody.[32]

Courts in states using an across-the-board discretionary approach typically consider several factors. First, they are more likely to reduce support payments to reflect unusually extensive visitation than to increase support to reflect unusually infrequent visitation. Second, they are likely to consider evidence of the relative financial impacts on both parents of the non-custodial parent's visitation. Third, they are likely to make adjustments when the visitation deviates significantly from the norm, even if it does not rise to the level of shared or joint custody; if deviations from the norm are less significant, they are likely to apply the guidelines without change.[33] In this regard, a circumstance where courts often adjust or abate support payments is the child's living with the non-custodial parent for an extended period during the summer vacation.[34]

States that fall in this discretionary category can vary from being fairly conservative about making adjustments for visitation to being quite receptive. New York, a moderately conservative state along this dimension, does not recognize extended (or abbreviated) visitation as a factor in calculating support, but its guidelines contain several discretionary considerations that might be used to adjust support in particular cases. These include 'extraordinary expenses' incurred by the non-custodial parent in exercising visitation, as well as expenses incurred by the non-custodial parent in extended visitation which 'substantially' reduce the custodial parent's expenses.[35] The extent to which this language supports adjustments of support obligations depends on the meanings that courts give to the quoted terms, which appear to limit somewhat the judicial flexibility to take visitation into account.[36]

Other states utilizing a discretionary approach display a more receptive attitude towards visitation adjustments. Tennessee's guidelines, for example, provide that in cases where overnight time is divided more equally than usual, the court can decide support on a case-by-case basis. In so doing, the court can decrease of the support obligations of a non-residential parent who exercises greater-than-normal visitation[37] or increase obligations in cases where the non-custodial parent's visitation is unusually infrequent.[38] Montana's guidelines, similarly, state that in determining the amount of child support, a court may consider the arrangement for custody;[39] although vague, this provision may provide discretion to trial courts to adjust awards to account for unusually extensive or infrequent visitation by the non-custodial parent.[40]

Other states more actively encourage courts to use their discretion to adjust support payments to reflect visitation. For example, Indiana's guidelines do not address adjustments for visitation, but the commentary recommends a reduction of up to 10 per cent in weekly support payments in cases of regular visitation, and additional reductions to account for extended visitation.[41]

Mandatory Adjustment

A fourth approach is to include an explicit adjustment for visitation in the state's general child suppport guidelines. California, long an innovator in family law issues, uses perhaps the most extensive methodology.[42] Its guideline apportions child support obligations between the parents on the basis of the percentage of time that each parent has primary physical custody over the children. The calculation is structured so as to award the non-custodial parent an accelerating credit as the amount of time with the children increases – presumably in order to take account of the greater fixed expenses the non-custodial parent must pay as the amount of visitation increases. For example, suppose that in a marriage with one child the mother's monthly disposable income is $300 and the father's monthly disposable income is $700. The father's monthly support obligation would decline at decreasing rates as time spent with children increases as shown in Table 8.1.

Table 8.1   Adjustment for visitation

Father's primary custody	Father's monthly payment
0%	$175
10%	$165
20%	$150
30%	$130
40%	$105
50%	$75

The fairness of California's scheme was challenged in a recent case, *In re Marriage of Denise & Kevin*.[43] The husband argued that application of the guidelines to his case would be unjust because he had physical custody only 1 per cent of the time, and therefore had to pay more than would be the case if he had custody a larger percentage of the time. The court rejected the argument, observing that 'both the fiscal and non-fiscal burdens of parenthood increase in proportion to the extent they are not shared with another parent'.[44]

New Jersey's approach is also tailored to account for visitation, although the adjustment is not contained in the guidelines themselves. The official commentary to New Jersey's guidelines assumes that 37 per cent of childcare expenditures are for variable costs (such as food), 38 per cent are for fixed costs (such as housing), and the remaining 25 per cent are for controllable costs (such as clothing and entertainment).[45] If a parent has the children during a regular visitation schedule, the parent is assumed to pay only variable costs; his or her support obligation may therefore be reduced by the variable costs assumed to be paid for the percentage of time the paying parent has visitation.[46] If the parent has visitation at a sufficient level to qualify for treatment as a 'shared-parenting' arrangement, the guidelines provide an additional adjustment for the payment of fixed expenditures by the non-custodial parent.[47] Unlike California, these factors are explicitly discretionary; however, courts may be inclined to follow them because of

the evident care with which they are drafted and the high degree of speci-
ficity they offer.

IV. RECOMMENDATIONS

In this section, I recommend the fourth approach to recognizing visitation
in the design of child support awards – the method that requires courts to
consider time spent with children, not only in cases of shared or joint
custody, but in all cases, and which explicitly adjusts the child support
award upward or downward to reflect the amount of time each parent
spends with the children. For ease of reference, I will refer to this as the
'California approach'.

The methodology could be implemented as follows. First, courts should
presume that non-custodial parents are entitled to the most liberal visitation rights possible consistent with the best interests of the child. Applying
this presumption, the non-custodial parent's request for visitation would be
granted if the court concludes that the non-custodial parent is a fit parent
who could provide a suitable environment for the child, and that the child
would not otherwise be harmed by the non-custodial parent's proposed visitation schedule. The burden would be on the custodial parent to prove that
the proposed schedule was not consistent with the child's best interests.

The court would then calculate child support in such a manner as to
account for time spent with each parent. The best approach would be to use
a scheme such as California's, which explicitly incorporates time spent with
parents into the basic child support guideline calculation. In the absence of
comprehensive legislation of this sort, however, a court could emulate the
result using the existing guidelines and judicial precedents. The court would
first determine the applicable support payment without considering the
anticipated visitation schedule, and then adjust the support figure upwards
or downwards to account for visitation that is either significantly below or
significantly above the norm, as well as fixed or extraordinary expenses that
a non-custodial parent must pay in order to sustain greater-than-normal
visitation. Because most divorces settle, the parties could engage in a
similar calculation in presenting an agreement to the court, demonstrating
the extent to which deviations from the guidelines are justified by the nature
of the noncustodial parent's visitation commitment.

The system endorsed here could be supplemented (as is already the case
in New Jersey) by *ex post* adjustments to account for changed or unfore-
seen circumstances. If non-custodial parents abused their promise by persistent absences and no-shows, custodial parents would be entitled to
return to court to seek an adjustment.[48] In the absence of a good excuse by

the non-custodial parent shown to be persistently absent, the court could, in such a proceeding, not only increase the support obligation to reflect the actual frequency of visitation, but also sanction the defaulting party by making the adjustment retroactive to the date of the initial decree. The sanction for failing to perform should be known in advance so that parties negotiating divorce agreements will think twice before making visitation commitments that they do not intend to keep.[49]

The California approach offers several advantages over other systems. Most importantly, it encourages and valorizes both parents remaining present in the lives of children after parental separation. As we have seen, fathers who remain present in the lives of their children appear likely to contribute significantly to their healthy emotional, social and intellectual development. By encouraging non-custodial parents – especially fathers – to remain involved with their children, the California approach offers the potential to improve the situation both of children and of society in general.

The incentives for continuing involvement in children's lives are partly financial in nature. In the absence of an adjustment, a non-custodial parent who exercises extensive visitation will have to incur additional expenses for time with the children – both the day-to-day costs of living, such as food and transportation, and larger costs such as providing a room in his or her home for children to occupy during sleepovers. Non-custodial parents will also incur potentially significant opportunity costs for the time that they spend with their children.[50] The adjustment of the non-custodial parent's support obligations provides a financial incentive that corrects for some of the penalty that the non-custodial parent would otherwise pay for exercising larger-than-normal visitation. By the same token, parents who would consider limiting their visitation in order to seek other sources of satisfaction – better jobs, new relationships or more leisure time – would have to evaluate the financial penalty from doing so.

The California approach is more equitable than the alternatives. When visitation patterns are not factored into the calculation, the result is to penalize non-custodial parents who remain actively involved in the lives of their children and to reward non-custodial parents who opt out. This is hardly a desirable result. Nor is it equitable to confer a windfall on the custodial parent who is relieved of the day-to-day costs during the time that an involved non-custodial parent spends with the children, or to impose a penalty on the custodial parent who incurs extra expenses because the non-custodial parent has disappeared. Whether the comparison is between involved and distant non-custodial parents, or between non-custodial parents and custodial parents, the equities favour adjusting support obligations to reflect time spent with the children by each parent.

The California approach has a compelling moral basis. If one accepts the proposition that parents owe a moral duty to participate in the lives of their children,[51] then, in the absence of strong considerations to the contrary, legal rules that encourage parents to remain involved after parental separation appear morally desirable. For similar reasons, rules that discourage parental involvement, such as regimes that award no credit (or impose no penalty) for visitation patterns, appear to be morally questionable.

The California approach holds the promise for enhancing public confidence in, and support of, the family law system – confidence that is sorely lacking in some circles. By providing a credit for involvement and explicitly recognizing the value of visitation, the California approach would potentially ameliorate the widespread perception among divorced parents – especially divorced fathers – that their support obligations are excessive and unjustified, or that they had been victimized during the divorce process.[52] Enhanced satisfaction with the legal system, in turn, is likely to increase involvement post-divorce because non-custodial parents feel less alienated from the process (Stone, 1998).

The California approach symbolizes and acknowledges the value of non-custodial parents remaining present in their children's lives. It honours their continuing involvement – a public statement that may be particularly meaningful for parents who often feel marginalized when their formerly central status in the family is replaced by the role of an occasional visitor (Greif, 1979; Keshetand and Rosenthal, 1978).[53] The public expression of state policy favouring visitation may also contribute to the shaping of cultural norms by endorsing the value of present parents. While state-sponsored attempts at norm-management are not always successful (consider Prohibition), the effort here seems to hold some promise, and carries with it a low risk of backfiring.[54]

The California approach could enhance the reliability of child support payments, for several reasons. Fathers who are induced to spend time with their children are likely to identify with their role as fathers. Such fathers are likely to make more regular child support payments without being compelled to do so by expensive and stressful judicial process (Lamb et al., 1983, p, 251).[55] Moreover, the paying spouse is likely to see his or her obligations as more 'fair' – an important ingredient in a parent's propensity to comply with support obligations (Nuta, 1986). And the California approach offers non-custodial parents a higher degree of control over funds that the state has designated for the benefit of the children: they get to spend some of the money themselves rather than giving it all to the custodial parent whom they may not trust to use the resources appropriately (Weiss and Willis, 1985). By alleviating this concern, the California system is likely to enhance compliance with support obligations.[56]

The California approach could be beneficial to custodial parents. It would to some extent relieve the burdens that come from the role of primary caretaker.[57] Increased visitation by the non-custodial parent should make it easier for custodial parents to work at higher-paying jobs with significant time demands. Increased visitation might also provide the custodial parent with opportunities to engage in dating and other activities that are precursors to remarriage (that is, spending the night with a potential partner). This could benefit custodial parents by reducing the severe difficulties they face in finding new life partners, especially if the children are young (Becker, 1991, p. 321).

The California approach may be beneficial for women. Because most custodial parents are women, California's approach advantages women to the extent that it helps custodial parents. But the potential benefits for women are greater. The California approach would encourage both parents to remain involved in the lives of girls, and girls – who will grow into women – are likely to benefit as a consequence. The California approach may also combat the stigma that mothers may feel, even today, if they do not act as residential caretakers after divorce (Greif and Pabst, 1988, pp. 147–9). More generally, by encouraging fathers to remain present in their children's lives, the California approach may encourage a culture of respect for women and women's rights.[58]

The California approach appears to mimic what the parties would agree to if they bargained over the matter. Peters et al. found in their analysis of data from the Stanford Child Custody Project that divorced couples frequently agree to informal modifications of support obligations when the non-custodial parent's time with the children differs substantially from what was anticipated at the time of the divorce (Peters et al., 1993, p. 729). Consistently with the California approach, non-custodial parents who spent more time with the children than originally specified paid significantly less – 19.3 per cent – than the amount paid by non-custodial parents with no change in custodial arrangements. Conversely, when the non-custodial parent spent less time with the children than originally anticipated, the amounts paid for support increased: these parents paid 11.8 per cent more than non-custodial parents with no change in custodial arrangement. The fact that parties appear voluntarily to adopt support modifications consistent with the California approach provides evidence that such an approach may be desirable as a matter of public policy.

The California approach does not appear to be subject to the problems that have led some authorities to question the desirability of joint physical custody arrangements (Emery, 1988). Presumably, because children would continue to be raised in a single home – albeit with more frequent contact with their non-custodial parent – there is a low likelihood that they would be confused or have a reduced sense of security in their environments.

The California approach appears to be superior to other methodologies. States that give little or no credit for visitation fail to recognize the value of the present parent, or to achieve the benefits that increased visitation can offer. States that allow adjustments only for shared or joint custody are likely to achieve some of these benefits, but because they may exclude adjustments for the more common situation of sole custody with visitation, they fail to go far enough. The across-the-board discretionary approach has the advantage of building in greater judicial flexibility to respond to the unique circumstances of each case, but because it does not include the factor of visitation in the basic support calculation, is unlikely to result in adjustments in a sufficient number of cases.[59] Of the states other than California discussed in this chapter, New Jersey comes closest to linking support to visitation; and New Jersey, unlike California, deals explicitly with the problem of fixed and variable costs. However, New Jersey does not include these considerations in its guidelines, but only offers them as considerations that courts may, but need not, employ when setting support levels. In this respect, California appears to be the best-designed system for achieving the goals identified in this paper.

Although the California approach has many advantages, it is not without problems. One concern is whether adjusting for visitation will actually impact upon the behaviour of the non-custodial parent. Not all fathers who would otherwise be absent would be induced to participate in their children's lives if the California approach were adopted. Yet some valuable effect can be anticipated, and, depending on the size of the adjustment, it may be relatively large.[60]

Another objection is that the state should not attempt to buy a parent's love. The idea that the law should compel fathers financially to do the right thing by their children may be morally or emotionally offensive to some people. Yet there should be nothing particularly surprising about the idea that people's behaviour is a function of their utility, and that their utility includes economic as well as non-economic features. The California approach does not attempt to buy a parent's love, but merely provides an incentive for parents to be present in a situation where love can blossom.

Another objection to the California approach is that even if it induces non-custodial parents to be present in the lives of their children, it only delivers them physically. It is up to the parent to provide a high quality of time. A parent who spends his or her visitation with children criticizing or ignoring them, or zoned out on the sofa in front of a television, is not going to contribute as much to their development as a parent who displays sensitivity to their needs and displays positive enjoyment of the parenting role. As already noted, the quality of paternal time is probably more salient than quantity in terms of its beneficial effects on child development. However, time spent with children is important for at least three reasons. First, quantity is a necessary condition for quality: if the parent is not physically present with his children, there will be no chance for positive parenting to occur. Second, even children whose visitation is not of the highest quality of time are still likely to benefit from the experience. Third, the law has little capacity to compel non-custodial parents to develop qualitatively positive relations with their children, but it can at least police to some extent the amount of time spent with them.

The California approach might be criticized if it resulted in visitation that was damaging to children. For example, if non-custodial parents are abusive or dangerous, or if visitation by the non-custodial parent results in extreme levels of conflict between the parents, increasing visitation may not benefit children. However, these problems can be handled on a case-by-case basis. Courts always have the power to deviate from the guideline calculations for good cause shown; and if visitation results in harm to the children, courts have power to set appropriate limits.

A potentially more serious problem is that the California approach provides non-custodial parents with an opportunity to manipulate the system in order to obtain reduced child support obligations. They can profess an earnest desire to spend as much time as possible with the children, and thereby obtain a decree awarding them liberal visitation – with the attendant reduction in child support obligations. Thereafter, they can default on their visitation commitments, leaving the custodial parent both inconvenienced and finally disadvantaged. The custodial parent is, of course, not without redress in this situation. In some states at least, she can petition the court to hold the non-custodial parent in contempt for his failure to comply with the orders in the decree.[61] And, as suggested above, a court should have the power to award retroactive support if the non-custodial parent persistently defaults on his visitation obligation.

Finally, the California approach does introduce some additional complexity into the system, and may to this extent be less desirable than simpler methodologies.[62] Moreover, if the approach required frequent re-litigation of support decrees – for example, because non-custodial parents were not, in fact, living up to the obligations they took on in the divorce – it could be seen as imposing an undesirable level of stress and cost. However, the the California statute does not appear excessively complicated when compared with other support guidelines. Overall, the arguments against the California approach do not appear sufficiently strong to outweigh its significant benefits.

CONCLUSION

This chapter has argued that, for a number of reasons, it may be desirable for states to adjust child support obligations to reflect patterns of visitation by non-custodial parents. Most importantly, such an adjustment encourages non-custodial parents to remain actively involved in the lives of their children after parental separation. A substantial body of social science literature suggests that such involvement can be beneficial to children's emotional, intellectual, social and moral development. Such an adjustment also appears to be more equitable than and morally superior to alternative approaches. In addition to helping children, it holds promise of serving other goals: enhancing public satisfaction with the family law system; increasing compliance with child support obligations; honouring parents who make a commitment to remain present for their children through difficult times; lightening the burdens on custodial parents; and providing benefits to women. Overall, the California system appears preferable to the alternatives. It warrants serious consideration by policy-makers and legislatures interested in improving the law of family relations.

NOTES

1. © 2002 Geoffrey P. Miller. I would like to thank Margaret Brinig, William Comanor, Ira Ellman, Sandra Langs, Wendy Parmet, and participants at the Conference on the Law and Economics of Child Support Payments at the University of California, Santa Barbara, 20 September 2002.
2. The importance of fathers is now widely accepted among scholars and policy-makers. Some of the better recent treatments include Adams et al. (1984); Biller (1993); Biller (1974); Blankenhorn (1995); Griswold (1993) McLanahan and Sandefur (1994); Popenoe (1996).
3. These figures are even more compelling when separated by race. Among European Americans, 21 per cent of all family groups with children under 18 are headed by women; among persons of Hispanic origin, the percentage is 30 per cent, and among African Americans, it is 57 per cent. Today, the majority of African American boys are being raised in fatherless homes.
4. These causes of father absence can be contrasted with the traditional causes of father absence in the United States – death of the father. During the eighteenth and nineteenth centuries, many families experienced loss of a parent due to death. In these families, at least for a period of time until the surviving parent remarried, the children would have only one parent. In 1900, the majority of all single-parent households were due to the death of a spouse: only 2 per cent of single-parent children lived with a divorced parent and 3.4 per cent lived with a never-married parent (Popenoe 1996, p. 22). It was only during the 1960s that the primary reason for an American child being deprived of a parent shifted from the parent's death to his or her divorce (Coney and MacKey, 1998).
5. The reasons for the increase in divorce since 1960 are not entirely understood, although the advent of no-fault divorce may have an influence. See Sugarman and Kay (1990); Brinig and Buckley (1998). But see Peters (1986) (bargaining among divorcing spouses should cancel the effects of no-fault divorce on the divorce rate).

6. Divorce may be self-perpetuating: children of divorce are themselves more likely to divorce. See Glenn and Kramer (1987); Wolfinger (1999). People entering marriage may also do so with less commitment because they are aware of the high failure rate. See Glenn (1991).
7. Although patterns may vary from state to state, it appears that, over all, mothers obtain sole physical custody as much as ten times more often than fathers. See Garrison (1990); Mnookin et al. (1990); Seltzer and Bianchi (1988); Weitzman and Dixon (1979).
8. Fewer than one in five of children surveyed by Furstenberg and Nord indicated that they had space in their non-residential father's homes to keep clothing or personal effects. If they visited their father's homes at all, many said that staying with their fathers was like 'visiting in someone else's home' (Furstenberg and Nord, 1985, p. 896). Children face similar difficulties in the United Kingdom (Lund, 1987, p. 220).
9. Non-resident mothers usually stay involved with their children's lives (Greif and Pabst, 1988; Seltzer and Bianchi, 1988, p. 670; Thompson, 1983, p. 88; Stewart, 1999). Furstenberg and Nord found that 35 per cent of non-custodial fathers had not seen their children in over five years, but only 3 per cent of mothers in the sample had failed to see their children for this period of time; 80 per cent of fathers never had their children sleep over at their homes, but only 42 per cent of mothers never had their children sleep over; and 55 per cent of fathers never spoke with their children over the telephone, compared with only 18 per cent of mothers (Furstenberg and Nord, 1985, p. 896).

    The frequency with which non-custodial mothers keep in contact with their children, as compared with non-custodial fathers, is all the more noteworthy when we consider the fact that the vast majority of mothers obtain custody of their children. Those mothers who do not get custody are presumably more likely than non-custodial fathers to have problems (emotional problems, drugs, alcohol and so on) that at least raise questions about their fitness as parents (McLanahan and Bumpass, 1988) (mothers in single-father families 'may have been declared "unsuitable" or have abandoned their children'.)

    Not all fathers drop out of their children's lives, of course; a significant proportion remain involved, and some may actually increase their personal investment in their children's lives after the separation. Fathers who do remain involved with their children tend to be ones who take gratification from and find meaning in their parental role (Bruce and Fox, 1999).
10. A mother may have varying motives for interfering with the father's visitation. She may herself want to avoid reminders of a failed marriage that the father's presence on the doorstep inevitably evokes. She may feel unresolved anger or hostility towards the father. She may believe that the father fails to provide adequate supervision for the children, or that he fails to comply with important policies (for example diet) that the mother has established for their welfare. She may believe that the activities she has scheduled are good for the children, and may have made a good faith effort to work around the father's schedule. Or she may consider the father to be dangerous or abusive towards the children and wish to protect them from what she perceives as a risk of serious harm.
11. This idealization of the mother–child bond is especially pronounced in the work of the eminent English psychiatrist John Bowlby (1951).
12. Perhaps the father's propensity to emphasize competition is an unhealthy response to social values that impose a rigid sex stereotype of achievement and physical courage on men, and the men's style of interaction with children is serving to perpetuate the stereotype rather than imparting something of lasting value to children.
13. It is surely plausible that both styles of parenting – the mother's calmer, more relational and soothing style, and the father's rougher, more abstract and stimulating style – are desirable. In life, a successful child will have to develop skills in relationships and in competition; in achieving intimacy and maintaining independence; in being calm and in being active when the situation demands.
14. Among children from intact families, those with active and involved fathers seem to do better in school than children with distant fathers (Harris et al., 1998).
15. Koestner and colleagues studied adults who had previously been subjects as five-year-olds. They found that one of the most important predictors of capacity for empathy in

later life was the amount of time the subjects spent with their fathers as children (Koestner et al., 1990).

16. Even in 'intact' families, increased father involvement predicts a lower level of delinquency (Harris et al., 1998). Obviously, father-absence is not a guarantee of anti-social behaviour in boys; many boys with absent fathers display good social adjustment, while some boys with present fathers become delinquent. However, father-absence is one factor, among others, that predicts adverse outcomes in the social dimension.

17. For a study concluding that the correlation between single-mother households and reduced educational and occupational success in children could be explained on socio-economic grounds alone, see Biblarz and Rafferty (1999).

18. Custody determinations are equally if not important in terms of maintaining a child's relationship with his or her father (or mother). However, because custody raises a variety of complex issues outside the scope of this chapter, I exclude it from the analysis here, and assume that the case falls in the usual pattern in which one parent (usually, the mother) obtains physical custody.

19. The federal government requires states to use pre-established formulas to determine the amount of child support. See Child Support Enforcement Amendments of 1984, P.L. 98–378, as amended by the Family Support Act of 1988, P.L. 100–485. For a general treatment of support guidelines, see Morgan (1996–present).

20. 750 Illinois Compiled Statutes § 5/505.

21. 750 Illinois Compiled Statutes § 5/505(a)(2).

22. *In re the Marriage of Demattia*, 706 N.E.2d 67, 302 Ill.App.3d 390 (1999).

23. See *In the Matter of the Marriage of Southwell*, 851 P.2d 599 (Or. App. 1993).

24. Virginia Code § § 20–108.2.

25. See New Mexico Statutes § 40–4–11.1D(3).

26. Pennsylvania Rule of Civil Procedure 1910.16–4 (1999).

27. Florida Statutes § 61.30(11)(g).

28. Washington Code § 26.19.075(a)[d].

29. Louisiana Statutes § 9:315.8E.

30. See, for example, *Falterman v. Falterman*, 702 So. 2d 781 (La. App. 1997) (refusing to adjust support in case where father had 40 per cent of time with children).

31. South Dakota, for example, recognizes as a factor potentially justifying deviation from the guidelines the 'effect of custody and visitation provisions including whether children share substantial amounts of time with each parent'; South Dakota Laws § 25–7–6.10, and authorizes abatement of an award of child support if the non-custodial parent actually spends at least ten days a month with the children. South Dakota Laws § 25–7–6.14.

32. In some cases it is clear from the guidelines or commentaries to the guidelines that adjustments are generally not permitted for visitation that falls short of qualifying for joint or shared custody. See, for example, Pennsylvania Rule of Civil Procedure 1910.16–4 (1999) (implying that adjustments are not ordinarily to be granted for non-qualifying custodial arrangements). Cf. *Langley v Langley*, 681 So. 2d 25 (La. App.), writ denied, 684 So 2d 935 (La. 1996) (failing to consider father's argument that his support obligation should be reduced to account for the ten days per month children spent with him); *Anzalone v. Anzalone*, 449 Pa.Super. 201, 673 A.2d 377 (1996) (reversing trial court's reduction of support when father spent 27 per cent of time with children, and noting that the 'non-custodial parent's support obligation should not be reduced absent a determination that the parent spends an unusual amount of time with the children').

33. See, for example, *In re Marriage of Toedter*, 473 N.W.2d 233 (Iowa App. 1991) (observing that deviations from guidelines are generally not favoured even for extended visitation, since custodial parent continues to bear the fixed expenses).

34. See, for example, *In re the Marriage of McElroy*, 475 N.W.2d 221 (Iowa App. 1991) (granting abatement for summer residence with noncustodial parent); *In re Marriage of Toedter*, 473 N.W.2d 233 (Iowa App. 1991) (same).

35. New York Domestic Relations Law § 240-1-b(f)(9).

36. New York cases do not appear particularly receptive to granting adjustments for unusually extensive visitation. See, for example, *Knapp v. Levy*, 245 A.D.2d 1027, 667 N.Y.S.2d

563 (1997) (no adjustment for one-third time spent with father); *Juneau v. Juneau*, 240 A.D.2d 858, 658 A.2d 736 (N.Y. App. 1995) (no adjustment allowed for extended visitation); *Bronstein v. Bronstein*, 203 A.D.2d 703, 610 N.Y.S.2d 638 (1994) (same).

37.   See, for example, *Gray v. Gray*, 885 S.W.2d 353 (Tenn. App. 1994).

38.   See *Dwight v. Dwight*, 936 S.W.2d 945 (Tenn. App. 1996).

39.   Montana Code § 40–4–204(2).

40.   See *In re Marriage of Corey*, 266 Mont. 304, 880 P.2d 824 (1994) (upholding downward reduction of father's support obligations for three-month period each year when father was sole custodian).

41.   Indiana Child Support Rules and Guidelines, Guidelines 3 and 6. The extent to which this non-binding recommendation is observed is unclear, however. Several opinions have adjusted the guideline computations to reflect extensive involvement by the non-custodial parent. See *Marmaduke v. Marmaduke*, 640 N.W.2d 441 (Ind. App. 1994) (adjusting support payments where father had physical custody close to half the time); *Terpstra v. Terpstra*, 588 N.E. 2d 592 (Ind. App. 1992) (father testified that he was with children approximately 50 per cent of the time; downward adjustment of support obligation upheld). However, other courts have refused to adjust the support payments to reflect extensive visitation. See *Matula v. Bower*, 634 N.E.2d 537 (Ind. App. 1994) (refusing to further adjust support payments when father had received 10 per cent credit, even though father had the children half the time). The state of the law in Indiana seems to be epitomized by *Garrod v. Garrod*, 590 N.E. 2d 163 (Ind. App. 1992), where the court upheld a trial court's refusal to make an adjustment for unusually extensive visitation, but also encouraged trial courts to give such a credit).

42.   See California Family Code § 4055.

43.   *In re Marriage of Denise & Kevin*, 67 Cal. Rptr.2d 508, 57 Cal.App.4th 1100 (1997).

44.   67 Cal.Rptr.2d at 513–14.

45.   See N.J. Court Rules, 1969 R. Appx. IX-A (1999) (Considerations in the Use of Child Support Guidelines), Para. 13(g)(1) (setting forth assumptions about various expense percentages).

46.   See N.J. Court Rules, 1969 R. Appx. IX-A (1999) (Considerations in the Use of Child Support Guidelines), Para. 13(b) (adjustments for regular visitation time). The custodial spouse can petition for a readjustment if the non-custodial spouse does not keep up with his visitation commitments. See N.J. Court Rules, 1969 R. Appx. IX-A (1999) (Considerations in the Use of Child Support Guidelines), Para. 13(d) (right to petition for readjustment in cases where noncustodial parent fails to adhere to visitiation schedule).

47.   See N.J. Court Rules, 1969 R. Appx. IX-A (1999) (Considerations in the Use of Child Support Guidelines), Para. 13(f) (shared-parenting arrangements).

48.   But see *Eddie v Eddie*, 201 Mich. App 509, 506 N.W.2d 591 (1993) (concluding that adjustment should reflect only father's formal visitation schedule, not amounts of visitation actually performed).

49.   The proposal to allow *ex post* adjustments for a non-custodial parent's persistent failure to comply with visitation obligations carries the risk that custodial parents, knowing that they can obtain an increase in support if they can demonstrate a persistent failure by other parent to meet the visitation schedule, may interfere with the non-custodial parent's visitation rights and thus reduce the frequency of visitation. However, it would be open to non-custodial parents to show, in any proceeding to increase support on grounds of persistent absence, that the reason for the absence was the custodial parent's unjustifiable conduct.

50.   For example, suppose a non-custodial father has an opportunity to take a well-paying job (such as being a partner at a corporate law firm) which, however, makes large and unanticipated demands on his time. To maintain an extended visitation schedule with his children, the father may elect to turn down the job and remain in one that pays much less but makes fewer demands on his time. The compensation difference between the jobs represents, in part, an opportunity cost to the father of sustaining his visitation with the child.

51. Such a duty could be based on a consequentialist theory, such as utilitarianism, on the principle that overall social welfare is improved if noncustodial parents remain involved in their children's lives; it could also be grounded in deontological ideas, such as the proposition that parents owe general duties of beneficence and care to their offspring.
52. Where fathers perceive the legal system to be fair, and where they believe that they have been heard and supported in the process, they evidence a higher degree of compliance with their support obligations (Mandell, 1995, pp. 88, 101).
53. There is evidence that when the law recognizes the importance of the paternal role, non-resident fathers retain greater involvement in the lives of their children after divorce. Seltzer, for example, found that holding other factors constant, the award of joint legal custody to non-resident fathers significantly increased paternal involvement: fathers with joint legal custody saw their children more frequently and had more overnight visits than fathers without joint legal custody (Seltzer, 1998. See also Stone, 1998).
54. For explorations of the possible role of the state in norm management, see, for example, Kahan (1998), Kahan (1997), Lessig (1995), Sunstein (1996).
55. A substantial body of literature indicates that paying child support and staying in contact with children are complementary activities (Seltzer (1991), Stephen et al. (1993), Peters et al. (1993), p. 730). Furstenberg and colleagues found that seven out of ten children whose fathers had not contributed any support also had no contact with their father for over a year, as compared with only one in five children whose father had contributed to their support (Furstenberg et al., 1983).
56. Nationally, only about one-half of resident parents with child support orders received the full amount due in 1991; one-quarter received nothing (US Bureau of the Census, 1995).
57. The legal and cultural bias in favour of present mothers is decried in some feminist literature as a yoke that keeps women tied to the home and reduces their ability to gain power and a competitive edge in the broader society. Carol Sanger makes this point most explicitly (for example, Sanger, 1996). Sanger observes that women who voluntarily separate from their children – for example, by going to work and putting their children in daycare – are likely to be judged adversely both by the culture, and by a judicial system that may take the woman's physical separation from the child as an indication of reduced bonding, and thus be more inclined to award custody to the father in divorce. Sanger recognizes the potential bearing of her work on the role of fathers, but excludes the paternal factor from her analysis.
58. Societies in which paternal involvement in child rearing is rewarded also display more positive attitudes towards the rights of women (Biller, 1993, p. 2). Conversely, in societies where parenting is more exclusively the woman's domain, men who are deprived of fathers as children are likely to compensate by displaying 'macho' behaviours – thus perpetuating patriarchal attitudes that harm women as well as men.
59. The discretionary approach also has the disadvantage of being vague, and accordingly may discourage efficient settlement bargaining by the divorcing parties (Mnookin and Kornhauser, 1979, pp. 954–6).
60. It would be interesting to see the results of an empirical study of the California approach – for example, by looking at visitation patterns by non-custodial parents before and after the California scheme was enacted, or by comparing visitation patterns in California with patterns in other states that do not allow adjustment for visitation.
61. See, for example, *In re James*, 79 Wy. App. 436, 903 P.2d 470 (1995).
62. Not surprisingly, court officials are apt to make more errors in calculating support obligations under statutory guidelines when the guidelines become more complex (Pirog-Good and Brown, 1995).

234   *The law and economics of child support payments*

REFERENCES

Adams, Paul L., Judith R. Milner and Nancy Schrepf (1984), *Fatherless Children*, New York: Wiley.
Amato, Paul R. and Joan G. Gilbreth (1999), 'Nonresident fathers and children's well-being: a meta-analysis', *Journal of Marriage and the Family*, **61**, 557–73.
Amato, Paul R. and Sandra J. Rezac (1994), 'Contact with nonresident parents, interparental conflict, and children's behavior', *Journal of Family Issues*, **15**, 191–207.
Angel, Ronald J. and Jacqueline L. Angel (1993), *Painful Inheritance: Health and the New Generation of Fatherless Families*, Madison, WI: University of Wisconsin Press.
Becker, Gary Stanley (1991), *A Treatise on the Family*, Cambridge, MA: Harvard University Press.
Bianchi, Suzanne M., Lekha Subaiya and Joan R. Kahn (1999), 'The gender gap in the economic well-being of nonresident fathers and custodial mothers', *Demography*, **36**, 195–203.
Biblarz, Timothy J. and Adrian E. Rafferty (1999), 'Family structure, educational attainment, and socioeconomic success: rethinking the "pathology of matriarchy"', *American Journal of Sociology*, **105**, 321–65.
Biller, Henry B. (1974), *Paternal Deprivation: Family, School, Sexuality, and Society*, Lexington, MA: Lexington Books and London: D.C. Heath.
Biller, Henry B. (1982),'Fatherhood: implications for child and adult development', in Wolman and Striker, pp. 702–25.
Biller, Henry B. (1993), *Fathers and Families: Paternal Factors in Child Development*, Westport, CT: Auburn House.
Biller, Henry B. and Margary Salter (1989), 'Father loss, cognitive and personality functioning', in Dietrich and Shabad, pp. 337–77.
Blanchard, Robert W. and Henry B. Biller (1971), 'Father availability and academic performance among third-grade boys', *Developmental Psychology*, **4**, 301–5.
Blankenhorn, David (1995), *Fatherless America: Confronting Our Most Urgent Social Problem*, New York: Basic Books.
Bowlby, John (1951), *Attachment and Loss (Vol. I: Attachment)*, New York: Basic Books.
Brinig, Margaret F. and F.H. Buckley (1998), 'No-fault laws and at-fault people', *International Review of Law and Economics*, **325** (18), 325–40.
Bronstein, P., M.F. Stoll, J. Clauson, C.L. Abrams and M. Briones (1994), 'Fathering after separation or divorce: factors predicting children's adjustment', *Family Relations*, **43**, 469–79.
Bruce, C. and G.L. Fox (1999), 'Accounting for patterns of father involvement: age of child, father-coresidence, and father role salience', *Sociological Enquiry*, **69**, 458–76.
Castro-Martin, T. and L. Bumpass (1989), 'Recent trends and differentials in marital disruption', *Demography*, **26**, 37–51.
Clingempeel, W. Glenn and N. Dickson Reppucci (1982), 'Joint custody after divorce: major issues and goals for research', *Psychological Bulletin*, **91**, 102–27.
Cohen, O. (1998), 'Parental narcissism and the disengagement of the non-custodial father after divorce', *Clinical Social Work Journal*, **26**, 195–215.
Coney, Nancy S. and Wade C. MacKey (1998), 'On whose watch? The silent separ-

ation of American children from their fathers', *Journal of Sociology and Social Welfare*, **25**, 143–78.

Dietrich, David R. and Peter C. Shabad (eds) (1989), *The Problem of Loss and Mourning: Psychoanalytic Perspectives*, Madison, CT: International Universities Press.

Dudley, J.R. (1991), 'Increasing our understanding of divorced fathers who have infrequent contact with their children', *Family Relations*, **40**, 279–85.

Easterbrooks, Ann and Wendy Goldberg (1984), 'Toddler development in the family: impact of father involvement and characteristics', *Child Development*, **55**, 740–52.

Emery, R.E. (1988), *Marriage, Divorce, and Children's Adjustment*, Beverly Hills, CA: Sage Publications.

Fitzgerald, Hiram E., Barry M. Lester and Michael W. Yogman (eds) (1982), *Theory and Research in Behavioral Pediatrics, Vol. 1*, New York: Plenum Press.

Fox, Greer Litton (1985), 'Noncustodial fathers', in Hanson and Bozett (eds), pp. 393–415.

Furr, L.A. (1998), 'Fathers' characteristics and their children's scores on college entrance exams: a comparison of intact and divorced families', *Adolescence*, **33**, 533–42.

Furstenberg, Frank F., Jr. (1988), 'Child care after divorce and remarriage', in Hetherington and Arasteh, pp. 245–61.

Furstenberg, Frank F., Jr. (1990), 'Divorce and the American family', *Annual Review of Sociology*, **382** (10), 379–403.

Furstenberg, Frank F., Jr. and Andrew J. Cherlin (1991), *Divided Families: What Happens to Children when Parents Part*, Cambridge, MA: Harvard University Press.

Furstenberg, Frank F., Jr. and Christine Winquist Nord (1985), 'Parenting apart: patterns of childrearing after marital disruption', *Journal of Marriage and the Family*, **47**, 893–904.

Furstenberg, Frank F., Jr., S. Philip Morgan and Paul D. Allison (1987), 'Paternal participation and children's well-being after marital dissolution', *American Sociological Review*, **52**, 695–701.

Furstenberg, Frank F., Jr., Christine W. Nord, James L. Peterson and Nicholas Zill (1983), 'The life course of children of divorce: marital disruption and parental contact', *American Sociological Review*, **48**, 656–68.

Garrison, Marsha (1990), 'The economics of divorce: changing rules, changing results', in Stephen D. Sugarman and Herma Hill Kay (eds) (1990), *Divorce Reform at the Crossroads*, New Haven, CT: Yale University Press, pp. 75–101.

Glenn, Norval D. (1991), 'The recent trend in marital success in the United States', *Journal of Marriage and the Family*, **36**, 261–70.

Glenn, Norval D. and Kathryn B. Kramer (1987), 'The marriages and divorces of children of divorce', *Journal of Marriage and the Family*, **49**, 811–25.

Goldstein, Joshua R. (1999), 'The leveling of divorce in the United States', *Demography*, **36**, 409–14.

Goldstein, Joseph, Anna Freud and Albert J. Solnit (1973), *Beyond the Best Interests of the Child*, New York: Free Press.

Gordon, Linda and Sara McLanahan (1991), 'Single parenthood in 1900', *Journal of Family History*, **16**, 97–116.

Greif, Geoffrey L. (1979), 'Fathers, children, and joint custody', *American Journal of Orthopsychiatry*, **49**, 311–19.

Greif, Geoffrey L. (1995), 'When divorced fathers want no contact with their children: a preliminary analysis', *Journal of Divorce and Remarriage*, **23**, 75–84.

Greif, Geoffrey L. and Mary S. Pabst (1988), *Mothers Without Custody*, Lexington, MA: Lexington Books.

Griswold, Robert L. (1993), *Fatherhood in America: A History*, New York: Basic Books.

Hanson, Shirley M.H. (1985), 'Single custodial fathers', in Hanson and Bozett, pp. 369–92.

Hanson, Shirley M.H. and Frederick W. Bozett (eds) (1985), *Dimensions of Fatherhood*, Beverly Hills, CA: Sage Publications.

Harris, Judith Rich (1998), *The Nurture Assumption: Why Children Turn Out the Way They Do*, London: Bloomsbury.

Harris, K.M., F.F. Furstenberg and J.K. Marmer (1998), 'Paternal involvement with adolescents in intact families: the influence of fathers over the life course', *Demography*, **35**, 201–16.

Hess, Robert D. and Kathleen A. Camara (1979), 'Post-divorce relationships as mediating factors in the consequences of divorce for children', *Journal of Social Issues*, **35**, 79–96.

Hetherington, E. Mavis (1972), 'Effects of father-absence on personality development in adolescent daughters', *Developmental Psychology*, **7**, 313–26.

Hetherington, E. Mavis and Josephine D. Arasteh (eds) (1988), *Impact of Divorce, Single Parenting, and Stepparenting on Children*, Hillsdale, NJ: Lawrence Erlbaum Associates.

Hetherington, E. Mavis, Martha Cox and Roger Cox (1982), 'Effects of divorce on parents and children', in Lamb (1982b), pp. 233–88.

Hetherington, E. Mavis, Martha Cox and Roger Cox (1985), 'Long-term effects of divorce and remarriage on the adjustment of children', *Journal of the Academy of Psychiatry*, **24**, 518–30.

Hetherington, E. Mavis et al. (1978), 'The aftermath of divorce', in Stevens and Matthews, pp. 149–76.

Hoffman, Martin (1971a), 'Father absence and conscience development', *Developmental Psychology*, **4**, 400–406.

Hoffman, Martin (1971b), 'Identification and conscience development', *Child Development*, **42**, 1071–82.

Japel, Christa, Richard E. Teremblay, Frank Vataro and Bernard Boulerice (1999), 'Early parental separation and the psychosocial development of daughters 6–9 years old', *American Journal of Orthopsychiatry*, **69**, 49–60.

Jenkins, J.E. and S.T. Zunguze (1998), 'The relationship of family structure to adolescent drug use, peer affiliation, and perception of peer acceptance of drug use', *Adolescence*, **33**, 811–22.

Kahan, Dan M. (1997), 'Social influence, social meaning, and deterrence', *University of Virginia Law Review*, **83**, 349–395.

Kahan, Dan M. (1998), 'Social norms, social meaning and the economic analysis of law', *Journal of Legal Studies*, **27**, 609–22.

Kelly, Joan B. (1993), 'Current research on children's postdivorce adjustment: no simple answers', *Family and Conciliation Courts Review*, **31**, 29–49.

Keshetand, H. and K. Rosenthal (1978), 'Fathering after marital separation', *Social Work*, **23**, 11–18.

King, V. (1994), 'Variation in the consequences of nonresident father involvement for children's well-being', *Journal of Marriage and the Family*, **56**, 963–72.

Koestner, Richard, Carol Franz and J. Weinberger (1990), 'The family origins of empathic concern: a 26-year longitudinal study', *Journal of Personality and Social Psychology*, **58**, 709–17.

Kotelchuck, Milton et al. (1975), 'Infant reaction to parental separations when left with familiar and unfamiliar adults', *Journal of Genetic Psychology*, **126**, 255–60.

Krein, S.F. and A.H. Beller (1988), 'Educational attainment of children from single-parent families: differences by exposure, gender and race', *Demography*, **25**, 221–34.

Kruk, Edward (1994), 'The disengaged noncustodial father: implications for social work practice with the divorced family', *Social Work*, **39**, 15–25.

Kurdek, Lawrence A. (ed.) (1983), *Children and Divorce*, San Francisco, CA: Jossey-Bass.

Kurdek, Lawrence A. and Berthold Berg (1983), 'Correlates of children's adjustment to their parents' divorces', in Kurdek, pp. 47–60.

Kurdek, Lawrence A., D. Blisk and A.E. Siesky, Jr. (1981), 'Correlates of children's long-term adjustment to their parent's divorce', *Developmental Psychology*, **17**, 565–79.

Lamb, Michael E. (1976a), 'Fathers and child development: an integrative overview', in Lamb (1976b), 1–70.

Lamb, Michael E. (ed.) (1976b), *The Role of the Father in Child Development*, New York: Wiley.

Lamb, Michael E. (1982a) 'The paternal influence in child development', in Lamb (1982b).

Lamb, Michael E. (ed.) (1982b), *Nontraditional Families: Parenting and Child Development*, Hillsdale, NJ: Lawrence Erlbaum Associates.

Lamb, Michael E. (1986a), 'The changing role of fathers', in Lamb (1986b), pp. 3–27.

Lamb, Michael (ed.) (1986b), *The Father's Role: Applied Perspectives*, New York: John Wiley & Sons.

Lamb, Michael E., Graeme Russell and Abraham Sagi (1983), 'Summary and recommendations for public policy', in Lamb and Sagi, pp. 247–58.

Lamb, Michael E. and Abraham Sagi (eds) (1983), *Fatherhood and Public Policy*, Hillsdale, NJ and London: Lawrence Erlbaum Associates.

Lessig, Lawrence (1995), 'The regulation of social meaning', *University of Chicago Law Review*, **62**, 943–1045.

Lewis, Charlie and Margaret O'Brien (eds) (1987), *Reassessing Fatherhood: New Observations on Fathers and the Modern Family*, London and Newbury Park, CA: Sage Publications.

Lund, Mary (1987), 'The non-custodial father: common challenges in parenting after divorce', in Lewis and O'Brien, pp. 212–24.

Maccoby, Eleanor E., Christy M. Buchanan, Robert H. Mnookin and Sanford M. Dornbusch (1993), 'Postdivorce roles of mothers and fathers in the lives of their children', *Journal of Family Psychology*, **29** (7), 24–38.

Mandell, Deena (1995), 'Fathers who don't pay child support: hearing their voices', *Journal of Divorce and Remarriage*, **23**, 85–116.

Manning, Wendy D. and Pamela J. Smock (1999), 'New families and nonresident father–child visitation', *Social Forces*, **78**, 87–116.

McLanahan, Sara (1985), 'Family structure and the reproduction of poverty', *American Journal of Sociology*, **90**, 873–901.

McLanahan, Sara (1988), 'Family structure and dependency: reproducing the female-headed family', *Demography*, **25**, 1–17.

McLanahan, Sara and Larry Bumpass (1988), 'Intergenerational consequences of family disruption', *American Journal of Sociology*, **94**, 130–52.

McLanahan, Sara S. and Gary D. Sandefur (1994), *Growing Up with a Single Parent*, Cambridge, MA: Harvard University Press.

Miller, Geoffrey P. (2000), 'Custody and couvade: the importance of paternal bonding in the law of family relations', *Indiana Law Review*, **33**, 691–736.

Mnookin, Robert H. and Lewis Kornhauser (1979), 'Bargaining in the shadow of the law: the case of divorce', *Yale Law Journal*, **88**, 950–97.

Mnookin, Robert H., Eleanor E. Maccoby, Catherine R. Albiston and Charlene E. Depner (1990), in Stephen D. Sugarman and Herma Hill Kay (eds) (1990), *Divorce Reform at the Crossroads*, New Haven, CT: Yale University Press, pp. 37–74.

Morgan, Lara W. (1996–present), *Child Support Guidelines: Interpretation and Application*, New York: Aspen Law and Business.

Mott, Frank L. (1990), 'When is a father really gone? Paternal–child contact in father-absent homes', *Demography*, **27**, 499–517.

Munsch, Joyce, John Woodward and Nancy Darling (1995), 'Children's perceptions of their relationships between co-residing and non-coresiding fathers', *Journal of Divorce and Remarriage*, **23**, 39–54.

Nuta, Virginia Rhodes (1986), 'Emotional aspects of child support enforcement', Family Relations, **35**, 177–81.

Pedersen, F.A. and K.S. Robson (1969), 'Father participation in infancy', *American Journal of Orthopsychiatry*, **39**, 466–72.

Pedersen, F.A., J. Rubinstein and L.J. Yarrow (1979), 'Infant development in father-absent families', *Journal of Genetic Psychology*, **135**, 51–61.

Peters, H. Elizabeth (1986), 'Marriage and divorce: informational constraints and private contracting', *American Economic Review*, **76** (3), 437–54.

Peters, H. Elizabeth, Laura M. Argys, Eleanor E. Maccoby and Robert H. Mnookin (1993), 'Enforcing divorce settlements: evidence from child support compliance and award modifications', *Demography*, **30**, 719–35.

Peterson, James and Nicholas Zill (1986), 'Marital disruption, parent–child relationships, and behavior problems in children', *Journal of Marriage and the Family*, **48**, 295–307.

Pirog-Good, Maureen and Patricia R. Brown (1995), 'Another factor to consider in choosing a child support guideline: errors in child support calculations', Institute for Research on Poverty Discussion Paper No. 1063–95.

Popenoe, David (1996), *Life Without Father: Compelling New Evidence that Fatherhood and Marriage are Indispensable for the Good of Children and Society*, New York: Martin Kessler Books.

Radin, Norma and Graeme Russell (1983), 'Increased father participation and child development outcomes', in Lamb and Sagi (1983b), 191–218.

Sanger, Carol (1996), 'Separating from children', *Colombia Law Review*, **96**, 375–517.

Santrock, John (1975), 'Father absence, perceived maternal behavior, and moral development in boys', *Child Development*, **43**, 455–69.

Seltzer, Judith A. (1991), 'Relationships between fathers and children who live apart: the father's role after separation', *Journal of Marriage and the Family*, **83** (53), 79–101.

Seltzer, Judith A. (1994), 'Consequences of marital dissolution for children', *Annual Review of Sociology*, **20**, 235–66.

Seltzer, Judith A. (1998), 'Father by law: effects of joint legal custody on nonresi-
dent fathers' involvement with children', *Demography*, **35**, 135–46.
Seltzer, Judith A. and Suzanne M. Bianchi (1988), 'Children's contact with absent
parents', *Journal of Marriage and the Family*, **50**, 663–77.
Seltzer, Judith A. and Yvonne Brandreth (1994), 'What fathers say about involvement with children after separation', *Journal of Family Issues*, **15**, 49–77.
Simons, Ronald L., Kuei-Hsiu Lin, Leslie C. Gordon, Rand D. Conger and
Frederick O. Lorenz (1999), 'Explaining the higher incidence of adjustment
problems among children of divorce compared with those in two-parent families', *Journal of Marriage and the Family*, **61**, 1020–33.
Simons, Ronald L., Les B. Whitbeck, Jay Braman and Rand D. Conger (1994), 'The
impact of mothers' parenting, involvement by nonresidential fathers, and parental conflict on the adjustment of adolescent children', *Journal of Marriage and
the Family*, **56**, 356–74.
Smith, Lee (1994), 'The new wave of illegitimacy', *Fortune*, **129**, 81–94.
Stephen, Elizabeth Hervery, Vicki A. Freedman and Jennifer Hess (1993), 'Near
and far: contact of children with their non-residential fathers', *Journal of Divorce
and Remarriage*, **184** (20),171–91.
Stevens, Joseph H. Jr. and Marilyn Matthews (eds) (1978), *Mother/child, father/
child relationships*, Washington, DC: National Association for the Education of
Young Children.
Stewart, Susan D. (1999), 'Non-resident mothers' and fathers' social contact with
children', *Journal of Marriage and the Family*, **61**, 894–907.
Stone, G. (1998), 'Nonresidential father involvement: a test of a mid-range theory',
Journal of Genetic Psychology, **159**, 313–36.
Sugarman, Stephen D. and Herma Hill Kay (eds) (1990), *Divorce Reform at the
Crossroads*, New Haven, CT: Yale University Press.
Sunstein, Cass R. (1996), 'Social norms and social rules', *Columbia Law Review*, **96**,
903–68
Thompson, Ross A. (1983), 'The father's case in child custody disputes: the contri-
butions of psychological research', in Lamb and Sagi.
Tschann, J., J. Johnston, M. Kline and J. Wallerstein (1989), 'Resources, stressors,
and attachment as predictors of adult adjustment after divorce: a longitudinal
study', *Journal of Marriage and the Family*, **51**, 1033–46.
Turkat, I.D. (1995), 'Divorce-related malicious mother syndrome', *Journal of
Family Violence*, **10**, 253–64.
US Bureau of the Census (1995), *Child Support for Custodial Mothers and Fathers:
1991, Current Population Reports*, Series P-60, No. 194.
US Bureau of the Census (1999), *Statistical Abstract of the United States 1999*,
Washington, DC: GPO.
Wallerstein, Judith S. and Joan Berlin Kelly (1976), 'The effects of parental divorce:
experience of the child in later latency', *American Journal of Orthopsychiatry*, **46**,
256–69.
Warshak, Richard A. (1992), *The Custody Revolution: The Father Factor and the
Motherhood Mystique*, New York: Poseidon Press.
Weiss, Yorem and Robert Willis (1985), 'Children as collective goods and divorce
settlements', *Journal of Labor Economics*, **3**, 268–92.
Weitzman, L.J. and R.B. Dixon (1979), 'Child custody awards: legal standards and
empirical patterns for child custody, support and visitation after divorce',
University of California Davis Law Review, **12**, 472–521.

Wolfinger, Nicholas H. (1999), 'Trends in the intergenerational transmission of divorce', *Demography*, **36**, 415–20.
Wolman, Benjamin B. and George Striker (eds) (1982), *Handbook of Developmental Psychology*, Englewood Cliffs, NJ: Prentice Hall.
Woodward, L., D.M. Fergusson and J. Belsky (2000), 'Timing of parental separation and attachment to parents in adolescence: results of a prospective study from birth to age 16', *Journal of Marriage and the Family*, **62**, 162–74.
Wu, Lawrence L. and Elizabeth Thomson (1998), 'Family change and early sexual initiation', Institute for Research on Poverty, Discussion Paper No. 1165–98.

9. Teenage delinquency: the role of child support payments and father's visitation

Heather Antecol and Kelly Bedard

1. INTRODUCTION

Single parenthood, stepfamilies and combined families have become commonplace in the United States. The number of children who spend all or part of their childhood apart from one or more biological parent increased from approximately 12 per cent to 40 per cent between 1960 and 1995 (McLanahan, 1997). Additionally, the fraction of out-of-wedlock births in 1997 was 26, 69 and 41 per cent of fertility among whites, blacks and Hispanics, respectively (Willis, 1999). Furthermore, Bumpass et al. (1995) point out that approximately 40 per cent of women and 30 per cent of all children are likely to spend some time in a stepfamily.[1]

Societal concerns surrounding this dramatic change in family structure is multifaceted. Firstly, single mothers are much more likely to fall below the poverty line, implying that increasing numbers of children may be exposed to poverty. While the incidence of this type of poverty can be reduced by support payments from the non-custodial parent (usually the father), many divorced fathers fail to volunteer adequate child support payments and/or comply with child support awards mandated by the courts (Weiss and Willis, 1985). The US Bureau of Census estimates that in 1997 6.3 million custodial mothers were due an average child support payment of $4200 but only an average of $2500 was received; in aggregate the difference amounts to a $10.6 billion deficit per year.[2] The low level of child support paid by non-custodial fathers is documented in numerous studies (see for example, Powers and Beller, 2002; Hanson et al., 1996; Garfinkel et al., 1994; Graham et al., 1994; Weiss and Willis, 1993; Beller and Graham, 1993; Garfinkel, 1992; Garfinkel and McLanahan, 1986).

Secondly, the absence of the biological father reduces the time that children spend with their father, making bonding and mentoring more difficult. By definition non-custodial fathers have less contact with their children because they reside at a different location. The non-residential status of non-custodial fathers means that all interactions are in the form of visitation that by its nature is limited in duration and bounded in terms of potential influence. There is growing empirical evidence suggesting a positive correlation between child support payment and visitation by the non-custodial father (examples include: McLanahan et al., 1994; Seltzer, 1991; Furstenberg et al., 1987). In other words, it is generally the case that fathers who pay child support have more contact with their children. Whether this is the result of paying child support, whether fathers who visit are more likely to make payments, or whether there are underlying factors that jointly determine both, is unclear. That being said, sound social policy depends on the true factors that determine youth outcomes. From a policy perspective, it is therefore clearly important that we fully understand the intricacies of the relationship between child support, visitation and youth behavior.

Unfortunately, understanding the impact of child support payments on child outcomes is further complicated by its impact on the relationship between the former spouses. McLanahan et al. (1994) point out that higher child support payments can either increase or decrease tension between the custodial and non-custodial parents depending on the circumstances. Conflict between the former spouses might be increased if the child support payment process is adversarial. On the other hand, it might reduce tensions and increase the custodial parent's willingness to grant visitation and involvement to the non-custodial parent.

Thirdly, the majority of single mothers remarry, changing the income status of the family and potentially introducing a new male role model. Perhaps surprisingly, McLanahan (1997) finds that the performance of children raised in stepfamilies is just as poor as those raised in single-parent families. This suggests that stepfathers are not a replacement for biological fathers and that factors in addition to income influence youth outcomes.

The concern about single parenthood and blended families is supported by a substantial body of recent research showing that children raised in non-traditional households tend to perform more poorly in school, exhibit behavioural problems, and are more likely to become sexually active, commit illegal acts and use illegal drugs at young ages (examples include: Antecol and Bedard, 2002; Painter and Levine, 2000; Comanor and Phillips, 2002, Wu, 1996; Garasky, 1995; McLanahan and Sandefur, 1994; Amato and Keith, 1991; Manski et al., 1992; Astone and McLanahan, 1991; Haveman and Wolfe, 1994; Flewelling and Bauman, 1990; and Matsueda and Heimer, 1987). The family structure effect, depending on the outcome measure, ranges from very small (cognitive achievement) to moderate (behavioural problems). For example, Antecol and Bedard (2002) estimate that the probability that a youth smokes regularly, engages in sexual intercourse, or is convicted before the age of 15 falls by 3.0, 5.4 and 0.6 percentage points if the biological father remains in the household for an extra five years.

While there is substantial evidence that children perform better, at least in terms of standard measures, when the family remains intact, we have less information regarding the impact of non-custodial behaviour on child outcomes once the family has disintegrated. Child support payments by non-custodial parents are an obvious starting point. It is well established that children raised in higher income families outperform poorer youth. As children raised in single-parent homes are substantially poorer on average, we would expect them to experience worse outcomes and be more likely to exhibit behavioural problems. Of course, such difficulties might be mitigated by child support payments made by the non-custodial parent. This leads to the obvious question: is a dollar a dollar regardless of where it comes from, or are child support dollars differentially valuable?

The importance of distinguishing child support payments from other sources of family income has received increased attention in the child support literature. In general, these studies find that both child support and income from other sources have a positive effect on educational attainment, but that the effect of child support receipt is larger (Knox, 1996; Knox and Bane, 1994; Graham et al., 1994; and Beller and Graham, 1993).[3]

While researchers have explored the importance and interaction of income, child support, male role models, the presence of the father and youth outcomes, the intricacies of the issues are not yet entirely understood. For example, is it the absence of a parent that has a negative impact on children or is it the associated poverty? Similarly, non-custodial male parents who pay child support also tend to visit their children more regularly. So, is it low income or the lack of contact that negatively impacts upon children? Disentangling these factors is complicated by the fact that child support payment and visitation may be correlated, in which case the measured effect of the former is largely describing the effect of the latter.

It is on these questions that we focus. In particular, we examine the impact of family structure, visitation by the non-custodial father and child support receipt on youth participation in smoking, sexual intercourse and crime before the age of 15, using single-equation probit models. To the best of our knowledge, this is the first study to examine the relationship between non-custodial visitation, child support receipt and youth participation in deviant behaviour. Previous studies have largely focused on the relationship between support payment on the part of the non-custodial father and the educational outcomes of children.

It is important that we make several qualifications before proceeding. The relationship between youth outcomes and family structure, visitation by the non-custodial father and father's support payment estimated in this chapter are correlational evidence, as opposed to causal. Stated somewhat differently, the same characteristics that cause a non-custodial father not to visit and/or pay child support may also be correlated with poor youth outcomes. In this case, the offspring of these men may have had bad outcomes even if the non-custodial father was more involved. As such, we are exploring the correlation between father's visitation and support payments and the prevalence of undesirable youth outcomes such as smoking, sexual activity and criminal behaviour among youth. Documenting these correlations is an important first step towards understanding the relationship between family structure, non-custodial parental behaviour and youth outcomes.

Using the National Longitudinal Survey of Youth (NLSY) and the NLSY Child Supplement, we find that the primary explanation for differences in teenage deviant behaviour is the presence of the biological father, rather than visitation by the non-custodial father or child support receipt. Single-equation probit estimates suggest that youth whose biological father is not always present are 3.1, 8.3 and 1.9 percentage points more likely to smoke on a regular basis, have sexual intercourse and be convicted of a crime, respectively, before the age of 15 than youth from traditional families, holding all else constant.

While the absence of the biological father is the most important family structure explanation for poor youth behaviour, there are interesting differences in youth behaviour within single-parent families across paternal visitation and child support payment. For example, youth who receive child support but rarely see their fathers are more likely to be sexually active and/or be convicted of a crime than other youth. This may reflect the fact that fathers with already deviant youth are more likely to pay but are unwilling to stay physically or emotionally in touch with such offspring. Or it may reflect the fact that youth whose fathers are committed enough to pay support but not committed enough to visit their children regularly are more likely to behave poorly. Interestingly, we find no difference in the propensity of youth to engage in deviant behaviour between youth from intact families and youth who receive no child support and rarely see their fathers. As this group is dominated by youth whose fathers were either never present or left at a very young age, this suggests that youth may not be affected by the absence of a father they never really had.

The remainder of the chapter is as follows. Section 2 describes the parental and youth data. Section 3 describes the relationships between family structure, visitation by the non-custodial father, child support receipt and youth outcomes. Section 4 concludes and discusses the ramifications of the results.

2. DATA

All youth, parental and family data are drawn from the National Longitudinal Survey of Youth (NLSY) and the NLSY Young Adult Supplement (NLSY-YAS). These data suit our purposes for a number of reasons. First, the NLSY-YAS allows us to include a wide range of youth outcomes, that is, participation in smoking, sexual intercourse and crime before the age of 15. Secondly, these data allow us to determine, for the sample of youth who did not live with their biological father for their entire life up to the age of 15, the amount of child support received and the frequency of their biological father's visitation.

The sample is restricted to children residing with their mother during their entire first 15 years of life. We restrict our attention to children living with their mother throughout their life because the small number of children raised by single biological fathers and alternate caregivers are too small to analyse reliably.

Since 1986 the children of NLSY women have been surveyed biannually. Child cognitive ability and development are assessed using tests and mothers are extensively surveyed to establish the quality of the home environment. In 1994 the survey was extended to survey 'youth' aged 15 and over directly. Each youth completes an interview focusing on education, employment and family-related behaviour as well as filling out a confidential questionnaire that focuses on substance use, sexual activity and other such sensitive issues. In particular, youth are asked how old they were when they first smoked cigarettes and how often they have engaged in this behaviour, engaged in sexual intercourse and were convicted of a crime other than a minor traffic offence. This information is used to construct variables indicating whether or not the respondent participated in a specified 'deviant' behaviour before the age of 15.[4] Behaviour is measured at age 14 to maintain a representative sample. In particular, older youth samples are less representative because they necessarily imply the over-sampling of individuals born to women who were very young at the point of childbirth.

Again to maintain the largest and most representative sample possible, the retrospective 'deviant' youth behaviour reports for 1998 are used. A youth is only included if they are 15 or older at the interview date so that behaviour occurring up until the end of age 14 is included. Table 9.1 reports the summary statistics for the sample.[5] Approximately 4 per cent of the sample are convicted of a crime before the age of 15, while 18 and 17 per cent become sexually active and smoke regularly, respectively.

The deviant behaviour variables are linked to youth and parental control variables measured in the year in which the youth is 15 years old. The

Table 9.1   Summary statistics

	Sample size	Mean	Standard deviation
Smoking	1101	0.170	0.376
Sex	1101	0.180	0.384
Conviction	1101	0.035	0.183
Proportion of youth in households that receive child support	599	0.515	0.500
Average annual child support (in $000's) including non-paying fathers	599	1.404	2.178
Average annual child support (in $000's) excluding non-paying fathers	262	2.727	2.369
Number of children in household	1101	2.596	1.079
First born child	1101	0.649	0.478
Male	1101	0.504	0.500
Black	1101	0.195	0.396
Race other than white or black	1101	0.023	0.149
Mother's years of education	1101	12.295	1.700
Mother's average weekly hours of work	1101	25.891	17.134
Mother's age at first birth less than 19	1101	0.225	0.418
Average annual net family income (in $000's)	1101	41.918	26.351
Stepfather present	599	0.365	0.482

Note:
All youth outcomes measure participation before age 15. Means and standard deviations calculated using 1998 youth sampling weights.

youth's gender and birth-order are obtained from the NLSY-YAS. The sample is evenly split between male and female children, with approximately 65 per cent of the sample being first-born children. The number of siblings that the youth has, the mother's years of education, the mother's current marital status, net family income, urban or rural residential location and the youth's region of residence at age 15 are drawn from the NLSY. Family income is measured by average net family income from the time the youth is 12 until age 15.[6] A mother is considered currently married to a stepfather if she reports being married at all times while the youth is between the ages of 12 and 15 for the sample of youth who did not live with their biological father for their entire life up to the age of 15. Of the eligible youth in our sample, those with an absent father, 37 per cent have a stepfather present. This three-year window is used to capture the environment experienced by the youth during the formative years with respect to deviant behaviour.

Combining the NLSY and the NLSY-YAS also allows us to measure the length of time that each youth lives with his or her biological father (the maximum is 180 months – their entire life up to the age of 15). Although these data do not allow one to directly link youth to their biological father, we are able to link them through the mother's marital status. In particular, a man is considered to be the youth's biological father if he was either married to the mother at the point of birth or married her within 36 months of the youth's birth. In both cases, the father is assumed to be present in the household from the point of birth. If the father marries the mother at or before the youth's birth, the number of months that the father is present is measured by the number of months that the marriage lasts. If, on the other hand, the father marries the mother after the youth's birth, the number of months that the father is present is measured by the number of months that the marriage lasted plus the number of months from the youth's birth until the marriage began. In all other cases, we assume that the youth never lives with his or her biological father. We use the measure of the length of time that each youth lives with his or her biological father to construct an indicator variable for the presence of the biological father which is coded as one if the youth spent less than their entire life up to the age of 15 with their biological father, and zero otherwise. Approximately 56 (44) per cent of the youth sample spent (less than) their entire life up to the age of 15 with their biological father (see Table 9.2).

Table 9.2   Youth behaviour by family structure, father's visitation and child support receipt

	% of sample	Smoking	Sex	Conviction
Overall	100.00	0.170	0.180	0.035
Father always present	55.88	0.165	0.120	0.026
Father not always present	44.12	0.176	0.255	0.045
See often & receive child support	19.48	0.135	0.205	0.021
See often & don't receive child support	16.40	0.167	0.279	0.036
See rarely & receive child support	32.00	0.234	0.295	0.076
See rarely & don't receive child support	32.11	0.148	0.233	0.035

Note:
1998 youth sampling weights used.

Finally, these data include the amount of child support received and the frequency of the father's visitation for youth with a non-custodial father. As with family income, child support and father's visitation are three-year averages while the youth is between 12 and 15 years of age. Visitation by the non-custodial father is reported categorically as almost daily, two to three times per week, about once per week, one to two times per month, once every two to three months, once per year and never. We define a non-custodial father as visiting often if he visited at least one or two times per month on average while the youth was between the ages of 12 and 15, otherwise the non-custodial father is defined as visiting rarely.

Perhaps surprisingly, only 52 per cent of the eligible youth in our sample, those with an absent father, actually receive child support. Conditional on receiving child support, the average level of child support is $2727 per mother per year.[7] Even more unsettling, only 36 per cent of non-custodial fathers visit their children on a regular basis (see Table 9.2). The next section provides a detailed examination of the distribution of family structures and the effect of child support and the incidence of the biological father's presence or visitation on youth outcomes.

3. FAMILY STRUCTURE, FATHER'S VISITATION, CHILD SUPPORT RECEIPT AND YOUTH OUTCOMES

3.1. Family Structure

Before examining the relationship between youth outcomes, child support payments and the visitation of non-custodial fathers, it is helpful to describe the distribution of family structures for our sample of 15-year-olds. Column 1 of Table 9.2 reports the frequency of family types for our sample. Fifty-six per cent of the youth live with their biological father during the entire first 15 years of their life. The remaining 44 per cent spend at least some fraction of their first 15 years in an alternate family structure – living with a single mother or with a stepfather present. Of the youth spending part of their life separated from their biological father, 19 per cent receive regular visitation and child support payments, 16 per cent receive regular visits but no child support, 32 per cent receive child support but infrequent visitation and 32 per cent are subject to infrequent visitation and no child support payments.[8]

These results are particularly interesting because they differ from previous studies. McLanahan et al. (1994), Seltzer (1991) and Furstenberg et al. (1987) find that child support payment and visitation are positively correlated. In contrast, our results, reported in Table 9.2, show no pattern across child support payment and visitation. For example, conditional on paying child support, 62 per cent of fathers visit rarely and conditional on not paying child support 66 per cent of non-custodial fathers visit rarely.

3.2. Youth Smoking, Sexual Activity and Criminal Conviction

The obvious question is: do father's presence, father's visitation and child support receipt affect youth outcomes? The last three columns of Table 9.2 reveal several interesting patterns. First, children who spend their entire childhood with both biological parents are less likely to smoke cigarettes, be sexually active and engage in criminal activity. While differences in the incidence of smoking are relatively small, the impact on sexual promiscuity and crime are substantial. More specifically, 25.5 per cent of youth who spend at least part of their life without their biological father are sexually active before the age of 15 compared to only 12.0 per cent of youth whose fathers are always present in the household. Similarly, 4.5 per cent of youth who spend at least part of their life without their biological father are convicted of a crime before the age of 15 compared to only 2.6 per cent of youth whose fathers are always present in the household.

The pattern of deviant behaviour across non-custodial father's visitation and child support payment generally reflects the fact that it is the absence of the biological father that is most detrimental, and not the decision of the father to withhold child support or visit his child infrequently. This is particularly true for teenage sexual behaviour. Regardless of father's child support payment or visitation, youth whose biological father is absent for part of their life are substantially more likely to have sex before the age of 15. While only 20.5 per cent of youth whose non-custodial father both visit regularly and pay child support have sex before age 15, approximately 30 per cent of youth whose non-custodial fathers either visit regularly but do not pay child support or pay child support but visit infrequently. At the same time, 23.3 per cent of youth whose non-custodial fathers neither pay child support or visit become sexually active before age 15. Comparing these outcomes to the 12 per cent of youth in intact families, it is clear that youth with non-custodial fathers of all types are more likely to become sexually active at a young age. The pattern of the results also tentatively suggests that a 'little' involvement (paying but not visiting, or visiting but not paying) may actually lead to worse outcomes for youth than either active involvement or no involvement at all on the part of non-custodial fathers.

The patterns across father's visitation and child support payment are less clear for smoking and conviction. While it is generally true that youth with absent fathers are more likely to smoke and be convicted of a crime, there are exceptions. For example, youth with non-custodial fathers who both pay child support and visit on a regular basis are less likely to smoke and be convicted than youth from intact families. At the other extreme, youth whose non-custodial fathers pay child support but visit rarely are much more likely to smoke and be convicted of a crime than any other group.

More specifically, these youth are 10 percentage points more likely to smoke and 5.5 percentage points more likely to be convicted than youth whose non-custodial fathers both pay child support and visit on a regular basis.

One might wonder if the differences in deviant behaviour across family structures differ across gender. Appendix Table 9.1 replicates Table 9.2 for boys and girls separately. Breaking youth into gender groups reveals that, at least for youth under the age of 15, there are no discernible differences between boys and girls. Therefore, the remainder of the analysis looks at the sample as a whole, but does include a gender indicator variable.

These results tentatively suggest that father's visitation and child support receipt play a limited role in explaining deviant youth behaviour. However, our inability to detect a child support effect may lie in the fact that child support payments comprise only a small fraction of net family income. More specifically, the average payment is only $2727 per mother per year and the average number of children per mother is 2.6 (see Table 9.1). This implies an average of about $90 per child per month,[9] which is approximately the price of a pair of Nike athletic shoes.

3.3. Child Support Receipt and Family Income

The economically insignificant impact of child support on family income can be seen in Table 9.3. All statistics reported in Table 9.3 refer only to youth with a non-custodial father; Panel A (B) includes the sample of youth who did not live with their biological father for their entire life up to the age of 12 (15). The results in Panels A and B are similar; therefore for the remainder of the discussion we focus on Panel A which matches more closely with our definitions of average net family income and average child support payments (averages from the time the youth is 12 until age 15).

Column 1 of Table 9.3 reports family income and child support receipt for the eligible youth sample, that is youth from non-traditional families. The average youth living in a non-traditional family receives child support in the amount of $1310 per year from the non-custodial father. Given an average family income of $31500, child support amounts to approximately 4 per cent of total income. If we restrict attention to youth with non-custodial fathers who actually pay child support, this percentage rises to 8 per cent. While it may seem important to distinguish between non-custodial fathers who pay child support and those who do not, no matter how we break up the sample child support accounts for only a small percentage of family income.

The relative unimportance of child support payments can more easily be seen by breaking the sample into households with and without a stepfather present (columns 2 and 3 in Table 9.3). As one might expect, child support is a more important income source for single mothers. The average youth living in a household where there is no stepfather present has a family income of $22700 with child support contributing approximately 7 per cent while the average youth living in a household with a stepfather present has a family income of $45000 with child support contributing approximately 2 per cent. Once again, a similar pattern emerges if we restrict attention to youth with non-custodial fathers who actually pay child support. In this case, the average youth living in a household where there is no stepfather present has a family income of approximately $24000 with child support contributing approximately 12 per cent while the average youth living in a household with a stepfather present has a family income of $49000 with child support contributing approximately 4 per cent.

The last three columns of Table 9.3 report family income and child support receipt by mother's educational attainment. Not surprisingly, family income is highest among mothers with more than a high school education ($35400), followed by high school graduates ($32800), and high school dropouts ($22500). Interestingly, child support payments contribute roughly the same amount to family income for all maternal educational groups: 4 per cent for both paying and non-paying fathers and 8 per cent for paying fathers only. This result may seem counter-intuitive given assortative mating: child support payments should make up a larger share of family income for the highly educated because their ex-partners would be more able to pay. However, as Weiss and Willis (1985) point out, low levels of child support payments and non-compliance are not restricted to non-traditional families below the poverty line.

3.4. The Impact of Father's Visitation and Child Support Receipt on Youth Outcomes

This section more formally estimates the relationship between family structure, father's visitation, child support receipt and youth outcomes in a discrete choice single-equation probit framework. Let the indicator variable Y_i $= 1$ if the youth participates in a specified deviant behaviour before age 15 and let $Y_i = 0$ otherwise. The choice problem is then described by the following latent variable model:

$$Y_i^* = X_i\beta = F_i\delta = \epsilon_i \qquad (1)$$

where Y_i^* is the propensity to participate in a deviant behaviour, X_i is a vector of individual characteristics (family size, birth order and gender), family characteristics (family income, mother's education and mother's race) and regional characteristics (metropolitan status and the youth's

Table 9.3 Family income and child support receipt by mother's characteristics

	Total	Stepfather not present	Stepfather present	Mother is a high school drop-out	Mother is a high school graduate	Mother has more than high school
			Panel A: Father present less than 144 months			
Both paying and non-paying fathers						
Average annual net family income (in $000's)	31.531	22.703	45.038	22.486	32.761	35.397
Average annual child support (in $000's)	1.310	1.559	0.927	0.757	1.393	1.528
Proportion of youth receiving child support	0.500	0.542	0.437	0.361	0.550	0.488
Correlation b/w family income & child support	**0.106**	**0.203**	**0.228**	0.058	0.040	**0.170**
Only paying fathers						
Average annual net family income (in $000's)	32.474	23.930	48.662	26.479	32.018	36.987
Average annual child support (in $000's)	2.617	2.879	2.120	2.098	2.532	3.127
Correlation b/w family income & child support	**0.147**	**0.249**	**0.326**	−0.147	0.115	**0.215**
Only non-paying fathers						
Average annual net family income (in $000's)	30.587	21.253	42.220	20.234	33.669	33.880
Average annual child support (in $000's)	0.000	0.000	0.000	0.000	0.000	0.000
			Panel B: Father present less than 180 months			
Both paying and non-paying fathers						
Average annual net family income (in $000's)	31.293	23.392	45.038	22.233	32.538	34.795
Average annual child support (in $000's)	1.404	1.678	0.927	0.736	1.547	1.539
Proportion of youth receiving child support	0.515	0.559	0.437	0.353	0.568	0.502
Correlation b/w family income & child support	**0.109**	**0.219**	**0.228**	0.065	0.037	**0.194**

Only paying fathers						
Average annual net family income (in $000's)	32.277	24.912	48.662	26.404	31.789	36.588
Average annual child support (in $000's)	2.727	2.999	2.120	2.082	2.722	3.065
Correlation b/w family income & child support	**0.147**	**0.251**	**0.326**	−0.142	0.106	**0.241**
Only non-paying fathers						
Average annual net family income (in $000's)	30.249	21.462	42.220	19.955	33.524	32.987
Average annual child support (in $000's)	0.000	0.000	0.000	0.000	0.000	0.000

Note:
1998 youth sampling weights used. Bold correlations are statistically significant at the 10 per cent level.

region of residence at age 15), F_i is a vector of family structure indicator variables and ϵ_{li} is a normally distributed disturbance term with mean zero and unit variance. The probability that the youth is observed engaging in the specified deviant behaviour is given by:

$$\text{prob } (Y_i = 1) = \text{prob } (X_i\beta + F_i\delta + \epsilon_i > 0) = \Phi(X_i\beta + F_i\delta) \qquad (2)$$

where Φ is the standard normal cumulative density function.

Equation (2) is estimated using a Probit model. Tables 9.4 to 9.6 report the estimated determinants of smoking, sexual activity and criminal conviction, respectively. In order to more easily describe the quantitative importance of the explanatory variables, all tables report the marginal effects ($\partial prob(Y_i = 1)/\partial X_i$) for continuous variables and average treatment effects for the discrete variables, in both cases evaluated at means, as well as standard errors calculated using the 'delta' method.

Tables 9.4 to 9.6 all have the same format. The first four columns include the indicator variable for youth whose biological father was not present for their entire first 15 years of life with columns 2 to 4 progressively adding the control variables described above. The second four columns have the same format as the first four columns, except that we replace the 'biological father not always present' indicator variable with four mutually exclusive family type indicators for families where the biological father is not always present: the father visits often and pays child support, the father visits often but does not pay child support, the father visits rarely but does pay child support, and the father visits rarely and does not pay child support. In all cases, the excluded category is the biological father present throughout the youth's entire 15 years of life.

Columns 2–4 and 6–8 add the control variables, other than family structure, progressively to assess the robustness of main result to model specification. More specifically, columns 2 and 6 add all control variables except family income and the presence of stepfathers in non-traditional households. Family income is added in columns 3 and 7 and the presence of a stepfather is added in columns 4 and 8. These last two variables are added in succession to help disentangle the relationship between family structure and family income, which is clearly affected by the presence of a stepfather in the case of non-traditional families (see Table 9.3).

3.4.1. Smoking
Family structure has a negligible impact on the smoking behaviour of youth. To begin, compare youth whose biological father is always in the household to youth whose biological father is absent for at least part of their life (Table 9.4, columns 1–4). When a dummy variable indicating that

the father is absent for at least some period is the only right-hand side variable it is positive, but statistically insignificant at conventional levels. Once the standard control variables, except family income and the presence of a stepfather are included, the indicator for father not always present becomes both larger in magnitude and is statistically significant. According to column 2, youth whose biological father is not always present are 5.9 percentage points more likely to smoke on a regular basis than youth from traditional families.

Holding father's presence constant, youth whose mothers are more educated are slightly less likely to smoke. For example, a youth whose mother holds an undergraduate degree is approximately 8 percentage points less likely to smoke on a regular basis than a youth whose mother only holds a high school graduation diploma. As is often found, first-born youth are less likely to engage in deviant behaviour. In this case, first-born youth are 9.9 percentage points less likely to smoke. Perhaps surprisingly, black youth are much less likely to smoke cigarettes than white youth. All of these results are similar to Antecol and Bedard (2002).

Column 3 adds family income to the list of regressors. The addition of family income reduces the point estimate of the father not always present indicator variable by 1.7 percentage points and renders it statistically insignificant. The father not always present indicator variable point estimate and statistical precision are reduced still further when a dummy variable indicating the presence of a stepfather is added. The insignificant impact of the biological father's presence once family income is controlled for suggests that in the absence of a family income measure, the father not always present variable is trying to absorb both family structure and income effects.[10]

While the inclusion of family income and stepfather presence wash out the effect of father's presence, they have little or no impact on the other coefficients in the regression. In fact, these coefficients are essentially the same regardless of the inclusion of family income and stepfather presence. In addition, once the indicator for stepfather is included, the coefficient on family income is negative and statistically significant. A $10 000 increase in family income reduces the probability of smoking by 1 percentage point.

Columns 5 to 8 break family structure into five categories: biological father always present; biological father not always present but visits often and pays child support; visits often but does not pay child support; pays child support but visits rarely; and does not visit often or pay child support. 'Father is always present' is the excluded category in all specifications. With the exception of the family structure variables, the coefficient estimates are almost identical under all specifications.

As in column 1, when the family structure variables are the only regressors they are neither individually nor jointly significant (column 5). The addition

Table 9.4 *Smoking probits (marginal effects)*

	(1)	(2)	(3)	(4)	(5)	(6)	(7)	(8)
Father not always present (FNAP)	0.011	**0.059**	0.042	0.031				
	(0.030)	(0.031)	(0.032)	(0.038)				
FNAP & see often & receive child support (CS)					−0.030	−0.003	−0.020	−0.023
					(0.050)	(0.052)	(0.051)	(0.050)
FNAP & see often & don't receive CS					0.002	0.046	0.034	0.026
					(0.055)	(0.061)	(0.059)	(0.067)
FNAP & see rarely & receive CS					0.068	**0.117**	**0.094**	**0.086**
					(0.048)	(0.054)	(0.053)	(0.058)
FNAP & see rarely & don't receive CS					−0.018	0.057	0.038	0.033
					(0.041)	(0.050)	(0.048)	(0.054)
Male		0.016	0.016	0.016		0.021	0.020	0.020
		(0.027)	(0.027)	(0.027)		(0.028)	(0.027)	(0.027)
Number of children in household		−0.008	−0.006	−0.006		−0.008	−0.007	−0.007
		(0.013)	(0.013)	(0.013)		(0.013)	(0.013)	(0.013)
First born child		**−0.099**	**−0.099**	**−0.099**		**−0.101**	**−0.101**	**−0.101**
		(0.034)	(0.034)	(0.034)		(0.034)	(0.034)	(0.034)
Black		**−0.177**	**−0.181**	**−0.181**		**−0.175**	**−0.180**	**−0.180**
		(0.021)	(0.021)	(0.021)		(0.021)	(0.021)	(0.021)
Race other than white or black		−0.083	−0.087	−0.087		−0.076	−0.081	−0.081
		(0.042)	(0.040)	(0.039)		(0.046)	(0.043)	(0.043)
Mother's years of education		**−0.020**	**−0.017**	**−0.017**		**−0.021**	**−0.017**	**−0.017**
		(0.009)	(0.009)	(0.009)		(0.009)	(0.009)	(0.009)
Mother's average hours of work		−0.001	0.000	0.000		−0.001	0.000	0.000
		(0.001)	(0.001)	(0.001)		(0.001)	(0.001)	(0.001)

Mother's age at first birth less than 19	−0.027 (0.034)	−0.026 (0.034)	−0.027 (0.034)	−0.023 (0.034)	−0.023 (0.034)	−0.023 (0.034)
Average net family income		−0.001 (0.001)	**−0.001** (0.001)		−0.001 (0.001)	−0.001 (0.001)
Stepfather present			0.023 (0.046)			0.012 (0.047)

Note:

Models (2)–(4) and (6)–(8) also include the youth's region of residence at age 15 indicator variables and metropolitan status indicator variables. Bold coefficients are statistically significant at the 10% level. The smoking outcome variable measures participation before age 15. 1998 youth sampling weights are used. The sample size is 1101 in all specifications. Heteroskedastic consistent standard errors are in parentheses.

Table 9.5 Sexual activity probits (marginal effects)

	(1)	(2)	(3)	(4)	(5)	(6)	(7)	(8)
Father not always present (FNAP)	**0.135**	**0.105**	**0.092**	**0.083**				
	(0.028)	(0.030)	(0.032)	(0.036)				
FNAP & see often & receive child support (CS)					**0.101**	0.081	0.063	0.060
					(0.060)	(0.055)	(0.055)	(0.056)
FNAP & see often & don't receive CS					**0.183**	**0.123**	**0.114**	**0.106**
					(0.061)	(0.061)	(0.061)	(0.073)
FNAP & see rarely & receive CS					**0.194**	**0.169**	**0.151**	**0.144**
					(0.053)	(0.053)	(0.055)	(0.056)
FNAP & see rarely & don't receive CS					**0.129**	**0.078**	0.061	0.056
					(0.045)	(0.046)	(0.046)	(0.051)
Male		-0.012	-0.011	-0.011		-0.009	-0.009	-0.009
		(0.027)	(0.026)	(0.026)		(0.026)	(0.026)	(0.026)
Number of children in household		**-0.026**	**-0.024**	**-0.025**		-0.028	**-0.026**	**-0.027**
		(0.013)	(0.013)	(0.013)		(0.013)	(0.013)	(0.013)
First born child		**-0.066**	**-0.065**	**-0.065**		**-0.067**	**-0.066**	**-0.065**
		(0.031)	(0.031)	(0.031)		(0.031)	(0.031)	(0.031)
Black		0.006	-0.005	-0.004		0.013	0.002	0.003
		(0.032)	(0.032)	(0.032)		(0.033)	(0.032)	(0.032)
Race other than white or black		0.087	0.079	0.079		0.094	0.086	0.085
		(0.078)	(0.076)	(0.076)		(0.081)	(0.079)	(0.079)
Mother's years of education		**-0.012**	-0.010	-0.009		**-0.013**	-0.010	-0.010
		(0.008)	(0.008)	(0.008)		(0.008)	(0.008)	(0.008)
Mother's average hours of work		-0.001	-0.001	-0.001		-0.001	-0.001	-0.001
		(0.001)	(0.001)	(0.001)		(0.001)	(0.001)	(0.001)

Mother's age at first birth less than 19	**0.089**	**0.087**	**0.086**	**0.090**	**0.088**	**0.087**
	(0.037)	(0.037)	(0.037)	(0.037)	(0.037)	(0.037)
Average net family income		−0.001	−0.001		−0.001	−0.001
		(0.001)	(0.001)		(0.001)	(0.001)
Stepfather present			0.019			0.010
			(0.040)			(0.041)

Note:
Models (2)-(4) and (6)-(8) also include the youth's region of residence at age 15 indicator variables and metropolitan status indicator variables. Heteroskedastic consistent standard errors are in parentheses. Bold coefficients are statistically significant at the 10% level. The sexual activity outcome variable measures participation before age 15. 1998 youth sampling weights are used. The sample size is 1101 in all specifications.

259

Table 9.6 Conviction probits (marginal effects)

	(1)	(2)	(3)	(4)	(5)	(6)	(7)	(8)
Father not always present (FNAP)	0.019 (0.014)	**0.020** (0.011)	**0.019** (0.012)	0.019 (0.013)				
FNAP & see often & receive child support (CS)					−0.007 (0.016)	−0.001 (0.011)	−0.002 (0.012)	−0.001 (0.012)
FNAP & see often & don't receive CS					0.012 (0.033)	0.008 (0.021)	0.008 (0.020)	0.011 (0.026)
FNAP & see rarely & receive CS					**0.051** (0.029)	**0.059** (0.030)	**0.056** (0.032)	**0.061** (0.036)
FNAP & see rarely & don't receive CS					0.010 (0.022)	0.009 (0.015)	0.008 (0.015)	0.009 (0.017)
Male		0.012 (0.010)	0.012 (0.010)	0.012 (0.010)		0.013 (0.009)	0.013 (0.009)	0.013 (0.009)
Number of children in household		0.001 (0.004)	0.001 (0.004)	0.001 (0.004)		0.000 (0.004)	0.000 (0.004)	0.000 (0.004)
First born child		**−0.042** (0.016)	**−0.042** (0.015)	**−0.042** (0.015)		**−0.040** (0.015)	**−0.041** (0.015)	**−0.041** (0.015)
Black		−0.007 (0.009)	−0.008 (0.009)	−0.008 (0.009)		−0.004 (0.008)	−0.005 (0.008)	−0.005 (0.008)
Race other than white or black		−0.008 (0.014)	−0.008 (0.014)	−0.008 (0.014)		−0.005 (0.015)	−0.005 (0.014)	−0.005 (0.014)
Mother's years of education		**−0.006** (0.002)	**−0.006** (0.003)	**−0.006** (0.003)		**−0.006** (0.002)	**−0.006** (0.002)	**−0.006** (0.002)
Mother's average hours of work		0.000 (0.000)	0.000 (0.000)	0.000 (0.000)		0.000 (0.000)	0.000 (0.000)	0.000 (0.000)

Mother's age at first birth less than 19	0.008	0.008	0.008	0.007	0.007	0.007
	(0.011)	(0.011)	(0.011)	(0.010)	(0.010)	(0.010)
Average net family income		0.000	0.000		0.000	0.000
		(0.000)	(0.000)		(0.000)	(0.000)
Stepfather present			0.000			−0.004
			(0.013)			(0.011)

Note:
Models (2)–(4) and (6)–(8) also include the youth's region of residence at age 15 indicator variables and metropolitan status indicator variables. Heteroskedastic consistent standard errors are in parentheses. Bold coefficients are statistically significant at the 10% level. The conviction outcome variable measures participation before age 15. 1998 youth sampling weights are used. The sample size is 1101 in all specifications.

of the remaining explanatory variables, column 6, does not change the joint statistical insignificance of the family structure variables. Interestingly, however, the coefficient on youth with absent fathers who pay child support but visit rarely is statistically significant and positive. In other words, it is youth with non-custodial fathers who pay child support but do not visit on a regular basis that are the most likely to smoke. As in columns 2–4, the addition of family income and the presence of a stepfather to the list of regressors reduce the family structure point estimates and the statistical precision of the coefficients.

3.4.2.   Sexual activity

The probit estimates for the sexual activity model are reported in Table 9.5. Before turning to the impact of family structure on teenage promiscuity, it is interesting to examine the correlation between the standard socioeconomic characteristics and youth sexual activity. In contrast to smoking, there is little evidence that mother's education effects teenage sexual behaviour. Once family income is included, mother's education is never statistically significant. However, this may be because family income and maternal education have very similar impacts on the sexual behaviour of their offspring. Just as with smoking, family income has a small negative impact on the probability that a youth becomes sexually active before the age of 15.

At the same time, the youth of mothers who began having children at younger ages are more likely to become sexually active before the age of 15. More specifically, the youth of mothers who had their first child before they were 19 years old are approximately 8.7 percentage points more likely to become sexually active before the age of 15. As with smoking, first-born children are less likely to be sexually promiscuous at young ages. Interestingly, youth raised with more siblings are less likely to be sexually active before the age of 15. Casual empiricism suggests that youths with fewer siblings have fewer positive family influences and have more free time available, and are therefore more likely to use that free time in ways that involve deviant behaviours.

In contrast to the limited impact of father's presence, visitation, or child support payment on their children's probability of smoking, these factors do deter early sexual activity in youth. Regardless of the control variables included, youth residing in households without a biological father are more likely to be sexually active before the age of 15 (columns 1–4). While the point estimate for the impact of an absent father is 13.5 percentage points when no other control variables are included, this point estimate falls to youth with an absent father being 8 percentage points more likely to be sexually active when the full set of controls are included.

Not surprisingly given the results in columns 1–4, the family structure variables in columns 5–8 are jointly significant at the 10 per cent level or better. Breaking paternal absence into four categories does, however, reveal the following noteworthy results. First, the propensity to engage in sexual intercourse before the age of 15 is 14.4 percentage points higher for youth whose fathers visit rarely but pay child support relative to youth from intact families (column 8). Secondly, there is little evidence that youth in non-intact families where the father visits often and pays child support, the father visits often but does not pay child support, and the father visits rarely and does not pay child support, differ in terms of their propensity to engage in sexual activity from youth in traditional families. Until the stepfather present indicator variable is included, the estimates show that both youth whose absent fathers pay child support but do not visit, and youth whose fathers visit but do not pay child support, are more likely to become sexually active before the age of 15. The fact that children who never lived with their father dominate the group for which the father neither pays support nor visits, suggests that the absence of either factor may only contribute to early sexual activity for youth who at some point resided with their biological father. On the other hand, the absence and lack of contact or financial support from a father that never really lived in the child's home has little impact on the sexual behaviour of youth.

3.4.3. Criminal conviction

The probit estimates for the conviction model are reported in Table 9.6. Similar to the pattern found for smoking, youth with more educated mothers are less likely to be convicted of a crime before the age of 15. However, the impact is fairly small. Holding all else constant, a youth with a college graduate mother is 2.4 percentage points less likely to be convicted of a crime compared to a youth whose mother is a only a high school graduate. The only other socio-economic variable that shows a statistically significant correlation with conviction is birth order. First-born children are approximately 4 percentage points less likely to be convicted of a crime before the age of 15 compared to later birth order children. Interestingly, there are no apparent differences across gender in the probability of conviction, nor smoking or sexual activity for that matter.

In contrast to the relationship between family structure and youth smoking, the presence of a biological father does reduce the probability that a youth is convicted of a crime. However, this relationship is not apparent until other socio-economic factors are controlled for (column 2). Once this is done, youth with an absent father are approximately 2 percentage points less likely to be convicted of a crime. In contrast to smoking and sexual activity, the magnitude of the coefficient on father not always present does not fall as family income and the presence of a stepfather are included; however, the point estimate does become statistically insignificant. The imprecision of the results is not surprising given the small number of youth committing crimes before the age of 15, only 3.5 per cent of the sample.

Breaking the father not always present category into four subcategories again reveals several interesting patterns. First, youth with an absent father who both pays child support and visits often are very similar to children with a resident father in terms of criminal conviction. In fact, it is only youth whose absent father pays child support but visits rarely that have a significantly higher probability of being convicted of a crime before the age of 15. This group of youth is approximately 6 percentage points more likely to be convicted of a crime than youth whose biological father is always present. This is a huge difference and suggests that youth with non-custodial fathers who are involved enough to pay child support but uninvolved to the extent that they visit infrequently are more likely to behave poorly compared to youth whose absent fathers either remain more involved through visitation or are completely uninvolved in the sense that they neither financially support their children nor bother to visit with any regularity.

4. DISCUSSION

This chapter contributes to the literature on the impact of child support receipt on child outcomes in two important ways. First, our sample includes youth from all family structures. This allows us to compare the deviant behaviour of youth in intact families from youth in non-traditional families with fathers who choose to be involved to various degrees, in terms of child support payment and visitation. Secondly, we examine the impact of family structure, the payment of child support by the non-custodial father, and visitation by the non-custodial father on the probability that youth engage in undesirable behaviours such as smoking, having sex and committing crimes.

We see the difference in teenage participation in deviant behaviour by youth with an absent father compared to youth with a present father as the primary finding of this chapter. In other words, paternal presence is the primary explanation for differences in teenage behaviour rather than the withholding of child support or visitation on the part of absent fathers. Once a father is absent from the household, his ability to deter deviant behaviour appears to be minimal.

While the absence of the biological father is the most important family structure explanation for poor youth behaviour, there are interesting differences in youth behaviour within single-parent families across paternal visitation and child support payment. For example, relative to other youth, youth receiving child support but who rarely see their fathers are more likely to smoke and engage in sexual intercourse and criminal activity than other youth. As discussed in section 1, the relatively poor performance of these youth may stem either from the fact that fathers with already deviant youth may be more likely to pay but be unwilling to visit such offspring, or it may reflect the fact that youth whose fathers are committed enough to pay support but not committed enough to visit their children regularly are more likely to behave poorly.

We view the results, and in some cases non-results, reported in this chapter as leading to important questions for future research. Firstly, why do non-custodial fathers choose to pay low levels of child support or none at all? Secondly, and probably more importantly, why do so many non-custodial fathers visit so rarely? The heterogeneity of fathers and the heterogeneity in the answers to these questions is likely part of the reason why it is difficult to obtain causal estimates of the impact of divorce, child support payment, and child visitation on child and youth outcomes. Despite the difficulties associated with obtaining such estimates, a sound understanding of the impact of family structure on children is clearly important.

NOTES

1. Bumpass et al. (1995) include cohabitation in their definition of stepfamilies.
2. See http://www.census.gov/hhes/www/childsupport/97tables/tab1.html.
3. A number of related studies look at the effect of family income on youth outcomes in single-parent families without attempting to isolate the child support component (see for example, Hill and Duncan, 1987; McLanahan, 1985; and Shaw, 1982).
4. A respondent is coded as participating in smoking before the age of 15 if they report participating for the first time before the age of 15 and have smoked cigarettes on more than 100 occasions.
5. 1998 youth sampling weights are used in all tables.
6. Respondents reporting family income of less than $1200 or more than $200000 per year in 1998 dollars are excluded from the sample.
7. Although the amount paid in child support seems low, it is consistent with the results reported in the child support literature. Examples include: Powers and Beller (2002), Hanson et al. (1996), Garfinkel et al. (1994), Graham et al. (1994), Weiss and Willis (1993), Beller and Graham (1993); Garfinkel (1992), and Garkinkel and McLanahan (1986).
8. As described in the previous section, these percentages reflect the average experience of the youth between the ages of 12 and 15.
9. This is only an approximation as some households are blended families and the reported child support is technically only for the support of a fraction of the children.
10. This is consistent with a number of studies, which find that the inclusion of family income reduces the magnitude of the presence of the father and in some cases renders it insignificant (see McLanahan, 1997 for a review of the literature).

REFERENCES

Amato, P.R. and B. Keith (1991), 'Separation from a parent during childhood and adult socioeconomic attainment', *Social Forces*, **70** (1), 187–206.

Antecol, H. and K. Bedard (2002), 'Does single parenthood increase the probability of teenage promiscuity, drug use, and crime?' Claremont Colleges Working Paper.

Astone, N.M. and S.S. McLanahan (1991), 'Family structure, parental practices and high school completion', *American Sociological Review*, **56** (3), 309–20.

Beller, A.H. and J.W. Graham (1993), *Small Change: The Economics of Child Support*, New Haven, CT and London: Yale University Press.

Bumpass, L.L., R.K. Raley and J.A. Sweet (1995), 'The changing character of step-families: implications of cohabitation and nonmarital childbearing', *Demography*, **32** (3), 425–36.

Comanor, W.S. and L. Phillips (2002), 'The impact of income and family structure on delinquency', *Journal of Applied Economics*, **5** (2), 209–32.

Flewelling, R.L. and K.E. Bauman (1990), 'Family structure as predictor of initial substance use and sexual intercourse in early adolescence', *Journal of Marriage and the Family*, **52** (1), 171–81.

Furstenberg, F.F., S.P. Morgan and P.D. Allison (1987), 'Paternal participation and children's well-being', *American Sociological Review*, **48** (5), 695–701.

Garasky, S. (1995), 'The effects of family structure on educational attainment: do the effects vary by the age of the child?' *American Journal of Economics and Sociology*, **54** (1), 89–105.

Garfinkel, I. (1992), *Assuring Child Support*, New York: Russell Sage Foundation.

Garfinkel, I. and S.S. McLanahan (1986), *Single Mothers and Their Children: A New American Dilemma*, Washington, DC: Urban Institute Press.

Garfinkel, I., S.S. McLanahan and P.K. Robins (1994), *Child Support and Child Well-Being*, Washington, DC: Urban Institute Press.

Graham, J.W., A.H. Beller and Pedro M. Hernandez (1994), 'The effects of child support on educational attainment', in I. Garfinkel, S.S. McLanahan and P.K. Robins (eds), *Child Support and Child Well-Being*, Washington, DC: Urban Institute Press.

Hanson, T.L., I. Garfinkel, S.S. McLanahan and C.K. Miller (1996), 'Trends in child support outcomes', *Demography*, **33** (4), 483–96.

Haveman, R.H. and B. Wolfe (1994), *Succeeding Generations: On the Effect of Investments in Children*, New York: Russell Sage Foundation.

Hill, Martha S. and Greg J. Duncan (1987), 'Parental family income and the socioeconomic attainment of children', *Social Science Research*, **16**, 39–73.

Knox, V.W. (1996), 'The effects of child support payments on developmental outcomes for elementary school-age children', *Journal of Human Resources*, **31** (4), 816–40.

Knox, V.W. and M.J. Bane (1994), 'Child support and schooling', in I. Garfinkel, S.S. McLanahan and P.K. Robins (eds), *Child Support and Child Well-Being*, Washington, DC: The Urban Institute Press.

Manski, C.G., G.D. Sandefur, S. McLanahan and D. Powers (1992), 'Alternative estimates of the effect of family structure during adolescence on high school graduation', *Journal of the American Statistical Association*, **87** (417), 25–37.

Matsueda, R.L. and K. Heimer (1987), 'Race, family structure and delinquency: a test of differential association and social control theories', *American Sociological Review*, **52** (6), 130–52.

McLanahan, S. (1985), 'Family structure and the reproduction of poverty', *American Journal of Sociology*, **90**, 873–901.

McLanahan, S. (1997), 'Parent absence or poverty: which matters more?' in G.J. Duncan and J. Brooks-Gunn (eds), *Consequences of Growing Up Poor*, New York: Russell Sage Foundation, pp. 35–48.

McLanahan, S. and G. Sandefur (1994), *Growing Up with a Single Parent: What Hurts, What Helps*, Cambridge, MA: Harvard University Press.

McLanahan, S., J.A. Seltzer, T.L. Hanson and E. Thomson (1994), 'Child support enforcement and child well-being: greater security or greater conflict?' in I. Garfinkel, S.S. McLanahan and P.K. Robins (eds), *Child Support and Child Well-Being*, Washington, DC: Urban Institute Press.

Painter, G. and D.I. Levine (2000), 'Family structure and youths' outcomes: which correlations are causal?' *Journal of Human Resources*, **35** (3), 524–49.

Powers, E.T. and A.H. Beller (2002), 'The problem of multiple fathers: family structure and the payment of child support', mimeo, University of Illinois at Urbana-Champaign.

Seltzer, J.A. (1991), 'Relationships between fathers and children who live apart: the father's role after separation', *Journal of Marriage and the Family*, **53** (1), 79–101.

Shaw, L.B. (1982), 'High school completion for young women: effects of low income and living with a single-parent', *Journal of Family Issues*, **3** (2), 147–63.

Weiss, Y. and R.J. Willis (1985), 'Children as collective goods and divorce settlements', *Journal of Labor Economics*, **3** (3), 268–92.

Weiss, Y. and R.J. Willis (1993), 'Transfers among divorced couples: evidence and interpretation', *Journal of Labor Economics*, **11** (4), 629–79.

Willis, R.J. (1999), 'A theory of out-of-wedlock childbearing', *Journal of Political Economy*, **107** (6), S33–S64.

Wu, L.L. (1996), 'Effects of family instability, income and income instability on the risk of premarital birth', *American Sociological Review*, **61** (3), 386–406.

Appendix Table 1 Youth behaviour by family structure, father's visitation and child support receipt by gender

	Percent of sample		Smoking			Sex			Conviction		
	M	F	M	F	D	M	F	D	M	F	D
Overall	100.00	100.00	0.172	0.167	0.005	0.171	0.189	−0.018	0.040	0.030	0.010
Father always present	0.588	0.529	0.169	0.159	0.010	0.105	0.138	−0.034	0.033	0.019	0.014
Father not always present	0.412	0.471	0.176	0.175	0.001	0.265	0.246	0.019	0.049	0.042	0.007
See often and receive child support	0.215	0.177	0.135	0.136	0.000	0.242	0.166	0.077	0.031	0.010	0.021
See often and don't receive child support	0.184	0.147	0.093	0.249	−0.155	0.291	0.267	0.024	0.000	0.077	−0.077
See rarely and receive child support	0.278	0.358	0.220	0.243	−0.024	0.280	0.306	−0.026	0.090	0.066	0.024
See rarely and don't receive child support	0.324	0.318	0.214	0.087	**0.127**	0.253	0.215	0.038	0.054	0.018	0.035

Note:
1998 youth sampling weights used. M, F and D are males, females, and the difference between males and females, respectively. Bold differences are statistically significant at the 10% level.

10. Family structure and child support: what matters for youth delinquency rates?

William S. Comanor and Llad Phillips

INTRODUCTION

Although there is a considerable literature on the effect of family structure on the performance of children, relatively little attention has been directed to the different alternatives that exist when a biological parent is absent. For the most part, earlier studies have focused on the presence or absence of a child's father, and asked whether his presence makes a difference for various measures of performance. Strikingly, there is near universal agreement that children who are raised in the presence of both mother and father do better along various dimensions as compared with those who live in alternative arrangements. In most cases, these studies assume that the child remains with his or her mother, for that is generally the case.

In our earlier paper on this subject,[1] we examined those issues using a data set from 1980. In that paper, we investigated whether the probability that a boy would be charged with a crime between the ages of 14 and 22 differed as between three alternate family structures: (1) mother and father together; (2) mother and no man present; and (3) mother and some other man present, be it stepfather or boyfriend. We reported that both the first and second categories had preferred outcomes in terms of lower probabilities of being charged with a crime as compared with the third. Those findings implied that the primary factor leading to a boy's delinquent behaviour was not so much the presence of his father in the household as the absence of another man. The similar coefficients for the 'father present', and the 'no man present' coefficients suggested that result.[2]

A separate issue, also explored in the chapter by Antecol and Bedard, is the role of child support payments. When a father is absent from the household, he pays child support in some instances but not in others. An important question is whether these payments make a difference for the child's performance.

The receipt of child support payments expands the resources available in the custodial parent's household and as such leads to increased 'average family income'. We therefore investigate the impact of this factor as well. However, child support payments may have a separate effect from other sources of income, and some earlier studies have found that to be the case.

In this analysis, our measure of a child's performance relates to delinquency, which is determined by whether a boy has been arrested for a crime by the age of 16. The primary explanatory factors that we investigate are the child's family structure, average income within the custodial household, and the presence or absence of child support payments. The critical issue we explore is whether family relationships or financial resources are more important for determining delinquency.

PRIOR STUDIES

There is a substantial literature on the determinants of child outcomes. Much of it is well reviewed by Haveman and Wolfe (1995). Rather than repeating their findings, we discuss here a few studies that have appeared more recently. In particular, we describe the measures used and the results obtained by Antecol and Bedard (2002), Harper and McLanahan (1998), and Painter and Levine (2000).

These studies use various measures of child performance. In their chapter in this volume, Antecol and Bedard employ three alternate measures: becoming sexually active before the age of 15, smoking regularly by that age, and also being convicted of a crime. This work followed an earlier study where they use five separate outcomes: measures of smoking, drinking, sexual intercourse, drug use and criminal behaviour, all before the age of 15 (Antecol and Bedard, 2002).

In contrast, others have used different measures. Harper and McLanahan (1998) focus on youth incarceration while Painter and Levine (2000) use three different variables: dropping out of high school, attending college after high school graduation and having a child out of wedlock.

These studies also employ different measures of family structure. Antecol and Bedard (2002) use the number of years that the biological father remained in the household. Harper and McLanahan (1998) simply distinguish between father-present and father-absent families, but also consider some other alternatives such as identifying father–stepmother households. Finally, Painter and Levine distinguish among three types of family structures: those with two biological parents, female-headed households and those which include a stepfather.

There are also differences in terms of which genders and ages are studied.

Antecol and Bedard include both genders, and measure deviant behaviour at age 14. Harper and McLanahan also include both genders but examine behaviour between ages 14 and 17. And Painter and Levine examine both genders for a sample generally aged 13 and 14, in 1988, with subsequent measurements at two-year intervals. All of these studies include boys and girls together even though some writers have suggested that the genders respond differently to a father's absence. Wilson (1993) for example, suggests that there is a greater adverse effect of family break-up on boys than on girls (p. 176). In the analysis below, we focus only on the contact that boys between the ages of 12 and 16 have with the criminal justice system.

A characteristic of most prior studies is that they employ probability models, which account for the role of endogenous explanatory variables by using two-stage models. Only Harper and McLanahan take a different approach by carrying out an event study that takes advantage of the panel data they have available. In the analysis below, we follow the first of these approaches since data for only a single year are available.

A striking feature of these recent studies is that despite differences in variables and methodologies, they all find that family structure is a significant factor leading to deviant behaviour. These effects are sufficiently strong that they appear in all of them.[3] In this regard, these studies are consistent with the earlier literature, as reported by Haveman and Wolfe. However, there still remain questions of how various family structures compare. In the analysis below, we pay particular attention to the many varieties and types of family structures that can arise when the original pairing of a biological mother and father is broken.

A second set of studies deals directly with the effect of child support payments on children's performance, although they appear to focus exclusively on educational outcomes. An example is the paper by McLanahan et al. (1994), which measures educational outcome by increases in grade point average (GPA). These authors estimate that a single dollar of child support income is worth \$22 of income from other sources (pp. 249–50). They seek to explain that finding by suggesting that 'child support is picking up some unobserved characteristic of the father, such as "family commitment," or to the fact that child support dollars have a symbolic value that enhances children's well-being' (p. 250).

A related study by Knox and Bane (1994) estimates the impact of child support payments on the number of grades completed by age 21. For this purpose, they estimate various models related to that effect. Their first model examines the impact of income received from all sources, where they find little support for the underlying hypothesis. The relevant coefficients are not even significant at the 10 per cent level (p. 296). In their second model, they separate income between two-parent years and mother-headed years, and find that 'income in two-parent years has a small positive effect ... whereas income in years of female headship has no impact' (p. 300). They conclude that these results are 'consistent with the hypothesis that unmeasured parent characteristics are more important than income' (p. 300).

In their third and fourth models, these authors separate child support income from income derived from other sources. In Model 3, they deal only with child support income, while in Model 4, they include child support income as well as income received from other sources. In both contexts, they find a significant impact of child support income on educational attainment. However, they also report that 'no other income source in female-headed years appears to have any effect on educational attainment' (p. 300). Again, they find that child support payments have an independent effect on educational attainment that is separate from that of family income. As with the previous study, these authors suggest that their observed effects 'may be partially attributable to unmeasured parental characteristics' (p. 302).

Finally, a third study compares educational achievement for children from two-parent and one-parent families. That study reaches a similar conclusion:

> Children who have spent at least part of their childhood living in a father-absent family have completed less schooling than average ... at least half of their schooling disadvantage appears to be related directly to the effect of family structure itself. We find, however, that at least half of this disadvantage is eliminated for those children whose mother has a child support award, and among these children, educational outcomes rise with the amount of child support received.
>
> There is strong evidence that the award of child support and the payment of larger amounts mitigates the negative effect of living in a mother-only family on a child's educational attainment. Furthermore, this effect cannot be duplicated from income from other sources, especially not welfare. (Beller and Graham, 1993, p. 245)

In this case also, the authors report that child support payments have an impact that is stronger than overall family income. However, in their study as well, there is little explanation as to why this should be. This question is particularly relevant since income received from child support payments by most single mothers is a relatively small share of their total income.

For the most part, these studies reach a similar conclusion: that child support dollars appear to have a significant positive impact on a child's performance even though average family income has little or no effect. Apparently, according to these studies child support dollars are 'super dollars' in that they have a greater impact than dollars received from other sources.[4]

AN ECONOMIC FRAMEWORK

Although economic agents are typically presumed to consider only their own utility, that presumption has never applied to actions related to family members.[5] In that setting, altruistic concerns are commonly assumed in which the actions of some family members affect the utility levels of others. One result, Becker writes, is that a member's 'concern about the welfare of other [family] members provide each . . . with some insurance against disasters.'[6] For this reason as well, familiar relationships are typically characterized by overlapping utilities.

In regard to parents and children, however, Becker suggests a pattern of asymmetric concerns in which the parent's utility function includes the children's consumption as well as his or her own, while the child's utility function depends only on its own consumption.[7] This structure leads to 'the rotten-kid theorem', which is well known but still warrants a brief review.

In Figure 10.1, the child's income is measured along the vertical axis while the parent's income is measured along the horizontal axis. The joint opportunity locus QQ reflects the aggregate income opportunities available

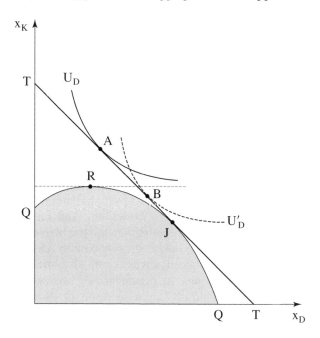

Source: Hirshleifer (1985), p. 57.

Figure 10.1   The Rotten Kid theorem

to the family when both parent and child agree on a final outcome. As Hirshleifer points out, a 'short-sightedly selfish' child will maximize his income at R.[8] In that case, the parent would reluctantly agree, so point R indicates the final outcome. However, the parent's altruism towards him is recognized by the child so that 'enlightened self-interest' leads him to maximize family income at J. From that point, his parent's benevolent motivations lead to an income transfer along the line TT. Furthermore, if the parent's utility function is represented by U_D, the resulting income distribution at A leads both parent and child to reach higher income levels than would be attained at R.

An important implication of this theorem is that if the parent is sufficiently benevolent towards the child, not only is the child better off but so is the parent. The child's enlightened self-interest leads him to a better outcome than he would gain from entirely selfish behavior. What is striking about this result is that the parent's utility level is also higher. Altruism benefits not only the recipient but also the provider.

To be sure, these results do not always hold. They require that the parent be sufficiently benevolent to the child. Suppose the parent's utility function is represented by U'_D in Figure 10.1. Then the desired outcome would be at B; and at that point the child would return to the completely selfish outcome at R. Thus, there is the important implication that both parent and child are better off when the parent is highly altruistic towards the child, but both parties are worse off when the degree of altruism is lower or absent.[9]

While this analysis is framed in terms of consumption levels and monetary transfers, it has broader implications than that. Individual and family objectives involve a larger set of concerns that reflect the entire gamut of activities pursued by family members. When a child agrees to sacrifice his private goals for those of his family, he does so in return for the broader scope of benevolence that follows from his parents' concern. When a child accepts the restrictions placed on his conduct by his parents, he does so with the understanding that ultimately he is better off. And his parents are willing to make the required effort because they too are better off.

Furthermore, the analysis is equally cogent when families disintegrate. Becker writes that 'altruism can benefit altruists only when there is substantial interaction between them and the beneficiaries'.[10] When interactions between parent and child diminish, say as a result of divorce and the father's absence from the home, an anticipated result is that the parent's benevolence for the child declines from what it would be otherwise. If the decline is sufficient, the child will accept its implications and move directly to the more selfish outcome at R rather than the outcome that maximizes joint family welfare at J. Both parent and child are worse off. A direct implication of the rotten-kid theorem is that increased altruism encourages good behaviour even on the part of a selfishly motivated child, while reduced or absent altruism encourages poor behaviour. The child's conduct turns critically on the anticipated benevolence of the parent.

When a family dissolves, a direct effect is lost proximity between the non-custodial parent and the child. As a result, 'the psychic returns from children' for that parent are greatly reduced; and even if they are not, both the time and monetary costs of maintaining close contact are substantially increased.[11] In either case, there is reduced concern by the absent parent for the child.[12]

In the empirical analysis below, we test an implication of this larger set of issues. In particular, we examine the impact of family structure on the delinquent behaviour of young boys. Where fathers are present in the home, we assume there is sufficient benevolence so that boys follow family objectives and do not respond to the temptations of lawlessness. On the other hand, where fathers are absent, we assume there is not sufficient altruism, so that boys more frequently search for their own pleasures without regard to family strictures, and are then more likely to come into contact with law enforcement officials. Following Becker's suggestion that altruism declines with the extent of interactions between altruist and beneficiary, we let family structure be a proxy for a parent's altruistic conduct toward his or her child, which then has the anticipated effect on the child's behaviour.

To be sure, other factors may be important as well. Among these additional factors is the level of family income, including that received from child support payments. To the extent that family incomes are higher, boys may see less need for criminal activity to achieve their goals. The suggestion here is not that boys in higher-income families are more likely to promote joint family objectives, but rather that they will have less need to engage in criminal activity to reach their individual goals. As a result, higher family incomes should be associated with lower rates of criminal activity. In the analysis that follows, we test these propositions for a sample of more than 4000 boys between the ages of 12 and 16.

DATA EMPLOYED AND SUMMARY STATISTICS

The data employed in this study are from the National Longitudinal Survey of Youth (NLSY), which is the same data source used by Antecol and Bedard. These data apply to 1997, when all respondents were between the ages of 12 and 16 on 31 December 1996. At these ages, we can assume that nearly all respondents lived in one of the family structures considered here, and typically with one or both parents. As a result, the reported data on household income directly measures the resources available to the respondent along with the other members of the household.

Because our measure of delinquency is the probability of being arrested for a crime by the age of 16, our data set is necessarily limited to boys. The reason is that girls are far less likely to commit a crime and be arrested, and their frequency in this data set is much lower. Because of data limitations, it would not be possible to study the effects on girls of alternate family structures beyond the two or three structures that are most common. Since we specifically want to examine various alternate structures, the empirical analysis here is limited to boys.

Finally, we measure child support payments by the simple distinction of whether any payments were ever received. In this data set, information on this question is available for most but not all of the respondents. Of the 4077 cases where this information was available for boys, payments were received in 990 cases, or 24.3 per cent.

The underlying data for this study is provided in Table 10.1, where we tabulate arrest rates and average income levels for various family structures. As can be seen, only just over half of all respondents lived with both biological parents; the rest lived with some other combination of parents and/ or adults. The second-largest category represents 'mother and no other man'; while the third most frequent group is 'mother and stepfather'. Following these categories are structures that include the biological father, first with no other woman and then with a stepmother.

The data on arrest rates, when cross-tabulated by family structure, suggests some interesting hypotheses. As expected, and consistent with the

Table 10.1   *Arrest rates and household incomes for various family structures*

Family Structure	Number of boys	Number arrested	Arrest rate	Average household income ($)
Mother–Father	2443	158	6.47	58977
Mother–No Man	1068	159	14.89	24756
Mother–Stepfather	415	55	13.25	44552
Father–No Woman	127	28	22.05	38884
Relative–No Man	58	14	24.14	25401
Father–Stepmother	105	15	14.29	61832
Mother–Boyfriend	65	9	13.85	29148
None–None	50	11	22.00	23938
All Other Combinations	422	46	16.55	–
Total	4753	495	10.41	46638

considerable literature on this subject, arrest rates are much lower when a boy remains with both his biological mother and father. Indeed, the arrest rates reported here are at least twice as high on average for all other cases.

For the remaining family structures, however, these data indicate that arrest rates fall generally into two other classes, which we refer to below as 'moderate risk' and 'high risk'. The 'moderate risk' category includes the following structures: 'mother–no man', 'mother–stepfather', 'mother–boyfriend', and 'father–stepmother'. All of these structures show relatively similar arrest rates. In contrast, there are three family structures where arrest rates are generally three times higher than those found for the 'mother–father' category. These include 'father–no woman', a 'female relative' and 'no man', and family structures that include neither his mother or father. Of particular interest is the substantial difference between 'father–no woman' and 'father–stepmother'. Note also that the arrest rate for the 'mother–stepfather' category is more than twice that for the 'mother–father' case. These summary data suggest that there may be three discrete risk classes.

These data also suggest the role played by household income. Although average household income for the 'father–stepmother' category is slightly higher than that for the 'mother–father' classification, the former still has a substantially higher arrest rate. More telling is the fact that the arrest rate for the 'father–stepmother' and the 'mother–no man' categories are approximately equal despite the fact that average household income in the latter case is less than half that of the former.

Note also that although average household income for the 'mother–no man' category and the 'female relative–no man' category are approximately equal, the arrest rate for the latter is substantially higher than for the former. These statistics suggest that average household income has little impact on arrest rates. What seems more important is the structure of the family with whom the boy is living rather than the income available to the household.

The NLSY data also provide information on the respondent's race. These data are reported in Table 10.2. In this tabulation, the 'other' group includes American Indians, Eskimos or Aleuts, Asians, Pacific Islanders and some small additional categories. In these tabulations, respondents of Hispanic ethnicity are included within the largest category. As can be seen, arrest rates are highest for black youths but relatively similar for white youths and 'others'. In addition, average household incomes are lowest for this classification, which could also contribute to the higher arrest rates. Furthermore, there may be differences in family structure as between these classifications, so the reported arrest rates could also be related to that factor. Note that there are 4563 respondents in this tabulation, which is

Table 10.2   Arrest rates and household incomes by racial categories

	Number of boys	Number arrested	Arrest rate	Average household income
White	2705	267	9.85	$55851
Black	1195	159	13.30	$30586
Other	663	67	10.11	$38094
Total	4563	493	10.80	

Table 10.3   Arrest rates and child support for various family structures

Family structure	No child support		Child support ever received	
	No. of boys	Arrest rate	No. of boys	Arrest rate
Mother–Father	2075	5.7	99	14.1
Mother–No Man	439	14.8	507	16.6
Mother–Other Man*	185	9.7	233	14.6
Father–No Woman	73	24.7	32	25.0
Father–Stepmother	56	19.6	35	8.6
Other**	69	26.1	19	5.3
	2997		925	

Notes:
* Includes both stepfather and a mother's boyfriend.
** Includes both the 'female relative–no man' and the 'none–none' family structures.

slightly lower than the number indicated in Table 10.1. The reason is that there are some records for which data on this classification is not available.

Another vantage point to approach these data is to distinguish between respondents who have ever received child support payments and those who have not. These tabulations are provided in Table 10.3. Overall, there is usable data for 3922 respondents, which is lower than the number provided in Table 10.1. As expected, the largest family structure category includes the boy's biological mother and father, and here the arrest rate is lowest. However, there were 99 boys, living with their mother and father, who at one time had received child support payments. We cannot explain why such payments were made, and the higher arrest rates indicated for this group are difficult to interpret.

An interesting feature of this table is that for all primary categories except one, the arrest rate is higher where child support payments are received than where they are not. The only classification where that pattern is reversed is the 'father–stepmother' category, where child support payments are associated with lower arrest rates. Those payments are presumably made by the boy's mother.

To be sure, in a number of categories, the differences are minimal so few conclusions should be drawn. This result applies to the 'mother–no man' and 'father–no woman' classifications. The arrest rates in these cases are essentially the same, and one might conclude only that there was little relationship between receipt of child support payments and arrest rates. On the other hand, for the 'mother–no other man' category, the arrest rate was approximately 50 per cent higher where child support payments were received than where they were not.

SOME EMPIRICAL ISSUES

An important empirical issue for estimating the effect of family structure on child performance relates to the endogeneity of the structural classifications. Some writers have suggested that the delinquency of children can influence the family structure classification since more difficult children make divorce more likely. See Wilson and Herrnstein, 1985. More likely, there are various reasons why family structure and children's outcomes might be jointly determined, which is an argument made by Manski et al. (1992). For example, drug or alcohol abuse could make divorce more likely and also lead to less effective parenting. In principle, there would then be unobserved variables, such as drug or alcohol abuse, that jointly influence both family structure and delinquency. As a result, there would then be a positive correlation between these variables.

Manski and his co-authors deal extensively with this issue, and develop various means to test for endogeneity between children's outcomes and family structure. In the end, however, they conclude that 'the exogeneity assumption is not far off the mark' (Manski et al., 1992, p. 35). However, their measure of children's outcomes is high school graduation rates rather than criminal activity. There could still be unobserved variables that link the latter factor with family structure despite Manski's conclusion.

To test this question further, we examine differences in arrest rates as between cases where the absent father is dead or alive. Presumably, a father who is absent from the household because he is dead did not die because of his son's performance. In this case, we use the father's death as an instrument to explain his presence or absence from the household.

Our findings are provided in Table 10.4. As can be seen, arrest rates are effectively the same regardless of whether the father is dead or alive, so long as he is absent from the household. At the same time, a boy's arrest rate is nearly twice as high when the father is absent as compared with when the father is present in the household. These results suggest that the critical factor is the father's presence or absence from the household, and not whether he is dead or alive. For this reason, the family structure variable can be considered an exogenous factor.

Table 10.4   Probabilities of boys being arrested between ages 12 and 16

	Father alive	Father dead
Father present in the household	0.077 (0.005) 2718	–
Father absent in the household	0.150 (0.009) 1610	0.143 (0.025) 203

Note:
Figures in parentheses are standard deviations of the estimated values, which are determined under the assumption of independence. The number of cases in each cell is the third figure given.

A second empirical issue is whether there are common risk factors for different family structures so that one can combine different structures into particular risk classes. Reviewing the findings provided in Table 10.1 suggests that result. For this purpose, we estimate a linear regression equation which corresponds to that table, where the dependent variable is an indicator for whether the respondent has ever been arrested, while the independent variables are the same classifications as before. Of course, the estimated coefficients for this equation are the same as reported in Table 10.1.

From these estimates, we can test whether certain coefficients are equal to each other. We first test whether the following four family structures have equal coefficients: 'mother–no man', 'mother–stepfather', 'mother–boyfriend', and 'father–stepmother'. The resulting Chi-Square coefficient is 0.859 with 3 degrees of freedom. As expected, we cannot reject the null hypothesis that these four classifications have the same coefficient.

We next carry out a similar test for three additional classifications: 'father–no woman', 'female relative–no man', and neither parent present. In this case, the Chi-Square coefficient is even smaller at 0.202 with 2 degrees of freedom. We conclude again that there are no significant differences among these classifications.

The next test is to determine whether there is a significant difference between the coefficient estimated for the 'mother–father' structure and the second set of family structures. The Chi-Square coefficient is now 58.2 with 3 degrees of freedom, which is statistically significant. Comparing the 'mother–father' classification with the final three structures, all associated with the highest risk category, leads to an even higher Chi-Square coefficient of 65.7 with 4 degrees of freedom, which again is highly significant.

These results confirm our earlier observation that there are three separate risk categories associated with the alternate family structures. The different structures should therefore be compressed into three categories. In the analysis below, we include these three classifications, and refer to them as low-risk, moderate-risk and high-risk family structures for childhood criminal activity. Although these classifications were determined by examining differences in delinquency rates, and various family structures were combined on that basis, we argue that the underlying classifications are largely exogenous from that vantage point; and therefore so are their combinations.

EMPIRICAL RESULTS

In this analysis, we estimate various regression equations where the dependent variable is an indicator of delinquency. It measures whether a boy between the ages of 12 and 16 has ever been arrested. Using this variable, we employ a binary probit model that rests on maximum likelihood methods. The results are provided in Table 10.5.

In the first of these equations, family structure is represented by the three categories described above, so we estimate coefficients for the first two categories. However, in the next two equations, we simply distinguish the 'mother–father' category from all others, and estimate only a single coefficient for family structure.

For these equations, we assume from the discussion above that the family structure variables are exogenous, but then we relax that assumption and admit endogeneity. In that case, we employ a two-stage procedure in which the family structure variables are predicted from a first-stage equation.[13] Even though there are strong reasons to assume that family structure is exogenous in relation to this dependent variable, we estimate equations under the alternative assumption to confirm our earlier findings.

As expected, arrest rates are lowest where the biological mother and father are both present in the household. However, they are somewhat higher in the four classifications linked together as 'moderate-risk' families. The omitted classification represents the highest risk category and thereby the highest arrest rates. Although household income has the expected negative sign, the

Table 10.5   Probit equations explaining whether boys between 12 and 16 have ever been arrested

	(1)	(2)	(3)	(4)+
Intercept	−4.42**	−4.62**	−4.63**	−4.47**
	(8.50)	(9.02)	(9.02)	(8.35)
Low-risk family	−0.599*	−0.422*	−0.409*	−0.577*
	(5.05)	(4.68)	(4.32)	(2.43)
Moderate-risk family	−0.300**	−	−	−
	(2.60)			
Age	0.250**	0.251**	0.251**	0.243**
	(7.49)	(7.55)	(7.56)	(7.24)
White	0.317**	0.326**	0.321**	0.315*
	(2.39)	(2.47)	(2.42)	(2.33)
Black	0.155	0.164	0.158	0.0881
	(1.12)	(1.19)	(1.14)	(0.58)
Household income	−0.00000227	−0.00000212	−0.00000213	−0.00000186
	(1.75)	(1.64)	(1.66)	(1.18)
PIAT test	−0.00388**	−0.00387**	−0.00392**	−0.00372**
	(3.12)	(3.12)	(3.16)	(2.94)
Single respondent household	−0.187**	−0.186**	−0.188**	−0.212**
	(2.45)	(2.44)	(2.47)	(2.71)
Neighbourhood gangs	0.439**	0.435**	0.432**	0.442**
	(5.22)	(5.19)	(5.15)	(5.22)
Safe schools	−0.282**	−0.284**	−0.282**	−0.287**
	(2.87)	(2.90)	(2.87)	(2.90)
Peers in gangs	0.0314	0.0269	0.0262	0.0304
	(0.36)	(0.31)	(0.30)	(0.35)
Child support	0.0817	0.0437	0.0288	0.154
	(0.87)	(0.49)	(0.31)	(1.75)
Had lived with father	0.0993	−	0.0643	0.223*
	(0.94)		(0.62)	(2.22)
N	2334	2337	2334	2308
Log likelihood	−678	−682	−681	−668

Notes:
** Statistical significance at 1% level.
* Statistical significance at 5% level.
+ This equation is estimated by two-stage least squares, where the 'low-risk family' variable is replaced by its projected value from the first-stage equation.

reported coefficients in all of the equations are not statistically significant at conventional levels. On the other hand, respondents with better scores in the PIAT test have lower arrest rates. These results are generally as expected.

A surprising result concerns the reported effect of ethnicity. As can be seen, the coefficient for white respondents is always positive and statistically significant, and on the order of twice the coefficient for black respondents, whose coefficient is never statistically significant. While these results may seem perverse, we note that others have found similar results in this data source, and we did as well in our earlier paper. For reasons which we can only guess at, this data set reports lower arrest rates for black respondents than would be expected on the basis of other data sources.

An interesting finding is the positive but non-significant coefficients reported for the child support variable. The figures are generally small, and approach statistical significance only in the final equation. However, in that case, there is the suggestion that respondents who had received child support payments were more likely to be arrested before the age of 16. Why that result might occur is difficult to explain.

Although the first equation deals with both low-risk and moderate-risk families, the latter three equations distinguish only between households with a biological mother and father and all others. And in the final equation, that variable is replaced by its instrument to account for possible endogeneity. Note that the coefficient does not change very much, although its t value declines substantially. The results do not seem dependent on whether or not we replace this variable by its instrument. Indeed, the overall findings presented here are not affected very much by the specifications of the equations.

Although the results provided above for the child support variable are suggestive, they are not conclusive because the largest category of respondents in these equations are those living with their biological mother and father, where child support payments are not indicated. A better test for this variable would be to limit the sample to family structures where child support might possibly be ordered. These categories include those where the child lives with his 'mother and no other man', his 'mother and stepfather', and his 'mother and boyfriend'. To be sure, child support payments are sometimes ordered where the child lives with his father and either a stepmother or 'no other woman'. However, there is evidence that custodial mothers are far more likely to have child support awards than are custodial fathers (Grall, 2002, p. 4) so we consider only circumstances where potential support payments are made by the father and not by the mother. These equations therefore do not employ the same risk categories as defined above. In all of these cases, the respondents live with their mother and not their father.

The results for this limited sample are provided in Table 10.6. As can be

Table 10.6   Probit equations explaining whether boys between 12 and 16 have ever been arrested, limited sample

	(1)	(2)
Intercept	−4.75**	−4.47**
	(6.10)	(5.98)
No man in household	0.025	−
	(0.19)	
Age	0.232**	0.224**
	(4.56)	(4.53)
White	0.349	0.223
	(1.58)	(1.72)
Black	0.154	−
	(0.71)	
Household income	−0.00000269	−0.00000308
	(1.11)	(1.31)
PIAT test	−0.0026	−0.00259
	(1.33)	(1.36)
Single respondent household	−0.176	−0.152
	(1.48)	(1.30)
Neighbourhood gangs	0.599**	0.571**
	(4.38)	(4.63)
Safe schools	−0.183	−0.169
	(1.25)	(1.19)
Peers in gangs	−0.019	−
	(0.14)	
Child support	0.084	0.074
	(0.68)	(0.60)
Had lived with father	0.185	0.160
	(1.52)	(1.33)
N	790	805
Log likelihood	−290	−295

Note:
** Statistical significance at 1% level.

seen, the only significant factors are the boy's age and whether there are neighbourhood gangs in his neighbourhood. No other variable approaches statistical significance at conventional levels, although some coefficients exceed their standard errors. We also find that whether or not the mother invites another man into the household has apparently no influence on prospects that her son will or will not be arrested. Of particular interest is the estimated effect of household income, which although negative is not statistically significant. While there is thus a suggestion that higher income levels lead to a lower probability of being arrested, that result is not confirmed in these equations.

Note that the child support variable is not statistically significant, and that the coefficient is substantially lower than its standard error. There is thus no indication in these data that higher child support payments lead to improved child performance. Despite the insistence by many that higher support levels lead to better child outcomes, those data do not support that result.

Overall, these findings are consistent with earlier studies that reported a significant influence of family structure on the performance of children. At the same time, our results regarding child support payments are largely negative. There is little indication here that these payments have a salutary impact on delinquency rates among boys who live apart from their fathers.

NOTES

1. Comanor and Phillips (2002).
2. See Comanor and Phillips (2002), Table 3, p. 223.
3. The only study reporting contrary findings is that by Lang and Zagorsky (2001). However, even there, the authors report significant effects of a father's presence on both of their measures of actual child performance: the Armed Forces Qualifying Test used to indicate cognitive ability and the highest grade completed at school. Their other measures, such as marriage rates and adult income, are indices of preferences and many other factors as well as child performance.
4. Similar findings are reported by Knox (1996) and Argys et al. (1998).
5. See Bergstrom's discussion of Adam Smith's views on these issues (1996, pp. 1904–5).
6. Becker (1974), p. 1076.
7. Becker (1981), p. 114.
8. Hirshleifer (1985), p. 57.
9. See also Bergstrom (1989).
10. Becker (1977), p. 507. See also Becker et al. (1972), pp. 1152–3.
11. See Weiss and Willis (1985), pp. 268–92. In a second paper, these authors find that because of agency problems, 'it costs the husband $5 to raise expenditures on his child by $1'. Reduced benevolence by an absent father follows directly. Weiss and Willis (1993), p. 665.
12. A father's absence from the home typically leads him to have little contact with his child. Fully 58 per cent of absent fathers saw their child fewer than several times a year, while only about one-quarter had contact more than once a week. Furthermore, parent–child contact diminished over time. While 28 per cent of absent fathers, separated for two years or less, saw their child fewer than several times a year, that percentage increased to 42 per cent between three and five years post-separation, to 62 per cent for six to ten years following the father's separation and to fully 72 per cent at 11 years or more. Seltzer (1991), Tables 1 and 4, pp. 86, 91.
13. The following instruments are employed in the first-stage equation: father alive or dead, mother alive or dead, household size, parent born in the United States, parental frequency of church attendance, parent lived with both parents until age 14.

REFERENCES

Antecol, Heather and Kelly Bedard (2002), 'Does single parenthood increase the probability of teenage promiscuity, drug use, and crime? Evidence from divorce law changes', unpublished paper, April.

Argys, Laura M., H. Elizabeth Peters, Jeanne Brooks-Gunn and Judith R. Smith (1998), 'The impact of child support on cognitive outcomes of young children', *Demography*, **35**, May, 159–73.

Becker, Gary S. (1974), 'A theory of social interactions', *Journal of Political Economy*, **82**, November, 1063–93.

Becker, Gary S. (1977), 'Reply to Hirshleifer and Tullock', *Journal of Economic Literature*, **15**, June, 506–7.

Becker, Gary S. (1981), *A Treatise on the Family*, Cambridge, MA: Harvard University Press.

Becker, Gary S., Elisabeth M. Landes and Robert T. Michael (1972), 'An economic analysis of marital instability', *Journal of Political Economy*, **85**, 1141–87.

Beller, Andrea H. and John W. Graham (1993), *Small Change: The Economics of Child Support*, New Haven, CT: Yale University Press.

Bergstrom, Theodore C. (1989), 'A fresh look at the Rotten Kid Theorem and other household mysteries', *Journal of Political Economy*, **97**, October, 1138–59.

Bergstrom, Theodore C. (1996), 'Economics in a family way', *Journal of Economic Literature*, **34**, December, 1903–34.

Comanor, William S. and Llad Phillips (2002), 'The impact of income and family structure on delinquency', *Journal of Applied Economics*, **5**, November, 209–32.

Graham, John W., Andrea H. Beller and Pedro M. Hernandez (1994), 'The effects of child support on educational attainment', in Irwin Garfinkel (ed.), *Child Support and Child Well-Being*, Washington, DC, pp. 317–54.

Grall, Timothy (2002), *Custodial Mothers and Fathers and their Child Support 1999*, Current Population Reports, US Census Bureau, October.

Harper, Cynthia and Sara S. McLanahan (1998), 'Father absence and youth incarceration', unpublished paper, August.

Haveman, Robert and Barbara Wolfe (1995), 'The determinants of children's attainments: a review of methods and findings', *Journal of Economic Literature*, **33**, December, 1829–78.

Hirshleifer, Jack (1985), 'The expanding domain of economics', *American Economic Review*, **75** (6), 57.

Knox, Virginia M. (1996), 'The effects of child support payments on developmental outcomes for elementary school-age children', *Journal of Human Resources*, **31**, Autumn, 816–40.

Knox, Virginia W. and Mary Jo Bane (1994), 'Child support and schooling', in Irwin Garfinkel (ed.), *Child Support and Child Well-Being*, Washington, DC: Urban Institute Press, pp. 285–316.

Lang, Kevin and Jay L. Zagorsky (2001), 'Does growing up with a parent absent really hurt?', *Journal of Human Resources*, **36**, Spring, 253–73.

Manski, Charles F., Gary D. Sandefur, Sara McLanahan and Daniel Powers (1992), 'Alternate estimates of the effect of family structure during adolescence on high school graduation', *Journal of the American Statistical Association*, **87**, March, 25–37.

McLanahan, Sara S., Judith A. Seltzer, Thomas L. Hanson and Elizabeth Thomson

(1994), 'Child support enforcement and child well-being: greater security or greater conflict?' in Irwin Garfinkel (ed.), *Child Support and Child Well-Being*, Washington, DC: Urban Institute Press, pp. 239–56.

Painter, Gary and David I. Levine (2000), 'Daddies, devotion and dollars: how do they matter for youth?', unpublished paper.

Seltzer, Judith A. (1991), 'Relationships between fathers and children who live apart', *Journal of Marriage and the Family*, **53**, February, 79–101.

Weiss, Yoram and Robert J. Willis (1985), 'Children as collective goods and divorce settlements', *Journal of Labor Economics*, **3**, July, 268–92.

Weiss, Yoram and Robert J. Willis (1993), 'Transfers among divorced couples: evidence and interpretation', *Journal of Labor Economics*, **11**, October, 629–79.

Wilson, James Q. (1993), *The Moral Sense*, New York: Simon & Schuster.

Wilson, James Q. and Richard J. Herrnstein (1985), *Crime and Human Nature*, New York: Simon & Schuster.

Index